The Disappearance of Writing Systems

Dedicated to the memory of Jeremy Black (1951–2004)

The Disappearance of Writing Systems

Perspectives on Literacy and Communication

Edited by

John Baines
John Bennet
Stephen Houston

Published by

Equinox Publishing Ltd.,

UK: 1 Chelsea Manor Studios, Flood Street, London SW3 5SR.

USA: DBBC, 28 Main Street, Oakville, CT 06779

www.equinoxpub.com

First published in the UK 2008

© John Baines, John Bennet, Stephen Houston and contributors 2008

Reprinted in paperback 2010

Library of Congress Cataloging-in-Publication Data

The disappearance of writing systems : perspectives on literacy and communication /
edited by John Baines, John Bennet, and Stephen Houston.

p. cm.

Includes bibliographical references and index.

ISBN 978-1-84553-013-6 (hb)

ISBN 978-1-84553-907-8 (pb)

1. Writing—History. 2. Language obsolescence.

I. Baines, John. II. Bennet, John, III. Houston, Stephen D.

P211.D57 2008

411.09—dc22

2008014610

British Library Cataloguing-in-Publication Data

A catalogue record for this book is available from the British Library.

Index by Jane Read, http://www.readindexing.co.uk/

Typeset by Queenston Publishing, Hamilton, Canada

Printed by Lightning Source, Inc., La Vergne, TN and
Lighting Source UK Ltd., Milton Keynes, UK.

Contents

List of Illustrations

List of Tables

Notes on Contributors

John Baines is Professor of Egyptology at the University of Oxford. His principal publications are on Egyptian art, literature, and religion. He has also focused on the role of writing in Egyptian society and on high-cultural legitimations and concerns of elites. His publications include *Visual and Written Culture in Ancient Egypt* (2007) and *High Culture and Experience in Ancient Egypt* (in preparation for Equinox).

John Bennet is Professor of Aegean Archaeology at the University of Sheffield, UK, and has received his doctorate from Cambridge University. He has held positions at the University of Wisconsin–Madison and Oxford University, where he was Sinclair and Rachel Hood lecturer in Aegean Prehistory. His research interests include the archaeology of complex societies, writing and administrative systems (especially Linear B), and diachronic landscape archaeology.

Jeremy Black† (1951–2004), who died entirely unexpectedly a month after the conference at which he presented his fully composed chapter for this book as a paper, was Lecturer in Akkadian in the University of Oxford. His primary research was on Sumerian literature, in which he published *Reading Sumerian Poetry* (1998) while developing the major collaborative project, the Electronic Text Corpus of Sumerian Literature (http://etcsl.orinst.ox.ac.uk). That project also yielded a volume of translations, *The Literature of Ancient Sumer* (2004), by Jeremy Black, Graham Cunningham, Eleanor Robson, and Gábor Zólyomi. Until 1988 Jeremy Black was the director of the British School of Archaeology in Iraq. He was the author of works on Sumerian grammar and editions of cuneiform texts. The present volume is dedicated to his memory.

Elizabeth Hill Boone, an art historian, has focused much of her research on the painted books and manuscripts of Aztec Mexico. She is author of *Stories in Red and Black: Pictorial Histories of the Aztecs and Mixtecs* and *Cycles of Time and Meaning in the Mexican Books of Fate*, and co-editor (with Walter Mignolo) of *Writing without Words: Alternative Literacies in Mesoamerica and the Andes*. Formerly Director of Pre-Columbian Studies at Dumbarton Oaks, she holds the Martha and Donald Robertson Chair in Latin American Art at Tulane University. She is the recipient of Mexico's Order of the Aztec Eagle and was named Andrew W. Mellon Professor at the US National Gallery of Art.

David Brown (Freie Universität Berlin) currently teaches mathematics in a Berlin school, and looks after his three young children. He maintains an informal affiliation with the Freie Universität Berlin and Wolfson College, Oxford, and continues to research the ancient exact sciences and cuneiform divination and religion. He studied physics at Trinity College, Cambridge, completing a doctorate in Assyriology on the evolution of astronomy in Mesopotamia. Thereafter, he spent four years in Oxford as a research fellow, publishing *Mesopotamian Planetary Astronomy-Astrology* in 2000. From 2002 to 2004, David was a full-time lecturer in Ancient History at University College, London, teaching Ancient Near Eastern History. He has been a Deutsche Forschungsgemeinschaft researcher for the last two years, and his new book *The Interactions of Ancient Astral Science* is forthcoming.

Chris Gosden is Professor of European Archaeology, University of Oxford, and a Fellow of the British Academy. He has carried out archaeological and ethnographic research in Britain, central Europe, Papua New Guinea, and Turkmenistan, and has run projects funded by large grants from the AHRC, ESRC, and Leverhulme Trust. He has published a number of books and articles, including works on cultural property and issues of postcolonialism. His current interests concern the nature of human intelligence. Recent works include *Archaeology and Anthropology: A Changing Relationship* (1999), *Prehistory: A Very Short Introduction* (2003), *Archaeology and Colonialism* (2004), *Collecting Colonialism: Material Culture and Colonial Change in Papua New Guinea* (with C. Knowles, 2001), 'Post-colonial Archaeology: Issues of Culture, Identity and Knowledge' (in I. Hodder, ed., *Archaeological Theory Today*, 2001).

J. David Hawkins was until his retirement in 2005 Professor of Ancient Anatolian Languages at the School of Oriental and African Studies, University of London. He is a Fellow of the British Academy. His teaching was principally the Hittite and Akkadian languages, and his main research interest the Luwian language and its hieroglyphic script. A second interest is the origin and dissemination of writing. He is the author of *Corpus of Hieroglyphic Luwian Inscriptions* (2 vols in 4, 1999–2000).

Stephen Houston, a specialist in Maya civilization, is Dupee Family Professor of Social Science at Brown University. Houston has authored many articles, book chapters, and reviews. The founding co-editor of *Ancient Mesoamerica*, he is also co-editor of a dozen technical monographs on archaeological work in Guatemala, and author or editor of twelve books, the most recent of which is *The Memory of Bones: Body, Being, and Experience among the Classic Maya* (with David Stuart and Karl Taube, 2006). His current research focuses on urbanism in Mesoamerica, the history of colour in the New World, Maya architecture, and the origins, development, and extinction of writing.

Kathryn Lomas is Senior Research Fellow in archaeology at University College London, and has research specialisms in the history and archaeology of early Italy and the western Mediterranean, ethnic and cultural identities in the ancient world, and the development of literacy in the ancient Mediterranean.

She is author of *Rome and the Western Greeks and Roman Italy, 338 BC – AD 200*, as well as editor of several volumes of collected papers, and has published numerous articles on her areas of interest. Her current research, sponsored by the AHRC, is on the earliest development of literacy in Etruscan Italy.

Michael Macdonald is a Fellow of Wolfson College, Oxford, and a Research Associate of the Faculty of Oriental Studies, University of Oxford. He works on the languages, inscriptions, and history of pre-Islamic Arabia and Syria, on literacy and the origins, development, and uses of alphabets, and on the history of the nomads of the ancient Middle East. He is a member of the Steering Committee for the Seminar for Arabian Studies, an annual international conference on all aspects of Arabia, and until 2005 edited its Proceedings.

John Monaghan is Professor and Department Head at the University of Illinois at Chicago. A socio-cultural anthropologist, Monaghan has carried out extended periods of ethnographic fieldwork among the Maya of Guatemala and the Mixtec of Mexico. He has published on a number of topics, including religion, economics, and ancient scripts. His current research examines the impact of liberal social and economic policies on the indigenous people of Mesoamerica.

Claude Rilly is a member of CNRS-LLACAN (Langage, Langues et Cultures d'Afrique Noire) in Paris. Since his doctoral thesis, defended in 2003, which brought long-awaited evidence classifying Meroitic as a member of a new branch of Nilo-Saharan languages he called 'Northern East Sudanic', he has been considered the most prominent specialist of this language. He is the current editor of the *Répertoire d'épigraphie méroïtique*, which was started in the 1950s under Jean Leclant. Besides numerous articles published on Meroitic, he has written two monographs which are currently in press: *La Langue du royaume de Méroé* and *Le Méroïtique et sa famille linguistique*.

Frank Salomon is the John V. Murra Professor of Anthropology at the University of Wisconsin–Madison. As an ethnohistorian he has conducted research on the subject peoples of the Inka empire in Ecuador and Peru, and as an ethnographer he focuses on the high villages of the central-Peruvian Andes. His books include *Ethnic Lords of Quito in the Age of the Incas* (1978), the English translation of the 1608 Quechua Huarochirí Manuscript, the South American volumes of the *Cambridge History of the Native Peoples of the Americas*, and, in 2004, *The Cord Keepers*, which concerns patrimonial khipus in Peru.

Richard Salomon is Professor of Asian Languages and Literature at the University of Washington and Director of the British Library/University of Washington Early Buddhist Manuscripts Project. His specialities are Sanskrit and Prakrit languages and literature, the languages and literature of Indian Buddhism, Indian epigraphy and palaeography, early Indian history, Gandhāran studies, and the world history of writing. He has published four books, including *Indian Epigraphy: A Guide to the Study of Inscriptions in the Sanskrit, Prakrit, and the other Indo-Aryan Languages* (New York, 1998) and *Ancient Buddhist Scrolls from Gandhāra: The British Library Kharosthi Fragments* (Seattle/London, 1999), as well as about one hundred articles on these subjects.

Martin Andreas Stadler holds master's degrees from the Julius-Maximilians-University in Würzburg in Egyptology, Classical Archaeology and History, and from the University of Oxford in Oriental Studies (Egyptology). In 2002 he obtained his DPhil from Würzburg, and is currently University Lecturer in Egyptology at the University of Würzburg. His principal research interests are Egyptian funerary art, demotic literature, and Egyptian religion including the Ptolemaic-Roman era, with a particular focus on the way in which Egyptians maintained their cultural identity during the periods of Greek and Roman rule.

Giovanni Stary (University of Venice) holds a PhD in Slavic languages and a diploma in Classical Chinese from the Oriental University, Naples, from where he went to Bonn University on a Humboldt scholarship. His specialisms are in Manchu language and literature, and Central and East Asian history. Stary is now Professor of Manchu Language and Literature at University of Venice, Italy, and is editor of the journals *Central Asiatic Journal*, *Aetas Manjurica*, and *Shamanica Manchurica Collecte*.

Preface

Decipherments of lost writing systems are among the most renowned achieve-ments of humanistic scholarship, involving Old Persian, Egyptian hieroglyphs, and cuneiform in the nineteenth century, through Linear B in the mid twen-tieth century, to the relatively recent, progressive solution of the challenges presented by Maya glyphs. For a script to need decipherment, it must have fall-en out of use, and knowledge of it must have been lost; yet the disappearance of writing systems and the meaning and implications of that loss have hardly been studied. This was the gap addressed in the conference held in Oxford on 26–28 March 2004. The papers from that conference are now published here, in revised form. So far as we know, this was the first focused meeting to be held on the topic.

In our planning we attempted to gather as many different cases as could be fitted into a weekend conference and a subsequent volume of reasonable size, seeking examples from throughout the world, setting themes as broadly as pos-sible, and including among the phenomena to be addressed some institutional-ized material practices that many people would not term 'writing'. We covered a temporal range down to the present day. This enabled us to see, for the case of Manchu, examples of a thoroughly documented script that now has only an emblematic existence in one region and is threatened in another. Further papers tackled the appearance and demise of often short-lived writing systems in small communities and the maintenance of social memory in societies with-out writing. Participants were given the published article of Stephen Houston, John Baines, and Jerrold Cooper as a position paper (2003, cited in several chap-ters). Some presentations addressed explicitly the categories and questions studied there, while other contributors chose their own routes through the issues.

We should emphasize that the chapters of this book treat only a fraction of the known range of writing systems that have disappeared—quite apart from the numerous systems likely to have been invented and lost again without leav-ing much vestige of their existence. For a couple of significant examples we were unable to find experts who could attend the conference. We hope that the spread of cases included in the conference and in this volume gives a sense of the potential range of issues raised by the phenomenon under study. We also hope that the essays collected here will stimulate others to look at questions of social change and transformation through the lens of the loss of writing and of other communication systems, both by revisiting materials covered in this book and by addressing others. This volume is no more than a first step.

The order of the first ten chapters in the book is the approximate chrono-logical order of the final eclipse of the writing systems under discussion. The subsequent chapters treat other usages that record or maintain social memo-ry (Elizabeth Hill Boone, Frank Salomon, Chris Gosden), broader issues of the standing of writing in smaller societies, mainly peripheral to large recent states (John Monaghan), a surviving script (Giovanni Stary), and a tentative synthesis (John Baines).

We are very grateful to all the participants for accepting our invitation to attend the conference, for offering papers of high quality, for engaging strongly in all of the proceedings, and for timely delivery of their papers and subsequent chapters. As organizers, the delayed appearance of this book is our fault and not theirs. We also owe a great deal to several bodies that provided financial support for the conference and the subsequent publication. The undertaking was sponsored by the Craven Fund in the Faculty of Classics and the Faculty of Oriental Studies at the University of Oxford, and by the Jesse Knight Univer-sity Professorship and the Institute for the Study and Preservation of Ancient Religious Texts at Brigham Young University. The conference was held at Keble College, Oxford, where the excellent organization and meals were coordinated by Janet Betts and the college staff. We should like also to thank Janet Joyce of Equinox very much for accepting to publish the book, Rebecca du Plessis for her editorial input, and Alison Wilkins for producing maps at very short notice.

John Baines
John Bennet
Stephen Houston

December 2007

Now You See It; Now You Don't!
The Disappearance of the Linear A Script on Crete[1]

John Bennet

Introduction: Background and Issues

This chapter explores the disappearance of one of the three scripts in use in the Aegean world (primarily the island of Crete, the southern mainland of Greece, and some of the Aegean islands) in the second millennium BC.

Arthur Evans, the excavator of the site of Knossos (see map Fig. 1.1), was keen to claim the Minoan 'civilization' of Crete, whose remains he had uncovered, as the first European civilization (e.g. Farnell 1927). One pressing motivation was the fact that Crete had only 'left' the shrinking Ottoman Empire in 1898, two years before Evans began his excavations at Knossos (see Brown 2000; 2001). For this first 'European' civilization to justify its status, it had to have a writing system, like the older 'Oriental' civilizations of Mesopotamia and Egypt. Indeed it was the existence of a so-called 'pictographic' writing system on stone seals acquired by Evans as keeper of Oxford's Ashmolean Museum in the 1880s that first led him to Crete, and they were a major piece of evidence for what Evans described in one of his early publications as a 'prae-Phoenician' writing system on the island (Evans 1895; see Bennet 2000). Another potent influence on Evans was the developing theory of evolution that had been adopted by British pre-historians, notably his own father, John Evans (see e.g. MacGillivray 2000: 30–3; Trigger 2006: 146).

These notions structured Evans' interpretation of cultural development, including that of script (first presented in Evans 1909), influencing the chronological framework he developed for his Minoan civilization. His chronology,

Figure 1.1 The Aegean, showing sites mentioned in the text.

subsequently modified extensively in detail, was a tripartite scheme, based on a perceived sequence of rise, florescence, and decline, and calibrated against a ceramic sequence loosely related to stratigraphy (Table 1.1). An absolute chronology was established by reference to the Egyptian 'historical' chronology through finds of Egyptian imports in Aegean contexts and of Aegean objects in Egypt (see Warren and Hankey 1989 for a fully documented exposition; also Kemp and Merrillees 1980). In this tripartite sequence, Evans divided the Bronze Age of Crete into three phases—Early, Middle, and Late—and gave it the overall term 'Minoan' (those on the Greek mainland and islands follow similar tripartite divisions, but are termed 'Helladic' and 'Cycladic' respectively). Each broad phase was divided into three—I, II, and III—and these in turn, where appropriate, subdivided into A, B, and C. As it is currently understood, therefore, the Bronze

Age began on Crete with the Early Minoan (EM) phase, continued through the Middle Minoan (MM), and ended with the close of the Late Minoan (LM).

Although Evans' system, with subsequent refinement, allows a fairly precise and narrow phasing of ceramics, major cultural shifts did not follow these neat, arbitrary divisions, necessitating the development of a broader, more descriptive terminology around the appearance of the complex architectural forms called 'palaces' (Table 1.1). Thus, the period covering the Early Minoan and the very beginning of Middle Minoan (phase MMIA), before the construction of the palaces, is called 'Pre-Palatial', while a major shift *within* the palatial phase is marked by the distinction between Proto- and Neo-Palatial. Many palatial and other sites suffered destruction at the end of the Neo-Palatial phase, but Knossos continued as a palatial centre for some generations, to which we now assign the term Final-Palatial (the era of Knossos' Linear B administration), followed by the Post-Palatial (the period after Knossos' destruction). Of greatest relevance to this chapter are the latest Pre-Palatial, when writing first appeared, and the end of the Neo-Palatial / beginning of Final-Palatial (Table 1.1), when Linear A disappears. While the relative chronology and thus the order in which developments occurred are not in dispute, Aegean archaeologists cannot yet agree on the absolute chronology of the first phase of the Late Bronze Age (Late Minoan IA–B). Conventional chronology would place this c. 1600–1450 BC (Warren and Hankey 1989: 137–46, 169, table 3.1), while recent work suggests that the beginning of the phase should be raised to c. 1710 BC, a difference of about a century (Manning *et al.* 2006). The effect of the 'high' chronology is to lengthen the Neo-Palatial phase, suggesting that developments took place over a longer timescale than the 'low' chronology allows (see Table 1.1).

A final element of the intellectual context created by Evans' legacy is the principle of Minoan primacy and supremacy in the Bronze Age Aegean. For Evans, civilization in Europe began on Crete and was brought to the rest of the Aegean by Cretans as a result of their naval supremacy. This analysis dominated the study of Aegean prehistory for the first half of the twentieth century and led to a profound difference of opinion between Evans and Alan Wace who, with Carl Blegen, established the second-millennium-BC cultural sequence on the Greek mainland (e.g. Blegen and Wace 1916–1918; also Wace 1956; Fitton 1995: 150–65). In terms of language, the logical conclusion of Evans' view was that the Minoan civilization, being of greater antiquity than that on the Greek mainland, must have used a language that preceded Greek. For him, this language was in use throughout much of the southern Greek mainland in the later second millennium BC (Evans 1935: 752–5; implicit also in Ventris 1940: esp. 494, 502). (On the contrary, Wace [e.g. 1956: xxiv] claimed that Greek-speakers arrived in mainland Greece at the beginning of the Middle Bronze Age). Logically for Evans, therefore, none of the three scripts he had identified could have notated the Greek language; for him, they more likely notated an 'older' language.

Dates (BC)	Pottery phase	Cultural phase	Script in use
2100–1900	Middle Minoan (MM) IA	Pre-Palatial	Archanes script
1900–1700	MM IB–III	Proto-Palatial	Cretan Hieroglyphic; Linear A
1700–1450	Late Minoan (LM) IA–B	Neo-Palatial	Linear A
1450–1350	LM II–IIIA1	Final-Palatial	Linear B
1350–1200	LMIIIA2–IIIB	Post-Palatial	Linear B

Table 1.1 Outline chronology of Minoan Crete, showing approximate absolute dates, pottery phases, cultural phases, and scripts in use (cf. Warren and Hankey 1989; Manning *et al.* 2006).

It was this understanding that led Michael Ventris to draw on Etruscan, a possible relict 'pre-Greek' language, as a basis for understanding the language behind Linear B (Ventris 1940; cf. Bennett 1989). Equally, it is against this background that we can better understand the comments which he describes as a 'frivolous digression' (Ventris 1988: 327) in his famous 'Work Note 20', immediately prior to his decipherment of Linear B in 1952, which he concludes with the following words (Ventris 1988: 331):

> If pursued, I suspect that this line of decipherment would sooner or later come to an impasse, or dissipate itself in absurdities; and that it would be necessary to revert to the hypothesis of an indigenous, non-Indo-European language. But this fantasy may be the excuse for us once more to ask ourselves the question: Which is historically more incongruous, a Knossos which writes Greek, or a Mycenae which writes 'Cretan'?

The importance of the demonstration that the language behind the Linear B script is Greek is akin to that of Evans' initial claim that Minoan civilization is European: it appears to show that Greek speakers (strictly only 'writers') existed not only on the Greek mainland, but also on the island of Crete, in the later phases of the Aegean Bronze Age. Furthermore, scholars like Wace and Blegen, vindicated in their view of the significance of mainland Greece in this period, interpreted the presence of the Greek language on Crete as evidence of mainland supremacy over Minoan. Some of these issues are made clear in Wace's foreword to the first major edition of a collection of Linear B texts published in 1956 (Wace 1956: xxxi):

> The importance of Mr Ventris' decipherment can hardly be over-estimated, for it inaugurates a new phase in our study of the beginnings of classical Hellas. We must recognize the Mycenaean culture as Greek, and as one of the first stages in the advance of the Hellenes towards the brilliance of their later amazing achievements … . In culture, in history and in language we must regard prehistoric and historic Greece as one indivisible whole.

Wace's words reveal an essentialist view of identity, in which language is of paramount importance. The 'proof' the decipherment offered that Greek speakers had taken over the Minoan civilization in the later second millennium BC made Evans' slightly dubious claim of Europeanness irrefutable, because prehistoric Greece was now directly linked to classical Greece by the thread of a single language. I would suggest not only that the polarization of the field in the first part of the twentieth century delayed the decipherment of Linear B, but also that its legacy has been a simplistic reconstruction of the changes that took place on Crete, especially at Knossos, in the fifteenth century BC. These have been interpreted as the consequence of a mainland invasion by Mycenaean Greeks, either learning to write upon their arrival, or, in the more extremely 'essentialist' view, bringing their own writing system with them. Among the changes that the fifteenth century BC saw on Crete is the disappearance of Linear A, which is the focus of this chapter.

A Brief History of Writing and Administration in the Aegean

Writing came relatively late to the Aegean world and is attested on Crete some time before its first appearance on the Greek mainland. It seems unlikely that Aegean writing was an independent invention, given the well-documented connections between the region and the eastern Mediterranean world that seem to have become more regular and intense in the later third millennium BC, facilitated by the introduction of the sailing ship (e.g. Broodbank 2000: 341–9; Sherratt 2000: 18–20). However, all three Aegean scripts are structurally distinct from those in neighbouring regions, being simple syllabaries, based on relatively small repertoires of phonetic signs, together with quite large numbers of logographic signs representing commodities. Evans, again in keeping with the intellectual climate of his time, saw the origins of script in Egypt (e.g. Evans 1909: 118–34), and this partly explains his label for its earliest manifestation, namely 'hieroglyphic', also known as 'pictographic'. Furthermore, he saw the development of the Cretan scripts in evolutionary terms, moving from 'pictographic' forms, often with recognizable prototypes in the material world, towards more conventionalized, 'linear' forms (Evans 1909: 8–18; 1952: 1–2). In particular, he identified an early script, now conventionally known as Cretan Hieroglyphic (e.g. Olivier and Godart 1996; Younger 1999; Karnava 2000) and itself divided into progressive variants—A and B (Evans 1909: 134–48)—that was superseded by the first 'linear' form: Linear A. This was replaced by the second—Linear B—but, according to Evans, only at Knossos, where it represented the most sophisticated, palatial variant, in contemporaneous use with the latest Linear A at Neo-Palatial sites of the same period (Evans 1909: 38–9).

Discoveries as well as systematic study and re-analysis since Evans have modified this evolutionary scheme. In the first instance, writing has been recognized on a small set of seals, bearing signs that have collectively become known as the 'Archanes script' (Olivier and Godart 1996: 31; Godart 1999), after the find-spot of

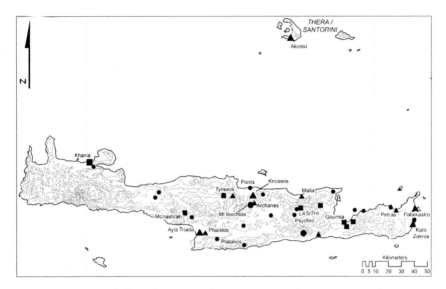

Figure 1.2 Crete and Thera/Santorini, showing sites producing Linear A documents. Sites mentioned in the text are named. Solid squares indicate sites with only administrative documents; solid circles, those with only non-administrative documents; and solid triangles, those with examples of both. Larger symbols indicate greater numbers of attested documents.

examples in the long-lived Fournoi cemetery near Archanes (Fig. 1.2), about 10 km south of Knossos in north-central Crete (Sakellarakis and Sapouna-Sakellaraki 1997: 326–30; Krzyszkowska 2005: 70–1). These belong in the final Pre-Palatial phase (Table 1.1) and therefore push back the history of writing in the region. It has become clear that, rather than constituting a distinct script whose use did not continue, the relatively small number of signs known in the Archanes script are best regarded as the earliest attestations of Cretan Hieroglyphic (Younger 1999: 380–1), itself regularly incised on stone seals, or even of Linear A (Godart 1999). Thus, the first true writing on Crete appears in an elite milieu, apparently unconnected with administration (see Schoep 2006: 44–8). However, we need to be aware of the taphonomy of writing in Crete: we are dependent on writing being applied to materials that are preserved archaeologically, such as stone or bone, *and* on conditions being favourable to the preservation of those materials. Since clay was in wide and regular use for the production of many types of administrative document in the Aegean and these were not deliberately baked, they are only preserved in burnt contexts, either destructions or accidental fires. This makes the observation of stages of development difficult. The absence of administrative documents in the Archanes script may simply be due to the absence of the appropriate depositional contexts.

There was a long tradition of the use of stamp seals in the Aegean, so we might expect seals to have been stamped on clay. Stamps are attested in the Aegean as early as the seventh millennium (Early Neolithic), becoming commoner by the sixth millennium (Papathanassopoulos 1996: 331–4; Krzyszkowska 2005: 33–5). By the third millennium BC (Early Bronze Age) direct evidence of their use is widespread in the form of impressed clay pieces (direct-object sealings), preserved by burning, that sealed various types of containers, both on the Greek mainland, at a number of sites in the Peloponnese, and, in smaller numbers, on Crete at the same time (Krzyszkowska 2005: 45–56, 76–8). Essentially the same system is attested in over 6000 stamped clay direct-object sealings preserved in the Proto-Palatial palace of Phaistos as well as several hundred at contemporary Monastiraki (Krzyszkowska 2005: 104–9) (Fig. 1.2). Although cylinder seals are known as artefacts from Pre-Palatial Aegean contexts, the style of sealing actually used on clay in the Aegean was always stamping, not rolling. This practice of stamp sealing further reminds us that administration is a practice that may or may not involve writing, and that accounts of change should include the broadest administrative context, not focus narrowly on its written manifestations (e.g. Palaima 1990).

The second modification to Evans' evolutionary scheme was the discovery of Linear A documents in Proto-Palatial contexts in the palace of Phaistos that were contemporary with the clay sealings mentioned above, long before the 'demise' of Cretan Hieroglyphic (e.g. Schoep 1995: 38–43). In that period, uses of Cretan Hieroglyphic and Linear A on clay documents seem to have had a complementary distribution: in the north and east of the island (particularly the sites of Knossos, Malia, and Petras), Cretan Hieroglyphic was used, while Linear A is attested in the south (currently only Phaistos; e.g. Schoep 1999a). Why both scripts should be in contemporaneous use is unclear. They may notate different languages, although similarities between the two scripts are such that some (e.g. Karnava 2005; Younger 1999: 387–8, 393) regard them as stylistic variants of a single script ('glyptic-derived' versus 'linear'), each embedded in different local administrative systems.

Finally, crucial for this analysis is Evans' chronological positioning of Linear B at Knossos. The recognition that the phase of the palace at Knossos in which the Linear B documents were preserved post-dated destruction levels at other Neo-Palatial sites, rather than being contemporary with them, emerged from the controversy that erupted in the early 1960s about the dating of the tablets (first summarized in Palmer and Boardman 1963). This controversy was sparked in part by a desire to 'tidy up' the cultural sequence in the area. The discovery of Linear B documents at Pylos in Messenia (Fig. 1.1), dating to the end of the Late Helladic IIIB period, c. 1200 BC, together with other discoveries at mainland sites of similar date, left the deposits at Knossos, belonging to a period a couple of centuries earlier, chronologically isolated. The fact that the Pylos documents were so similar to those at Knossos, combined with Leonard Palmer's scepticism about the quality of Evans' recording of the excavation, led him to propose that the Pylos and Knossos tablets were contemporary, a view vigorously denied by John Boardman. Re-study of the Knossos material by Mervyn Popham (1970) and others, plus newly excavated contexts, demonstrated that the Knossos documents were indeed much earlier than those at Pylos, but belonged to a phase that clearly post-dated the end of the Neo-Palatial period. The situation is quite involved, as one would expect with a large building complex in use over several centuries, but it now seems that the oldest surviving Linear B documents at Knossos were preserved in an area called the 'Room of the Chariot Tablets' (Driessen 2000). These belong early in the LMIIIA1 period (see Table 1.1), perhaps around 1400 BC, while the majority of the rest of the archive dates a generation or two later, in early LMIIIA2, although some small groups may date later still (the situation is summarized in Driessen 1990; 1997a).

Linear A in Use: Neopalatial Minoan Administration

As noted above, the Linear A script was in use on Crete from at least the Middle Minoan IIB phase (c. 1800 BC). In the Neo-Palatial period (c. 1700–1450 BC), Linear A became predominant, and it is the sole script attested by its latest phase. From this period Linear A is also attested at a number of sites off the island, mostly in the Cycladic islands to the north (Karnava 2008).

We know of almost 1500 inscriptions in Linear A (Schoep 2002: 13–22, from which the statistics in this paragraph are drawn). Of these, 113 (7.5%) can be categorized as 'non-administrative', appearing on a range of objects, such as ceramic vessels (both incised and painted), stone vessels (Fig. 1.3), and gold and silver items of personal adornment (Table 1.2). A few of these may have had some relation to economic administration, such as the 42 that were incised before firing on large-scale ceramic storage vessels, including the example from Kato Zakros (Fig. 1.1) with signs numbering at least 24, plus the logogram for 'wine', followed by the figure 32 (ZA Zb 3: Godart and Olivier 1982: 112–13). Others represent longer, continuous text, without logograms or numerals. Among these are the 42 examples incised on stone vessels, many of them deposited in sanctuaries (alongside much larger numbers of uninscribed examples), such as that on the peak of Mt Iouchtas c. 15 km south of Knossos (Fig. 1.2). One vessel from this context bears an inscription of over 37 signs (IO Za 2: Godart and Olivier 1985: 18–19), while another example, from the far-eastern site of Palaikastro (Fig. 1.2), has 45 signs (PK Za 11: Godart and Olivier 1982: 32–5). Rarer are precious-metal objects deposited in tombs, such as a gold ring from the Mavrospelio cemetery at Knossos with 19 signs arranged in a spiral (KN Zf 13: Godart and Olivier 1982: 152–3), or a silver pin from a tomb at Platanos (Fig. 1.2) in south-central Crete, with at least 24 signs (PL Zf 1: Godart and Olivier

1982: 161). Although we may classify these as non-administrative documents, on the basis of material and find contexts, they were certainly bound up with practices of the elite, who may well have seen no distinction between recording on clay and inscribing on metal or stone.

The vast majority of preserved Linear A inscriptions can be considered 'administrative', and were inscribed on clay media specifically shaped to reflect their function within that system: tablets, and seal-impressed clay pieces in a range of forms (Table 1.2). About 1370 inscribed administrative documents are known, of which the majority were preserved in the burnt destructions of various major sites, notably Ayia Triada in south-central Crete, Khania in the northwest, and Kato Zakros on the east coast (Fig. 1.2). They therefore belong at the end of the Late Minoan IB phase, c. 1450 BC (Schoep 1995; Hallager 1996: 39–77). Of 330 known tablets, 147, the largest single group, come from Ayia Triada. This is the only class of document designed exclusively as a support for writing. Linear A tablets occur in only one form, with the proportions of a playing-card, and bear, on average, 16.1 signs per tablet (Schoep 2002: 38).

All other classes of document involve seal-impressions, but do not *require* writing. With one exception (Younger 1999: 384–5), Linear A writing does not appear on seals, unlike the situation with Cretan Hieroglyphic; rather, seals contain pictorial scenes, sometimes of considerable elaboration (e.g. Hallager 1985). By the Neo-Palatial period, all writing is incised or painted; it was not formed by

Figure 1.3   Linear A inscribed stone offering table from cave sanctuary at Psychro
(PS Za 2: Godart and Olivier 1982:52–5). Max. W. approx. 40 cm.

Type	Classification*	Medium	Style of mark	Function
tablet	[site + no.]		incision	
roundel	Wc			
one-hole hanging nodule	Wa	clay	incised/stamp	administrative
two-hole hanging nodule	Wd		stamp/incised (rare: c. 5%)	
nodulus	We/Wf			
flat-based nodule	Wb	clay + parchment	stamp/incised (very rare: < 1%)	
vessel	Zb	clay	incised pre-firing	administrative?
	Zc		painted pre-firing	non-administrative
			painted post-firing	
	Za	stone	incised	
architectural block	Ze			
personal adornment	Zf	metal		
wall	Zd	plaster		administrative?
miscellaneous	Zg	various	incised or painted	non-administrative

*For classification of sealed document types (W-), see Hallager 1996: 21–9; Schoep 2002: 16–21; for other types (Z-), see Godart and Olivier 1982; Schoep 2002: 13–16.

Table 1.2   Types of inscription in Linear A, indicating media, function, and style of marking.

the process of stamping. The commonest type of seal-impressed document is a simple clay nodule, formed around the knotted end of a cord, and referred to as a 'single-hole hanging nodule'. Of these 983 are known (936 from Ayia Triada alone), 878 of them bearing inscriptions, almost exclusively comprising a single Linear A sign. At Ayia Triada, these were found in large numbers, concentrated in the northwest quarter of the main building, almost certainly fallen from an upper storey (Hallager 1996: 43; Schoep 2002: 194). The most plausible interpretation offered to date is that these—perhaps in pairs—sealed rolled papyrus documents, which have not themselves survived (Hallager 1996: 159–99, esp. 198–9; Krzyszkowska 2005: 158–60). A second large group of 761 sealings (only seven bearing inscriptions, however) reveal, under microscopic examination, the imprint of animal skin and therefore seem to have sealed tightly folded and bound parchment documents or 'packets', again not preserved (Pini 1983:

560–2; Hallager 1996: 135–58; Krzyszkowska 2005: 155–8). This probable indirect attestation of other writing media reminds us that traditions parallel to that attested on clay must have existed (supported by the existence of longish ink inscriptions on the inside of two cups found at Knossos—KN Zc 6 and 7: Godart and Olivier 1982: 118–25), and that we need to be as much aware of what we are *not* observing as of what we are observing.

Three other types of documents bear seal-impressions. 'Roundels' are known in 180 examples, of which 139 bear inscriptions, usually single signs, it seems used logographically to denote a commodity. As their name suggests, these were small disks of clay, inscribed usually on one face, with varying numbers of identical seal-impressions round the edge. These were probably receipts, held by the issuing party, the number of seal-impressions corresponding to the quantity of the commodity issued (Hallager 1996: 79–120; Krzyszkowska 2005: 163). The two remaining types, *noduli* and two-hole hanging nodules, are rarely inscribed (less than 5% of examples: Table 1.2). *Noduli* are simply small pieces of clay with one or more seal-impressions, depending on their shape. Their exact function is unclear, but may have included that of 'dockets' or 'tokens' (perhaps to allow passage, or to receive accommodation), although some may have been issued to receivers as receipts *from* an authority (Hallager 1996: 121–33; Krzysz-kowska 2005: 161–3). Two-hole hanging nodules were formed around a knotted cord that protruded on both sides (hence 'two-hole'); they seem to have tagged or labelled objects, possibly valuables (Hallager 1996: 159–61; Krzyszkowska 2005: 160–1).

Understanding the administrative process to which these documents attest is not easy, given both that the script is undeciphered and that longer, pre-sumably summarizing and potentially 'archival' documents on papyrus and/or parchment are absent. Schoep divides the process into: 'primary' documents, for information-gathering, among which she includes the *noduli*, some tab-lets, some roundels, and some flat-based nodules (i.e. parchment documents); 'intermediate' documents, for information-processing, chiefly tablets, but also some roundels and some flat-based nodules; and 'final' documents, the papyri implied by the large numbers of single-hole hanging nodules, although she also allows a role here for roundels and flat-based nodules, and perhaps for the two-hole hanging nodules (summarized in Schoep 2002: 193–9, esp. fig. 4.4). Pietro Militello (1991), basing his study on the largest surviving 'system' at Ayia Triada, develops a similar reconstruction, moving from 'data-collection' through 'data-elaboration' to 'data-archiving'. However, he distinguishes proc-esses taking place within the central complex and those that happened outside, reflecting the centre's interaction with a territory. Unlike the situation with Linear B administration, no hierarchy is obvious within the documentation on tablets, although it is clear, for example, from tablets that have multiple topics and formats that they drew data from other sources (Schoep 2002: 194). The overall picture strongly suggests that we are missing a summary stage that presumably existed originally on the perishable documents.

A total of forty-five sites on Crete, the islands (Thera/Santorini, Melos, Keos, Samothrace), and the Greek (Ayios Stefanos) and Anatolian (Miletos) mainlands have produced Linear A inscribed material (Fig. 1.1), although only eleven of those sites have both administrative *and* non-administrative types. More significantly, sites at either end of Crete—Khania in the west, and Kato Zakros in the east—plus Ayia Triada in south-central Crete, have the full repertoire of administrative document types in the LMIB phase (Schoep 1995). This suggests that the administrative 'reach' of any one of these various centres did not extend over the majority of the island, although the existence of flat-based nodules in non-local clay at some sites implies administrative or diplomatic interaction. That the scale of administration was regional, rather than island-wide, is also supported by the overall figures attested in the better-preserved collections of documents (Schoep 1999b; 2002: 199). A surprising gap in the record of Linear A documents preserved in the LMIB phase is Knossos itself. Although the site produced examples of administrative and non-administrative documents, those that can be given relatively clear contexts—especially the clay documents—belong to earlier phases, mostly LMIA (Schoep 1995: 31–4). The significance of this absence is difficult to gauge, especially given that unbaked clay documents are preserved only where they have been burnt, but if it were real, it could be relevant to the disappearance of Linear A more generally.

Over 1000 inscriptions in Linear A belong to the end of the LMIB phase. It is therefore striking that only three definitively Linear A inscriptions are known from later contexts. Two of these may actually have been manufactured and inscribed in or before LMIB: a ceramic storage jar with six signs incised pre-firing on its shoulder that was found in the Unexplored Mansion near the palace at Knossos (KN Zb 40: Godart and Olivier 1982: 83; Popham, Pope, and Raison 1976) is LMII by context, while a handle found in a closed LMII–IIIA deposit at the eastern site of Palaikastro bears a single, incised sign (PK Zb 24: Schoep 1998). The third, and most convincing, example is a clay female figure, LMIIIA1 by style, bearing an inscription painted before firing on her skirt, and recovered from the Knossian harbour site of Poros (PO Zg 1: Dimopoulou *et al.* 1993). None of these three examples can be categorized as administrative documents. A fourth possible example also falls into this category: the two signs incised on an architectural block forming part of the entrance to a tholos tomb (a type of Late Bronze Age tomb, with a circular chamber constructed in corbelled stone blocks, approached by a narrow corridor, or *dromos*: e.g. Cavanagh and Mee 1998: 44–6) at the location named Kephala, north of the palace at Knossos (Preston 2005). Godart and Olivier include this in their catalogue of Linear A inscriptions (KN Ze 16: Godart and Olivier 1982: 138; cf. Preston 2005: 62), but the signs involved are attested in both scripts and the more likely construction date for the tomb is LMII (Preston 2005: 83–6). If we accept the inscription as Linear A, then it is another example of the continued use of the script in a non-administrative context; if we consider it Linear B, then it would be a highly unusual use.

We should also note, in passing, the puzzling example of a stone plaque dated to the Hellenistic (third century BC) or Roman periods and commonly thought to have been recovered from the Psychro cave sanctuary in east-central Crete, or possibly from the village of Ini. This object bears an alphabetic inscription in the so-called Eteocretan language found mainly in inscriptions of the seventh to third centuries BC, but also has three signs that bear a striking resemblance to the Linear scripts (Duhoux 1982: 95–111, 328, pl. 27). Since a Bronze Age Linear A inscription is known from this site (PS Za 2: Godart and Olivier 1982: 52–5), it is possible that the inscription, if genuine (see Duhoux 1982: 110–11), copied signs from an ancient object encountered in the cave (cf. Alcock 2002: 116–7; Watrous 1996: 55).

If this disappearance of Linear A represented the (almost complete) disappearance of writing on Crete, then the situation would be relatively clear, but the Linear B script is attested there and, in later contexts, on mainland Greece, as we observed above. Moreover, the Linear B script is evidently an adaptation of Linear A, with modifications to the syllabic and logographic repertoires, and to the system of recording weights and measures. The earliest known Linear B documents are from the Room of the Chariot Tablets area of the palatial complex at Knossos (Driessen 1990; 2000), and, although their precise dating remains controversial, they appear to belong two to three generations after the end of LMIB, at the beginning of the LMIIIA phase, perhaps around 1400 BC. Linear B documents are not yet attested anywhere else on Crete until the mid-LMIIIB phase, c. 1250 BC. Moreover, with one striking exception, Linear B inscriptions are confined to the administrative world of tablets and clay sealings.

We seem, then, to be dealing with the 'replacement', within a script community, of Linear A by Linear B, rather than with the former's true disappearance. The replacement raises significant issues, since it is absolute, which is striking when, earlier in Crete's history, Linear A and Cretan Hieroglyphic had been in contemporaneous use.

The Relationship between Linear A and Linear B

Evans' observations about Linear B—that it was a Knossian variant of Linear A—are understandable, because the scripts bear a considerable resemblance to one another: '[t]he occurrence in both of similar sign-groups seems at any rate to prove that the language itself of those who used the one or the other Script was essentially the same' (Evans 1909: 38). However, it had become clear, even before the decipherment, that there were differences. With the decipherment came the realization that one important, underlying difference was language.

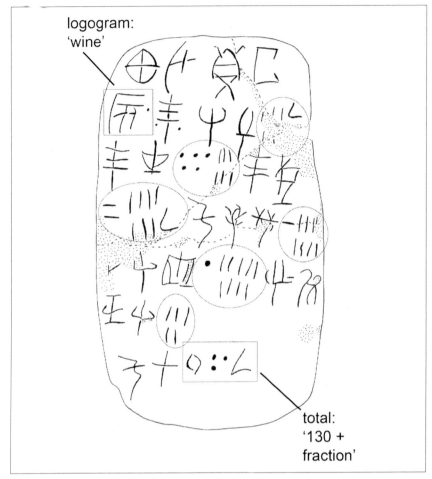

Figure 1.4 Linear A tablet from Ayia Triada (HT 13), annotated to show components of the script. Circles indicate numbers and fractions. H. 10.5 cm.

Relations in script

Both scripts are similar in structure, comprising a relatively small number of syllabograms in comparison to Hittite or Mesopotamian logo-syllabic systems (Figs. 1.4–1.6). In Linear B, the core syllabic repertoire is about 59 signs, while that of Linear A may number as high as 100 (Palaima and Sikkenga 1999: 600). In the case of Linear B, it is clear that the majority of signs are either pure vowels (*a, e, i, o, u*) or open consonant (C) + vowel (V) combinations (e.g. *da, de, di, do, du*). There are also a few C + glide + V combinations (e.g. *nwa, dwe, rya*). Nothing in the Linear A syllabary suggests that it was structurally dissimilar, although it appears that the phonetic structure of the language behind Linear

A differed from that of Greek. This is evident when comparing the two sign repertoires: many Linear B syllabic signs are recognizably similar in form to signs in Linear A. Scholars disagree about the exact number of Linear B signs with formal parallels in Linear A, but a figure of 75% overall is plausible; this percentage is even higher (85%) if only the core signs are taken into account (based on Palaima and Sikkenga 1999: 607, table 1). The signs that appear to 'innovate' are not randomly distributed across the grid of Linear B values. Most striking is that seven of thirteen core signs representing C+*o*, and two of the C+*e* series, are 'new' (e.g. Palaima and Sikkenga 1999: 603), while the C+*a*, C+*i*, and C+*u* series all have formal parallels in Linear A. This suggests a different vowel system behind Linear A, most plausibly a three- rather than five-vowel system. In addition to differences in the vowel system, there are some indications that the consonantal system of the language behind Linear A differed from that of Greek. For example, there is a possible *d/l* confusion in the Linear A script (Palaima and Sikkenga 1999: 604, n. 16), and Linear A may contain signs for C + glide + V (C^w+V; C^y+V) (Schrijver 2001). Similarly, Linear B appears to have retained some 'inherited' signs whose value cannot yet be determined with certainty, notably Linear B *22 and *56 (see Melena 1987); these possibly reflect sounds in the 'Linear A language', and are particularly common in personal and place-names (Palaima and Sikkenga 1999: 603). The fact that no sign-series in Linear B is entirely new, combined with the probable difference in consonant values, suggest that *some* modification of phonetic values of borrowed signs took place, meaning that great caution should be exercised in using Linear-B-derived values to 'read' Linear A inscriptions (e.g. Younger 2000).

As well as syllabic signs, both Linear A and B used a range of logograms, sometimes referred to as 'ideograms', to denote people, materials, commodities, and objects. Although there is some overlap between the scripts (e.g. Palmer 1995; Schoep 2002: 91–3), Ilse Schoep (2002: 29) estimates that 80% of around 180 Linear A logograms (including multiple variant forms) did not continue into Linear B. The creators and early users of Linear B devised a new logographic repertoire comprising around 140 signs and variants (e.g. Ventris and Chadwick 1973: 50–1), among which are numerous representational or 'iconic' logograms, for example those for 'horse' and 'deer', for vessels, for 'chariots', and for a range of vessel forms, elements of armour, and weapon types. Also Linear B used some syllabic signs in isolation as new logographic signs on the acrophonic principle: e.g. *KO*, abbreviating *koriadna*, 'coriander'; some 'monograms' were created from syllabic signs that spelled words in Greek: e.g. *ME+RI* for *meli*, 'honey' (Ventris and Chadwick 1973: 52–3; Schoep 2002: 29). In the Linear A script logograms are often ligatured—some frequently, such as that conventionally read as 'barley'— with syllabic signs, or fractions (Schoep 2002: 29–30). All of these practices are seen in examples of Linear A logograms that continue into Linear B, such as the cloth logogram with various infixed syllabograms (e.g. Melena 1975: 107–17) or the 'wool' logogram, which is probably a monogram created in Linear A from the signs which have the syllabic values *ma* and *r/lu* in Linear B, or the logogram for 'figs', which has the syllabic value *ni* in Linear B, possibly an abbreviation for *nikúleon*, a word attested in later Greek lexicographers (e.g. Ventris and Chadwick 1973: 563).

While the system of numerals is identical in Linear A and B (both are decimal, as was Cretan Hieroglyphic, and both use the same symbols for units, tens and hundreds: Schoep 2002: 30–1), the way in which the two scripts handled weights and measures differs radically. Linear A has an extensive range of around 17 'simple' and 30 'composite' signs denoting fractional quantities, conventionally referred to as 'klasmatograms' (Schoep 2002: 31). Thus, a weighed quantity of a commodity might be expressed as '50¾' 'talents'. In Linear B, by contrast, weights and dry and liquid volume measures were notated in three series, using a hierarchy of quantities: major unit, plus four smaller units for weights, and three each for dry and liquid volumes (e.g. Ventris and Chadwick 1973: 54–60, 393–4). Thus, the same '50¾' quantity might be expressed in Linear B, on the lines of pre-metric British weights, as '50 cwt 84 lbs'. Some of the Linear A 'klasmatogram' signs were re-used in this system, but not, as far as we can tell, systematically with the same fractional ratios. This change in practice suggests a revision to accommodate a new, or external, system, seemingly sexagesimal (e.g. Petruso 1978; De Fidio 2002; generally Michailidou 2001).

Relations in administration

At the higher level of administrative practice, differences between the two administrative communities are still clearer (see Palaima 2003 for a concise summary of Linear B practice). The range of documents produced in Linear B is much more restricted (Table 1.3). The only class of texts other than clay-based administrative documents was painted, before firing, on to about 160 examples of a type of transport/storage vessel called the stirrup-jar. The vast majority of

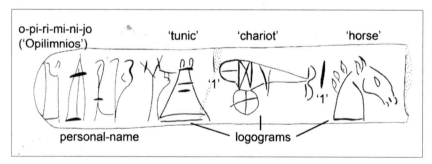

Figure 1.5   Linear B single-entry tablet from the Room of the Chariot Tablets deposit at Knossos (KN Sc 230), indicating combination of phonetic signs, numerals and logograms. W. 13 cm.

Type	Classification*	Medium	Style of mark	Function
tablet (page)	An–z			
tablet (elongated)	Aa–m		incision	
label	Wa–b	clay		
string nodule	Wm; Wo			administrative
regular/irregular string nodule	Wr–y		stamp/incision (rare: c. 14%)	
nodulus	Wn			
flat-based nodule	Wb [only RCT at Knossos]	clay + parchment		
vessel	Z	clay	painted pre-firing	administrative?
weight?	Zh	stone	incision	non-administrative?

* For classification of tablets, see Ventris and Chadwick 1973: 50–1; for sealed document types (W), see Hallager 2005: 249–58.

Table 1.3 Types of inscription in Linear B, indicating media, function and style of marking.

the vessels were not inscribed, and they were probably manufactured on Crete, but were found widely distributed at sites on Crete and the Greek mainland; most date to the later fourteenth and thirteenth centuries (e.g. Van Alfen 1997; Haskell *et al.* in press). There are a handful of inscriptions on stone (including, perhaps, that on the Kephala tholos tomb, mentioned above), or incised on ceramics other than stirrup-jars, but nothing like the quantity attested in Linear A, despite the fact that Linear B written administration is attested not only on Crete but also at a number of mainland sites (Pylos, Mycenae, Tiryns, Midea, and Thebes: Fig. 1.1).

As with Linear A, Linear B administrative documents include tablets and a range of other clay documents, many of them stamped by seals. Among the approximately 5,500 documents attested in Linear B, the vast majority are tablets that exist in two forms, unlike those in Linear A: elongated (or 'palm-leaf'), and page-shaped. The former, a type not attested in Linear A, were used predominantly to record single units of information, single 'rows' of data as in a computer spreadsheet (Fig. 1.5). Page-shaped tablets, on the other hand, had multiple rows of data, sometimes clearly summarizing information recorded elsewhere on individual documents, either elongated tablets or string nodules (Fig. 1.6). There is thus a clear hierarchy and progression of data-recording within the clay media, and scholars sometimes refer to Linear B as more obsessed with paperwork (or 'claywork'); such a hierarchy is far less obvious in Linear A (e.g. Schoep 2002: 193; see also Militello 1991; Driessen 1997b). What is far from clear in Linear B administration is whether there was a top level of summary

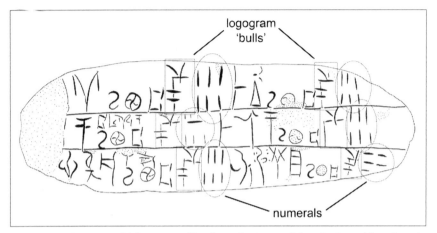

Figure 1.6 Linear B multiple-entry tablet from the Room of the Chariot Tablets deposit at Knossos (KN Ce 59), indicating 'working' male oxen at six places in central and western Crete. W. 14 cm.

recording on perishable material, although many scholars assume that this was so (e.g. Palaima 2003: 171–2; Driessen 1997b; contrast Bennet 2001). There are only seven examples of flat-based nodules, all from the Room of the Chariot Tablets deposit at Knossos, the earliest attested Linear B (e.g. Driessen 1990; 1997a; 2000), although they differ in detail from Linear A examples, leading to the suggestion that they might not have sealed parchment documents like their Linear A counterparts (Hallager 2005: 252). No single-hole hanging-nodules are known, implying that papyrus documents, if they existed, were not sealed in the same way as they had been in the Neo-Palatial period.

Equally, the sealing system of Linear A administration is simplified in Linear B (see Hallager 2005 for an excellent summary): roundels disappear altogether, while *noduli*, only in one type, become very rare. Single-hole hanging-nodules also disappear, as noted above, while the two-hole variety is split into two types: regular and irregular string nodules. Of these, only the former bear inscriptions, in about 50% of preserved examples. Regular string nodules were probably attached to commodities both within and outside the palatial centres, while the irregular examples (all found broken, probably in antiquity) may have been attached to commodities that had arrived in the palatial buildings themselves, and were broken when no longer required (Hallager 2005: 257–8).

In terms of 'administrative reach', the Linear B documents seem to operate at a higher level, often recording large quantities, either individually or collectively across sets of documents. The loss of the roundel might reflect a distancing of the administration from those to whom it issued goods. The clearest evidence, however, is a product of the decipherment: the fact that we can read and recognize some place-names. These suggest that the 'reach' of Knossos extended as far as Khania in western Crete, over much of west-central and central Crete (including the region of Ayia Triada and Phaistos), to the east-central part of the island, if probably not to the far east (e.g. Bennet 1985; 1987; 2009). It is possible that the extent of this reach might not have been as great at the time of the earliest administration attested in the Room of the Chariot Tablets deposit, nor might control have been continuous over a single, undifferentiated territory (e.g. Driessen 2001). However, the Linear B documents confirm, for the first time in Crete's prehistory, that Knossos exercised some form of control over the greater part of the island.

Knossos and Crete in the Fifteenth Century BC: The Disappearance of Linear A

It is clear from the above that a new script (Linear B) and administrative system was created at some point before its attestation around 1400 BC in the Room of the Chariot Tablets within the palace at Knossos. This observation raises four questions: how, when, where, and why was Linear B created? The first we have largely answered above in outlining the relationship between the two scripts and their related administrative practices. We can give a *terminus ante quem* to the second question: no later than Linear B's earliest attestation, c. 1400 BC. A more considered date can only be proposed if the third question is answered first.

There are broadly two possibilities for the locus of creation of Linear B: mainland Greece, among a community of Greek speakers, or on Crete, probably at Knossos itself, in an environment, probably bilingual, where Greek was either prestigious or strategically advantageous. In the first instance, the adaptation can be seen as part of the appropriation of exotic materials and knowledge by the early Mycenaean elite, most prominent in the period of the Shaft Graves at Mycenae (see Wright 1995; Palaima 1995; Bennet 2004). It is easy to see how the mid-twentieth-century view of identity, with its emphasis on language, would favour the creation of a Greek-based administration in a Greek-speaking milieu, and its subsequent introduction to Crete by conquering 'Mycenaean' mainlanders. However, with a single possible exception discussed below, there is no evidence for writing on the Greek mainland prior to the LHIIIA2 (mid to late fourteenth century BC) tablet recently discovered in the Petsas House at Mycenae (Shelton 2006). There are fairly numerous examples of Cretan seals deposited in early Late Bronze Age mainland tombs, often in pairs (Rehak and Younger 2000), but no writing. Indeed, it has been argued that the need for complex administration only arose with the earliest palatial structures on the mainland (e.g. Palaima 1988: 336–42), perhaps around the same time as the earliest attested examples of Linear B at Knossos.

Why should the converse be more likely, however: namely the creation of a Linear B script and administration at Knossos on Crete? First, the Linear A and B scripts and administrative systems show considerable similarities, and indeed they seem to diverge with time, the Room of the Chariot Tablets system representing a closer approximation to Linear A practice than later patterns (e.g. Driessen 2000: 224–8). It is not difficult to imagine a situation in which bilingual administrators, in the cosmopolitan major Aegean centre that Knossos was in the second millennium BC, could have adapted Linear A to record the Greek language. Modifications to the administrative system would have been made to reflect the recently enlarged area administered from Knossos—essentially moving administrative activity up to a higher level—and also the centralization of administrative control at Knossos itself.

In support of this scenario, we can first note that we have no evidence for the use of Linear A at Knossos in the immediately preceding LMIB period, although this may simply be a taphonomic issue: no burnt contexts at the site that would have preserved unbaked documents. If so, it is surprising that Linear A documents of all types are so widely attested elsewhere, even if in very small numbers at most individual sites. It is possible, therefore, that a new script may have been adapted from Linear A already in LMIB. Second, we observe quite profound changes in burial practice and material culture, centred on Knossos itself, beginning in the LMII period. Laura Preston has summarized the burial practices, which include new tomb types, especially built examples, like the Kephala tholos tomb (Preston 2005), and new locations for burial, in prominent ridge-top locations north of the palace, on routes to its harbour-town at Poros (Preston 1999). Although the new tomb types have been seen as mainland-derived, and therefore as further evidence for mainland incursions, their range of resonances is more complex, indeed drawing on mainland themes and forms, but also combining them with local Cretan symbols, or even materials, in the case of the re-used ashlar blocks in the Kephala tholos (Preston 1999; 2005). Similarly, new vessel types, particularly the stemmed drinking cup, imply a shift in styles of display on commensal occasions. It is even possible to read the application of an inscription to the entrance of the Kephala tholos as drawing on a Cretan tradition of inscribing on stone and using 'mason's marks'. Moreover, if we were to read the inscription as Linear B, and therefore Greek, it reads *a-pi*, a possible imperative form, 'Go away!' (see Nagy 1963: 205).

We can suggest that the cultural changes at Knossos that began with the LMII period and included the adaptation of administration to form a new system were part of an active construction of a new identity for the Knossos elite on a pan-Cretan, possibly an Aegean stage (see also Driessen 2002; Driessen and Langohr 2007). Similar situations might be the shifts in administrative practice, and language, introduced in Mesopotamia in the Sargonic period in the mid third millennium BC, and then again with the establishment of the Ur III dynasty a century or so later (e.g. Van de Mieroop 2007: 63–84; Michalowski 1991; Postgate 1994: 40–3).

The ease with which an administrative shift such as this could have been achieved becomes clearer when we consider the likely size of the script-using communities involved. Analysis of scribal hands in the Ayia Triada Linear A documents suggests a possible minimum number of tablet-writers of eighteen (e.g. Godart and Olivier 1985: 83–6; Schoep 1996: 335–55). More 'hands' are identified on the single-hole hanging nodules, but it is difficult to estimate how many individuals this represents, since these are almost all single-sign inscriptions. In the Knossos Room of the Chariot Tablets, Driessen identifies nine major and four minor Linear B 'scribes' responsible for about 650 surviving documents (Driessen 2000: 71–99), against a possible total of around sixty for the much larger corpus attested elsewhere in the palace of Knossos and in later contexts (Driessen 2000: 150–1; see also Olivier 1967). If we accept the idea that Aegean writers were not merely secretaries, but were themselves active in administration (Bennet 2001; see also Palaima 2003: 175–7), then the possibility of a deliberate and active adaptation of the script is still more likely. Moreover, there is no reason for this to have taken a long time (e.g. Palaima 1988: 341); it could certainly have been accomplished within a generation. (Achieving administrative control over much of Crete may have taken longer, of course.) The hypothesis of a relatively quick creation also militates against the idea of a longer 'gestation' on the mainland, prior to the script's introduction, fully formed, to Crete.

There is one small, but potentially significant, piece of evidence against the suggestion that Linear B was adapted on Crete: the discovery, on 1 April 1994, of a small pebble bearing a Linear B inscription at the site of Kafkania, near Olympia in the northwestern Peloponnese (Arapojanni *et al.* 2002). The context for this object is given as late Middle Helladic, perhaps c. 1600 BC (earlier on the high chronology: Table 1.1), but certainly at least two centuries earlier than the Room of the Chariot Tablets at Knossos. The object is peculiar: unique in form and style of inscription, and in its early date, as well as being on stone (but see Adrimi-Sismani and Godart 2005: 59–65), not to mention its place of discovery, well away from the 'heartland' of early Mycenaean developments in the Argolid and Messenia, respectively in the northeastern and southwestern Peloponnese. Thomas Palaima has outlined these and further difficulties with the inscription, drawing attention, among other things, to its precocious sign-forms, which resemble closely Pylos 'hands' some 400 years later in date (Palaima 2006). Although this object cannot be ignored, so long as it remains unique, it cannot be used by itself to overturn the wealth of evidence for the later adaptation of Linear B, whether this occurred on the mainland or, as I argue, on Crete.

If we accept the probability that Linear B was created at Knossos on Crete, then the date is likely to be between c. 1450 and 1400 BC. As to why it was created, I would argue that it was part of a major cultural realignment among the

Knossian ruling elite (including those who used writing), no doubt bilingual, who chose to differentiate themselves through a range of cultural materials and practices drawing on both local and mainland traditions. This realignment included the adaptation of a script that was already at least 300 years old (and so perhaps distanced from spoken forms of its language) to a new written language. It also involved the redesign of indigenous administrative practice for a new context, in which Knossos was expanding its control on the island, control it was to exercise for a further seventy-five or 100 or so years. Seen in this perspective, Linear A did not simply disappear; rather, it was killed. Mid-twentieth-century attitudes to ancient identity and its essentialist link to language led to mainland Greek speakers ('Mycenaeans') being 'framed' for this murder. More probably the guilty party was within the family, so to speak. We can better appreciate the mid-fifteenth-century BC changes on Crete as telling us about how elite notions of identity were constructed and played out in public, than by trying to read modern concepts of identity, shaped by our belonging within modern nation-states, into the material record of a period that is as 'foreign' as any other in the distant past.

Note

1. I should like to thank my fellow editors for proposing and helping to organize the original meeting in Oxford, and for their extraordinary patience in waiting for this chapter; both also offered valuable comments, some at long distance, using the latest technology. I am also grateful to Paul Halstead and Debi Harlan for reading and commenting on the final version, as I am to Artemis Karnava and Peter Schrijver for sharing copies of material in advance of publication. None of them should be held responsible for the use to which I have put—or not put—their advice. Finally, I would also like to thank the staff at Keble College, Oxford, for creating such a pleasant physical environment for our meeting and my former colleagues there for offering a stimulating intellectual environment during the tenure of my fellowship.

References

Adrimi-Sismani, Vasso, and Louis Godart
    2005   'Les inscriptions en Linéaire B de Dimini/Iolkos et leur contexte archéologique'. *Annuario della Scuola Archaeologica di Atene* 83: 47–70.

Alcock, Susan E.
    2002   *Archaeologies of the Greek Past: Landscape, Monuments, and Memories.* Cambridge: Cambridge University Press.

Arapojanni, Xeni, Jörg Rambach, and Louis Godart
    2002   *Kavkania: die Ergebnisse der Ausgrabung von 1994 auf dem Hügel von Agrilitses.* Mainz: von Zabern.

Bennet, John
> 1985 'The Structure of the Linear B Administration at Knossos'. *American Journal of Archaeology* 89: 231–49.
>
> 1987 'The Wild Country East of Dikte: The Problem of East Crete in the LM III Period'. In John T. Killen, José L. Melena, and Jean-Pierre Olivier (eds), *Studies in Mycenaean and Classical Greek Presented to John Chadwick. Minos* 20–22. Salamanca: Ediciones Universidad de Salamanca, 77–88.
>
> 2000 'Linear B and Linear A'. In Davina Huxley (ed.), *Cretan Quests: British Explorers, Excavators and Historians.* London: British School at Athens, 129–37.
>
> 2001 'Agency and Bureaucracy: Thoughts on the Nature and Extent of Administration in Bronze Age Pylos'. In Sofia Voutsaki and John Killen (eds), *Economy and Politics in the Mycenaean Palace States: Proceedings of a Conference held on 1-3 July 1999 in the Faculty of Classics, Cambridge.* Cambridge Philological Society Supplement 27. Cambridge: Cambridge Philological Society, 25–37.
>
> 2004 'Iconographies of Value: Words, People and Things in the Late Bronze Age Aegean'. In John C. Barrett and Paul Halstead (eds), *The Emergence of Civilisation Revisited.* Sheffield Studies in Aegean Archaeology 6. Oxford: Oxbow, 90–106.
>
> 2009 'The Geography of the Mycenaean Kingdoms'. In Yves Duhoux and Anna Morpurgo Davies (eds), *A Companion to Linear B: Mycenaean Greek Texts and their World.* Bibliothèque des Cahiers de l'Institut de Linguistique de Louvain 120. Leuven: Peeters.

Bennett, Emmett L., Jr.
> 1989 'Michael Ventris and the Pelasgian Solution'. In Yves Duhoux, Thomas G. Palaima, and John Bennet (eds), *Problems in Decipherment.* Bibliothèque des cahiers de l'Institut de Linguistique de Louvain 49. Leuven: Peeters, 9–23.

Blegen, Carl, and Alan J. B. Wace
> 1916–18 'The Pre-Mycenaean Pottery of the Mainland'. *Annual of the British School at Athens* 22: 175–89.

Broodbank, Cyprian
> 2000 *An Island Archaeology of the Early Cyclades.* Cambridge: Cambridge University Press.

Brown, Ann
> 2000 'Evans in Crete before 1900'. In Davina Huxley (ed.), *Cretan Quests: British Explorers, Excavators and Historians.* London: British School at Athens, 9–14.
>
> 2001 *Arthur Evans's Travels in Crete 1894-1899.* British Archaeological Reports, International Series 1000. Oxford: Archaeopress.

Cavanagh, William, and Christopher Mee
> 1998 *A Private Place: Death in Prehistoric Greece.* Studies in Mediterranean Archaeology 125. Jonsered: Paul Åströms Förlag.

Chadwick, John, Louis Godart, John T. Killen, Jean-Pierre Olivier, Anna Sacconi, and Iannis Sakellarakis
> 1986 *Corpus of Mycenaean Inscriptions from Knossos*, vol. 1 (1–1063). Incunabula Graeca 88. Cambridge/Rome: Cambridge University Press/Edizione dell'Ateneo.

De Fidio, Pia
  2002   'On the Tracks of Aegean Bronze Age Wool and Weights'. In John Bennet and Jan Driessen (eds), *A-NA-QO-TA: Studies Presented to J. T. Killen*. *Minos* 33–34 (1998–1999). Salamanca: Ediciones Universidad de Salamanca, 39–63.

Dimopoulou, Nota, Jean-Pierre Olivier, and Georges Réthémiotakis
  1993   'Une statuette en argile avec inscription en Linéaire A de Poros/Irakliou'. *Bulletin de Correspondance Hellénique* 117: 501–21.

Driessen, Jan
  1990   *An Early Destruction in the Mycenaean Palace at Knossos: A New Interpretation of the Excavation Field-Notes of the South-East Area of the West Wing*. Acta Archaeologica Lovaniensia Monographiae 2. Leuven: Katholieke Universiteit Leuven.
  1997a 'Le Palais de Cnossos au MR II–III: combien de destructions?' In Jan Driessen and Alexandre Farnoux (eds), *La Crète mycénienne: Actes de la Table Ronde Internationale organisée par l'Ecole française d'Athènes (26-28 mars 1991)*. Bulletin de Correspondance Hellénique Supplément 30. Athens: Ecole française d'Athènes, 111–34.
  1997b 'Data Storage for Reference and Prediction at the Dawn of Civilization? A Review Article with Some Observations on Archives before Writing'. *Minos* 29–30: 239–56.
  2000   *The Scribes of the Room of the Chariot Tablets at Knossos: Interdisciplinary Approach to the Study of a Linear B Deposit*. Minos Supplement 15. Salamanca: Ediciones Universidad de Salamanca.
  2001   'Centre and Periphery: Some Observations on the Administration of the Kingdom of Knossos'. In Sofia Voutsaki and John Killen (eds), *Economy and Politics in the Mycenaean Palace States: Proceedings of a Conference held on 1-3 July 1999 in the Faculty of Classics, Cambridge*. Cambridge Philological Society Supplement 27. Cambridge: Cambridge Philological Society, 96–112.
  2002   '*Kretes* and *Iawones*: Some Observations on the Identity of Late Bronze Age Knossians'. In John Bennet and Jan Driessen (eds), *A-NA-QO-TA: Studies Presented to J. T. Killen*. *Minos* 33–34 (1998–1999). Salamanca: Ediciones Universidad de Salamanca, 83–105.

Driessen, Jan, and Charlotte Langohr
  2007   'Rallying Round a "Minoan" Past: The Legitimation of Power at Knossos during the Late Bronze Age'. In Michael L. Galaty and William A. Parkinson (eds), *Rethinking Mycenaean Palaces II*, second edition. Cotsen Monograph 59. Los Angeles: Cotsen Institute of Archaeology, 178–89.

Duhoux, Yves
  1982   *L'Etéocrétois: les textes, la langue*. Amsterdam: Gieben.

Evans, Arthur J.
  1895   *Cretan Pictographs and Prae-Phoenician Script; with an account of a Sepulchral Deposit at Hagios Onuphrios near Phaestos in its relation to Primitive Cretan and Aegean Culture*. London: Bernard Quaritch.
  1909   *Scripta Minoa: The Written Documents of Minoan Crete with Special Reference to the Archives of Knossos*, vol. 1: *The Hieroglyphic and Primitive Linear Classes*. Oxford: Clarendon Press.

1935   *The Palace at Knossos*, vol. 4, part 2. London: Macmillan.

1952   *Scripta Minoa: The Written Documents of Minoan Crete with Special Reference to the Archives of Knossos*, vol. 2: *The Archives of Knossos*, ed. John L. Myres. Oxford: Clarendon Press.

Farnell, Lewis R.

1927   'Preface'. In Stanley Casson (ed.), *Essays in Aegean Archaeology Presented to Sir Arthur Evans in Honour of his 75th Birthday*. Oxford: Clarendon Press.

Fitton, J. Lesley

1995   *The Discovery of the Greek Bronze Age*. London: British Museum.

Godart, Louis

1999   'L'écriture d'Arkhanès: hiéroglyphique ou Linéaire A?' In Philip P. Betancourt, Vassos Karageorghis, Robert Laffineur and Wolf-Dietrich Niemeier (eds), *Meletemata: Studies in Aegean Archaeology Presented to Malcolm H. Wiener as He Enters His 65th Year*, vol. 1. Aegaeum 20. Liège: Université de Liège, 299–302.

Godart, Louis, and Jean-Pierre Olivier (eds)

1976   *Recueil des inscriptions en Linéaire A*, vol. 1: *Tablettes éditées avant 1970. Etudes Crétoises* 21:1. Paris: Paul Geuthner.

1982   *Recueil des inscriptions en Linéaire A*, vol. 4: *Autres documents. Etudes Crétoises* 21:4. Paris: Paul Geuthner.

1985   *Recueil des inscriptions en Linéaire A*, vol. 5: *Addenda, corrigenda, concordances, index et planches des signes. Etudes Crétoises* 21:5. Paris: Paul Geuthner.

Hallager, Erik

1985   *The Master Impression: A Clay Sealing from the Greek-Swedish Excavations at Kastelli, Khania*. Studies in Mediterranean Archaeology 69. Gothenburg: Paul Åströms Förlag.

1996   *The Minoan Roundel and Other Sealed Documents in the Neopalatial Linear A Administration*. 2 vols. Aegaeum 14. Liège: Université de Liège.

2005   'The Uniformity in Seal Use and Sealing Practice during the LH/LM III Period'. In Anna Lucia D'Agata and Jennifer Moody (eds), *Ariadne's Threads: Connections between Crete and the Greek Mainland in Late Minoan III (LM IIIA2 to LM IIIC)*. Athens: Scuola archeologica italiana di Atene, 243–65.

Haskell, Halford W., Richard E. Jones, Peter M. Day, and John T. Killen (eds)

In press Transport Stirrup Jars of the Bronze Age Aegean and Eastern Mediterranean. Philadelphia, PA: INSTAP Academic Press.

Karnava, Artemis

2000   'The Cretan Hieroglyphic Script of the Second Millennium BC: Description, Analysis, Function and Decipherment Perspectives'. Unpublished PhD thesis, Université libre de Bruxelles.

2005   'Tradition and Innovation: The Scripts in the Old Palatial Period'. Paper delivered to the London Mycenaean Seminar, 12 January. [abstract: *Bulletin of the Institute of Classical Studies* 50 (2007): 199–200]

2008   'Written and Stamped Records in the Late Bronze Age Cyclades: The Sea Journeys of an Administration'. In Neil J. Brodie, Jennifer Doole, Giorgos Gavalas, and Colin Renfrew (eds), *Horizon: A Colloquium on the Prehistory of the Cyclades*. Cambridge: McDonald Institute, 377–86.

Kemp, Barry J., and Robert S. Merrillees
  1980   *Minoan Pottery in Second Millennium Egypt.* Deutsches Archäologisches Institut, Abteilung Kairo. Mainz: von Zabern.

Krzyszkowska, Olga
  2005   *Aegean Seals: An Introduction. Bulletin of the Institute of Classical Studies.* Supplement 85. London: Institute of Classical Studies.

MacGillivray, J. Alexander
  2000   *Minotaur: Sir Arthur Evans and the Archaeology of the Minoan Myth.* London: Jonathan Cape.

Manning, Sturt, Christopher Bronk Ramsey, Walter Kutschera, Thomas Higham, Bernd Kromer, Peter Steier, and Eva M. Wild
  2006   'Chronology for the Aegean Late Bronze Age 1700–1400 BC'. *Science* 312: 565–9.

Melena, José L.
  1975   *Studies on Some Mycenaean Inscriptions from Knossos Dealing with Textiles. Minos* Supplement 5. Salamanca: Ediciones Universidad de Salamanca.
  1987   'On Untranslated Syllabograms *56 and *22'. In Petar Ilievski and Ljiljana Crepajac (eds), *Tractata Mycenaea: Proceedings of the Eighth International Colloquium on Mycenaean Studies, Held in Ohrid (15-20 September 1985).* Skopje: Macedonian Academy of Sciences and Arts, 203–32.

Michailidou, Anna (ed.)
  2001   *Manufacture and Measurement: Counting, Measuring and Recording Craft Items in Early Aegean Societies.* Meletemata 33. Athens: National Hellenic Research Foundation.

Michalowski, Piotr
  1991   'Charisma and Control: On Continuity and Change in Early Mesopotamian Bureaucratic Systems'. In McGuire Gibson and Robert D. Biggs (eds), *The Organization of Power: Aspects of Bureaucracy in the Ancient Near East*, second edition. Studies in Ancient Oriental Civilization 46. Chicago, IL: Oriental Institute, 45–57.

Militello, Pietro
  1991   'Per una classificazione degli archivi nel mondo egeo'. *Sileno* 17: 327–47.

Nagy, Gregory
  1963   'Greek-like Elements in Linear A'. *Greek Roman and Byzantine Studies* 4: 181–211.

Olivier, Jean-Pierre
  1967   *Les Scribes de Cnossos.* Incunabula Graeca 17. Rome: Edizioni dell'Ateneo.

Olivier, Jean-Pierre, and Louis Godart (eds)
  1996   *Corpus Hieroglyphicarum Inscriptionum Cretae.* Etudes Crétoises 31. Paris: de Boccard.

Palaima, Thomas G.
  1988   'The Development of the Mycenaean Writing System'. In Jean-Pierre Olivier and Thomas G. Palaima (eds), *Texts, Tablets and Scribes: Studies in Mycenaean Epigraphy and Economy Offered to Emmett L. Bennett, Jr. Minos* Supplement 10. Salamanca: Ediciones Universidad de Salamanca, 269–342.

1995   'The Nature of the Mycenaean Wanax: Non-Indo-European Origins and Priestly Functions'. In Paul Rehak (ed.), *The Role of the Ruler in the Prehistoric Aegean.* Aegaeum 11. Liège: Université de Liège, 119–42.

2003   '"Archives" and "Scribes" and Information Hierarchy in Mycenaean Greek Linear B Records'. In Maria Brosius (ed.), *Ancient Archives and Archival Traditions: Concepts of Record-Keeping in the Ancient World.* Oxford: Oxford University Press, 153–94.

2006   'OL Zh 1: quousque tandem?' *Minos* 37–38 (2002–2003): 373–85.

Palaima, Thomas G. ed.
1990   *Aegean Seals, Sealings and Administration: Proceedings of the NEH-Dickson Conference of the Program in Aegean Scripts and Prehistory of the Department of Classics, University of Texas at Austin January 11-13, 1989.* Aegaeum 5. Liège: Université de Liège.

Palaima, Thomas G., and Elizabeth Sikkenga
1999   'Linear A > Linear B.' In Philip P. Betancourt, Vassos Karageorghis, Robert Laffineur, and Wolf-Dietrich Niemeier (eds), *Meletemata: Studies in Aegean Archaeology Presented to Malcolm H. Wiener as He Enters His 65th Year*, vol. 2. Aegaeum 20. Liège: Université de Liège, 599–608.

Palmer, Leonard R., and John Boardman
1963   *On the Knossos Tablets: The Find-Places of the Knossos Tablets; the Date of the Knossos Tablets.* Oxford: Clarendon Press.

Palmer, Ruth
1995   'Linear A Commodities: A Comparison of Resources'. In Robert Laffineur and Wolf-Dietrich Niemeier (eds), *POLITEIA: Society and State in the Aegean Bronze Age*, vol. I. Aegaeum 12. Liège: Université de Liège, 133–55.

Papathanassopoulos, George A. (ed.)
1996   *Neolithic Culture in Greece.* Athens: Nicholas P. Goulandris Foundation.

Petruso, Karl M.
1978   'Systems of Weight in the Bronze Age Aegean'. PhD dissertation, Indiana University.

Pini, Ingo
1983   'Neue Beobachtungen zu den tönernen Siegelabdrücken von Zakros'. *Archäologischer Anzeiger* 1983: 559–72.

Popham, Mervyn R.
1970   *The Destruction of the Palace at Knossos: Pottery of the Late Minoan III A Period.* Studies in Mediterranean Archaeology 12. Gothenburg: Paul Åströms Förlag.

Popham, Mervyn R., Maurice Pope, and Jacques Raison
1976   'An Inscribed Pithoid Jar from Knossos'. *Kadmos* 15: 102–7.

Postgate, J. Nicholas
1994   *Early Mesopotamia: Society and Economy at the Dawn of History.* London: Routledge.

Preston, Laura

 1999 'Mortuary Practices and the Negotiation of Social Identities at LM II Knossos'. *Annual of the British School at Athens* 94: 131–43.

 2005 'The Kephala Tholos at Knossos: A Study in the Reuse of the Past.' *Annual of the British School at Athens* 100: 61–123.

Rehak, Paul, and John G. Younger

 2000 'Minoan and Mycenaean Administration in the Early Late Bronze Age: an Overview'. In Massimo Perna (ed.), *Administrative Documents in the Aegean and Their Near Eastern Counterparts: Proceedings of the International Colloquium, Naples, February 29—March 2, 1996*. Turin: Centro internazionale di ricerche archeologiche antropologiche e storiche, 277–301.

Sakellarakis, Yannis, and Efi Sapouna-Sakellaraki

 1997 *Archanes: Minoan Crete in a New Light*. 2 vols. Athens: Ammos Publications.

Schoep, Ilse

 1995 'Context and Chronology of Linear A Administrative Documents'. *Aegean Archaeology* 2: 29–65.

 1996 'Minoan Administration on Crete: An Interdisciplinary Approach to Documents in Cretan Hieroglyphic and Linear A (MM I/II–LM IB)'. Unpublished PhD dissertation, Katholieke Universiteit Leuven.

 1998 'A Note on the Inscribed Material of the 1994 Excavations.' *Annual of the British School at Athens* 93: 264–8.

 1999a 'The Origins of Writing and Administration on Crete'. *Oxford Journal of Archaeology* 18: 265–76.

 1999b 'Tablets and Territories? Reconstructing Late Minoan IB Political Geography through Undeciphered Documents'. *American Journal of Archaeology* 103: 201–21.

 2002 *The Administration of Neopalatial Crete: A Critical Assessment of the Linear A Tablets and their Role in the Administrative Process*. Minos Supplement 17. Salamanca: Ediciones Universidad de Salamanca.

 2006 'Looking beyond the First Palaces: Elites and the Agency of Power in EMIII–MMII Crete'. *American Journal of Archaeology* 110: 37–64.

Schrijver, Peter

 2001 'Structure and Affiliation of Minoan'. Seminar paper, Somerville College, Oxford, 23 October.

Shelton, Kim S.

 2006 'A New Linear B Tablet from Petsas House, Mycenae'. *Minos* 37–38: 387–96.

Sherratt, E. Susan

 2000 *Catalogue of Cycladic Antiquities in the Ashmolean Museum*. Oxford: Oxford University Press.

Trigger, Bruce G.

 2006 *A History of Archaeological Thought*, second edition. Cambridge: Cambridge University Press.

Van Alfen, Peter G.

 1997 'The LM IIIB Inscribed Stirrup-Jars as Links in an Administrative Chain'. *Minos* 31–32: 251–74.

Van de Mieroop, Marc
  2007   *A History of the Ancient Near East ca. 3000–323 BC*, second edition. Oxford: Blackwell Publishing.

Ventris, Michael
  1940   'Introducing the Minoan Language'. *American Journal of Archaeology* 44: 494–520.
  1988   *Work Notes on Minoan Language Research and Other Unedited Papers*, ed. Anna Sacconi. Incunabula Graeca 90. Rome: Edizioni dell'Ateneo.

Ventris, Michael G. F., and John Chadwick
  1973   *Documents in Mycenaean Greek*, second edition. Cambridge: Cambridge University Press.

Wace, Alan J. B.
  1956   'Foreword'. In Michael G. F. Ventris and John Chadwick, *Documents in Mycenaean Greek*. Cambridge: Cambridge University Press, xvii–xxxi.

Warren, Peter, and Vronwy Hankey
  1989   *Aegean Bronze Age Chronology*. Bristol: Bristol Classical Press.

Watrous, L. Vance
  1996   *The Cave Sanctuary of Zeus at Psychro: A Study of Extra-Urban Sanctuaries in Minoan and Early Iron Age Crete*. Aegaeum 15. Liège: Université de Liège.

Wright, James C.
  1995   'From Chief to King in Mycenaean Greece'. In Paul Rehak (ed.), *The Role of the Ruler in the Prehistoric Aegean*. Aegaeum 11. Liège: Université de Liège, 63–80.

Younger, John G.
  1999   'The Cretan Hieroglyphic Script: A Review Article'. *Minos* 31–2: 379–400.
  2000   *Linear A Texts in Phonetic Transcription*. http://www.people.ku.edu/~jyounger/LinearA/, last accessed 13 November 2007.

2

The Disappearance of Writing Systems:
Hieroglyphic Luwian

J. David Hawkins

Terminology

In addressing the disappearance of the hieroglyphic script of Anatolia ('Hittite hieroglyphs'), we need to begin with a brief survey of the script's designation, origin, character, use, and extent. The designation 'Hittite hieroglyphs' is still valid to the extent that, for the first part of the script's known history, it was primarily employed by and attested in the Hittite kingdom of Hattusa, and after the dissolution of that polity, it continued to be used by dynasties generally termed (Neo-)Hittite: the heirs of Hattusa in the first millennium BC. The label 'Hieroglyphic Hittite' for the language written by the script has however been rendered obsolete by the gradual recognition, now completed, that the language is in fact a form of Luwian; it is therefore termed 'Hieroglyphic Luwian', to distinguish it from 'Cuneiform Luwian', the small group of texts found among the clay tablet archives of Boğazköy-Hattusa. Thus no *language* other than Luwian is found written in the hieroglyphs, although personal names from other language groups—Hittite, Hurrian, and Semitic, as well as Luwian—may be rendered in the script. These hieroglyphs, perhaps best termed 'Anatolian', appear primarily as a glyptic and monumental script in the Hittite kingdom. The intriguing problem remains as to why the Hittite kings wrote their royal library and archives on clay tablets in the cuneiform script principally in their own language Hittite, but their monumental inscriptions on stone in hieroglyphic in the Luwian language. The implications that this has for the range of Hittite and Luwian as spoken languages have been variously assessed, as have the implications for the origin of the hieroglyphic script in relation to Luwian.

Origin and Development under the Hittite Empire

Signs certainly identifiable as hieroglyphs are first found on seals (usually known only from impressions on clay sealings) from the Old and Middle Kingdom periods of Hattusa and in smaller quantities from other sites, also of unknown provenance, c. 1650–1450 BC (Güterbock 1942; Boehmer and Güterbock 1987). These cannot be shown to connect with seals of the earlier periods as known from Kültepe, Acemhöyük, and Karahöyük–Konya, nor can they usually be dated very precisely within their own period. The most common signs are the *triangle*, representing 'good' (= cuneiform SIG_5); the *ankh*, borrowed from Egypt, 'life' (= cuneiform TI); and the sign 'scribe', recording the profession of most of the seal-holders. Other hieroglyphs render the owners' names, but while many can be identified with their later forms, not many convincing names can be collected from these readings. It is not certain that these early occurrences represent a fully developed system of writing (Mora 1991).

Royal seals begin to be known from impressions on legal texts during this period, but up to the end of the Middle Kingdom, their inscriptions are in cuneiform only, typically written in two circles around a central rosette, to which may be added on occasion the hieroglyphs *triangle* and *ankh*. The outer cuneiform circle normally reads 'Seal of Tabarna the Great King', to which, in the Middle Kingdom, the king's personal name is added (Otten 1987; Neve 1991, 1992); the inner circle reads 'who changes (his word) will die'. The seals without the added personal name ('anonymous Tabarna seals') are shown by a recent prosopographical study of the legal texts probably not to antedate Telipinu, the last king of the Old Kingdom (Wilhelm 2005).

A seal impression from Tarsus shows the seal of Telipinu's contemporary, Išputahšu, king of Kizzuwatna, on which a single ring of cuneiform surrounds a centre with four hieroglyphs, the signs *ankh* and *triangle* flanking the signs 'Storm-God' and 'King'. The reading and significance of these latter signs is not clear. If they could be shown to represent the king's name in any way, this would be the earliest example of a 'digraphic' royal seal on which the cuneiform name of the outer circle corresponds to a hieroglyphic writing in the centre, but such a correspondence cannot be demonstrated. So it may be that this digraphic practice originated with Tudhaliya I of Hattusa whose digraphic seal is known from a recently discovered impression (Otten 2000). Thereafter it becomes a regular feature of royal seals followed by all kings of the Empire dynasty from Tudhaliya I to Suppiluliuma II. It seems that this format was reserved for royalty: princes and officials have only hieroglyphic inscriptions on their seals, and the addition of cuneiform is very rare. The digraphic seals of the kings of Hattusa are the only place where the two scripts, cuneiform and hieroglyphic, overlap. It is perhaps also worth noting that a different type of digraph is found on the legal texts of Ras Shamra-Ugarit and Meskene-Emar under the Hittite provincial administration c. 1320-1200 BC. There, the local witnesses impressed their seals, on which their predominantly West Semitic and Hurrian names were written in hieroglyphic, and these were identified by cuneiform epigraphs 'seal of So-and-so, son of So-and-so' (see Laroche 1956; Beyer 2001).

With the advent of Hittite monumental sculpture on rock and dressed stone monuments, hieroglyphs also appear in monumental form to provide the epigraphs identifying human or divine figures. No such monuments or inscriptions can definitely be dated earlier than the thirteenth century BC in spite of attempts to push some examples back to the fifteenth century (Neve 1994). Most such monuments with inscriptions are specifically linked to the last three generations of the Hattusa dynasty in the thirteenth century BC, beginning with the brothers Muwatalli II (rock relief SİRKELİ) and Hattusili III (rock relief FRATKTİN) and their first cousin Talmi-Sarruma of Aleppo (inscription ALEPPO 1). In the short inscriptions of the latter two, the first phonetically written Luwian words are recognizable, indicating that the still largely logographic texts should be read in that language. It is only in the next two generations that longer monumental inscriptions in hieroglyphic are found, specifically the work of Hattusili's son Tudhaliya IV and grandson Suppiluliuma II (the last known king of the dynasty). The best examples from each king are YALBURT and BOĞAZKÖY 21 (SÜDBURG), both acquisitions of the last twenty years, though other inscriptions have long been known: the EMİRGAZİ altars text, and the badly eroded NİŞANTAŞ (see Poetto 1993; Hawkins 1995).

Here should also be mentioned the 'wooden documents', referred to in Cuneiform Hittite texts along with 'scribes on wood'. No such inscribed document has survived, though a small two-leafed, hinged writing board without inscription was recovered from the Uluburun/Kaş shipwreck (see Symington 1991). We can only speculate as to the script(s) and languages committed to such documents. It is possible, though evidence is lacking, that besides cuneiform (for which see Singer 1983: 40-1), hieroglyphic could also have been written on these, and so might the Luwian language. If this is the case, it would mean that practical documents such as the Iron Age lead strips of ASSUR and KULULU (see below) were already being written in the Empire period, perhaps in a linear incised form of the script, the existence of which may be suggested by certain relief sign forms which appear 'cursive' (e.g. mu), as well as by the incised silver bowl text (see below). Epigraphs incised on building slabs at Boğazköy and especially on a boulder found in the lower city gateway give scribes' names with professional title and imply the existence of public scribes writing documents, on perishable material such as wood, for common people (Bittel 1957; Dinçol and Dinçol 2002).

Inscribed objects are rare in the Hittite record, but one such demands consideration in the context of the development of the hieroglyphic script: a silver bowl with a three-clause inscription in what appears to be a rather developed form of the script, stating that the object was made in the year 'when Labarna Tudhaliya smote the land Tarwiza'. Although our knowledge of the script's development as outlined above would naturally lead to the identification of Tudhaliya IV, there are significant arguments which could point to Tudhaliya I as author. This would mean that the script was sufficiently developed for a coherent inscription to be written six generations earlier than might have been supposed, but it does not seem possible to exclude completely such a view (see Hawkins 1997, reprinted with additions 2005; Mora 2007).

To summarize, Anatolian hieroglyphs are used to write names and titles on seals from perhaps 1600 BC down to 1200 BC, and the same script identifies figures on monumental stone sculpture for a period perhaps 1300–1200 BC. Though these names may be recognizable as belonging to specific language groups—Hittite, Luwian, or Hurrian—these short epigraphs cannot be said to be written 'in' any language. Extended stone inscriptions clearly written in Luwian are attributable only to Tudhaliya IV and Suppiluliuma II, having begun in a small way only in the preceding generation. The silver bowl inscription discussed above, if indeed attributable to Tudhaliya I rather than Tudhaliya IV, would raise the date of recognizably Luwian inscriptions by six generations.

The fall of the Hittite Empire c. 1200 BC saw the destruction of its leading cities and the dissolution of its system of royal and imperial administration. Along with this dissolution went the writing system associated with it—cuneiform on clay tablets—and this may indeed serve as a simple and clear example of the disappearance of a writing system. At this point it should be noted that the previous excavator of Boğazköy argues on the basis of the archaeological evidence that the traditional view of a sudden and violent end of Hattusa is better replaced with the concept of a slower withdrawal and abandonment (Seeher 2001). In this discussion the apparent sudden and total end of the cuneiform writing tradition must find its place. A slow decline hardly seems adequate to account for it: unless we are to envisage a possible future discovery of post-Hattusa cuneiform archives, some kind of violent termination seems more probable.

The Iron Age

The end of the cuneiform tradition of Hattusa however was not the end of its tradition of Anatolian hieroglyphic inscriptions. In the provinces of the former empire in south-east Anatolia and northern Syria independent successor states survived or re-established themselves: the so-called Neo-Hittite states of the Iron Age. These preserved traditions of art and architecture from the Hittite

Empire, and along with these the practice of writing monumental inscriptions in Hieroglyphic Luwian. The discovery of a handful of letters and economic texts written on lead strips in the same script/language shows that these states also continued a system of literacy in everyday documents which have mostly failed to survive.

These Neo-Hittite states have yielded to excavation, official or irregular, groups of monuments including hieroglyphic inscriptions. These are dated to various points in the period c. 1000–700 BC principally by association with the absolute chronology of Assyrian historical sources, but also partly by their own internal chronologies. The preceding period, c. 1200–1000 BC, has traditionally been seen as a hiatus in civilization, a dark age lacking monuments and inscriptions, but evidence is gradually accumulating for centres of continuity linking the Hittite Empire with the Neo-Hittite period.

Neo-Hittite Centres of Literacy

Karkamiš on the river Euphrates, as the seat of the Hittite viceroyalty of Syria under the Empire, appears to have escaped serious destruction at the end of the Bronze Age, and might have been expected to represent a centre of cultural continuity in the transitional period to the Iron Age. The earliest monuments recovered here however do not appear to date earlier than c. 1000 BC, but from this period on, most phases of development down to the late eighth century BC are represented. A smaller group of monuments from the neighbouring Til Barsip (modern Tell Ahmar), only 20 km downstream, belongs closely with the earlier Karkamiš material of the tenth century BC.

For the sculpture and inscriptions of Malatya, new evidence now re-establishes the early dating to the 'dark age', c. 1150–1000 BC, connecting it with the Empire period dynasty of Karkamiš and providing evidence for cultural continuity. In Gurgum (modern Maraş) irregular excavation has produced a group of inscribed sculpture, including the Maraş lion with an inscription recording a seven-generation dynasty, and enough other pieces attributable to this dynasty's members to give valuable dating criteria.

Smaller groups of inscriptions, both the work of father–son dynasties, have been found at Hamath (modern Hama), c. 860–810 BC, and Kummuh (classical Commagene), c. 810–775 BC. The Kingdom of Unqi (modern Amuq, Plain of Antioch) has yielded at its capital Tell Tayinat (ancient Kunulua?) fragmentary remains of ninth/eighth-century sculpture and inscriptions, presumed smashed at the Assyrian capture of the city in 738 BC.

The recent discovery on Aleppo Citadel of the Temple of the Storm-God with reliefs and a dedicatory inscription belonging apparently to the period 1100–1000 BC, throws further light on the 'dark age'. The name of the author and his country, already known from other monuments from Hama and the

Amuq, suggest the existence at this period of a large kingdom centred on the Plain of Antioch.

On the former Hittite heartland, the Anatolian plateau itself, known to the Assyrians as Tabal, two chronologically distinct groups of monuments are known: first the Karadağ-Kızıldağ group, which now seems to date c. 1200 BC, either shortly after or even shortly before the fall of the Hittite Empire; and secondly some later eighth-century BC monuments, the work of two father-son dynasties, from Tabal proper in the north (modern Kayseri, Nevşehir) and Tuwana in the south (classical Tyana, modern Niğde). Despite the gap of some four centuries separating the two groups, the later does show links, real or pretended, with the earlier.

The other integral part of the Hittite Empire, Cilicia, had until recently produced only the great KARATEPE bilingual in Phoenician and Hieroglyphic Luwian (the longest text in either corpus; Fig. 2.1), but in 1998 there was found in a field near Adana a colossal limestone figure of the Storm-God with a basalt base, his bull-drawn chariot, which itself bore a short bilingual inscription in Phoenician and Luwian. This ÇİNEKÖY inscription is the work of the king of Cilicia, apparently the same as is named in KARATEPE as the patron of the author, and who here claims descent from the hero Mopsos of Greek legend. ÇİNEKÖY is thus a generation earlier than KARATEPE, and they date late eighth to early seventh centuries BC (Tekoğlu and Lemaire 2000).

Style and Content of the Neo-Hittite Inscriptions

The hieroglyphic inscriptions are rendered in two different styles: the 'relief monumental', in which the signs are in relief with the background cut away and generally more pictographic in appearance; and the 'incised cursive', where the signs are simplified to unrecognizable linear forms suitable for incision. The boundaries between these styles are not sharply demarcated; thus monumental pictographic forms may appear in incised inscriptions, and cursive linear forms in relief. Nor is the distinction entirely one of date, though incised inscriptions are rare in the Empire period and become more common towards the end of the Late period. It seems that the incised cursive forms may represent hand-written documents, though such are unattested in the Empire period and represented only by the few lead strips in the Late period. It is noteworthy that the stone monuments of Tabal are prominently executed in this style, 'Kululu', as it may be termed from the site with which it seems most closely associated.

The stone inscriptions on which Hieroglyphic Luwian predominantly comes down to us are by their very nature commemorative or dedicatory, and are closely linked to building and sculpture. Thus they were executed primarily by those with resources to build and deeds to commemorate, mostly rulers. They were frequently placed on building elements, orthostats and door jambs, otherwise

Figure 2.1 Pair of lions from the entrance to the lower North Gate of the fortifications of Karatepe, Turkey, bearing part of the Phoenician and the Hieroglyphic Luwian inscriptions of Azatiwada (c. 700 BC).

as free-standing stelae with or without sculpture. Rock inscriptions might mark frontiers, routes, or local events. A specialized monument was the inscribed commemorative statue, described in a cuneiform text of the late twelfth century BC but with no surviving example until the ninth century. From the latter period, too, inscribed memorials of private persons begin to be found, which doubtless served as tombstones. Also written on stone are a few legal texts, land grants, and sales, comparable with Mesopotamian *kudurrus*. In general the content and purview of these stone inscriptions is strictly parochial, being restricted to the affairs of the author, his buildings, and his relations with the gods.

As noted, the survival of a few letters and economic texts written on lead strips implies a more widespread use of the script for such commonplace purposes on perishable materials. Although nothing of the sort survives for the Empire period, contemporary cuneiform texts do contain references to wooden documents, which may well have been, in part at least, inscribed in hieroglyphic.

The end of the hieroglyphic tradition

This survey of the development, extent, and use of the hieroglyphic script should have positioned us to assess the manner of and reason for its disappearance. We have seen how the cuneiform script and its clay tablets, used as a tool of the Hittite royal and imperial administration, disappeared with the dissolution of that administration. Yet the hieroglyphic script with the Luwian language was preserved, along with the associated traditions of sculpture and architecture, in a cultural continuity that is now beginning to become apparent. On the evidence of the lead strips late in the Neo-Hittite period, these states must have used the script and language for practical purposes as well as for display inscriptions. Yet it is not possible to be certain of the language(s) and ethnicity of the dynasts, let alone of the bulk of the population of the area from south-east Anatolia to north Syria. A shift in the language of the inscriptions of Til Barsip and Hamath from Hieroglyphic Luwian to Aramaic seems to show a change of dynasty but tells us little certain about the composition of the general populations.

Fate of the Neo-Hittite states: Assyrian annexation

The overall history of the Neo-Hittite states in the period c. 900–700 BC is drawn from the Assyrian historical records, in which they, along with the Arameans, Phoenicians, Hebrews, and others, appear as the victims of Assyrian depredations. In the most aggressive phase of Assyrian imperialism, c. 745–705 BC, these states were attacked, conquered, and annexed as Assyrian provinces. Their ruling classes, craftsmen, artisans, and much of the general population were regularly deported and resettled elsewhere in the Assyrian Empire, their places taken by other deportees. Destruction of the local monuments, including inscriptions, has been noted by excavators at several sites.

The dates of these annexations are methodically reported in the annals of the Assyrian kings Tiglath-pileser III and Sargon II: Unqi, 738; Karkamiš, 717; Malatya, 712; Gurgum, 711; Kummuh, 708. These historical events adequately explain the disappearance of epigraphic Hieroglyphic Luwian as being a result of the removal of the local dynasties who had set up the inscriptions in the first place. Little evidence survives of the extent to which the displaced peoples continued to write their own documents in Hieroglyphic Luwian. Only the hieroglyphic letters on lead strips discovered at Assur suggest that they might have done so, since the other end of the correspondence appears to be Karkamiš and it is possible that these are to be dated after the annexation. But even if Hieroglyphic Luwian lingered on after the deportation of its writers, it is likely that it gave way in the seventh century BC to the Aramaization which was taking over Assyrian administration and culture.

Surviving Neo-Hittite states

The disappearance of Hieroglyphic Luwian writing in those states annexed to the Assyrian Empire and attested as Assyrian provinces in the seventh century BC is hardly surprising. Certainly no Hieroglyphic Luwian inscriptions in any of the deported kingdoms are found later than the Assyrian annexations. But the situation in the states most remote from Assyria where the conquest may have been ephemeral is not so clear cut: Malatya had been conquered by Sargon in 712 BC, and though a conquest of Que (Plain Cilicia) is not recorded, an Assyrian governor is attested in 715 BC; likewise Sargon had been actively interfering in the affairs of Tabal, and in 713 BC he deposed the ruler, his own son-in-law, and seemingly left his daughter in charge. In Tuwana the local king Warpalawa was still in place in 710–709, but under pressure.

The death of Sargon in battle in 705 BC, apparently in Tabal, shook Assyrian control in their north-western provinces and in some cases terminated it, especially in Tabal, Malatya and Que. Sennacherib (704–681 BC) sent campaigns led by generals against Que (696 BC), and Tilgarimmu, a western province of Malatya (695 BC), but while no lasting results may have been achieved in Tilgarimmu, the situation in Que may have been different, for the KARATEPE bilingual inscription may mostly easily be fitted into the historical context of this period. Its author Azatiwada, according to his own account, had been a subordinate ruler promoted by the king of Adana, and had gained wide authority over the country, acting as regent to the royal family, the house of Mopsos. The narrative is difficult to accommodate in the reign of Sargon, when there was an Assyrian governor in the land, but could well fit into the circumstances of Sennacherib's reign if Azatiwada were an Assyrian client. If this dating, which fits also with the Phoenician and hieroglyphic palaeography of the texts, is correct, KARATEPE would be the latest Hieroglyphic Luwian inscription by quite a margin, and the only one written later than 700 BC.

Although Sennacherib may have succeeded in maintaining or regaining the Assyrian control of Que, the same does not seem to have been the case for Hilakku, Tabal, and Malatya. Esarhaddon's enquiries of the Šamaš oracles show that he considered them to be menacing enemies, and he names independent dynasts of Malatya and Tabal (Starr 1990), as does Assurbanipal also for Hilakku.

Environment of the Script's Final Disappearance

The main external political powers in eighth-century Anatolia had been Urartu and, later in the century, Phrygia, and these continued into the seventh century though probably weakened by Cimmerian incursions, which would also be pressing on the Neo-Hittite states. Would these conflicting pressures have been enough to terminate their literate tradition as represented by the Hieroglyphic Luwian inscriptions? It is certainly the case that monumental hieroglyphic inscriptions are not found here after c. 700 BC. It should be noted however that capital cities of the period are poorly known. Kululu, clearly an important centre which has yielded eighth-century inscriptions and sculpture to surface survey, has not been properly investigated (Özgüç 1971). Göllüdağ, a dramatic mountain-top site, has produced monumental buildings and sculpture which may date down to the seventh century BC, but is notably without inscription (Schirmer 1993). Kerkenes Dağ, another massive mountain-top site currently under survey and investigation, has been proposed as the Median site of Pteria, but has recently surprised by producing a still-fragmentary Phrygian inscription from one of its monumental gates (Summers *et al.* 2003). While this has as yet to be assessed and dated, it may have relevance to our present problem.

Even if monumental hieroglyphic inscriptions do actually cease in seventh century Anatolia, we have to ask whether the art of writing everyday documents, as attested by the KULULU lead strips for the late eighth century BC, was abandoned, and if so, why. Social decline, and the collapse of the political system which sustains the writing, might explain such a disappearance, though evidence for such disruption is lacking. Could it have been that the Anatolian dynasts attested in seventh-century Assyrian sources not only ceased to erect the monumental commemorative inscriptions that their predecessors had, but also gave up writing for the purposes of communication and administration? Of course such documents, unless committed to some durable material, do not appear in the archaeological record, which is in any case highly defective for this period.

At this time the epigraphic void of central Anatolia was surrounded by literate political powers. Throughout the seventh century BC, the Assyrian Empire preserved the cuneiform tablet tradition, although, significantly, the administration was increasingly conducted by means of the Aramaic parchment or papyrus, which does not survive in normal circumstances. At the same time the Urartian kingdom continued to erect its monumental cuneiform inscriptions and has left scanty but sufficient traces of everyday literacy (see e.g. Zimansky 1985: 80–3). In the south, alphabetic writing had spread from the Phoenicians to the Greeks, and the presence of these peoples trading in Cilicia must have meant that their documents would have been circulating there. Indeed, Phoenician had spread from Cilicia up to Tabal at the end of the eighth century BC, as shown by the bilingual royal inscriptions ÇİNEKÖY and İVRİZ 2, but this practice is not known to have continued later than KARATEPE. To the west, Phrygia too had been using the alphabet, having received it, as is now known, not later than c. 800 BC, though its fine monumental inscriptions seem to be concentrated in the period of Midas (later eighth century BC). At this time Phrygian writing penetrated the Neo-Hittite area at Tuwana, as seen by the 'Black Stone', but a substantial number of graffiti mainly on ostraca attest to its continuation as a writing system of Anatolia down to the fourth century BC (Brixhe and Lejeune 1984).

Conclusion

We have seen that at least half of the question of the disappearance of the Anatolian hieroglyphic script was straightforwardly answered as being a result of the destruction by the Assyrians of the states, or perhaps more specifically the dynasties which used it. But for the more remote states, Hilakku, Malatya and Tabal, which did not remain under Assyrian control during the seventh century, the Assyrian depredations may not be a sufficient explanation for the cessation of hieroglyphic documents, since these states soon reappeared under their own native dynasts who, by the reign of Assurbanipal, are sending embassies, surely not illiterate, to Assyria. Even if they gave up writing monumental stone inscriptions, the known circumstances of the period hardly suggest that, surrounded as they were by literate neighbours, they would simply have given up writing altogether. It would thus seem most probable that they would have continued to write their script on a medium which has not survived, or possibly adopted the alphabetic script of their neighbours the Phoenicians and Phrygians, but again on perishable material. It is even possible that future excavation might turn up some evidence for seventh-century Anatolian writing. As the seventh century BC faded into the sixth, the period of Lydo-Median and then Persian domination of Anatolia, there can be surely no question of the survival of the Hittite script, yet kingdoms of Cilicia and Cappadocia existed at that time. As earlier, the extent and nature of their literacy is quite unknown, though it seems no more likely that they had simply lapsed into illiteracy than their forebears of the seventh century.

References

Beyer, Dominique
    2001   *Emar IV: les sceaux.* Fribourg and Göttingen: Editions Universitaires and Vandenhoeck and Ruprecht.

Bittel, Kurt
    1957   'Vorläufiger Bericht über die Ausgrabungen in Boğazköy im Jahre 1956.' *Mitteilungen der Deutschen Orient-Gesellschaft* 89: 18–19.

Boehmer, Rainer Michael, and Hans Gustav Güterbock
    1987   *Glyptik aus dem Stadtgebiet von Boğazköy.* Boğazköy-Hattusa XIV. Berlin: Gebr. Mann.

Brixhe, Claude, and Michel Lejeune
    1984   *Corpus des inscriptions paléo-phrygiennes.* Paris: Editions Recherche sur les civilisations.

Dinçol, Ali M., and Belkis Dinçol
    2002   'Die "Anzeigen" der öffentlichen Schreiben in Hattuscha.' In *Anatolia Antica. Studia in Memoria di F. Imparati.* Florence: LoGisma, 207–15.

Güterbock, Hans Gustav
    1942   *Siegel aus Boğazköy* II. Teil. *AfO* Beiheft 7. Berlin: Selbstverlag E. H. Weidner.

Hawkins, J. David
    1995   *The Hieroglyphic Inscription of the Sacred Pool Complex at Hattusa.* Studien zu den Boğazköy-Texten Beiheft 3. Wiesbaden: Harrassowitz.
    1997   'A Hieroglyphic Luwian Inscription on a Silver Bowl in the Museum of Anatolian Civilizations, Ankara.' *Anadolu Medeniyetleri Müzesi 1996 Yıllığı.* Ankara: T. C. Kültür Bakanlığı. Reprinted with additions in *Studia Troica* 15 (2005): 193–204.
    2000   *Corpus of Hieroglyphic Luwian Inscriptions* volume I, 3 parts. Berlin, New York: de Gruyter.

Kohlmeyer, Kay, and J. David Hawkins
    forthcoming 'The Hieroglyphic Luwian inscription of the Temple of the Storm-God at Aleppo.'

Laroche, Emmanuel
    1956   'Documents hiéroglyphiques provenant du palais d'Ugarit.' In C. L. A. Schaeffer, *Ugaritica* III. Paris: Geuthner, 97–160.

Mora, Clelia
    1991   'Sull'origine della scrittura geroglifica anatolica.' *Kadmos* 30: 3–28.
    2007   Three metal bowls. In Metin Alparslan, Meltem Doğan-Alparslan, and Hasan Peker (eds), *Belkis Dinçol ve Ali Dinçol'a armagan VITA: Festschrift in Honor of Belkis Dinçol and Ali Dinçol.* Istanbul: Yayınları, 515–21.

Neve, Peter
    1991   'Die Ausgrabungen in Boğazköy-Hattusa 1990.' *Archäologischer Anzeiger*: 331–5.
    1992   'Die Ausgrabungen in Boğazköy-Hattusa 1991.' *Archäologischer Anzeiger*: 311–16.

1994   'Zur Datierung des Sphinxtores in Alaca Höyük.' In Manfried Dietrich and Oswald Loretz (eds), *Beschreiben und Deuten in der Archäologie des Alten Orients: Festschrift für Ruth Mayer-Opificius*. Münster: Ugarit-Verlag, 213–26.

Otten, Heinrich
1987   'Das hethitische Königshaus im 15. Jahrhundert v. Chr.' *Anzeiger der phil.-hist. Klasse der Österreichischen Akademie der Wissenschaften* 123 (1986): 21–34.
2000   'Ein Siegelabdruck Duthaliyas I.(?).' In Jürgen Seeher, 'Die Ausgrabungen in Boğazköy-Hattusa 1999.' *Archäologischer Anzeiger*, 375–6.

Özgüç, Tahsin
1971   *Kültepe and its vicinity in the Iron Age*. Ankara: Türk Tarimi Kurumu.

Poetto, Massimo
1993   *L'Iscrizione luvio-geroglifica di Yalburt*. Studia Mediterranea 8. Pavia: Gianni Iuculano.

Sams, G. Kenneth
2003   'Review of Eva-Maria Bossert, *Die Keramik Phrygischer Zeit* (Boğazköy-Hattusa XVIII).' *American Journal of Archaeology* 107: 677.

Schirmer, Wulf
1993   'Die Bauanlagen auf dem Göllüdağ in Kappadokien.' *Architectura: Zeitschrift für Geschichte der Baukunst*: 121–31.

Seeher, Jürgen
2001   'Die Zerstörung der Stadt Hattusa.' In Gernot Wilhelm (ed.), *Akten des IV. Internationalen Kongresses für Hethitologie*. Studien zu den Boğazköy-Texten 45. Wiesbaden: Harrassowitz, 623–34.

Singer, Itamar
1982   *The Hittite KI.LAM Festival* 1. Studien zu den Boğazköy-Texten 27. Wiesbaden: Harrassowitz, 40–1.

Starr, Ivan
1990   *Queries to the Sungod: Divination and Politics in Sargonid Assyria*. State Archives of Assyria IV. Helsinki: Helsinki University Press.

Summers, Geoffrey, Françoise Summers, David Stronach, and Scott Branting
2003   *Kerkenes News* 6. Ankara: METU Press.

Symington, Dorit
1991   'Late Bronze Age Writing-Boards and their Uses: Textual Evidence from Anatolia and Syria.' *Anatolian Studies* 41: 111–23.

Tekoğlu, Recai, and André Lemaire
2000   'La bilingue royale louvito-phénicienne de Çineköy.' In *Comptes rendus de l'Académie des Inscriptions et Belles-Lettres*. Juillet–octobre 2000: 963–1007.

Wilhelm, Gernot
2005   Zur Datierung der älteren hethitischen Landschenrungsurkunden. *Altorientalische Forshungen* 32: 272–9.

Zimansky, Paul E.
1985   *Ecology and Empire: The Structure of the Urartian State*. Chicago, IL: The Oriental Institute.

3

The Obsolescence and Demise of Cuneiform Writing in Elam

Jeremy Black†[1]

Introduction

Elam is the historical name for the region of south-western Iran closest to Iraq, covering both the mountainous area and the plain. It was anciently the region of the Elamite civilization, with its own language, which was written in cuneiform script for almost 2000 years.[2]

Uniquely, three distinct cuneiform writing systems were used in south-western Iran in ancient times: Mesopotamian cuneiform, writing various phases of Akkadian language; the adaptation derived from that used to write Elamite; and Old Persian cuneiform, invented to write this early Indo-European language.[3]

While the focus of this chapter will be on the writing of the Elamite language, the whole question of obsolescence and abandonment cannot be answered for the region without reference to the other writing systems used in Iran. Yet it is problematic to separate the history of writing systems from the viability and survival of spoken languages. Equally, in the case of ancient languages, modern knowledge of them is exclusively based on what is written. I will not attempt to describe the whole history of cuneiform writing in Elam; but it will be convenient to document the ways in which it was different from Mesopotamian writing, before concentrating on its gradual obsolescence. Also it is difficult to describe the demise of cuneiform without considering the rise of the new alphabetic systems, specifically Aramaic.

The emphasis of this volume is more than justified in the case of Elamite, in that the standard work on Elamite palaeography (Steve 1992), while describing in detail the origin and subsequent development of writing in ancient Elam, makes no mention of its demise, and there is little consideration of this in any other publication. The material is confusingly heterogeneous and diffuse, and I can do no more than suggest some interpretations.

Historical Background

The ancient evidence of writing for Elam is spread unevenly across periods and regions, and frustratingly there are phases for which none currently exists. During most of its history, material from Susa (the urban centre on the plain opposite southern Iraq) outstrips in quantity and variety that from other centres (for a historical overview, see Stolper 2004: 61–5). This could give a false impression of the significance of Susa in the history of Elam, when it is known that other centres further north and east of there played an equally important role in political development, in particular Anshan (modern Tall-i Malyan; Carter and Stolper 1984: 3–4). In general, the database for the study of writing in Elam, and especially of writing in the Elamite language, is very uneven as a basis from which to draw broad conclusions.

An independent writing system conventionally known as 'Proto-Elamite' was first developed in Elam for administrative recording perhaps as early as 3200 BC, almost certainly under the influence of early proto-cuneiform writing in adjacent southern Mesopotamia (Englund 2004). The very earliest documents have numerical signs and seal impressions only, and have been found at Susa, but also at Chogha Mish, Tepe Sialk, Tall-i Ghazir, and Godin Tepe V. Dating from shortly after these, the earliest tablets with pictographic signs (so-called Proto-Elamite A) are written in an undeciphered signary of 400–800 signs in up to 5000 variants. Again the majority of tablets have been found at Susa; others at Tepe Sialk, Tepe Yahya, Tall-i Malyan (at a time when Malyan was five times the size of Susa), and almost 1000 km east of Susa at Shahr-i Sokhta.

What appears to be a late survival of this script was still in use as the 'Linear Elamite' (or Proto-Elamite B) script as late as c. 2200 BC. It seems plausible that Linear Elamite and, by extension, Proto-Elamite recorded earlier forms of the Elamite language. Only just over 100 signs are attested in Linear Elamite writing, on fewer than two dozen inscribed objects, most from Susa. Others are from Shahdad and the Marv Dasht (Carter and Stolper 1984: 5–9). It is too early to assess reports (in February 2004) of an inscribed clay seal found at Jiroft in the Halil Rud region of Kerman province (some 480 km to the east of Tall-i Malyan/ Anshan) and provisionally dated to this chronological horizon.

It might have seemed as if at this point Linear Elamite was poised to become the 'national' writing of Elam (Steve 1992: 4); but in fact its attested history extends no further. Instead, Mesopotamian cuneiform writing was introduced to Elam alongside Linear Elamite around 2300 BC, to write Sumerian and Old

Akkadian, and was quickly adapted to the phase of the local language now known as Old Elamite.

The Elamite confederation of provinces tended to be ruled by one provincial dynasty at a time. In the epoch of the Akkadian dynasty of southern Mesopotamia, this was Anshan (Westenholz and Sallaberger 1999: 90). However, during the reigns of the Akkadian kings Narām-Suen (c. 2260–2223 BC) and Šar-kali-šarrī (c. 2223–2198 BC) the Susa plain was fully annexed to their Mesopotamian kingdom. An Old Akkadian brick inscription of Narām-Suen was found at Susa (Malbran-Labat 1995: no. 1), and documents in Old Akkadian from Susa of this period demonstrate commercial and political ties between Elam and southern Mesopotamia (Foster 1993). A treaty between Akkadian and Elamite rulers found at Susa is written in Old Elamite in Mesopotamian cuneiform (Hinz 1967: 66–96), and is the earliest Elamite in cuneiform, written in what is essentially a borrowed Mesopotamian syllabary. However, about ten of the signs exhibit somewhat archaic features which have been taken to argue for a prototype borrowing at an earlier date, possibly as early as the conquest of Sargon some eighty years previously, or as a result of even earlier contacts (Steve 1992: 4 and n. 8, and for Elamite sources in general 19–24).

Several of the Old Akkadian kings of southern Mesopotamia held some sort of control at least over lowland Elam, and Maništūšu (2275–2260 BC) had not only controlled Susa but had campaigned farther east, towards Anshan. After the collapse of Akkadian expansion and the reduction of Akkad to a small city-state, most of Elam appears to have fallen under the control of the state of Awan. Some of the inscriptions of Puzur-Inšušinak, the last king of Awan, found mostly at Susa, were written in Old Akkadian. A few were in Linear Elamite (Carter and Stolper 1984: 10–16). The third dynasty of Ur (c. 2112–2004 BC) controlled Susa under Šulgi (for whom it is claimed that he could speak Elamite) and his two successors, Amar-Suena and Šu-Suen (Carter and Stolper 1984: 16–17, nn. 90, 107). A brick of Šu-Suen from Susa is inscribed in Akkadian (Malbran-Labat 1995: no. 3).

However, the preserved amount of Old Elamite writing in cuneiform is small. At Susa the display inscriptions on bricks even of native Elamite rulers of the dynasties of Awan and Šimaški (c. 2500–1970 BC) were still written in Sumerian (Malbran-Labat 1995: nos. 4–5, 8–9), or bilingually in Sumerian and Akkadian (nos. 6–7); or else simply in Akkadian (nos. 10–18, often with many logograms). Rulers of the Sukkalmaḫ period (c. 1970–1500 BC) generally also used Akkadian (nos. 10–18), and administrative documents from Susa of this date are in Akkadian (see Carter and Stolper 1984: 24, n. 169). In the following centuries, a local variant of Akkadian was used at Susa with certain characteristic Susa spellings, such as *šà* regularly for *ša/šá* (Malbran-Labat 1995: nos. 19–20; Labat, Edzard, and Ghirshman 1974; von Soden 1991: introduction sub 9(a) 'Elam'; De Meyer 1962 has little on orthography).

Only in the Middle Elamite period, from the fourteenth century BC, did the Elamite language begin to be written again at Susa in official contexts. Elamite was widely used in royal inscriptions on stone, on bricks, and on statues throughout the period c. 1500–1100 BC. Yet over 600 administrative documents from Haft Tepe were written in Akkadian in the fourteenth century BC (Carter and Stolper 1984: 32–5), including the so-called 'Mālamīr' documents. From then on, with the flourishing of the Middle Elamite state, there were abundant building and dedicatory inscriptions, mostly in Elamite but occasionally in Akkadian (Steve 1967: I–VIII; Scheil 1908: 85–6; Carter and Stolper 1984: 36–44). Even where Akkadian is used, in this period the sign forms are always distinctively Elamite, and this continues down to the time of Šutruk-Naḫḫunte II (716–699 BC). Only later, in the Achaemenid period, is the script of Akkadian inscriptions, for example in the monumental inscriptions of Darius I at Bisitun, distinctively Akkadian with Babylonian sign forms. Bilingual bricks, that is, with the titulature and dedication in Elamite and the curse formulae in Akkadian, or wholly Akkadian bricks, are apparently common at Dur-Untaš-Napiriša but rare at Susa (Malbran-Labat 1995: 77–8, no. 31). One brick begins with a version of a much older inscription in Old Babylonian Akkadian (mostly in Sumerian logograms, some of them using unconventional spellings), followed by a Middle Elamite text of Šilḫak-Inšušinak I (Malbran-Labat 1995: no. 49).

Evolution of Elamite Cuneiform Writing

The above details serve to illustrate the complex inherited tradition of written language use in Elam. The development of Elamite writing itself is rather gradual. From the early second millennium BC, Mesopotamian cuneiform was adapted and developed as an independent Elamite variant to the point where many signs would no longer have been recognizable to a Mesopotamian reader. This differentiation from the Akkadian syllabary becomes evident already from the very early second millennium BC (Steve 1992: 4).

The two writing traditions diverged progressively in the number and shapes of signs, the values assigned to the signs, and the frequency of logograms, with the syllabary used in Elam to write Akkadian developing more rapidly and along more perceptibly Mesopotamian lines, but nevertheless with certain regional features (Steve 1992: 1). Thus by the eighteenth century BC there were two parallel graphic systems in use, different, yet derived from the same source. Bricks of Untaš-Napiriša (1340–1330 BC) from Dur-Untaš-Napiriša carry identical inscriptions in either Akkadian or Elamite and, although the sign forms are very similar, certain logograms, spellings, and syllabic values are used only in the Akkadian, leading Marie-Joseph Steve (1992: 5) to hypothesize the existence of two schools of scribes in this period.

The Old Akkadian syllabary from which Elamite was borrowed comprised 323 signs, of which only 106 are found attested in Old Elamite sources; however, the small body of data does not allow the conclusion that the syllabary was deliberately reduced in size when it was borrowed. But the overall size of the sign inventory had stabilized at around 130 by the end of Middle Elamite or the beginning of Neo-Elamite. By comparison, the contemporary Neo-Babylonian phase of Akkadian writing used about 400 signs, and Mesopotamian writing in general about 600 (see Labat 1988).

Elamite used considerably fewer logograms—that is, historic Sumerian signs used to represent whole words—than Akkadian writing. According to Steve (1992: 11, fig. 1), the number and proportion of distinct logograms or signs with logographic values in Elamite writing increased gradually from eight out of 107 attested signs (7.5 per cent) in Old Elamite writing to 90 out of 131 signs in Achaemenid Elamite writing (69 per cent). But Steve's statement to this effect (also Gragg 1996: 59) was intended to rebut Gelb's remarks (1963: 196) about the progressive elimination of logograms from Elamite writing, and needs nuancing, since it might be taken to imply that Elamite writing became more complex (see Vallat 1996a). As regards the total of 87 logograms recorded by Steve for Neo-Elamite II, no individual document or group of documents has as many as the 28 logograms of one particular tablet of omens (Scheil 1917). These observations are relevant, of course, to the question of the later decline of cuneiform in Elam.

In fact the numbers of logograms used in non-administrative documents remained small and even declined; only 26 are attested in the inscriptions of Darius I, a mere three in the inscriptions of Xerxes I, and only one (KAM, used for ordinal numbers) in an inscription of Artaxerxes II. However, in the more than 200 Neo-Elamite administrative documents from Malyan, 56 different logograms are in use; in the 299 immediately pre-Achaemenid administrative documents from Susa there are 64 logograms, but only as many as six in any other individual group or text from the same phase (for example the two texts in Lambert 1977). In the 4935 edited documents from Persepolis Fortification (509–494 BC; Hallock 1969) and Treasury (492–458 BC; Cameron 1948), the numbers rise even further, to 84 (see Fig. 3.1 for an example of such a document). But the number of these documents preserved by accident also increases with time, and by comparison with the surviving contemporary inscriptions, they deal with a very wide range of realia which are well suited to logographic writing. Thus the number of logograms employed is not simply a function of the high degree of education of the scribes, and it is misleading to present it as an overall gradual increase.

Steve noted a significant change in the forms of a number of signs around the beginning of the Neo-Elamite phase in the first half of the first millennium, starting with the administrative documents from Malyan, which brought them closer to the contemporary Assyrian forms. He may have been correct to link

this to the decline of centralized Elamite power about this time and the concomitant growth in political and military significance of Assyria around the
turn of the first millennium BC (Steve 1992: 12).

Seventeen new signs were added after the Malyan phase documented by the
Malyan tablets, including eight (mostly CVC signs) which occur for the first
time in the documents from Susa (Scheil 1907). This is also the period in which
the greatest alteration in shape is seen in the Elamite sign forms, away from
their Akkadian predecessors. From this period to the later Achaemenid signs
the changes are very small, and include the replacement of some horizontal
wedges by *Winkelhaken* (reverse tailless wedges) or a combination of horizon-
tals and diagonals: but such alterations occur already in the pre-Achaemenid
Elamite documents found at Nineveh, and cannot therefore be attributed to the
introduction of Iranian scribes. There do not appear to have been any additions
to the syllabary thereafter; some signs which occur in the Susa (Scheil 1907) and
Nineveh documents are no longer found, probably for practical reasons (Steve
1992: 13). However, some twenty-seven logograms are unique to the documents
from Persepolis, doubtless reflecting the specific requirements of the administration operating there.

Characteristics of Elamite Writing

Elamite writing was borrowed from a system originally more or less suited to
Sumerian, and later adapted to Semitic Old Akkadian. Neither of these languages is related genetically to Elamite. The Elamite syllabary has a full set of CV
and VC signs for the vowels a, i and u and all the consonants hypothesized for
Elamite (b, d, g, ḫ, k, l, m, n, p, r, s, š, t, z). There are also signs for *ya*, and for *qa* and
qu (whatever these signify), and a limited number of syllabograms specialized
to the vowel *e* (*e, be, me, ne, še, te, el, en*; otherwise iC/Ci signs are used). All in all,
it is likely that the borrowed writing system was not very well suited to the phonetic system of Elamite, and Elamite phonology can be assumed to have evolved
further during the history of the language. Little separation is made in Elamite
writing between CV signs which in Akkadian distinguish voiced and voiceless
stops, leading to the conclusion that this feature may not have been distinctive,
at least in later Elamite; however, some words are consistently spelled with one
or the other (Gragg 1996: 60). The distinction *z–s* is usually maintained, but may
not have corresponded to presence or absence of voice. Already in Neo-Elamite,
the signs with *ḫV* frequently alternate with the corresponding V signs, suggesting that the phoneme transliterated as *ḫ* was in the process of disappearing (Vallat 1996a: 387). So-called 'broken writings' are characteristic of Elamite writing,
for example, for *pe-ul* read /pel/, where the different vowel of the second sign
(always *u* or *i*) is disregarded. Probably this results from the incompleteness of
the sign inventory, but some of these writings may have a phonological basis

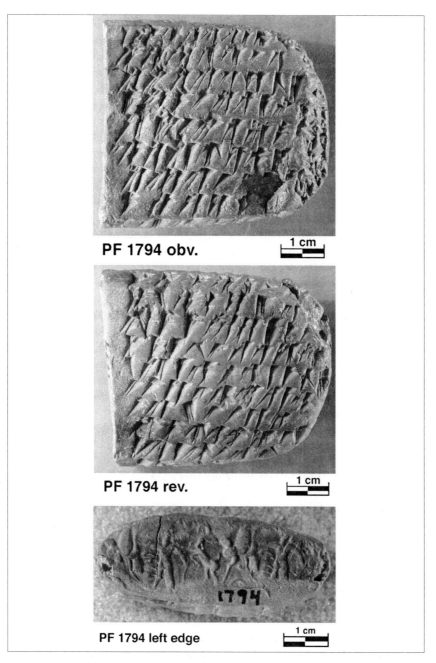

PF 1794 obv.   1 cm

PF 1794 rev.   1 cm

PF 1794 left edge   1 cm

Figure 3.1   Typical Elamite cuneiform of the Achaemenid period: Persepolis Fortification Tablet 1794, with seal impression on edge.

(Stolper 2004: 67, 72). They do not occur in Middle Elamite (apart from Ci-eC writings). As far as I can establish, they first occur in inscriptions of Hallutaš-Inšušinak (698–693 BC; see the copy in Malbran-Labat 1995: 137), exactly when certain other changes that are noted by Vallat (1996a: 387–8, 390) are first attested. They occur in the Elamite omens (placed in the mid-seventh century BC by Steve, 1992: 22) and become much more commonplace in Achaemenid Elamite (Paper 1955: 9–15).

About twelve determinatives (classifiers written at the ends of words) are used, reduced to fewer than ten in Achaemenid Elamite. These include some not used in Mesopotamian cuneiform: AŠ = location; ḪAL before countries or regions; MEŠ, adapted in Achaemenid Elamite to indicate that the preceding sign is a logogram. BE for persons, attested from later Neo-Elamite on, does occur rarely in other cuneiform (Van Soldt 1991: 428–9).

There is an incomplete range of CVC signs. A few developments in Achaemenid Elamite served to disambiguate confusing writings (Vallat 1989: 219–22). About seven signs have CVC readings that are unique to Elamite: mostly it is difficult to guess the reason for these developments, although the reading /nap/ for the sign DINGIR (Sumerian 'god') is clearly derived from the Elamite lexeme *nap* 'god'. In Achaemenid Elamite, there often seems to be uncertainty as to the vowel quality, so that, for example, *tur* alternates with *tar*, or *muš* with *mi-iš*. Since these writings occur especially in the writing of Iranian names, this development may be attributable to an improperly understood alien vocalic system, and can be taken as the first indication of the mutual encounter between the Elamite and Persian phonetic systems (Steve 1992: 18). However, they also occur in the writing of native Elamite words.

All the evidence shows that the writing system was functional and still evolving in the Achaemenid period, its last attested phase.

The Neo-Elamite Phase

To identify the beginning of the obsolescence of Elamite writing and language, it is necessary to return to the Neo-Elamite phase of Elamite history (c. 1000–539 BC). The Neo-Elamite period represents the apogee of Elamite writing. It is also, perhaps, the critical phase because it coincides with the extinction of the ethnic and political independence of Elam; and possibly the decline of the Elamite language, though this is a more problematic question.

Despite many upheavals and more or less violent political and military interventions in and from Babylonia, by the eighth century BC Elam was again an independent state which used its own tradition of cuneiform writing to record the Neo-Elamite phase of its national language. The chronological seriation of Neo-Elamite materials is difficult and often rests on similarities of orthography assumed to represent a gradual evolution, supported by prosopographic data (see Steve 1992: 21–3 for the sources; Stolper 2004: 63 and the revisions of Vallat 1996a for a partial re-dating and some additions). What follows is therefore a tentative summary of the work of others: the review by Henkelman (2003) demonstrates the complexities of historical reconstruction.

At the highland centre Tall-i Malyan, a varied collection of over 200 administrative documents in Neo-Elamite has been recovered from a single building. They date to c. 1000–900 BC and exhibit strong Akkadian influence in language and writing practice. So far, 114 have been published (Stolper 1984). Some of the inscriptions of Šutruk-Naḫḫunte II (717–699 BC) from Susa are written in Elamite; others are in Akkadian, but always written in Elamite sign forms, including using the uniquely Elamite logogram ESSANA for LUGAL 'king' (Malbran-Labat 1995: nos. 55–6). The stela of an official called Šutruru from Susa records various benefices, and a local ruler called Ḫanni son of Taḫḫiḫi left rock inscriptions near Izeh.

As Assyrian military power in the region increased, the power and stability of Elamite rulers declined. Assurbanipal was responsible for an Assyrian sack of Susa in 653 BC and a 'tour of looting and destruction around the adjoining plains of Khuzestān' (Stolper 2004: 63) that led to the death of the Elamite ruler known to the Assyrians as 'king' Te-Umman. Among the tributaries who brought gifts to Assurbanipal in 646 BC, several of them from highland regions east of Elam, was Kuraš king of Parsumaš, that is, Cyrus the Persian (but not Cyrus I, according to Vallat, 1996a: 392). Yet some Elamite successor states continued after this. In the post-Assurbanipal period, c. 646–c. 539 BC (Vallat 1996a), a ruler named Ururu set up a bronze plaque at Persepolis originally with a ninety-eight-line inscription (Cameron 1957: 64–65, pl. 28; Vallat 1996a: 386 n. 14 notes that this has not been published). Various inscribed cylinder seals also survive from this period.

An important group of about 300 palace administrative documents was found at the citadel of Susa; some of these must have originated from other towns or regions. A group of twenty-five fragmentary Late Elamite letters is written in the same script style, with some of the same personal names. These were excavated in the South-West Palace at Nineveh, dating well before 612 BC, and are probably from around the time of Sin-šumu-ukīn (625–620 BC; Reade 1992, 2000, and pers. comm.; Weissbach 1902: 168–202; Vallat 1998: 95–106; further references in Jones and Stolper 2004: 2 n. 6). How did they get to Nineveh? It is possible that they were written there, or were captured by the Assyrians in Elam, or were brought to Nineveh by an Elamite official or refugee.

A tablet recording a selection of divinatory omens drawn from celestial phenomena of the type known from Mesopotamia as *enūma Anu Ellil* was found at Susa (Scheil 1917: 29–59). It has been described as 'the only literary text in Elamite' (Reiner 1969: 63). Possibly related, however, is an Elamite hemerology (Scheil 1925: 157–8), an abbreviated listing of (presumably favourable) days for twelve months of the year, similar to Mesopotamian hemerologies. These indicate the use of Elamite at this time for a full range of literary scribal purposes and show that more contact with Mesopotamia must have occurred on the cultural level than is attested by this meagre evidence. Possibly contemporary, and equally intriguing, is a tablet of dream omens in Akkadian language but Elamite script from Susa, with an extraordinary arrangement of the columns on the tablet surface (Scheil 1912: 49–59; Oppenheim 1956: 256–61).

Inscribed cylinder seals were among the finds from a substantial tomb excavated in 1981–1982 at Arjān, 10 km north of Behbehan. In a sarcophagus in the tomb were a bronze cup with an Elamite inscription (Bashash 1990: 63), and a gold 'ring' inscribed 'Kidin-Hutran son of Kurluš'. This object, too small to be an armlet, was perhaps a cultic object to be held in the hand (Alizadeh 1985: 53, 66–76, and pl. 28:2; Towhidi and Khalijian 1982: 266, fig. 45).

During the same period, Šutur-Naḫḫunte, Hallutaš-Inšušinak, and Atta-ḫamiti-Inšušinak, local rulers at Susa, left dedicatory inscriptions there.

A group of silver objects of uncertain provenance, several inscribed in Elamite, has turned up in recent years. They may all be a hoard from the Kalmakareh cave. The Elamite inscriptions include the names of Ampiriš King of Samati, his son Unzikitaš, and others. Among these was also a silver bucket, presumably inherited loot, bearing an Akkadian inscription of Esarhaddon (680–669 BC) with dedication to the deity Adad of Guzana in Syria (photo: Seipel 2000: 205–6, no. 117). The Elamite inscriptions have been assigned to the early sixth century BC (Vallat 1996a: 391 n. 42; Vallat 1996b; Donbaz 1996).

From the period c. 585–539 BC, there are more building inscriptions in Elamite of local rulers of Susa, including Šilḫak-Inšušinak II and Tepti-Ḫumban-Inšušinak (redated to this period by Vallat 1996a). These (corresponding to the phases NIIIA, NIIIB of Steve 1992) show the revival of a political and administrative centre at Susa following the end of the Assyrian Empire, and the existence of an Elamite principality in the uplands contemporary with the Neo-Babylonian dynasty (626–539 BC) in southern Mesopotamia, before the Achaemenid conquest (Carter and Stolper 1984: 54–5). However, the area of Anshan (around Malyan) was probably already under the control of Cyrus by this date.

The Achaemenid Period

The initial chronology of this period of major upheaval cannot yet be exactly computed (Vallat 1996a). During the early part of the Achaemenid Empire (from the mid-sixth century BC), three forms of cuneiform were in use: the local Elamite tradition as described above; 'normal' Mesopotamian cuneiform, used at this date by the Achaemenid rulers to record versions of their royal inscriptions in the prestigious Neo-Babylonian dialect of Akkadian; and alongside these, Old Persian cuneiform, an entirely independent alphasyllabic writing system specifically devised for the dynastic language of the time.

There are inscriptions of all the Achaemenid rulers down to Artaxerxes III in all three languages (occasionally also Egyptian) from a variety of sites in Iran and some other locations including Lake Van and the ancient canal from the Nile Delta to Suez (Kent 1953; Schmitt 2000; Stolper 2004: 60). The kings in question are:

Darius I	522–486
Xerxes I	485–465
Artaxerxes I	465–423
Darius II	423–405 (no Elamite inscriptions so far)
Artaxerxes II	404–359
Artaxerxes III Ochos	358–338

Old Persian cuneiform is a script with only thirty-six phonetic signs, five logograms, a word divider (elsewhere found only in Old Assyrian and Ugaritic cuneiform), and numerals. Although there are no VC or CVC signs, there is a full set of Ca signs, which can also be used with the signs /i/ and /u/ to supplement the limited number of Ci or Cu signs, i.e. *pa-i* for /pi/. This practice might be derived from the broken writings of Elamite, or from the use of the *aleph, yod*, and *waw* letters used to write long vowels in Aramaic. Most phonetic signs have three or four wedges (up to a maximum of five—much simpler than Mesopotamian cuneiform, in which signs may have up to twenty wedges). The sign for /la/ bears some resemblance to the Elamite/Mesopotamian /la/, but no other sign is significantly similar to any from an earlier cuneiform system. As a writing system, Old Persian cuneiform is ambiguous and unsatisfactory for writing the language it is used for; but this is true of most ancient writing systems, and it would be anachronistic to expect a format based on a systematic modern phonological analysis.

The script was used only for Old Persian, for inscriptions on expensive materials for display: stone slabs, walls, and columns in palaces, statues, gold tablets, doorknobs, weights, and seals; but (remarkably for a cuneiform script) was almost never written on clay tablets or used for straightforward administrative purposes [for the sole administrative tablet identified so far, see Stolper and Tavernier 2007 (eds)]. On small objects, Old Persian writing often forms part of the design, and this decorative function is a significant aspect of its character.

While the new script may conceivably have been used to a limited extent in a simpler form before Darius I, it seems most likely to have been devised ad hoc at his request to write the Bisitun inscription in Old Persian. A couple of seals inscribed with the names of private individuals are the only non-royal inscriptions (Schmitt 1981; Kaptan 2002). Supposed earlier Old Persian cuneiform inscriptions of Cyrus at Pasargadae have been demonstrated to have been written after the Bisitun inscription (Stronach 1990), while others purporting to be by Ariaramnes and Arsames, ancestors of Darius, show linguistically late features, and appear to be spurious (Schmitt 1999: 105–11).

Elamite was maintained for display purposes, and Achaemenid royal inscriptions were normally provided with an Elamite version alongside the Old Persian, often also Akkadian. Royal inscriptions in Elamite are less numerous than those in Old Persian (Kent 1953). The earliest version of the great inscription at Bisitun was put up in Elamite because 'Elamite was the premier historical written language of western Iran' (Stolper 2004: 2). But apart from using the Elamite language, the Achaemenids 'did not give the Elamite history from which they had emerged any other prominence' (Stolper 2004: 63). It is significant that fragments of two Aramaic versions of Darius' Bisitun inscription survive on papyrus from Elephantine (in Egypt). This confirms the inscription's statement that copies were sent to the provinces in other languages and on other writing material ('both on clay tablets and on parchment': Brosius 2000: 39); there are also two versions from Babylon in the form of large display inscriptions in Akkadian on stone (Von Voigtlander 1978: 63–6, 67). Some royal inscriptions add a fourth version in Egyptian hieroglyphic script, in addition to the Old Persian, Elamite, and Akkadian.

Elamite continued to be used also for administrative purposes at the royal institutions at Persepolis and beyond (see Jones and Stolper in press), probably because a scribal class of bureaucrats trained in Elamite writing already existed. But in the wider context the limited amount of inscribed objects (statues, seals, etc.) may well underline the symbolic rather than functional use of Elamite writing.

A few inscriptions survive in all three languages on clay tablets, perhaps drafts of the versions on stone (Vallat 1970: 149–60). A stone statue was excavated in the Apadana at Susa, with a quadrilingual inscription in Elamite, Akkadian, Old Persian, and Egyptian hieroglyphic. The display of Egyptian hieroglyphic writing at Susa can hardly have served any functional purpose (Vallat 1974: 211, fig. 27; 254, pl. VIII). Inscriptions of Artaxerxes II are found at Susa, of which three are trilingual, including Elamite, and one is in Old Persian only. A black diorite column base from Ecbatana (Hamadan) is inscribed in Elamite and Akkadian. Another fragmentary inscription is in Akkadian and Old Persian (Walker 1980: 81). Among inscriptions excavated at Babylon, there are fragments of two copies of a three-line Elamite inscription. At least four further (unattributable) fragmentary Elamite inscriptions on marble, and approximately five in Old Persian, have also been found there, mostly from the central Kasr or Procession Street areas (Wetzel *et al.* 1957: 48–9).

Several inscribed cylinder seals and seal impressions are known, including the impressions of an heirloom seal of Cyrus I with a six-line Elamite inscription on two Darius administrative tablets from Persepolis (Hinz 1976: 53, fig. 16; Amiet 1973; Jones *passim* in Garrison and Root 2001). A seal of Darius I with a trilingual Old Persian, Elamite, and Babylonian inscription was found at Thebes in Egypt, and may have belonged to an Egyptianized Persian noble (Wiseman *et al.* n.d.: 100; Walker 1980: 79–81).

A piece of silver 17.5 mm^2 bears three signs from the Elamite version of an inscription of Darius I or Xerxes, probably cut from a bar-ingot either for melting down or as a form of currency. Such bar-ingots were often inscribed. Somehow it found its way to Afghanistan, where it was discovered as part of the Kabul hoard, dated about 380 BC, consisting largely of coins of the sixth and fifth centuries BC (Schlumberger 1953: 41, pl. V [III.12], with commentary by René Labat, p. 45; Hulin 1954; Henning 1956; Bivar 1971: 102, fig. 1; 107). Another similar fragment of cut silver ingot currency from a hoard at Nush-i Jan bears a fragmentary cuneiform inscription, but it is not possible to say if the signs on this piece are Elamite, Old Persian, or Akkadian (Bivar 1971). Standardized weights are found, inscribed in Akkadian, Elamite, and Old Persian (Schmidt 1957: 105–6), and there are 'a few seal impressions, enameled ornamental nails and decorative tiles inscribed with a royal name, fragments of a gold plaque with the remains of a few lines of inscription' (Reiner 1969: 65).

In addition to the royal and other public inscriptions, there exists from this period an enormous body of Elamite administrative documents. The vast majority of these are from the Fortification and the Treasury at Persepolis, although most short documents found there were actually drafted at other sites and brought to Persepolis for auditing or compilation into journals or for storage (Jones and Stolper 1986: 248), a fact which bears on the question of the geographical extent of competence in Elamite. However, it seems plausible that every Elamite document from Persepolis was also tagged onto a rolled-up Aramaic document on parchment, held in a sealed clay ring (Cameron 1948: 25–9). The parchment documents were destroyed by fire. This pattern of use has a crucial bearing on modern assessment of the dominance of Elamite writing in the Persepolis administration. The number of Elamite documents recovered from the Fortification (509–494 BC) has been estimated as perhaps 30,000 tablets including fragments, of which c. 4810 have been published or studied. The Fortification also produced hundreds of monolingual Aramaic tablets, a few in Akkadian, Greek, and probably Phrygian (see now Brixhe 2004: 118–26), and thousands of uninscribed, sealed tablets. The much smaller number of documents from the Treasury (492–458 BC) is estimated at 750, of which 125 are published, dating to the reigns of Darius I, Xerxes I, and the beginning of Artaxerxes I (Cameron 1948). The figures above are based on Jones and Stolper (in press: 1; see also Cameron 1948: 18–19) and show that so far only a fraction of the available Achaemenid Elamite administrative material has been researched.

Much smaller numbers of Elamite administrative documents are known from other sites. One document from Susa bears a seal impression of the Achaemenid king, and is inscribed 'year twenty-two' of Darius (Scheil 1911: 101, no. 308). A document resembling those from the Persepolis Treasury is registered as 'Sippar, Babylonia' but unlikely to come from there (BM 56302, Walker 1980: 79 and fig. 4). A fragment of an Elamite letter bears the same, probably misleading, registration (BM 62783, Walker 1980: 79 and fig. 4). Other tablets also resemble those from the Fortification, but are perhaps from other sites (YBC 16813: Jones and Stolper 1986: 249). A fragmentary tablet (perhaps a letter) and two administrative documents were excavated at the Urartian site Argištiḫenele (modern Armavir-blur in Armenia) in an eighth- or seventh-century BC stratum corrupted by later intrusions. Although it has been claimed that these tablets did not belong to an intrusion, graphically they are identical to the tablets from the Persepolis Fortification and Treasury and should probably be evaluated with them (Diakonoff and Jankowska 1990: 102–23; Steve 1992: 24; Reade 2000; Jones and Stolper in press: 1–2, n. 4).

Jones and Stolper (in press) survey other isolated finds, mostly (it is presumed) dating from the reign of Darius I and originating from the Persepolis Fortification, including three tablets excavated at Old Kandahar in Afghanistan in secondary contexts, but likely to have been written there (ibid.: 5–6), and one found at Qaṣr-i Abu Naṣr (6 km east of Shiraz) but probably brought there in modern times from Persepolis. One may also have been found on the surface at Chogha Mish (Jones and Stolper 1986). Taken together, the above evidence suggests the existence of several administrative archives other than those at Persepolis.

The Growth of Aramaic Language and Writing

To what extent can this narrative be correlated with the growth in the use of alphabetic scripts, and with political pressures that imposed new administrative and display languages? If obsolescence in Elamite writing began to set in from the Neo-Elamite phase onwards, then it is impossible to exclude from this the growth in alphabetic Aramaic writing, which became increasingly widespread throughout the Achaemenid Empire. The earliest surviving written sources for the Aramaic language are from about the ninth century BC in north-eastern Syria; its spread may have been accelerated by Assyrian and Babylonian policies of deporting large populations from the ninth to sixth centuries BC, as well as by spontaneous population movements during the same epoch. Ancient Aramaic existed in two forms (Beyer 1986: 11–14): the 'original' western Aramaic of Syria, written from the eighth century BC (also attested on looted objects found in Assyria), and an eastern form written already from the mid-ninth century BC at the Aramaean states of Sam'al and Gozan (notably the inscribed statue from Tell Fakhariyah).

Late Ancient Aramaic had already by the eighth century BC become a *lingua franca* across the Near East, with various local forms, such as that found in letters and inscriptions from Egypt (especially sixth century BC). It is found in inscriptions on two bronze dishes from Luristan in central western Iran from around 700–600 BC (Teixidor 1967: nos. 73, 72 = Gibson 1975: no. 12), for which one can compare the Elamite and Akkadian inscriptions on similar objects mentioned above. There is a private letter written on an ostrakon from Assyria from the mid-seventh century BC in which an Assyrian official Bēl-ēṭir, who is well known as the author of letters in Akkadian cuneiform, writes from Babylonia to his brother in Aššur (Donner and Röllig 2002: no. 233 = Gibson 1975: no. 20). Seven debt-notes survive, inscribed in Aramaic on clay tablets from Aššur. These private documents, dating mostly from the second half of the seventh century BC, exhibit the same structure as contemporary Akkadian documents in cuneiform. Some of the personal names are Assyrian and some Aramaic (Donner and Röllig 2002: nos. 234–6; Fales 1986). Annotations on Assyrian and Babylonian cuneiform documents written on clay tablets of the seventh and sixth centuries BC are either incised, in which case they must have been written at the same time as the document, or written in ink (Beyer 1986: 13 n. 7).

It was probably the Late Ancient Aramaic of Babylonia which became widely employed as a language of the Achaemenid royal administration, especially in the western parts of the Achaemenid Empire from around 500 BC, when Elamite was still current in the Iranian region. The use of Aramaic, already established as a *lingua franca*, was pragmatic, resulting from the earlier spread of the language, and the extent to which it was imposed by the Achaemenids has been questioned by several authorities (Greenfield 1985: 698; Briant 1996/2002: 981/956; Graf 2000). Thereafter it was to remain the most widespread commercial and literary language until, after the fall of the Achaemenid Empire, it was gradually replaced by Greek, Middle Persian, later vernacular forms of Aramaic, and ultimately, Arabian languages. The earliest documents in this Imperial Achaemenid Aramaic survive especially from Egypt (Beyer 1986: 14–19), including versions of parts of the Bisitun inscription and Darius' tomb inscription at Naqš-i Rustam. (One may here perhaps note the role of climate in the preservation of inscribed materials.) Thereafter it spread to Palestine, Jordan, northern Arabia, Asia Minor, and to Babylonia (where it was used for annotations on cuneiform tablets), gradually spreading further east into the areas where hitherto Elamite had been the administrative language. In Elam itself, similar Aramaic annotations are written on Elamite cuneiform tablets from the Persepolis Fortification (509–494 BC; Hallock 1969: 82), and there are some 163 Aramaic ink inscriptions on stone Zoroastrian ritual objects from the Treasury (479–435 BC; Bowman 1970; Naveh and Shaked 1973: 445–57; Teixidor 1974: no. 152), in addition to the monolingual Aramaic tablets alluded to above. As already mentioned, it is possible that thousands of fifth to fourth century BC Aramaic parchment documents went up in smoke when the Persepolis archives were destroyed by fire.

Later, Aramaic reached even to Afghanistan, where five inscriptions of the Indian ruler Aśoka (268–233 BC) have been found in different places. To some extent the enormous predominance of material from Egypt and relative paucity from Iran is due to conditions of discovery and preservation, but many private letters survive on damaged ostraka from Babylonia (fifth to third centuries BC).

Recent and as yet largely unpublished discoveries of Aramaic documents in Bactria (north-eastern Iran) indicate the use of Aramaic there for official Achaemenid administrative purposes already during the fifth and fourth centuries BC (Shaked 2004; Naveh and Shaked forthcoming). These documents fall into four groups. The earliest are ten letters, many fragmentary, of unclear purpose, from the fifth century BC. Then there are ten documents on parchment, some lengthy: these are orders from the governor Akhvamazda to one Bagavant, with dates in the fourth century BC. One example is dated year eleven of Artaxerxes (II or III). One order, dated November/December 330 BC, mentions a figure called Bessos, with a royal title, and refers to him facing Alexander and his generals. Thirdly, there are eighteen inscribed tally sticks, recording dated supplies of provisions to servants of the satrap, giving the names of recipient and donor or officer, with notches cut to confirm that the item had been supplied. One of these is dated year three of Darius III, that is, 333/2 BC. There are other instances of dated texts in each collection. Finally, a number of documents on parchment, some also long, include one with several columns of twenty lines each, listing agricultural products to be distributed to various named individuals. This is dated 324 BC. One is dated year seven of 'king Alexander'. When the scribes' names are given, they are all Persian, suggesting trained Persian administrators sent out to Bactria. There are no names that obviously reflect other non-Persian Iranian elements, and remarkably there are no Semitic names. According to Shaked (2004) the Aramaic is highly standardized, and contains numerous Iranian loan words.

Apparently, then, Aramaic was the alternative language used increasingly for administration under the late Achaemenids, even if it never achieved the status of an official language in the peripheral regions of the Achaemenid Empire, but was only one element in a multicultural environment in which provincial regional languages were still used and interpreters played an important role (Graf 2000). The Seleucids used Greek and Aramaic for both administration and display, but no form of Iranian writing. After Old Persian, Iranian languages were not written until Parthian (first century BC). Later, Arsacid Aramaic (Beyer 1986: 28–30), which is often close to Imperial Achaemenid Aramaic but was increasingly influenced by vernacular forms, became the official language of the Parthian Empire from c. 200 BC; and its script forms and over 600 logograms were in due course taken over as features of the writing of the Iranian language Pahlavi, which became the official language of the Sassanians from 224 AD (e.g. the Aramaic logogram MLK' used to write Pahlavi *šāh*, 'king').

Discussion

In approaching the question of the obsolescence of cuneiform in Elam, a number of research problems must be taken into account. Assyriologists—those who study the Akkadian language and Mesopotamian cuneiform—inevitably do so from a Mesopotamian point of view. Elam ('Susa'), along with other areas of Akkadian language use outside Mesopotamia, is conventionally considered as 'peripheral'. Doubtless this goes some way towards explaining why there is still no survey of Akkadian language use in the region. The study of Rössler (1938) is confined to the Akkadian of the Bisitun inscription. De Meyer (1962) describes the language of the Old Babylonian contracts from Susa only, and Salonen (1962) considers also the Mālamīr documents, which may be as early as 1500 BC.

On a broader scale, despite the fact that some of the Achaemenid trilingual inscriptions are published in modern editions that reproduce them in trilingual format, no overarching trilingual (or, to include Egyptian, Aramaic, and others, multilingual) survey of language and writing use within the Achaemenid Empire exists. The description by Pierre Briant (1996/2002: 523–6/507–10) of 'Imperial administration and multilingualism' does not mention Elamite. Graf (2000) usefully surveys Aramaic usage in peripheral regions of the empire. Most of the more detailed research studies have been written by specialists in one language or another—and most of the languages are unrelated—or by specialists who have agreed for editorial reasons to concentrate on one language. Specialists in Elamite may not necessarily have detailed knowledge of Old Persian; specialists in Aramaic rarely know Elamite or Old Persian. (The writer is content to acknowledge no competence in Old Persian or Aramaic and only a modest knowledge of Elamite.)

As for Elamite itself, there is a small group of genuine specialists, and Elamite studies are visibly still in an evolving stage. While there are some excellent and detailed publications of certain groups of documents, other groups of material, in some cases considerable, are still unstudied. As so often, reconstructions of history are determined by the languages and writing systems in which the sources survive, and for a variety of reasons modern studies fail to succeed in crossing the boundaries that these throw up. In addition, the whole field of Elamite language studies is a classic case of limited and unevenly distributed data, on the basis of which generalizations have to be made.

Clearly there was a complex interplay of prestige between the Elamite, Akkadian, and Old Persian languages. 'When Darius I had the first edition of his apologia composed for Bisitun, he did not hesitate to display it in the heart of Media first as a monolingual Elamite text, not only because Elamite was the historical written language of Persia proper, but also because Elamite was the premier historical written language of western Iran' (Jones and Stolper in press: 2). However, other inscriptions are presented in one, two, three, or four languages, and the precise implications of the choice of languages in each case have not been studied. When considering the implications of 'display' as a motive for language choice, due consideration must be given to the implications of display in places where a particular language is unlikely to have been understood. It is possible both that there were Egyptian speakers in Susa and Elamite speakers in Babylon, but it seems more likely that these choices were motivated by a propagandistic aim to announce that Egyptian, or Elamite, were official languages of the Achaemenid Empire, which was therefore independent of any consideration of successful communication in the particular location of display or distribution. (One is reminded of instruction booklets in fifteen European languages.)

Which registers and functions of cuneiform writing were the first to become obsolete in Elam, and which survived longest? It will be of particular importance to focus on the functionality and distribution of the latest Achaemenid uses of cuneiform Elamite. Literary use of the written language did not outlive the seventh century BC. The latest attested usage for administrative purposes seems to be the documents from the Persepolis Treasury, where it was already functioning as an adjunct to Aramaic (492–458 BC), but—again on the basis of attested materials—the writing system continued to be used for display purposes for another century until the reign of Artaxerxes III (358–338 BC). The trilingual Elamite/Akkadian/Old Persian inscription on Grave V (the 'Southern Tomb') at Persepolis is now attributed to Artaxerxes III (Schmitt 1999: 1–25; 2000). As far as Old Persian is concerned, cylinder seals and a vase with Old Persian inscriptions are also dated to Artaxerxes III. The Hadish Wall/Tacara West staircase inscription in Old Persian at Persepolis appears also to belong to Artaxerxes III, in 'a perfect example of the degenerated language of the late Achaemenid period' (Schmitt 1999: 91–104; 2000: 114–18). It may well be merely accidental that the remaining eight years until the arrival of Alexander—the reigns of Artaxerxes IV (338–336 BC) and Darius III (336–330 BC)—have so far produced no cuneiform evidence. All three cuneiform systems in Elam die much earlier, and for different reasons, than cuneiform in Babylonia.

The choice of written language is inescapably bound up with the question of living language use and language death. While there is a growing literature on language death in linguistics, this almost exclusively concerns the documented demise of various modern spoken languages, where it is possible to establish more or less exact numbers of the competent speakers of a language. The data for ancient languages are inevitably different both in extent and nature (Houston *et al.* 2003: 432–43). How can it be established to what extent vernacular usage of the Elamite language was already restricted by c. 550 BC? This may have been a critical factor in the obsolescence of Elamite as a written standard. Probably the use of Elamite cuneiform does not at any point truly *prove* the wide oral use of the Elamite language, although we assume it for Middle and Neo-Elamite. The great mass of private documents available from Mesopotamia is lacking. Still, letters are usually a good indicator, and these exist down to the late seventh century BC letters from Nineveh, in a period when divination manuals and hemerologies were also written in Elamite. It is more difficult to establish whether Elamite was still a living language for the scribes of the Persepolis administration. They must by then have become a restricted group of specialists, since Aramaic was being used increasingly. Elamite cuneiform was still used for display purposes at its latest date of use, but who could read it? Evidence of evolution or disintegration in a language's phonology is not unequivocal evidence of its day-to-day viability, precisely because it may be the result of interference from another language. But there is evidence that, even if it was the first language in which the Bisitun inscription was displayed, the Elamite of the bi- and trilingual Achaemenid royal inscriptions already represents a translation language: it contains many Old Persian loan words, and some syntax and even some morphology tracks Old Persian constructions (Reiner 1960; 1969: 67).

Once the extent of the Achaemenid Empire had broken its Iranian boundaries, it must have been only a matter of time before Elamite was replaced. The Achaemenid rulers' eventual adoption of Aramaic as a chancery language can be attributed to the growth in the direction and geographical extent of the Achaemenid Empire, whereas knowledge of the Elamite language seems to have been geographically quite restricted, even if documents are found from as far away from its Iranian homeland as Assyria, Urarṭu, and Afghanistan. This would have a bearing on the training of new scribes. As elsewhere in the cuneiform world, among Elamite 'scribes' one must include not only writers on clay tablets but also stonemasons and other craftsmen, since cuneiform is found inscribed on metal, stone, and precious stones; to what extent this presupposes full comprehension of a given inscription by a craftsman is unclear.

Languages that exist or survive in a written form may be tied closely, even exclusively, to one writing system or technology. This association can have the effect that once a writing system becomes obsolete, the language itself is under threat, and some languages do not survive the transition to new writing systems. Successful modern examples of such transitions (Turkish, Malay) are mainly of changes from one alphabetic system (Arabic) to another (Roman). There is as yet no overwhelming pressure for Chinese or Japanese to romanize, but their native writing systems, although laborious to learn, have certain advantages for those languages and also carry with them an enormous cultural message. Similarly Burmese orthography, while hopelessly unsuited to contemporary spoken Burmese, is retained because of its 'impersonal, timeless qualities', which are perceived as contributing to Burmese cultural identity (Wheatley 1992).

But Aramaic alphabetic writing had many practical advantages over cuneiform. Cuneiform is both a writing system and a writing technology. Alphabetic writing was superior even to the much simplified Old Persian cuneiform system, which seems never to have been used for anything other than display purposes. Writing in ink on parchment, stone, clay, or papyrus also has certain advantages to writing with a reed impressed on clay, especially in some regions. Just after the middle of the fourth century BC, none of the three cuneiform writing systems are no longer attested in Iran, and by the beginning of the Seleucid Empire in the late fourth century, cuneiform had been entirely replaced in Iran by the Aramaic and Greek writing systems, used to write Aramaic and its dialects, Greek, and in due course various forms of Middle Persian (Parthian, Bactrian). Thus functionally speaking, cuneiform in Iran and Elamite in particular did not survive the demise of the Achaemenid Empire. Presumably knowledge of Elamite was geographically extremely limited. Competence in Old Persian seems to have collapsed—possibly the spoken language had changed too much—while Akkadian was irrelevant in Iran for the Seleucids.

The afterlife of the Elamite language is entirely uncertain. A population group known as Elymeans seem to have maintained their autonomy into Parthian times (late third century), and when central control by the Seleucids declined, a local ruler captured Susa. His name (or title) was Kamnaskires (perhaps Achaemenid Elamite *kapnuškir* 'treasurer'). It has been suggested that this exiguous evidence might indicate a survival of a form of the Elamite language (Le Rider 1965: 349–58; Carter and Stolper 1984: 58–9; Stolper 2004: 64, 90).

A range of factors has been suggested as structural features of script obsolescence, in the context of possible similarities to or differences from language death (Houston *et al.* 2003: 435). Have there been simplifications (loss of complexity) or reductions (defectiveness) in the expressiveness of the communicative system? This is certainly not true on the technical level for Elamite cuneiform writing, although not as untrue as has been suggested (Steve 1992). The evidence shows that it was still developing productively in its last attested phases, and so the explanation for the abandonment of Elamite writing is not to be sought in this area. Is there a sociolinguistic explanation, relating to loss of prestige of the obsolescent system? This is not relevant for Elam until after the conquest of Alexander. So far as is known, cuneiform was, in its latest forms in Iran, associated exclusively with the Achaemenid government and therefore enjoyed the ultimate prestige; but consequently disappeared when that polity was overwhelmed. (The situation in Babylonia was quite different.) Can the decline be explained in terms of restricted linguistic transactions, and a diminished sphere of exchange? This concept is more relevant for Elamite, since one of the reasons for its obsolescence must have been that it was not widely spoken or functional beyond Iran at a time when the organizational horizon of the Achaemenid Empire had spread as far as the Aegean in the west, and the borders of India in the east. Or is the demise to be explained in demographic terms, as a reduced number of writers and readers leading to a lack of transmission of the writing system? This is a partial explanation for the demise of Elamite writing, in that it can be hypothesized—although there is no evidence of this—that inability to produce sufficient numbers of scribes trained in Elamite must have weakened the power of Elamite chanceries to take on the potential task of administering the growing extent of the Achaemenid realm, if this had ever been a serious possibility.

Finally, can the obsolescence be attributed to the loss of a native elite who valued the writing (Houston *et al.* 2003: 467)? The Achaemenid elite employed Elamite, Akkadian, Aramaic, and even Egyptian for a variety of prestige and practical purposes, but if they valued any writing system for cultural reasons it was probably that which had been specially devised for their own Persian language. This writing system was inefficient and, perhaps precisely because it was devised at a juncture between the demise of Elamite and the unstoppable rise of Aramaic, was doomed not to 'catch on' as anything other than a display script. To this extent, the earlier collapse of the Elamite polities must have been one more signal of the imminent demise of the Elamite cuneiform writing system.

With the background of these typological factors, the following possibly more contingent points can be added. First, the geographical horizon of the politico-cultural unit to which Elamite writing belonged (in this case the Achaemenid Empire) increased and with it the range of competing cultures which were alien to Elam and to which Elam was alien. A practical result of this will have been an insufficiency in the availability of trained Elamite scribes and communicators. Elamite became marginalized. There is some evidence in any case for a decline in the vernacular usage of Elamite, which may have been a critical factor in the obsolescence of its use as an official form of communication. Second, and concomitantly, the natural growth in the use of a specific competing language (Aramaic) brought with it a writing technology which was superior to, and which ultimately superseded, that of cuneiform. Elamite was apparently unable to transfer to a pen-written alphabetic script. Third, Elamite cuneiform writing exhibited a gradual reduction in the registers for which it was used, with first literature and then administrative functions disappearing, leaving it in the end exclusively as a mode of display. This more or less social phenomenon resembles aspects of language death, but does not appear to be related (in the case of Elamite) to impoverishment of the technical possibilities of the writing system itself. Languages and writing systems can continue to be used for display even when they are no longer widely understood, and they may be actively retained for ideological (symbolic) reasons, or passively retained through inertia caused by the weight of tradition. This effect of tradition may go some way to explain not why cuneiform writing was abandoned in Elam, but why it survived so long.

Notes

1. Jeremy Black died before producing a final version of this chapter. Where necessary I have corrected the few typographical errors and slips, and completed the bibliography. Otherwise the text is as it was when submitted to the editors prior to the conference, modified only with normal adjustments of copy-editing. Black left some questions unanswered, and would no doubt have cut some of the earlier sections in order to reduce the word count to that originally stipulated. David Brown, Berlin, 21 September 2004. [Some updates have been made in the proof (eds)].

2. For the precise geographical range of historical 'Elam' and assumed spread of the Elamite language, see Stolper 2004: 60–1.

3. Different dialects and phases of the Semitic language Akkadian, spoken in Mesopotamia, are conventionally referred to as Assyrian, Babylonian, Old Akkadian, Archaic Old Babylonian, Middle Babylonian, Neo-Babylonian, etc. For convenience here they are all referred to as Akkadian.

References

Note: The journal *NABU, Nouvelles assyriologiques brèves et utilitaires*, which is the source of a number of references below, is known by its acronym rather than its full title. Articles/notes in the journal are cited by article number, not by page(s).

Alizadeh, Abbas
   1985   'A Tomb of the Neo-Elamite Period at Arjān near Behbahan.' *Archäologische Mitteilungen aus Iran* 18: 49–73.

Amiet, Pierre
   1973   'La glyptique de la fin de l'Elam.' *Arts Asiatiques* 28: 3–44.

Bashash, R.
   1990   'Inscriptions on a Bronze Cup from Arjān.' *Athar* 17, 63, special edition on Arjān; in Persian.

Beyer, Klaus
   1986   *The Aramaic Language: Its Distribution and Subdivisions.* Trans. John F. Healey. Göttingen: Vandenhoeck and Ruprecht.

Bivar, A. D. H.
   1971   'A Hoard of Ingot-Currency of the Median Period from Nush-i-Jan, near Malamir.' *Iran* 9: 97–111, with a note by John A. Brinkman: 107.

Bowman, Raymond A.
   1970   *Aramaic Ritual Texts from Persepolis.* University of Chicago Oriental Institute Publications 91. Chicago, IL: University of Chicago Press.

Briant, Pierre
  1996/2002 *Histoire de l'empire perse de Cyrus à Alexandre.* Paris: Fayard. Trans. Peter T. Daniels 2002, *From Cyrus to Alexander: A History of the Persian Empire.* Winona Lake, IN: Eisenbrauns.
Brixhe, Claude
  2004 'Corpus des inscriptions paléo-phrygiennes: Supplément II.' *Kadmos* 43: 1–130.
Brosius, Maria
  2000 *The Persian Empire from Cyrus II to Artaxerxes II.* LACTOR 16. Kingston upon Thames: London Association of Classical Teachers.
Cameron, George G.
  1948 *The Persepolis Treasury Tablets.* University of Chicago Oriental Institute Publications 65. Chicago, IL: University of Chicago Press.
  1957 'An Elamite Bronze Plaque.' In Erich F. Schmidt, *Persepolis II: Contents of the Treasury and Other Discoveries.* University of Chicago, Oriental Institute Publications 69. Chicago, IL: University of Chicago Press, 64–5.
  1959 'The "Daiva" Inscription of Xerxes: In Elamite.' *Die Welt des Orients* 2: 470–6.
Carter, Elizabeth, and Matthew W. Stolper
  1984 *Elam: Surveys of Political History and Archaeology.* University of California Near Eastern Studies 25. Berkeley: University of California Press.
De Meyer, Leon
  1962 *L'Accadien des contrats de Suse.* Leiden: Brill.
Diakonoff, Igor M., and N. B. Jankowska
  1990 'An Elamite Gilgameš text from Argištiḫenele, Urarṭu (Armavir-blur, 8th century B.C.).' *Zeitschrift für Assyriologie* 80: 102–20.
Donbaz, Veysel
  1996 'A Median (?) Votive Inscription on Silver Vessel.' *NABU* 1996: 43.
Donner, Herbert, and Wolfgang Röllig
  2002 *Kanaänische und aramäische Inschriften* I–III. 5th ed. Wiesbaden: Harrassowitz.
Englund, Robert K.
  2004 'The State of Decipherment of Proto-Elamite.' In Stephen D. Houston (ed.), *The First Writing: Script Invention as History and Process.* Cambridge: Cambridge University Press, 100–49.
Fales, Frederick Mario
  1986 *Aramaic Epigraphs on Clay Tablets of the Neo-Assyrian Period.* Studi Semitici n.s. 2. Rome: Università degli studi 'La Sapienza'.
Farber, Walther
  1975 'Eine elamische Inschrift aus der 1. Hälfte des 2. Jahrtausends.' *Zeitschrift für Assyriologie* 64: 74–86.
Foster, Benjamin
  1993 '"International" Trade and Sargonic Susa (Susa in the Sargonic Period III).' *Altorientalische Forschungen* 20: 59–68.
Garrison, Mark B., and Margaret C. Root
  2001 *Seals on the Persepolis Fortification Tablets* I: *Images of Heroic Encounter.* Uni-

versity of Chicago Oriental Institute Publications 117. Chicago, IL: Oriental Institute, University of Chicago. (With studies of the seal inscriptions by Charles E. Jones; the inscriptions on the seals in the next two volumes are in preparation.)

Gelb, Ignace J.
  1963 *A Study of Writing*, revised edition. Chicago, IL: University of Chicago Press.

Gibson, John C. L.
  1971 *Textbook of Syrian Semitic Inscriptions*. Oxford: Clarendon Press.
  1975 *Textbook of Syrian Semitic Inscriptions* II: *Aramaic Inscriptions Including Inscriptions in the Dialect of Zenjirli*. Oxford: Clarendon Press.

Graf, David F.
  2000 'Aramaic on the Periphery of the Achaemenid Realm.' *Archäologische Mitteilungen aus Iran und Turan* 32: 75–92.

Gragg, Gene B.
  1996 'Elamite Cuneiform.' In Peter T. Daniels and William Bright (eds.), *The World's Writing Systems*. New York and Oxford: Oxford University Press, 58–61.

Greenfield, Jonas
  1985 'Aramaic in the Achaemenian Empire.' In Ilya Gershevitch (ed.), *Cambridge History of Iran* II. Cambridge: Cambridge University Press, 698–713.

Hallock, Richard T.
  1969 *The Persepolis Fortification Ttablets*. University of Chicago Oriental Institute Publications 92. Chicago, IL: University of Chicago Press.

Henkelman, Wouter
  2003 'Defining "Neo-Elamite History" ' (review of Matthew W. Waters, *A Survey of Neo-Elamite History*). *Bibliotheca Orientalis* 60: 251–63.

Henning, Walter Bruno
  1956 'The "Coin" with Cuneiform Inscription.' *Numismatic Chronicle*: 327–8.

Hinz, Walther
  1967 'Elams Vertrag mit Naram-Sin von Akkade.' *Zeitschrift für Assyriologie* 75: 66–96.
  1976–79 *Darius und die Perser: eine Kulturgeschichte der Achämeniden*, 2 vols. Baden-Baden: Holle.

Houston, Stephen, John Baines, and Jerrold Cooper
  2003 'Last Writing: Script Obsolescence in Egypt, Mesopotamia and Mesoamerica.' *Comparative Studies in Society and History* 45: 430–79.

Hulin, Peter
  1954 'The Signs on the Kabul Silver Piece.' *Numismatic Chronicle*: 174–6.

Jones, Charles E., and Matthew W. Stolper
  1986 'Two Late Elamite Tablets at Yale.' In Leon De Meyer, Hermann Gasche, and François Vallat (eds.), *Fragmenta historiae aelamicae: Mélanges offerts à M.-J. Steve*. Paris: Editions Recherche sur les civilisations: 243–54.
  In press 'A Survey of Scattered Achaemenid Elamite Administrative Texts.' *Papers of the First International Conference on Iran and Western Asia in Antiquity, Tehran,*

August 2003, 1–10. See in interim Henkelman, Wouter F. M., Charles E. Jones, and Matthew W. Stolper 2004. *Clay Tags with Achaemenid Seal Impressions in the Dutch Institute of the Near East (NINO) and Elsewhere*. ARTA: Achaemenid Research on Texts and Archaeology: http://www.achemenet.com/ressources/enligne/arta/pdf/2004.001/2004.001.pdf.

Jones, Charles E., and Matthew W. Stolper
2006   *Fortification Texts Sold at the Auction of the Erlenmeyer Collection*. ARTA: Achaemenid Research on Texts and Archaeology: http://www.achemenet.com/ressources/enligne/arta/pdf/2006.001.Jones-Stolper.pdf.

Kaptan, Deniz
2002   *The Daskyleion bullae: Seal Images from the Western Achaemenid Empire*. 2 vols. Achaemenid History XII. Leiden: Nederlands Instituut voor het Nabije Oosten.

Kent, Roland G.
1953   *Old Persian: Grammar, Texts, Lexicon*. 2nd ed. New Haven, CT: American Oriental Society.

King, Leonard W., Reginald Campbell Thompson, and Ernest A. W. Budge
1907   *The Sculptures and Inscriptions of Darius the Great on the Rock of Behistûn*. London: British Museum.

Labat, René
1988   *Manuel d'épigraphie akkadienne*. 6th ed., ed. Florence Malbran-Labat. Paris: Geuthner.

Labat, René, Dietz O. Edzard, and Roman Ghirshman
1974   *Textes littéraires de Suse*. Mémoires de la Délégation Archéologique en Iran 57. Paris: Geuthner.

Lambert, M.
1974   'Deux textes élamites du IIIᵉ millénaire', *Revue d'Assyriologie* 68: 3–14.
1977   'Deux textes élamites de la fin du septième siècle', *Journal Asiatique* 264: 221–5.

Le Rider, George
1965   *Suse sous les Séleucides et les Parthes: les trouvailles monétaires et l'histoire de la ville*. Mémoires de la Mission Archéologique en Iran 38. Paris: Geuthner.

Malbran-Labat, Florence
1995   *Les Inscriptions royales de Suse*. Paris: Editions de la Réunion des musées nationaux.

Miroschedji, P. de
1982   'Notes sur la glyptique de la fin de l'Elam.' *Revue d'Assyriologie* 76: 51–63.

Naveh, Joseph, and Shaul Shaked
1973   'Ritual Texts or Treasury Documents.' *Orientalia* 42: 445–57.
forthcoming. *Aramaic Documents from Ancient Bactria*. London: Nour Foundation.

Oppenheim, A. Leo
1956   *The Interpretation of Dreams in the Ancient Near East*. Transactions of the American Philosophical Society 46:3. Philadelphia, PA: American Philological Society.

Paper, Herbert Harry
    1954   'Note préliminaire sur la date de trois tablettes élamites de Suse.' In Roman Ghirshman, *Village perse-achéménide*. Mémoires de la Délégation Archéologique en Iran 36, Mission de Susiane. Paris: Presses universitaires de France: 79–82.
    1955   *The Phonology and Morphology of Royal Achaemenid Elamite*. Ann Arbor: University of Michigan Press.

Potts, Daniel T.
    1999   *The Archaeology of Elam: Formation and Transformation of an Ancient Iranian State*. Cambridge: Cambridge University Press.

Reade, Julian E.
    1992   'The Elamite Texts from Nineveh.' *NABU* 1992: 119.
    2000   'Elam after the Assyrian Sack of Susa in 647 BC.' *NABU* 2000: 80.

Reiner, Erica
    1960   'Calques sur le vieux-perse en élamite achéménide.' *Bulletin de la Société de linguistique de Paris* 55: 222–7.
    1969   'The Elamite Language.' In B. Spuler (ed.), *Altkleinasiatische Sprachen*. Handbuch der Orientalistik I, 2, 2. Leiden: Brill, 54–118.

Rössler, O.
    1938   'Untersuchungen über die akkadische Fassung der Achämenideninschriften.' Unpublished doctoral dissertation, University of Berlin.

Salonen, Erkki
    1962   *Untersuchungen zur Schrift und Sprache des Altbabylonischen von Susa mit Berücksichtigung der Mâlamir-Texte*. Studia Orientalia 27, 1. Helsinki: Societas Orientalis Fennica.

Scheil, Vincent
    1907   *Textes élamites—anzanites*, 3rd series. Délégation en Perse, Mémoires 9. Paris: Leroux.
    1908   *Textes élamites—sémitiques*, 4th series. Délégation en Perse, Mémoires 10. Paris: Leroux.
    1912   *Textes élamites—sémitiques*, 5th series. Mémoires de la Mission archéologique de Susiane 14. Paris: Leroux.
    1917   'Déchiffrement d'un document anzanite relatif aux présages.' *Revue d'Assyriologie* 14: 29–59.
    1925   'Hémérologie élamite.' *Revue d'Assyriologie* 22, 157–8.
    1927   'Vers l'écriture nucléiforme.' *Revue d'Assyriologie* 24, 43.
    1928   'Sparsim.' *Revue d'Assyriologie* 25, 40.

Schlumberger, Daniel
    1953   'L'argent grec dans l'empire achéménide.' In Raoul Curiel and Daniel Schlumberger, *Trésors monétaires d'Afghanistan*. Mémoires de la Délégation archéologique française en Afghanistan 14. Paris: Imprimerie nationale; Klincksieck: 1–64.

Schmidt, Erich F.
    1953   *Persepolis I: Structures, Reliefs, Inscriptions*. University of Chicago Oriental Institute Publications 68. Chicago, IL: University of Chicago Press.

1957   *Persepolis II: Contents of the Treasury and Other Discoveries.* Oriental Institute Publications 69. Chicago, IL: University of Chicago Press.

Schmitt, Rüdiger
1981   *Altpersiche Siegel-Inschriften.* Vienna: Österreichische Akademie der Wissenschaften.
1993   'Die Sprachverhältnisse im Achämenidenreich.' In R.B. Finazzi and P. Tornaghi (eds), *Lingue e culture in contatto nel mondo antico e altomedievale: Atti dell'VIII Convegno internazionale di Linguisti.* Brescia: Paideia, 77–102.
1999   *Beiträge zu altpersischen Inschriften.* Wiesbaden: Reichert.
2000   *The Old Persian Inscriptions of Naqsh-i Rustam and Persepolis.* Corpus Inscriptionum Iranicarum Part I: I, Texts II. London: School of Oriental and African Studies.

Seipel, Wilfried, ed.
2000   *7000 Jahre persische Kunst: Meisterwerke aus dem Iranischen Nationalmuseum in Teheran: Kunsthistorisches Museum, 22. November 2000 bis 25. März 2001.* Exhibition catalogue. Vienna and Milan: Kunsthistorisches Museum; Skira.

Shaked, Shaul
2004   *Le Satrape de Bactriane et son gouverneur: documents araméens du IVe s. avant notre ère provenant de Bactriane.* Persika 4. Paris: de Boccard.

Steve, Marie-Joseph
1967   *Textes élamites et accadiens de Tchoga Zanbil.* Mémoires de la Délégation en Perse 41 = *Tchoga Zanbil (Dur Untash)* III. Paris: Geuthner.
1992   *Syllabaire élamite: histoire et paléographie.* Civilisation du Proche-Orient II, Philologie I. Neuchâtel and Paris: Recherches et publications.

Stolper, Matthew W.
1984   *Texts from Tall-i Malyan I: Elamite Administrative Texts (1972-1974).* Philadelphia: Babylonian Fund of the University Museum.
2004   'Elamite.' In Roger D. Woodard (ed.), *The Cambridge Encyclopedia of the World's Ancient Languages.* Cambridge: Cambridge University Press, 60–94.

Stolper, Matthew W. and Jan Tavernier
2007   'From the Persepolis Fortification Archive Project, 1: An Old Persian Administrative Tablet from the Persepolis Fortification.' ARTA 2007.001. Online at http://www.achemenet.com/.

Stronach, David
1990   'On the Genesis of the Old Persian Cuneiform Script.' In François Vallat (ed.), *Contribution à l'histoire de l'Iran: Mélanges Jean Perrot.* Paris: Recherche sur les civilisations, 195–203.

Teixidor, Javier
1967   'Bulletin d'épigraphie sémitique 1967.' *Syria* 44: 163–95.
1974   'Bulletin d'épigraphie sémitique 1974.' *Syria* 51: 299–340.

Towhidi, F., and A. M. Khalijian
1982   'Report on the Study of the Objects Originating from the Tomb of Arjān, Behbehan.' *Asar* 7-9: 266, fig. 45 (in Persian).

Vallat, François
    1970   'Table élamite de Darius Iᵉʳ.' *Revue d'Assyriologie* 64: 149–60.
    1974   'Les textes cunéiformes de la statue de Darius.' *Cahiers de la Délégation archéologique française en Iran* 4: 161–70.
    1989   'Les compléments phonétiques ou graphiques en élamite achéménide.' *Annali dell'Istituto Universitario Orientale di Napoli* 49: 219–22.
    1996a 'Nouvelle analyse des inscription néo-élamites.' In Hermann Gasche and Barthel Hrouda (eds), *Collectanea orientalia: Histoire, arts de l'espace et industrie de la terre, études offertes en hommage à Agnès Spycket*. Neuchâtel: Recherches et publications, 385–95.
    1996b 'Le royaume néo-élamite de Samati.' *NABU* 1996: 31.
    1998   'Le royaume élamite de Zamin et les "lettres de Ninive".' *Iranica Antiqua* 33: 95–106.

Van Soldt, Wilfred
    1991   *Studies in the Akkadian of Ugarit: Dating and Grammar*. Alter Orient und Altes Testament 40. Neukirchen-Vluyn: Neukirchener Verlag; Kevelaer: Butzon und Bercker.

Von Soden, Wolfram
    1991   *Das akkadische Syllabar*. 4th ed. Analecta Orientalia 42. Rome: Pontifical Biblical Institute.

Von Voigtlander, Elizabeth Nation
    1978   *The Bisitun Inscription of Darius the Great: Babylonian Version*. Corpus Inscriptionum Iranicarum I, 2, 1. London: Lund Humphries.

Walker, Christopher B. F.
    1980   'Elamite Inscriptions in the British Museum.' *Iran* 18: 75–81.

Weissbach, Franz Heinrich
    1902   'Susische Thontäfelchen.' *Beiträge zur Assyriologie* 4: 168–202.

Westenholz, Aage, and Walther Sallaberger (eds)
    1999   *Mesopotamien: Akkade-Zeit und Ur III-Zeit*. Orbis Biblicus et Orientalis 160. Fribourg and Göttingen: Universitätsverlag; Vandenhoeck und Ruprecht.

Wetzel, Friedrich, Erich Schmidt, and Alfred Mallwitz
    1957   *Das Babylon der Spätzeit*. Ausgrabung der Deutschen Orient-Gesellschaft 62. Berlin: Gebrüder Mann.

Wheatley, Julian K.
    1992   'Burmese.' In William Bright (ed.), *International Encyclopedia of Linguistics*. New York and Oxford: Oxford University Press, 206–10.

Wiseman, Donald J., and Werner and Bedrich Forman
    n.d.   *Cylinder Seals of Western Asia*. London: Batchworth.

Yoyotte, Jean
    1972   'Les Inscriptions hiéroglyphiques, Darius et l'Egypte.' *Journal asiatique* 260: 253–66.

4

Increasingly Redundant: The Growing Obsolescence of the Cuneiform Script in Babylonia from 539 BC[1]

David Brown

Introduction

In 539 BC Cyrus conquered Mesopotamia. No subsequent ruler of the land claimed to be Mesopotamian, or claimed a common heritage with the populace,[2] though being 'king of Babylon' continued to hold great significance throughout the Achaemenid period and well into the Hellenistic (Sherwin-White 1987: 8–9).[3] Between 334 and 331 BC, Alexander the Great swept across Asia, initiating Macedonian/Greek rule in Mesopotamia until c. 143 BC.[4] After a period of uncertainty Mesopotamia fell under stable Parthian rule from 125 BC. Following Roman involvement from AD 115–199, Mesopotamia came to be controlled by the Sassanians from AD 226 until AD 642, when the Arab caliphs came to power.

Timeline

There was no 'end' as such to Mesopotamian civilization (Rempel and Yoffee 1999: 386). Scholars such as Kuhrt and Sherwin-White (1994) stress the continuity in legal, administrative, and cultural-religious traditions from Neo-Babylonian into Achaemenid times, and thence to Hellenistic ones, as well as the continuity of Hellenistic traditions in these areas under the Arsacid Parthians (Oelsner 1986: 63; 2002a: 24–8; 2002b: 53; 2002c: 195; 2003: 286). Continuities in the plastic arts, architecture, and town-planning can be traced to much later times (Van De Mieroop 1999: 245). In the present context, continuities in law,

Neo-Babylonian period and dialect (NB)	c. 1000–539 BC
Late-Babylonian period and dialect (LB)	c. 539 – c. 90 BC (n. 21)
Standard-Babylonian (a literary) dialect (SB)	c. 1500 BC – c. AD 75 (n. 19)
Achaemenid/Persian rule over Babylonia (ruling house named after founder Achaemenes)	539–331 BC
Macedonian/Greek rule over Babylonia	331–141 BC
Seleucid Era (SE; house named after founder Seleucus I Nikator)	Begins 3 April 311 BC
Arsacid/Parthian rule over Babylonia	125 BC – AD 226
Arsacid Era (AE; ruling house named after founder Arsaces)	begins 15 April 247 BC

Table 4.1   Salient dates in first millennium BC Babylonia.

administration, and 'religion', broadly defined, concern us particularly, especially the latter, for it was in the temples that writing survived the longest. Aspects of Mesopotamian religion continued well into the first millennium AD (Dalley 1998: ch. 2),[5] but, although an argument largely from silence, it has become commonplace to state that it was with the arrival of the Sassanians in the early third century AD that the temples in the heartland finally ceased their traditional activities.[6] The evidence from Assur, that Aššur, his spouse, Nabû, Nannai, and Nergal were worshipped at least until the end of the Parthian period is, however, based solely on the existence of Aramaic dedications on votive plaques. Clearly, in this case, the cult continued without recourse to cuneiform, and the same was true of the cult of Nabû in Egypt (Dalley 1998: 38) and in many other places, and may well have been true in Babylonia itself. Oelsner (2002c: 192–3), points out that Babylonian theophoric elements appear in the names of people resident in Uruk recorded in Greek inscriptions as late as the second century AD, more than a century after the latest datable cuneiform tablet from there. Thus, Geller's hypothesis (1997: 62) that 'cuneiform was in use so long as the temples were in use' cannot readily be accepted. Oelsner's emendation (2002a: 30) that Akkadian and Sumerian were likely to have been used as long as the temples were in use, but in the latest phase were written in an alphabetic script on perishable materials, may well be true (the alternative being that the cult employed Aramaic or Greek), but does not answer the question as to why, finally, cuneiform was abandoned.

Changes in Macro-Economic Structures

One thing that does have a bearing on the end of cuneiform usage is the general economy of the region. I call the following the macro-economic explanation for the demise of cuneiform.

Van De Mieroop (1999: 229–30) addresses the wider economic picture in his discussion of the eclipse of the Mesopotamian city. He describes briefly the 'Bedouinization' of Assyria after the fall of that empire in c. 612 BC, the area a victim of numerous military incursions and political uncertainty. Its sparse population was largely semi-nomadic and the few important urban centres, such as Hatra, existed on the basis of caravan trade and their strategic importance in the conflicts between great powers (see map Fig. 4.1). No cuneiform of a very late date is attested from northern Mesopotamia (except the text edited by Black 1997), and we may account for its absence simply because of the land's new demography.

The middle Euphrates valley was also an area that changed hands politically many times after c. 330 BC, and yet it thrived economically at least until Sassanian times. Many centres in Syria attest to the continued practice of Babylonian religion. New cities, such as Dura-Europus (founded 303 BC), have provided us with inscriptions in which inhabitants with Babylonian names are recorded (Geller 1997: 62), but no cuneiform. This picture may yet change.

Babylonia proper, the area south of Baghdad, was wealthy and heavily urbanised through to the eighth century AD. From the early seventh century BC, more and more land was brought into production through collective ac-

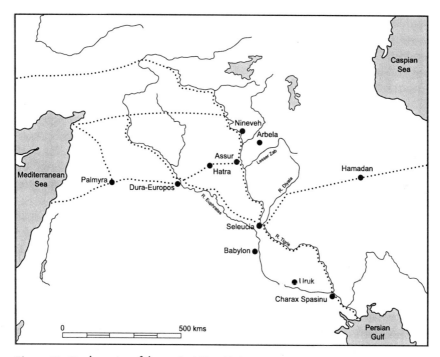

Figure 4.1 Trade routes of the ancient Near East.

tion on irrigation, and it is only after AD 700 or so that we see abandonment of the land and collapse of the agricultural economy. Seleucid, Parthian, and Sassanian periods saw a high percentage of people living in urban centres. New cities were founded, notably Seleukeia on the Tigris around 300 BC. The Parthians later built Ctesiphon opposite Seleukeia, and to the Sassanians the developed complex was called Veh-Ardashir. The area was later known to the Arabs as *al-Mada'in*, 'the cities' (Van De Mieroop 1999: 232-3). The old cities of Babylonia also continued at first to maintain populations under foreign rule. Babylon, Uruk, Larsa, and Nippur all have substantial Parthian remains, and Kish a large Sassanian town. Why then does cuneiform become redundant some time during the period after AD 75? The macro-economic explanation is that while analysis of settlement patterns shows that a well-managed agricultural base sustained a large urban population well beyond AD 75, that population was not located in the same towns and cities. The new foundations reflect a gradual and ultimately fundamental alteration of the socio-economic structure of the area, which in due course came to marginalize many traditional Babylonian centres, the places where cuneiform was last written.

The Tigris River was increasingly exploited as a trade route, and a move eastwards of the urban population ensued. This change began with Persian rule: Darius I established Susa, the ancient Elamite centre, as capital of his empire, and the royal road to Sardis passed from it, through Arbela,[7] to the east of Nineveh, without travelling through Babylonia. The Persian unification of the east led to an increased circulation of goods, to the profit of some entrepreneurial Babylonians, but it removed Babylonia from the main axis of trade (Joannès 1995: 1475). While scholars are right to stress that the Persians altered little in Babylonia (Dalley 1998: 39; Kuhrt 1987; Sherwin-White 1987: 8; Oelsner 2002a: 7; 2002b: 53), it is also true that after the uprisings under Darius and Xerxes the economy of Babylonia was heavily exploited, and the area experienced 'pronounced inflation characterised by the increase in prices in the most ordinary products' (Joannès 1995: 1475). Babylonia may have been one of the richest satrapies of the Persian Empire, but it had become merely a colony on the margins of power.

Macedonian rule further emphasized the increasing marginalization of those ancient cities located on the Euphrates. Alexander's alleged plan to turn Babylon into Asia's capital foundered upon his death, and his Seleucid successors ensured that while Babylon and other ancient cities were supported, a new capital would sit upon the new main trade routes running both alongside the Tigris, and across the deserts to the Mediterranean coast. These latter trade routes were made possible by a new technology, which must also be mentioned as an indirect factor in the demise of cuneiform: the camel. Its domestication and use as a pack animal in the early first millennium BC, if not earlier, had opened up new trade networks previously impossible with beasts of burden that required constant access to water (Van De Mieroop 1999: 238). Shortcuts across deserts became possible, and oasis cities such as Palmyra and Hatra were able to become substantial trading *entrepôts*. Seleukeia, and then Ctesiphon, were located at a nodal point in this transit-trade network, on the 'silk route' travelling east up the Diyala to Hamadan, and on into Afghanistan, India, and China, and west to the Mediterranean, as well as on the 'Tigris route' from Charax Sapsinu (the Persian Gulf harbour for sea trade from the east that supplanted Ur's role in such trade), north and west to Anatolia and the Mediterranean. Babylon was not such a nodal point, and nor were any of the other ancient Babylonian cities.

In c. AD 50 Pliny wrote that: 'Besides, the town (Babylon) has turned into a barren waste, exhausted by its proximity to Seleukeia.'[8] A similar statement had already been made by Strabo in c. AD 20.[9] Emperors Trajan and Septimus Severus found Babylon deserted and destroyed in AD 115 and AD 199 respectively (Geller 1997: 51; Oelsner 2002a: 25). However, a late-second-century AD Greek inscription on the amphitheatre in Babylon, the second-century AD Parthian buildings recovered archaeologically in the Amran area of the city, and the evidence of Rabbi Rav (fl. c. AD 219), who wrote that the temples of Bēl at Babylon and Borsippa's Nabû temple were flourishing in his day, all indicate that parts of Babylon, and certainly the temples, were still functioning in some capacity well after AD 75 (Oelsner 2002a: 27).

We may draw from this evidence some justification for the macro-economic explanation for the demise of cuneiform. The temple of Marduk (Bēl) in Babylon had traditionally been sustained by the tithes (*ešrû*) of the population and the occasional rebuilding efforts of kings or governors. With a depleted population we might imagine that the temple limped on as best it could for some decades, perhaps even centuries, but that one of the consequences of its reduced income was an inability to fund the necessary education to keep the cuneiform scribal tradition going. The cults, therefore, outlived cuneiform. Attractive though this model is, there is no direct evidence that this was what in fact happened.

The question is raised as to why the temples and cults survived at all, once rulership had passed into foreign hands. The temples were integral to the life of the cities in which they were located, acting not only as the intermediary between royal and divine spheres, but also between royalty and the community. They were located in central parts of the city, and were the focus of citizen-wide festivals and rituals, as well as being vital economic centres. The prebendary systems linked the temples directly to a wide, urban elite, blurring distinctions between civic and religious offices, and indeed between private and temple business (Kuhrt 1995: 62). Secondly, and more prosaically, the temples were generally useful to colonizers as ready sources of income, especially during crises, as van der Spek argues (1994: 19). Their work was supervised by the colonial administrators, and the foreign rulers posed as pious benefactors, participating in religious ceremonies and supporting temple refurbishment, but always helping themselves to a share of the taxes already being raised by the institutions (MacGinnis 1995: 6–7).[10] The Persians allowed the temples to function as important economic units (Kuhrt 1995: 671; MacGinnis 1995: 7). Greek support for the temples is well attested, particularly in the early period of their hegemony, though textual references to rebuilding or repairing the temples occur as late as the end of the second century BC (Oelsner 2002a: 18–23; 2002c: 186–7). The long-argued-for connection between the arrival of the Parthians and the archaeologically attested burning of the Uruk temples has had to be rethought with the publication by Kessler (1984) of a text dating to 108 BC, which shows the institution functioning as normal under the Parthians, and with the same families *in situ* (Sherwin-White 1987: 2).[11] The Uruk temples remained useful to the Parthians too, one must assume.

No particular pressure that was put on the existence of the temples by Persian, Greek, or Parthian rulers can thus account for cuneiform falling into disuse. While it remains possible that the Babylonian cults were suppressed later under the Sassanians, I suggest that cuneiform had already by then fallen into disuse, as we shall see. Further, the gradual diminution in economic activity in Babylonia does indeed provide the backdrop to the increasing obsolescence of cuneiform, but there is also no direct evidence that this alone accounts for the script's ultimate demise.

Scripts, media, and languages

Another macro-scale explanation we should consider in looking at cuneiform's demise is the notion that alphabetic scripts were easier to use than logo-syllabic ones.[12] Most of the very latest texts where signs were indicated by impressed strokes of a reed stylus on clay, which we call cuneiform, wrote Akkadian or Sumerian in logograms and syllables. The co-existence of alphabetic and logo-syllabic scripts since c. 1700 BC suggests, however, that alphabetic scripts played little or no role in the demise of cuneiform. Alphabetic cuneiform scripts are known as early as the late Bronze Age, but even logo-syllabic cuneiform scripts were capable of rendering a language very efficiently. Only seventy-odd signs were commonly used for Old Assyrian, for instance. Two hundred signs were perhaps sufficient for normal run-of-the-mill transactions in Akkadian, and 400 for literary texts in that language.

The medium upon which cuneiform was written explains, in part, its attraction. Clay was plentiful, cheap, and extremely durable, a factor not to be ignored when it comes to promissory notes, legal judgements, or indeed treasured works of literature—and certainly astronomical data records. Tablets were also very easy to seal, and if kept moist, could be added to or changed over the course of some days. Cursive scripts are harder to write on clay, though by no means impossible. Indeed, clay tablets were adopted by those writing Greek for recording public documents (Sherwin-White and Kuhrt 1993: 160). The virtual exclusivity of cuneiform to clay, and alphabetic scripts to other media,[13] however, probably does account for why no hybrid alphabetic script based on cuneiform values took hold in Mesopotamia in the late period, such as happened with Coptic in Egypt, for example.

In some instances, the cuneiform logo-syllabic script itself contained part of the meaning of what was being transmitted. Much has been made of punning in Mesopotamia, some of which was purely graphic (for some late examples, see Beaulieu 1995). The full meaning of a logo-syllabic text could not be gleaned from merely pronouncing the words. Some of the richness of such literature is lost through translation *and* through transliteration, which would perhaps account in part for a particular attachment to the logo-syllabic script.

However, so little has survived of the media upon which alphabetic scripts were written, that it is quite possible that Akkadian or Sumerian were indeed commonly rendered in such scripts,[14] that much of the 'literary' material was translated and has simply been lost. We know, for example, that Darius's Bisitun inscription was translated from the cuneiform (logo-syllabic Elamite or Akkadian, or alphabetic Old Persian) into alphabetic Aramaic and propagated around the empire, as a papyrus from Elephantine has shown (Sims-Williams 1981). Perhaps the royal cuneiform inscriptions of the Hellenistic period monarchs were similarly transmitted to the far reaches of the empire, and have been lost because survival conditions for such media outside Egypt are not favourable. It may be a factor, however, that the earliest Semitic alphabets did not indicate vowels, which would have made them unsuitable for rendering Akkadian or Sumerian. This is not true of the Greek alphabet, of course.

Alphabetic cuneiform scripts, in which a small number of signs are used as syllables/consonants/vowels, were used in Ugarit before 1200 BC, and again in order to write Old Persian from the late sixth century BC. Cuneiform was occasionally used to write languages with long traditions of an alphabetic script—namely Greek and Aramaic (see n. 13). Cursive Aramaic and Greek are also found on clay tablets (Oelsner 1986: §§3.2, 4.1.2). Cuneiform was certainly written on waxed boards throughout the first millennium BC, and perhaps on other easily perishable materials (Brown 2000: 30; Oelsner 2002a: 16–17). There are overlaps in all directions, and it is hard to draw any conclusions as to the effect alphabetic-cursive scripts had on cuneiform. The fact is, the part-syllabic, part-logographic cuneiform script survived alongside alphabets, with its own infrastructure of seal-cutters and scribes, and possessed enough momentum to carry it through to the first century AD. Levels of literacy were probably very low at all times in Mesopotamia during the period of concern, and we cannot escape the conclusion that cuneiform's very exclusivity, and perhaps even its difficulty, were positive advantages, at least so far as the scribal guilds that made their living out of it were concerned.

A third macro-scale explanation for the redundancy of cuneiform is that it was, in the end, tied to the languages of Sumerian and then Akkadian, the latter of which, in its Late Babylonian (LB) form, eventually died out. It is not clear, though, when Babylonian died out as a spoken language, and more importantly, cuneiform had always previously been adapted to write new languages, or preserved to render dead ones. Indeed, as far as our sources allow us to judge, cuneiform texts written in the 'vernacular' LB end before those written in Standard Babylonian (SB), a purely literary dialect. The fact that fewer and fewer people actually spoke Babylonian is largely irrelevant to the question of why and when cuneiform became redundant (Oelsner 2002b: 58–60).

The script had been in existence in southern Mesopotamia for more than 2500 years prior to the Persian conquest, spreading during the course of the third millennium as far as the Levant and Iran, and still further during the second millennium deep into Anatolia and Egypt. Initially adapted to write the Sumerian language, so far as we can judge, it was subsequently used to write other local languages. To name only the most important, these were Elamite, Akkadian, Eblaitic, Hurrian, Hittite, and Urartian, all of which largely maintained the sign shapes and some values of logo-syllabic Sumerian cuneiform, as well as alphabetic Ugaritic and Old Persian, both of which used the script, but adapted the shapes of the signs and gave them many new values. Given that background, the question must arise as to why cuneiform was not more commonly adapted to render Aramaic, other North-West Semitic languages, and Greek. The existence of a few Greek personal names and technical terms proves only that Greek, too, could be written in cuneiform. We also have enough material from Achaemenid and Hellenistic times to be fairly confident that the reason why we have found so little Greek and Aramaic is because they were mostly *not* written in cuneiform.

It therefore seems reasonable to argue that cuneiform was able to supplant other scripts in earlier times because of the high regard in which Assyro-Babylonian culture was held, and because the alternative scribal infrastructures were not sufficiently well embedded to resist change. For example, Anatolian hieroglyphic traditions used in Urartu were supplanted in the course of the ninth and eight centuries BC by Assyrian-style cuneiform and not by Phoenicio-Aramaic-style alphabets, probably due to the status of the Neo-Assyrians at that time. Old Persian was first written in an alphabet (if there had been an earlier native Old Persian script it has not survived), but a cuneiform alphabet, probably in part because of the cultural value the Persians attached to the Babylonians and Elamites. In the Late Babylonian period, Aramaic and Greek were not extensively written in a cuneiform script, firstly because Babylonia's star had by then fallen, and secondly because a substantial scribal infrastructure *already* existed, underpinning the rendering of those languages in cursive alphabets by the time the peoples who used them came to dominate, in cuneiform's last stronghold. One has to suppose that this infrastructure was first able to take hold because of the difficulties of the 'dark age' after 1200 BC and the consequent loss of cuneiform centres such as Ugarit, Emar, Alalakh, and thus the end of cuneiform as the *scripta franca* between the great powers of the Near East and Mediterranean. Alphabetic cuneiform had arisen by then, no doubt, because of a complex interplay between the efficiency of the alphabet and the prestige of the clay-based script. Had cuneiform's prestige survived the dark ages, and had alphabetic cuneiform taken hold in the Levant instead of the cursive Phoenician alphabet, might the Greeks have written their language in a version of cuneiform?

By the time of the Assyrian revival in the ninth century BC, Aramaic had an associated script infrastructure which ensured its survival alongside the cuneiform writing emerging from Assyrian schools, temples, and royal courts, as well as thereafter. By the sixth century BC, the Greek scribal tradition itself was strong enough to begin to influence back into the Near East, in Phrygia, Lydia, Caria, and Lycia, to such an extent that Luwian, a language which had at one time been written in logo-syllabic cuneiform, came to be written in a version of the Greek alphabet (see further Hawkins in this volume). Cuneiform could no longer threaten the Greek scribal tradition in the period after Greek hegemony in Babylonia.

With the elimination of Assyria in c. 612–609 BC, the cuneiform scribal infrastructure in the north also collapsed shortly thereafter.[15] A hatred of all things Assyrian probably played the major role in this, rather than anything intrinsically superior about the cursive script associated with Aramaic, which by and large replaced it. Later, in the south, despite some flirtations, cuneiform failed to enjoy a sustained relationship with the dominant languages of Aramaic and Greek. They remained true to cursive alphabetic scripts. Cuneiform had been a wonderfully flexible script, and had adapted well to the challenges of many new languages over the millennia, at least until the sixth century BC, but perhaps its relative difficulty, when compared to the cursive alphabetic scripts, together with the low status of Babylonia at that time, meant that its attractions could not supplant those of the well-established cursive scripts. It survived for some centuries thereafter, rendering, almost without exception, only Akkadian and Sumerian; but with no prospect of its being used to write Greek and Aramaic, its days were numbered.

Without that link to the living, politically important languages, one would expect cuneiform's demise, when it came, to be sudden and absolute. Also, until that 'tip' (Houston *et al.* 2003: 468) into obsolescence—and we shall turn to that shortly—one would expect cuneiform to have been used for as wide a range of texts as possible, given the limitations imposed by the colonial powers, since that would have been to the advantage of those who continued to make their living from it. Indeed, the script was used for legal, administrative, scientific, literary, cultic, historical, and personal texts throughout the centuries of Persian, Macedonian, and Parthian rule. New texts were composed and old texts copied and preserved. The temples, and even private families, conducted business in both cursive and cuneiform scripts, for the discovery of some 25,000 bullae from Seleukeia and about 1000 from Uruk reveals that extensive archives in Aramaic and Greek must have been kept alongside cuneiform archives in Babylonia at this time (Oelsner 1986: 257–8; 2003: 295).

A detailed study of what has survived shows us that immediately prior to the 'tip' some text-types ceased to be written in cuneiform before others. The reasons for this piecemeal extinction can be put down to the direct or indirect demands of the colonial administration. I turn now to these changes, before focusing attention on the final 'tip', and the end of cuneiform writing.

Administrative changes

One might suppose that the first application of cuneiform to disappear would be that used by the powers that were, given that they were now foreign. In Assyrian times the king surrounded himself with scholars who both wrote to him on a daily basis, and composed letters on his behalf, and this practice continued under the Neo-Babylonian (NB) kings, though our evidence is only indirect (Rochberg 2000: 364–5). We have few 'state' documents from NB times (Oelsner 2002b: n. 21). MacGinnis (1995: 2) suggests that they may have been cleared out by the incoming Persians. It seems most probable that royal correspondence would have been written for Persian rulers in Elamite (the language of Persepolis administration) or Aramaic, and for the Seleucid and Parthian rulers in Greek or Aramaic.

Once Babylonia had become a colony, probably no more correspondence was written to or for the king in cuneiform, but much else continued to be written for him, or on his behalf (Sherwin-White 1987: 24).[16] Beginning with the *Cyrus Cylinder*, via Darius's Bisitun inscriptions, through to the last cuneiform king list dating to c. 138 BC, chronographic writing in cuneiform, and in the literary dialect Standard Babylonian, continued to be undertaken. Such texts copied old patterns and were continued both for the sake of tradition and for practical political ends.

Foreign rule did have an effect on other types of text being written. Initially after 539 BC cuneiform was written throughout Babylonia. We have Late Babylonian temple archives from the Ebabbara in Sippar and the Eanna in Uruk, and many private archives. However, private and temple documents become much rarer after the early years of Xerxes, perhaps in the wake of the suppression of revolts in 481 and 479 BC (MacGinnis 1995: 2). This applies particularly to the archives of the Egibi family from Babylon (archives date from c. 690–480 BC) and Ea-ilutu-bani family from Borsippa (687–487 BC), and Sippar temple (MacGinnis 1995: 17). The Eanna temple archives end somewhat earlier in 520 BC. However, Nippur's Murašû family, and Babylon's Kasr family continued to use cuneiform until the last decades of the fifth century BC (Oelsner 2002b: 56; 2003: 285), and two small temple archives from Babylon and Borsippa include material that can be dated to the second half of the fourth century BC (Oelsner 2002b: 55). A few other texts, found scattered throughout Babylonia, can be dated to the final years of Achaemenid rule.

This dramatic overall reduction in the usage of cuneiform in Babylonia was presumably brought about in part as a result of administrative reform imposed from above. However, it is also clear that the changes were piecemeal, and that while Aramaic gained an unassailable foothold amongst the literate of the land, cuneiform survived into the Seleucid period largely unscathed. The several hundred cuneiform tablets found in the south-east of Uruk, in the so-called Planquadrat Ue XVIII, stem from private houses and date from c. 400–316 BC, thus spanning the arrival of Macedonian rule in Babylonia (Oelsner 2002b: 63), as does the archive documenting the economic activity of the 'barber' (*gallābu*) family in Ur (Oelsner 2003: 286–7).

Under Achaemenid rule, the cuneiform archives of the great trading houses, such as the Egibi or Murašû indicate their involvement in financing international trade. The Hellenistic cuneiform archives do not attest the same, however; they are more concerned with temple lands, and the private individuals involved are probably all connected to the temples in some capacity. The distinction between private and temple blurs totally during the Hellenistic period (Oelsner 2003: 288), and the wider outlook then of those still writing in cuneiform has shrunk noticeably. It is inconceivable that there were not many Babylonians involved in international trade at this time, however. One must presume that their transactions were recorded on perishable materials in cursive scripts.

Rempel and Yoffee (1999: 393–4) suggest that while that the Seleucids were patronizing traditional Mesopotamian cultural institutions, they were simultaneously devaluing them by imposing an entirely different mode of interaction in the political realm. They point to Anu-uballiṭ Nicharkos, who received his second and Greek name from Antiochus II (261–246 BC), and records this prominently on the foundation inscription for the Bīt Rēš building in Uruk. They also point to the scholar Berossus, who wrote his history of Babylonia in Greek for Antiochus I (281–261 BC), and to the sealings in which Greek motifs are used by Babylonians. Becoming Greek became a route to power, and this, they suggest, worked rapidly to undermine the relevance of 'being Mesopotamian', which may in turn have undermined support for a temple-based cuneiform scribal tradition that served to preserve ancient Mesopotamian forms. It would seem likely, however, that under the Parthians 'being Greek' was no great advantage, though being able to write it may have still been. Indeed, it is worth proposing that the change of foreign rule around 125 BC sustained 'being Mesopotamian' for a while longer, spinning out cuneiform's existence for another couple of centuries or more.

Doty (1977: 'abstract' and fig. 15), showed on the basis of some 300 'private' contracts from Uruk that in c. 274 BC 'all sale documents involving slaves or arable land had to be written on papyrus or parchment, rather than cuneiform tablets, and registered with the Seleucid notary officer (*chreophylax*)'. It remains true to this day that no slave-sale contracts are attested from Uruk after SE 37 (274 BC). Property sales were not taxed and contracts continued to be written in cuneiform. This is another significant administrative cause of cuneiform's increasing redundancy, comparable with the changes brought about under Darius and Xerxes.

It is tempting to blame cuneiform's demise on administrative changes imposed on the final users of that ancient script by the foreign powers. Certainly, restrictions do appear to have been imposed that limited the script's use (Oelsner 2003: 290), and it is more than likely that cuneiform was not used in communication with the colonial rulers. The realities of international commerce also meant that cuneiform was of little use to merchants. Despite all these limitations, other legal and commercial transactions and administrative undertakings continued to be recorded in cuneiform, ancient texts recopied, and new scientific texts composed. Still, the script did become redundant in due course. We turn finally to the texts themselves in order to see which types become redundant first, and see that therein lies a clue as to why cuneiform finally fell out of use—evidence for the 'tip' into redundancy which, to my knowledge, has not been aired before.

The Last Texts

In Babylonia the following ancient cities had a scribal tradition lasting into the Hellenistic period:

Babylon, Uruk, Borsippa, Cutha, Kish/Hursagkalamma, Nippur, Larsa, Ur, and Dēr (Oelsner 2003).

One might expect in the course of time to find texts from this period from Marad, Tell al 'Aqar, Udanna, Telloh, and Sippar (Linssen 2003: 1). A little cuneiform has also been unearthed in Seleukeia (Oelsner 1986: 236).

More than 2200 cuneiform texts dating to the period after 330 BC are known, over half of which are astronomical in some form. Large numbers are attested only from Babylon and Uruk (e.g. Fig. 4.2), however, and I will restrict discussion to these two sites. The tradition in Uruk ends long before that in Babylon. We find SB and LB texts together, suggesting a blurring of the private–temple distinction. Texts are very hard to date on palaeographic criteria (Oelsner 1986: 192), but context and prosopography help. Some are dated by regnal year, and many astronomical examples can be dated.

Texts in Late Babylonian (LB)[17]

Legal and administrative

Uruk—c. 700 Hellenistic period texts, which come from the Rēš and Irigal temples, and from private houses (Oelsner, 2003: 287–8):

Last slave sale contract (BRM 2, 10) dates to 274 BC;
Last slave dedication contract (A3689) dates to 127 BC;
Latest house plot sale (BRM 2, 52) dates to 138 BC;
Latest prebend sale (VS 15, 37) dates to 140 BC;
Latest contract (W 18568) dates to 108 BC.[18]

Babylon[19]—c. 200 legal and administrative texts and letters (Oelsner 1986: 195–7; Kessler 2000), only half of which are published, and almost all of which were excavated illegally. Oelsner (2003: 289) argues that some come from private houses:
Private legal contracts come to an end in 155 BC (Oelsner 1986:197);
The last administrative texts, probably from the Gula temple, date to 93–2 BC (Oelsner 1986:198; Kessler 2000: 218),[20] and one from the Esaggila temple dates to 90 BC (Kessler 2000: 223; Oelsner 2003: 291).

Letters

Uruk—only five letters are known, the latest dating to c. 171 BC (NCBT 1969 and ARRIM 6 35f, updating Oelsner 1986: 153).
Babylon—Rm 844 dates to 87 BC (Oelsner 1986: 196). Letter orders are attested until 147 BC (Oelsner 1986: 198), though most are from 261–252 BC.

There are very few late letters. Since we have recovered private archives, this scarcity suggests that after Alexander, correspondence was mostly conducted in cursive scripts, and increasingly so. The many hundreds of LB contracts exhibit the grammar of the vernacular, but are also very formulaic in their structure. They show cuneiform being used to render the last version of the oral Akkadian language into the early first century BC, but do not prove that Akkadian was still learned at the breast this late. The latest oral version may already have been hundreds of years old by this time, and being kept alive only by specialists as a 'male language' (Houston *et al.* 2003: 451).

The last LB texts come from the archives of relatively important individuals and families associated with the temples, though not necessarily in any religious capacity. It is not clear that the texts from Babylon denoted as 'private' by Oelsner (1986: 197) do not actually deal with temple business, however indirectly. Doty (1977: 155) notes that individuals with Greek names, and whose ancestries also contain only Greek names, get involved in transactions recorded in cuneiform in Uruk in the period after 165 BC, though only in small numbers.

Figure 4.2 High-quality astronomical tablet of the Seleucid period, with information on
new moons from 193–191 BC. From Uruk. Berlin, Vorderasiatisches Museum
VAT 7809.

He suggests that this was because a Greek community in the vicinity came to be
interested in similar business opportunities. This suggests that cuneiform, even
in its near-latest manifestations, was not restricted to any particular social class
(for example, the older families), but was theoretically open to all. Nevertheless,
cuneiform was restricted somewhat in its use by Greek rulers, was rarely used
for correspondence during the Hellenistic period, and ceased to be a medium of
administrative or legal record throughout Babylonia around 90 BC. The latest
datable LB texts coincide more or less with the complete end of cuneiform in
Uruk. In Babylon, however, SB texts persist thereafter.

Texts in Standard Babylonian (SB)[21]

Babylonian temples flourished with Macedonian support during the early Hellenistic period (Sherwin-White 1987: 28). Macedonian kings took an active part
in the cult (Linssen 2003: 1.3) and were also probably the subject of a ruler cult
(Linssen 2003: 127–30). This cult represented a change in temple function, and
attests to these institutions' continued vitality. Temple ritual texts were not
simply copied for antiquarian purposes but do reflect the reality on the ground,
at least until the first century BC (Oelsner 2002c: 188–9). The cult may not have
needed the script, but a well-funded cult with an unbroken tradition would
have been more likely than a poor one to afford upkeep for ancient scribal practices.

Chronographic texts

New contemporary material was written, and old material treated again (Oelsner 1986: 204–5). The latest 'chronographic' material is attested in the astronomical Diary of 63 BC, though the statement 'year 241 of the Arsacid Era' is

attested in LBAT 1195 (namely AD 7), and years are dated by royal reigns up to then. The last chronicles date to near the end of the third century BC (Del Monte 1997: 203), and the king list BM 35603 to at least the period of the reigns of Demetrios II and Mithridates I Arsaces V (c. 145–138 BC; Del Monte 1997: 208 and 259).

'Literary' texts

From Uruk, the texts published in van Dijk and Mayer (1980), of which many are literary, include ones datable to between 297 and 162 BC. W 18567, a school tablet fragment, was found with the latest known contract (see n. 16), and may date to around 108 BC (Oelsner 2002a: n. 14).

From Babylon, the latest known literary text is an unpublished prayer to Marduk, BM 45746, written in 35 BC.[22]

The Graeco-Babylonian Texts

Geller (1983: 114) argued that based on palaeography HSM 1137, a zi-pà incantation with a Greek transliteration, is 'unlikely to be earlier than the first century AD'. He later suggested (Geller 1997: 46; 76) that the text may be even younger. He also provides (1997: 64–8) a detailed analysis of the orthography and phonology of the eighteen texts of this sort known. He suggests that 'the same system was in use for transliterating Akkadian and Sumerian into Greek letters as was used by Origen in the third century AD for transliterating Hebrew into Greek', and on this basis dates texts 6, 7, 8, and 14 to the first century AD, or later. All other examples are dated to the first century BC, which is a more plausible date given the school-curriculum-like contents of the tablets, and in view of the latest dated exemplars noted above. Given the date of the youngest astronomical text, a date for some of these texts in the first century cannot be excluded. However, the table of Greek scripts provided by Geller (1997: 95) indicates that not much weight can be placed on the palaeographic dating, and I hesitate to date any of these fascinating texts to a period after the latest attested good-quality SB pieces, namely around the time of Christ, as we shall see below.

It is not clear why these texts were written. Oelsner's suggestion, quoted by Geller (1997: 48), that the cuneiform was transcribed into Greek and not Aramaic, because the Greek alphabet shows the vowels, is probably sound. Oelsner goes further (2002a: 16; 2002c: 191), arguing that the Graeco-Babylonian texts were written to assist scholars in transmitting what was written on tablets in cuneiform into a cursive, alphabetic, fully vocalic script written on perishable materials. Oelsner sees this as a significant cause of cuneiform's demise, rather than a symptom. Even if true, it still does not explain why a change in writing materials was thought necessary. The answer may lie amongst the largest surviving cuneiform text group from the Hellenistic period, to which we now turn.

Astronomical texts

Sachs (1955) listed some 1648 late 'astronomical' texts, most of which are Hellenistic in date. Astronomical texts were written by scholars associated with the temples in Uruk and Babylon. According to CT 49 144, some scholars around 119 BC were paid a ration by the temple to make observations and to produce ephemerides (here used to refer to tables of calculated positions and dates of each of the seven planets visible to the naked eye) and almanacs—a fair cross-section of the full repertoire of attested astronomical texts (Rochberg 2000: 369).

Fully developed lunar ephemerides include predictions dating to 263–42 BC, for System A from Babylon; 258–68 BC for System B from Babylon; 188–185 BC for System A from Uruk; and 208–150 BC for System B from Uruk (Neugebauer 1955; Hunger and Pingree 1999: 221). The latest texts were written some years before the youngest dates indicated above, since the texts constitute predictions of future scenarios. Attested planet ephemerides include predictions from 307–7 BC, though this last figure is for a tablet from Uruk (U.179 = Neugebauer 1955: No. 401) predicting the phenomena of Venus from 136 BC to 7 BC, and thus was written around 136 BC. The bulk of the ephemerides from Uruk were written c. 211–161 BC, and those from Babylon ca.180–41 BC. One very late ephemeris from Babylon preserves lunar and solar eclipse predictions for 13 BC and AD 43, but the beginning is broken away and it too was probably written before c. 40 BC (Neugebauer 1955: 7).

Horoscopes are attested between 410 and 69 BC (Rochberg 1998).

Astronomical Diaries, mostly from Babylon, are attested until 61 BC (Sachs and Hunger and 1988; 1989; 1996). One tablet now in the British Museum, BM 140677, dates to 99–97 BC, making it the latest Uruk text known.

Observational records of:

Mercury are regularly attested until 102 BC
Venus to 73 BC
Mars to 103 BC
Jupiter to 136 BC
Saturn to 125 BC
Moon to 41 BC
Sun—an observation of a solar eclipse recorded in BM 35606 dates to
30 June 10 BC (Steele 2001).

The Almanacs and Goal Year texts, which date to still later periods, were based on contemporary observations.

Goal-Year Texts: Attested from 235–56 BC. One late one is perhaps Sachs (1955: No. 1305), dated provisionally to AD 41 (Hunger and Pingree 1999: 172).

Normal Star Almanacs: Attested from 292–77 BC (Hunger and Pingree 1999: 161).

Almanacs: Attested for virtually every year from 184–6 BC; the five latest date to (Sachs 1976; Sachs 1955: Nos. 1197–1201):

   AD 31/32 Met. Museum 86.11.354
   AD 36/37 DT 143 (in the British Museum)
   AD 44/45 BM 45982
   AD 61/62 BM 40083 and duplicate BM 40084
   AD 74/75 Dropsie College Text (Fig. 4.3).

The astronomical texts reach their greatest level of sophistication under late Seleucid rule, c. 200 BC. Their evolution can be traced back into Achaemenid times, indeed the Diaries take us back to Neo-Assyrian times. Dating to c. 200 BC, from both Uruk and Babylon, a wide variety of text types is attested, utilizing a number of different methods to calculate planetary and luni-solar configurations. Why this occurred is hard to answer simply, but that it is a remarkable last flowering of the cuneiform tradition is clear.

New 'literary' pieces were composed in SB during the Hellenistic period, albeit following standard formats, and old compositions copied, but these uses combined are far outweighed by the use to which cuneiform was put in the service of astronomy-astrology. This fact alone should suggest to us that such texts, rather than their being a by-product of the survival of cuneiform for cultural, religious, or administrative purposes, may instead have been a significant factor in why cuneiform survived for so long at all.

It is hard to understand these astronomical-astrological texts as serving some direct cultic purpose within the temples, though the rise of astral religion in the LB period may have provided some impetus to their production;[23] it is much easier to imagine that they provided a private income for the scholars who wrote them. The attestation of two Greek names in the horoscope corpus and of the name of a senior member of the temple staff (Rochberg 1998: Nos. 10, 12, and 9), suggests that this part of the astronomy-astrology industry was indeed serving a need of both local and colonial dignitaries.[24] It was an income, I suggest, which not only ensured that their trade survived over the centuries but was also one of the major reasons why texts for the cult and new compositions for the king continued to be produced in cuneiform rather than in another script. It was one, perhaps the major, reason why the 'stream of tradition' was preserved for so long in cuneiform, and possibly prolonged the survival of LB cuneiform administrative and legal writing. I propose that those cuneiform scribes with no association with the temple-based astronomy-astrology industry were the first to abandon cuneiform. This explains the narrowing of the focus of LB texts over time onto temple-linked matters. Indeed some of the latest LB texts were found in what may have been an astrologer's archive (n. 20). The overarching importance of astronomy-astrology for those writing cuneiform may also explain why scribes belonging to guilds of the chanter (*kalû*), the exorcist (*āšipu*), as well as astrologers (*ṭupšar Enūma Anu Ellil*) wrote astronomical tablets in the late period.

The rich and wide usage of cuneiform, bar a few administrative restrictions, continues throughout most of the second century BC, but begins to falter during the end of the second and start of the first centuries BC. In Uruk the last contract dates to 108 BC, the last Diary to 99–97 BC, and last ephemeris to c. 136 BC. SB and LB seem to end there more or less at the same time, while both were still going strong. This suggests to me that cuneiform writing was brought to an end in Uruk as a result of external factors.

In Babylon the last private contracts end in the mid-second century BC, but vernacular LB continues in administrative contracts connected to temples until c. 90 BC. It is outlived by texts in SB and Sumerian (Emesal). 'Stream of tradition' compositions can be dated to as late as 35 BC, more or less coincident with the latest Horoscopes, Diaries, and Ephemerides. Thereafter, however, the only astronomical-astrological texts attested are the non-sophisticated, observation-based, and largely non-mathematical Goal Year Texts and Almanacs. These continue for another century, but exhibit certain revealing characteristics.

For example, ab is written for áb, meaning 'month', in one exemplar of the Almanac for 7/6 BC (Sachs and Walker 1984: 50). In LB astronomical texts áb for month is common, because áb = *arhu* 'cow' is homophonous with itu = *arhu* 'month'. This use of ab is unique. It suggests that the scribe was still aware of the Sumerian pronunciation of the signs, but not their Akkadian readings. It is as if he were translating directly from Sumerian into his native language, without passing through Akkadian. Furthermore, the late Almanacs indent the second line due to overflow attesting a carelessness of preparation. They exhibit unusual terminology: múl or babbar for múl.babbar 'Jupiter'; múl for múl.múl 'the Pleiades'; maš for maš.maš 'Gemini'; bat for dele-bat 'Venus'; gu_4 for gu_4-ud 'Mercury'; ku_{10} for an-ku_{10} 'eclipse'(Sachs 1976: 380). Again, it appears as though the scribes were writing out the cuneiform signs without any longer understanding their etymology. They treat them as signs for planets, zodiacal constellations, and so forth, without appreciating that they are part of a wider network of signifiers that accounts for their particular usage in certain contexts. The latest Almanacs exclude certain kinds of data (the Sirius, equinox, solstice, and eclipse data), though not consistently; the latest one omits them all; they contain many errors in terms of the zodiac sign (Hunger and Pingree 1999: 166). All in all, they are suggestive of a dying art.[25]

The evidence provided by the distribution of surviving, datable astronomical-astrological texts suggests that those scholars capable of producing advanced astronomical texts in cuneiform, who would also have been those with a profound understanding of the wider cuneiform tradition, begin to cease working in that medium in the last third of the first century BC. I suggest that the last non-astronomical SB texts, including the so-called Graeco-Babyloniaca texts,

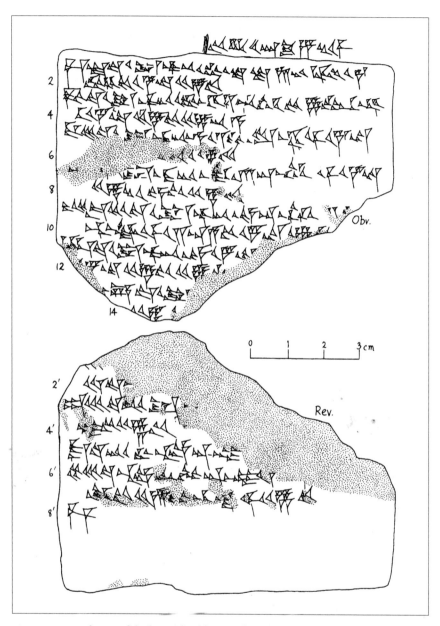

Figure 4.3 Hand copy of the latest datable cuneiform text, by Abraham Sachs (1976: 398; Dropsie College Text). The tablet comes from Babylon and is a so-called astronomical almanac. For those familiar with late-Babylonian astronomical tablets and Sachs' copies, it is clear at first glance that the text is in a very poor hand.

were likely written within a generation or so of the date of the latest ephemeris, and should also be dated before AD 1. These latter texts hint at why, finally, the cuneiform scribal tradition had become sufficiently unattractive that no great scholars were interested in mastering it anymore. That is, I suggest, that the secrets and techniques of the Babylonian astronomer-astrologers had been copied over into cursive scripts by this time, and, what is worse, new rival methods of doing the same sorts of thing were beginning to be put into forms that a merely average astrologer could use.

Drawing up Greek-style horoscopes, for example, requires the use of some handy astronomical tables, and a little astrological know-how. Babylonian horoscopes, however, were originally drawn on the basis of predicted locations determined by constant recourse to the records of actual observations. The creation and preservation of such observational records had been the work of an institution. Once the need for such records had been dispensed with, any sufficiently well-informed scribe could write horoscopes, and the role of the temple as preserver or creator of a database that made horoscopy possible became redundant. Was this the 'tip' that made the script's 'disuse relatively painless for most people' (Houston *et al.* 2003: 468)?

Translations and rivals

Mesopotamian astronomical-astrological expertise spread to the West from perhaps as early as the seventh century BC, and transmission continued thereafter, accelerating in the Hellenistic period (Dalley 1998: 39; Pingree 1998: 129). Hipparchus (fl. c. 150 BC), the first Greek astronomer to have applied the strictures of movement in circles to his models with some predictive success, was so intimate with Babylonian methods that it has been suggested that he had probably been tutored in them by a temple scholar (Toomer 1988: 359).

By this time horoscopic and related astrology had begun to be practised in earnest in Greece and Egypt, as far as our surviving records allow us to judge. Earlier transmissions of certain Babylonian astronomical-astrological ideas seem to have been for the benefit only of an elite few. The first known Greek 'horoscope' deals with a birth in 72 BC (Neugebauer and van Hoesen 1959 Nos. 9; L71). The earliest Egyptian Demotic one was cast for a native born in 38 BC (Jones 1999: 5). The first recorded natal chart to make use of an ascendant (the point on the ecliptic rising above the horizon at the moment of birth, from which the astrological 'houses' are counted) is in Greek and dates to 4 BC (P Oxy IV 804, cited by Jones 1999: 308). It is also only in the first century BC that a substantial number of sources in Egypt attest to Babylonian astronomical methods that would have been used in constructing horoscopes (Jones 1999: 301). All but four of the fifteen planetary epoch tables attested in the papyri from Oxyrhynchus use Babylonian methods (Jones 1999: 114).

Although, thanks to Hipparchus, Greek kinematic-trigonometric astronomy was now capable of making many of the necessary calculations (though seemingly not those for the star-planets, Toomer 1988: 361) those who wrote horoscopes in cursive scripts did not in general avail themselves of such methods, but rather used Babylonian and Babylonian-style arithmetic techniques. Cursive horoscopes were heavily inspired by cuneiform ones, though adapted to an Aristotelian framework, and with innovations such as the ascendant. One can only assume, however, that kinematic-trigonometric techniques were considered by the average astrologer to be too difficult to use.

Conclusions

Irrespective of earlier piecemeal transmissions which served to stimulate the upper echelons of the Greek astronomical establishment from Meton to Apollonius and Hipparchus, it was during the first century BC that the arithmetic methods used in the Babylonian temples were widely translated into Demotic and Greek and came to be applied to the construction of horoscopes in Greece, Egypt, and elsewhere, no doubt including Babylonia itself.[26] These methods were not merely used in addition to Greek ones. As far as we are able to judge they were far and away the most popular ones, even beyond the late second century AD, when Ptolemy's *Handy Tables* finally simplified the results of kinematic astronomy for an eager, but less able audience of astrologers.

Why were the Babylonian methods so popular? Part of the reason was, of course, that zodiacal astrology too had its roots in Babylonia. Partly, though, it was because Babylonian arithmetic methods were easier to use than kinematic-trigonometric ones, while being also very good. Their parameters were often highly accurate, and why this was so points to perhaps the major reason for the prolonged usefulness of cuneiform. The accurate parameters that astrologers demanded in their pursuit of ever more refined interpretations of the configurations of the heavens were derived from records of celestial phenomena taken down in cuneiform sometimes hundreds of years earlier. Britton (2002: 46) shows, for example, how the extraordinarily accurate value for the length of the month determined around 300 BC was probably based on records dating back some 350 years! Many other parameters key to the accuracy of cuneiform arithmetic astronomy were determined in the same way. Only an institution such as the temple could have provided the continuity to be able to make and keep such records, and to train the scribes able to use them centuries later.

However, by the mid-first century BC, translation, with small adaptations to local calendars and tastes alike, had broken the near-monopoly the Babylonian temples had had. With competition from those not versed in cuneiform lore, the last means to bankroll the cuneiform scribal tradition in hostile times was gradually lost. I suggest that those with both the depth of understanding required to produce the marvellous ephemerides and with them horoscopes, as well as a profound knowledge of cuneiform, died out around the time of Christ. In my model, scholars with good astronomical skills had, during the course of the second and first centuries BC, written in cursive scripts, in the languages of a far larger group of potential consumers, but had thereby undermined cuneiform's last stronghold. The temples learned to do without cuneiform and survived for some centuries longer, either by transliterating Akkadian and Sumerian into a cursive script (probably Greek) on perishable materials, or by translating the texts necessary for the practice of the cult into a living language (probably Aramaic). Cuneiform, however, only limped on into the first century of the Christian era, not because of its association with the temples, but because some who worked there could still exploit a shrinking market for old-fashioned Babylonian astrology in cuneiform. The tradition ended, thereby, with badly trained scribes composing simple Almanacs and Goal Year texts in bad cuneiform.

The end was hastened by the macro-economic changes that were turning Babylon into a ghost city, but testimony cited above suggests that the temples outlived cuneiform. Cuneiform Greek and Aramaic were not useful enough to compete with their cursive-alphabetic versions, so the former script's days were always numbered. The final 'tip' into obsolescence came, though, when the astronomical skills and astrological notions first developed in cuneiform, and which I propose helped preserve the usefulness of that script for much longer than one would otherwise expect, were widely translated into cursive scripts. Through being translated, though, some of those same methods and ideas avoided obsolescence altogether.

Notes

1. This work was conducted as part of a project of research into the transmission of astronomical knowledge in the ancient world, funded by the Deutsche Forschungsgemeinschaft, and conducted at the Freie Universität, Berlin. Many thanks to Jerrold Cooper and Andrew George for two stimulating exchanges of ideas on the demise of cuneiform, and to John Baines and Stephen Houston for their careful editorial work on this chapter.

2. Aside from the very brief reigns of Nebuchadnessar III (= Nidintu-Bēl) and Nebuchadnessar IV (= Arahu) during the early years of the usurper Darius I (521–486 BC), and Bēl-šimmani and Šamaš-eriba in the first few years of the reign of Xerxes I (485–465 BC).

3. 'Hellenistic period' in Babylonia is used here to refer to the interval from 331 BC to AD 226.

4. Oelsner states (1986: 64) that Arsacid rule was first recognised in Babylonia between 2 and 8 July 141 BC.

5. Geller (1997: 53) surveys the evidence for the survival of cults to Babylonian gods in Palmyra, Edessa, Harran, Hatra, and Assur until, in some cases, the sixth century AD. This is, he writes: 'suggestive (but certainly not conclusive) evidence for the existence of temple cults in Babylonia at the same time' (p.56).

6. See, for example, Geller (1997: 63–4), who argues that Aramaic magic bowls from Babylonia, of the fourth century AD and later, show no trace of Babylonian personal names, and that archaeology reveals little evidence of the survival of Babylonian temples after the mid-third century AD. The argument is that the Sassanian rulers instigated a new policy of religious intolerance towards all non-Mazdaean practices, though Geller reminds us not to overstate the case, citing instances where Judaism, Christianity, and other religions did survive under Sassanian rule. See also Van De Mieroop (1999: 244), and Oelsner (2002a: 32; 2002c: 195): 'one may conclude that not Hellenization, but Iranization, is to be held responsible for the end of the Babylonian culture'.

7. Another centre where Mesopotamian religion flourished well into the first millennium AD, and whence no cuneiform from that period comes (Dalley 1998: 38).

8. Pliny, *Naturalis Historia* VI 122. Translation, based on Brodersen 1996.

9. Strabo, *Geographica* XVI.1.16: 'And in ancient times Babylon was the metropolis of Assyria; but now Seleukeia is the metropolis.' Translation, Jones 1932. For further non-cuneiform references to the state of Babylonia in the Parthian period see Oelsner 2002a: 24-26.

10. Cyrus ended the tithe the state had to pay the temple, and Cambyses obliged the Eanna to provide sheep, and many other goods *ana naptāni ša šarri*, 'for the table of the king'. Where once the state had supported the temple financially, under the Achaemenids the reverse became true.

11. The Gareus temple was built on the same site after the destruction, c. 100 BC, which perhaps did signal the end of the cuneiform tradition in Uruk. Oelsner 2002a: 20 believes that after this destruction the traditional gods were no longer worshipped in Uruk, though the survival in personal names of the names of traditional Babylonian gods may suggest otherwise, as mentioned above. See below for late astronomical texts from Uruk.

12. E.g. for Sherwin-White and Kuhrt (1993: 160), cuneiform is 'cumbrous'. Is this also the implicit reason behind Oelsner's argument (2002a) that cuneiform's demise was caused by a shift of writing medium, and concomitant shift from a logo-syllabic script to an alphabetic one?

13. Oelsner (1986: 246) discusses TU 58, a Hellenistic text from Uruk in which Aramaic is written in cuneiform. It is, to my knowledge, unique.

14. One piece of evidence for this is cited by Oelsner (1986: 244; 246).

15. See Black (1997: 229–30) for references to material younger than 609 BC; Radner (2002) for Assyrian texts of NB date from Dūr Katlimmu. The one tablet, IM 95332, to confound this idea of a more or less clean break in the cuneiform scribal tradition is from Tell Fisna, 45 km north of Mosul, and was found in a Hellenistic level. It is not a counterfeit. It looks Hellenistic, is flat and turns like a page of a book. It records events during the course of the year in months. Black (1997: 231) argues that it was most likely a late development from Assyrian, which suggests the survival of a pocket of cuneiform scholars, but it is equally likely an import from the south. The criterion upon which Black suggested an Assyrian origin is that the undeciphered writing has the upright style of Assyrian. This style, however, also characterizes some Babylonian Hellenistic texts (e.g. Sachs 1976), so perhaps IM 95332 is a late import to the north. Like the latest datable texts, the Tell Fisna text is most likely an astronomical almanac, as Black suggests.

16. The existence of a royal or official seal on a slave sale contract with a legend in cuneiform dating to the reign of Antiochus I (281–261 BC), for example, indicates the extent to which cuneiform was adopted by the Greeks for administration (Oelsner 2002c: n. 13).

17. The language of correspondence and of legal and administrative contracts had evolved into Assyrian and Babylonian dialects by the early second millennium BC and diverged thereafter. In Babylonia at the end of the first millennium BC, a top scribe would write Sumerian or SB for literary texts, and LB for correspondence, all in a LB ductus (though he might sometimes employ an archaizing hand), and very likely spoke Aramaic at home. He probably wrote both Aramaic and Greek, in addition.

18. This text (Kessler 1984) attests to the continued existence after the Parthian takeover of the temples of Uruk, and of the involvement of the Ah'ūtu family. Bagā, whose other name is Nikanōr, and Anu-bēl-šunu, otherwise Heraklides, oversee the quit claim. The former is presumably an Iranian Parthian. The latter was probably a local with a temple association, who had taken a Greek name in his official capacity, perhaps under the former regime.

19. It is hard to distinguish texts from Babylon, Borsippa, Cutha, or Marad (Oelsner 1986: 195).

20. In AB 244 (published by McEwan 1981), a certain Xenon receives rations, showing that a man with a Greek name is involved with the temple at this late time. Line 13 has the word *gi-na-ni-e*. *Ginānê* is a LB plural form of *ginû* 'regular offering' in the genitive; thus good LB grammar is exhibited as late at 92 BC. In AB 245 (McEwan 1981), also dating to 92 BC, an account is given of gold being re-melted, suggesting that the temple was still an important economic entity at this time. The eclipse ritual text AB 249 (Linssen 2003: 324) was probably also from this archive, and is perhaps to be linked with the astrologer Murānu named in AB 247 (McEwan 1981).

21. Standard Babylonian is the name given by Assyriologists to that version of the Old Babylonian (c. 1700 BC) dialect in which the majority of what Oppenheim (1977: 13),

famously called the 'stream of tradition' was written. It and Sumerian (long since dead) were the languages of epics and myth, of omen literature, apotropaic ritual, incantations, lexical texts, fables, proverbs, and so forth, that had been copied and recopied, edited, and commented upon over the centuries, by students and by advanced scholars alike. Standard Babylonian was also the language in which royal inscriptions and related chronographic material in both Assyria and Babylonia were written throughout the first millennium.

22. Oelsner (2002a: n. 26–7) lists the youngest published and unpublished literary texts from Babylon, citing examples of cult songs, fragments of the Gilgamesh Epic, the fable of the dug.dug bird, the series known as tin.tir.ki, and some omen texts. Oshima 2003 describes BM 45746 in more detail, though in n. 25 has mixed up Arsacid and Seleucid Eras and assigned the text an earlier date. Reference courtesy of A. George.

23. On the rise of astral religion in late Achaemenid Uruk see Frahm 2002.

24. Rochberg (1999: 12) argues instead that the 'association with the temple was [...] key to the survival of Babylonian astronomy after it had become defunct in the political sphere', but this fails to explain why cursive Babylonian astronomy could spread to other cultures so easily. I doubt whether Babylonian astronomy was developed merely for its own sake, or that it ever became defunct in the real world. See further Brown (2000: 220, 243, n. 381) and Oelsner (2002c: n. 29).

25. It is within this context that we should interpret the oddities of the Tell Fisna text (n. 15). Are these 'the scribbles of rememberers' sought in vain by Houston *et al.* (2003: 469)?

26. Strabo's reference to astrologers in Uruk and Borsippa in *Geographica* 16.1.6 in c. AD 20 suggests strongly that although cuneiform was then no longer written in those centres, scholars with the relevant skills were still working there, no doubt writing only in cursive scripts. For evidence of the continuity in Uruk of many 'Babylonian' elements into the second century AD see Oelsner 2002c: 192-3.

References

Beaulieu, Paul-Alain
    1995   'An Excerpt from a Menology with Reverse Writing'. *Sumer*: 1–14.

Black, Jeremy
    1997   'Hellenistic Cuneiform Writing from Assyria: The Tablet from Tell Fisna'. *Al-Rāfidān* 18: 229–40.

Britton, John
    2002   'Treatments of Annual Phenomena in Cuneiform Sources'. In John Steele and Annette Imhausen (eds), *Under One Sky*. Alter Orient und Altes Testament 297. Kevelaer and Neukirchen-Vluyn: Butzon and Bercker; Neukirchener Verlag: 21–78.

Brodersen, Kai (ed. and trans.)
  1996   *Plinius Secundus d. A. Naturkunde. Lateinisch-deutsch. Buch VI. Goegraphie Asien.* Roderich König and Gerhard Winkler series editors. Zürich and Düsseldorf: Artemis and Winkler.

Brown, David
  2000   *Mesopotamian Planetary Astronomy-Astrology.* Groningen: Styx.

Dalley, Stephanie (ed.)
  1998   *The Legacy of Mesopotamia.* Oxford: Oxford University Press.

Del Monte, Giuseppe
  1997   *Testi dalla Babilonia Ellenistica—Volume I: Testi Cronografici.* Rome: Istituti editoriali e poligrafici internazionali.

Doty, Laurence
  1977   'Cuneiform Archives from Hellenistic Uruk'. Unpublished doctoral dissertation, Yale University.

Frahm, Eckart
  2002   'Zwischen Tradition und Neuerung: Babylonische Priestergelehrte im achämenidenzeitlichen Uruk'. In Reinhard Kratz, ed., *Religion und Religionskontakte im Zeitalter der Achämeniden.* Veröffentlichungen der Wissenschaftlichen Gesellschaft für Theologie 22. Gütersloh: Kaiser, Gütersloher Verlag-Haus, 74–108.

Geller, Mark
  1983   'More Graeco-Babyloniaca'. *Zeitschrift für Assyriologie* 73: 114–25.
  1997   'The Last Wedge.' *Zeitschrift für Assyriologie* 87: 43–95.

Houston, Stephen, John Baines, and Jerrold Cooper
  2003   'Last Writing: Script Obsolescence in Egypt, Mesopotamia, and Mesoamerica'. *Comparative Studies in Society and History* 45: 430–79.

Hunger, Hermann
  1968   *Babylonische und assyrische Kolophone.* Alter Orient und Altes Testament 2. Kevelaer and Neukirchen-Vluyn: Butzon and Bercker; Neukirchener Verlag.

Hunger, Hermann, and David Pingree
  1999   *Astral Sciences in Mesopotamia.* Leiden: Brill.

Joannès, Francis
  1995   'Private Commerce and Banking in Achaemenid Babylon'. In Jack Sasson *et al.* (eds), *Civilizations of the Ancient Near East.* New York: Scribner, 1475–85.

Jones, Alexander
  1999   *Astronomical Papyri from Oxyrhynchus.* Philadelphia: American Philosophical Society.

Jones, Horace Leonard (trans.)
  1932   *The Geography of Strabo.* London, Cambridge, MA: Loeb Classical Library, Heinemann, Harvard University Press.

Kessler, Karl-Heinz
  1984   'Eine arsakidenzeitliche Urkunde aus Warka'. *Baghdader Mitteilungen* 15: 273–81.

2000   'Hellenistische Tempelverwaltungstexte—eine Nachlese zu CT 49.' In Joachim Marzahn and Hans Neumann (eds), *Assyriologica et Semitica, Festschrift für Joachim Oelsner*. Alter Orient und Altes Testament 252. Münster: Ugarit Verlag, 213–41.

Kuhrt, Amélie
1987   'Survey of the Written Sources Available for the History of Babylonia under the late Achaemenids'. In Heleen Sancisi-Weerdenburg (ed.), *Achaemenid History* I: *Sources, Structures, Synthesis*. Leiden: Nederlands Instituut voor het Nabije Osten, 147–57.
1995   *The Ancient Near East c. 3000–330 BC*. London: Routledge.

Kuhrt, Amélie, and Susan Sherwin-White
1994   'The Transition from Achaemenid to Seleucid Rule in Babylonia: Revolution or Evolution'. In Heleen Sancisi-Weerdenburg, Amélie Kuhrt, and Margaret C. Root (eds.), *Achaemenid History* VIII: *Continuity and Change*. Leiden: Nederlands Instituut voor het Nabije Osten, 311–27.

Linssen, Marc J. H.
2003   'The Cults of Uruk and Babylon—the Temple Rituals as Evidence for Hellenistic Cult Practices'. Dissertation, Vrije Universiteit, Amsterdam.

McEwan, Gilbert J. P.
1981   'Arsacid Temple Records'. *Iraq* 43: 131–43.

MacGinnis, John
1995   *Letter Orders from Sippar and the Administration of the Ebabbara in the Late-Babylonian Period*. Poznań: Bonami Wydawnictwo.

Neugebauer, Otto
1955   *Astronomical Cuneiform Texts*. London: Lund Humphries.

Neugebauer, Otto, and Henry B. van Hoesen.
1959   *Greek Horoscopes*. Transactions of the American Philosophical Society 48. Philadelphia, PA: American Philosophical Society.

Oelsner, Joachim
1986   *Materialien zur babylonischen Gesellschaft und Kultur in hellenistischer Zeit*. Budapest: Eötvös Lorand University.
2002a   *'Sie ist gefallen, sie ist gefallen, Babylon die große Stadt'. Vom Ende einer Kultur*. Sitzungsberichte der Sächsischen Akademie der Wissenshaften zu Leipzig, Philologisch-historische Klasse 138/1. Stuttgart and Leipzig: S. Hirzel, 5–36.
2002b   'Babylonische Kultur nach dem Ende des babylonischen Staates'. In Reinhard Kratz (ed.), *Religion und Religionskontakte im Zeitalter der Achämeniden*. Veröffentlichungen der Wissenschaftlichen Gesellschaft für Theologie 22. Gütersloh: Kaiser, Gütersloher Verlag-Haus, 49–73.
2002c   'Hellenization of the Babylonian Culture'? In Antonio Panaino and Giovanni Pettinato (eds), *Ideologies as Intercultural Phenomena*, Melammu Symposia III. Milan: Università di Bologna and IsIAO, 183–96.
2003   'Cuneiform Archives in Hellenistic Babylonia: Aspects of Content and Form'. In Maria Brosius (ed.), *Ancient Archives and Archival Traditions: Concepts of Record-Keeping in the Ancient World*. Oxford: Oxford University Press, 284–301.

Oppenheim, A. Leo
  1977   *Ancient Mesopotamia: Portrait of a Dead Civilisation,* second edition, revised by Erica Reiner. Chicago, IL: University of Chicago Press.

Oshima, Takayoshi
  2003   'Some Comment on Prayer to Marduk, no. 1 lines 5/7'. *NABU* 4 §99: 109–11.

Pingree, David
  1998   'Legacies in Astronomy and Celestial Omens'. In Stephanie Dalley (ed.), *The Legacy of Mesopotamia.* Oxford: Oxford University Press, 125–37.

Pliny. See Brodersen.

Radner, Karen
  2002   *Die neuassyrischen Texte aus Tall Šēh Hamad.* Berichte der Ausgrabung Tall Seh Hamad Dur-Katlimmu 6/2. Berlin: Dietrich Reimer.

Rempel, Jane, and Norman Yoffee
  1999   'The End of the Cycle? Assessing the Impact of Hellenization on Mesopotamian Civilization'. In Barbara Böck, Eva Cancik-Kirschbaum, and Tomas Richter (eds), *Minuscula Mesopotamica: Festschrift für Johannes Renger.* Alter Orient und Altes Testament 267. Münster: Ugarit Verlag, 384–98.

Rochberg, Francesca
  1998   *Babylonian Horoscopes.* Transactions of the American Philosophical Society 88. Philadelphia, PA: American Philosophical Society.
  2000   'Scribes and Scholars: The *ṭupšar Enūma Anu Enlil*'. In Joachim Marzahn and Hans Neumann (eds), *Assyriologica et Semitica.* Alter Orient und Altes Testament 252. Münster: Ugarit Verlag, 359–75.

Sachs, Abraham
  1955   *Late Babylonian Astronomical and Related Texts copied by T. G. Pinches and J. N. Strassmaier* (with the cooperation of J. Schaumberger). Providence, RI: Brown University Press
  1976   'The Latest Datable Cuneiform Tablets'. In Barry Eichler, Jane W. Heimerdinger, and Åke Sjöberg (eds), *Kramer Anniversary Volume: Cuneiform Studies in Honor of Samuel Noah Kramer.* Alter Orient und Altes Testament 25. Kevelaer and Neukirchen-Vluyn: Butzon and Bercker; Neukirchener Verlag, 379–98.

Sachs, Abraham J., and Hermann Hunger
  1988   *Astronomical diaries and related texts from Babylonia, vol. 1: Diaries from 652 B.C. to 262 B.C.* Vienna: Verlag der Österreichischen Akademie der Wissenschaften.
  1989   *Astronomical diaries and related texts from Babylonia, vol. 2: Diaries from 261 B.C. to 165 B.C.* Vienna: Verlag der Österreichischen Akademie der Wissenschaften.
  1996   *Astronomical diaries and related texts from Babylonia, vol. 3: Diaries from 164 B.C. to 61 B.C.* Vienna: Verlag der Österreichischen Akademie der Wissenschaften.

Sachs, Abraham, and Christopher Walker
  1984   'Kepler's View of the Star of Bethlehem and the Babylonian Almanac for 7/6 BC'. *Iraq* 46: 43–55.

Sherwin-White, Susan
  1987   'Seleucid Babylonia: A Case Study for the Installation and Development of Greek Rule'. In Amélie Kuhrt and Susan Sherwin-White (eds), *Hellenism in the East.* Berkeley: University of California Press, 32–56.

Sherwin-White, Susan and Amélie Kuhrt
  1993   *From Samarkhand to Sardis: A New Approach to the Seleucid Empire.* London: Duckworth.

Sims-Williams, Nicholas
  1981   'The Final Paragraph of the Tomb-Inscription of Darius I (DNb, 50–60): The Old Persian Text in the Light of an Aramaic Version'. *Bulletin of the School of African and Asian Studies* 44: 1–7.

Spek, Robartus J. van der
  1994   '*... en hun machthebbers worden weldoeners genoemd': Religieuze en economische politiek in het Seleucidische Rijk.* Amsterdam: Vrije Universiteit Amsterdam.

Steele, John
  2001   'The Latest Dated Astronomical Observation from Babylon'. In Alan R. Millard (ed.), *Archaeological Sciences '97.* Oxford: Archaeopress, 208–21.

Strabo. See Jones, Horace Leonard.

Toomer, Gerald J.
  1988   'Hipparchus and Babylonian Astronomy'. In Erle Leichty, Maria De J. Ellis, and Pamela Geradi (eds), *A Scientific Humanist: Studies in Memory of Abraham Sachs.* Philadelphia, PA: Occasional Publications of the Samuel Noah Kramer Fund 9, 353–62.

Van De Mieroop, Marc
  1999   *The Ancient Mesopotamian City.* Oxford: Oxford University Press.

van Dijk, Jan, and Werner Mayer
  1980   *Texte aus dem Rēš-Heiligtum in Uruk-Warka.* Baghgader Mitteilungen Beiheft 2. Berlin: Mann.

Postscript

Redundancy Reconsidered:
Reflections on David Brown's Thesis

Jerrold Cooper

David Brown, drawing upon his profound knowledge of late astronomical-astrological cuneiform texts, has pointed out that the latest of these, from the late first century BC and the first century AD, are unsophisticated products that are more aberrant than I had realized (in Houston *et al.* 2003: 454–5). He rightly correlates this reduced scribal competence with the fact that production of tablets with compositions from the 'stream of tradition', which provided the fodder for scribal education for millennia, ceased around the middle of the first century BC, meaning that traditional cuneiform schooling ceased then as well. Soon after, higher quality astronomical texts disappeared and the only cuneiform texts that were still inscribed are the products of unschooled astrologers who continued to practise their craft late into the first century AD.

Why had cuneiform persisted and even flourished in the last centuries BC, resisting a variety of political, economic and linguistic pressures that might be expected to have led to a much earlier demise? Brown suggests that it was the cuneiform records of centuries of celestial observation, as well as the horoscopic techniques developed by cuneiform astronomers, that assured the continued utility of cuneiform. This, together with the inertia inherent in any scribal culture, facilitated the transmission of cuneiform in an age when there was no longer an Akkadian mother-tongue community, and nearly all aspects of life were documented in alphabetic scripts. But in the first century BC, from which Babylonian astronomical and horoscopic methods are first attested in Greek and Demotic, demonstrating that these methods had spread beyond the cuneiform community, cuneiform schooling—that is, the institutional support of cuneiform study and learning—ceased. After a couple of generations in which individual astrologers probably passed on what cuneiform knowledge was necessary to perform their one narrow task, the writing of cuneiform ceased altogether.

Brown is certainly right, but his thesis raises two important questions. First, as he himself has summarized so beautifully, the Babylonian astronomical techniques that reached their apogee in the Seleucid period around 200 BC originated a half millennium earlier, around 700 BC, when prediction became an all-important skill to the astronomers who practised astrological divination in the service of the Assyrian kings (Brown 2003). Only later, beginning in the fifth century BC when Babylonia was an Achaemenid Persian province, were predictive techniques used to calculate personal horoscopes (Brown 2003: 10–11).

Traditional Mesopotamian astrological divination was concerned with affairs of state and the well-being of the king (e.g. Pongratz-Leisten 1999). Yet there is no evidence that the Achaemenid kings or their Seleucid and Parthian successors communicated with the cuneiform astronomers who by then were attached to the temples of the major traditional Babylonian urban centres.[1] It is telling that, in contrast to the many hundreds of inscriptions of Assyrian and Babylonian kings testifying to royal construction and support of temples, after 539 BC we have only a few building inscriptions of Cyrus and one of Antiochus I (281–261 BC). Persian and Greek rulers seem not to have been great patrons of Babylonian temples or of their personnel.[2]

Horoscopic astrology, in contrast to traditional astrological divination, was concerned with the destiny of the individual. If the income from horoscopy provided the incentive, as Brown suggests, for the temples to maintain the elaborate educational enterprise needed to train scribes in cuneiform, then it is surprising that only a few dozen cuneiform horoscopes survive. The absence or paucity of documentation in both instances—for royal consultation of temple astronomers and for individual horoscopes—could easily be explained by the accidents of recovery, but should be kept in mind nonetheless.

The second question raised by the notion that cuneiform was kept alive in large part for its astronomical and astrological value has to do with the temple cult. Among the Standard Babylonian texts preserved from the fifth through first centuries BC are many liturgical compositions and temple rituals, and it has always been thought that, like Latin or Hebrew or Arabic in their respective religious traditions, the ancient Sumerian and Akkadian languages were essential to the Babylonian temple cult. But if the successful transmission of Babylonian astronomical and astrological techniques to vernacular languages led to the abandonment of Sumero-Akkadian learning in the first century BC, then the Babylonian cults and temples, which by all accounts persisted at least into the third century AD, must have also been using the vernacular by the first century BC, and probably somewhat earlier.[3] That the vernacular was used in the cult, and that it was Aramaic and not Greek, is strongly suggested by the following: when, at the end of the third century BC, the highest official in Seleucid Uruk, who bore both an Akkadian name, Anu-uballit, and a Greek name, Cephalon, rebuilt the temple of Ishtar, he had his double name inscribed neither in Akkadian cuneiform nor in Greek, but in Aramaic, on the glazed brick façade of the temple's cult niche (Sherwin-White 1987: 24).[4] Any Aramaic liturgical texts would have been written on perishable materials and, like Aramaic documents in general from Babylonia, would not have survived.[5]

The abandonment of traditional cuneiform education in the mid-first century BC, then, ushered in a period of a century and a half or so during which cuneiform writing was a niche technology practised by astrologers with diminished scribal competence, but I think Brown would agree that none of the latest cuneiform astronomical-astrological texts are the products of 'semi-literates'.[6] Brown has set forth a very plausible description of how and why 'fewer and fewer students ... studied cuneiform, until finally there were none and the script community died with its last members' (Houston *et al.* 2003: 456).

Notes

1. For Classical traditions regarding the warnings given to Alexander by Babylonian diviners, see Spek 2003: 332–5.

2. Two building inscriptions from the Rēš-temple in Uruk recording building by the local governor 'for the life' of the Seleucid kings (Linssen 2004: 107–8, 125) do not suggest royal initiation or support of the rebuilding, but rather the opposite (cf. McEwen 1981: 184), and the temples in Babylon seem to finance their own repairs and reconstruction under the Seleucid's Arsacid successors (Spek 1985: 547). For the project of rebuilding the Marduk temple precinct in Babylon begun under Alexander, see Spek 2003: 335–6; Linssen 2004: 108.

   Although there is a role for the king in many of the ritual texts of the Seleucid period (Linssen 2004: 18), these were copied or adapted from older compositions going back to the Neo-Babylonian period some centuries earlier, and it is not possible to know if the Seleucid or even Achaemenid monarchs ever participated in ceremonies, say, in the temples of Uruk. The same Antiochus I who left our only Seleucid royal building inscription, and who had been his father's viceroy for the east before his own accession, is reported by cuneiform chronicles to have worshipped at the ruins of Esagil (Spek 2004a) and in the temple of Sin in Babylon (Spek 2004b), and an astronomical diary records that Antiochus III (222–187) participated in the New Year ceremony there (Linssen 2004: 84), but there is no evidence that royal participation in the cult at Babylon was anything but infrequent. Most frequently, when the diaries record offerings made in Esagil, they are made by military commanders or high officials.

3. There must have a long period of transition when both the traditional Sumerian and Akkadian liturgy and Aramaic materials were employed. Colophons of Hellenistic cult texts explicitly state that they were copied for chanting (*ana zamāri*) in the temples (Linssen 2004: 14).

4. Anu-uballit was probably honoured with a Greek name by his Seleucid overlords (as was his earlier namesake, Anu-uballit Nicarchus; Sherwin-White 1987: 29), and would have used Greek in his dealings with the government in Seleucia. At the same time, he chose Aramaic, not Greek, letters for his temple inscription. Compare the situation at Palmyra from the late first century BC to the third century AD: 'Aramaic was considered the appropriate language for the linguistic domain of religion ... Greek ... is associated with public activities, whether the running of the city and its dependent territories, or the public honouring of notable citizens and foreign dignitaries' (Taylor 2002: 319–20).

5. The Aramaic tale of the seventh-century-BC civil war between the Assyrian king Ashurbanipal and his brother Shamash-shum-ukin, preserved only on a single manuscript in Demotic transliteration (Steiner 1997), and the sayings of Ahiqar, a sage in the service of Ashurbanipal's father Esarhaddon, preserved in manuscript fragments at Elephantine (Lindenberger 1983), imply a large and almost entirely lost pagan literature in Aramaic (see now also Holm 2007: 220–4).

   Lost, too, are all late cuneiform texts written on wax-covered writing boards (Oelsner 2002: 15) and scrolls. In Houston *et al.* 2003: 455–6, I rather cavalierly dismissed the one Akkadian reference to a text written on a scroll, but Eckart Frahm has indicated to me that he has seen three more Akkadian colophons referring to copying texts from scrolls (see for now Frahm 2005: 45, and the thoughts of Oelsner 2007: 221; Westenholz 2007: 278–80; and cf. Clancier 2005: 90 n. 23). I hope to show elsewhere that these references must be to writing in cuneiform, and not to transliterations into Aramaic or Greek script. In any case, the kinds of compositions said to be copied from those scrolls, as the compositions found on the Graeco-Babyloniaca (Houston *et al.* 2003: 454–6; Brown, above; and the new treatment by Westenholz 2007), all belong to the 'stream of tradition', and should thus be no later than the mid-first century BC, i.e., they would not belong to the corpus of the latest cuneiform texts (but cf. Westenholz 2007, who dates the Graeco-Babyloniaca to 50 BC–50 AD, and Oelsner 2007: 221, who suggests 1st cent. BC–1st cent. AD).

6. The Tell Fisna tablet (Houston *et al.* 2003: 454 n. 5; Brown, above n. 15), however, may well, as Brown suggests (above n. 23), represent 'the scribbles of rememberers'.

References

Brown, David
   2003   'The Scientific Revolution of 700 BC'. In Alasdair A. MacDonald, Michael W. Twomey, and Gerrit J. Reinink, (eds), *Learned Antiquity: Scholarship and Society in the Near-East, the Greco-Roman world, and the Early Medieval West*. Leuven: Peeters, 1–12.

Clancier, Phillipe
   2005   'Les scribes sur parchemin du temple d'Anu'. *Revue d'Assyriologie* 99: 85–104.

Frahm, Eckart
   2005   'On Some Recently Published Late Babylonian Copies of Royal Letters'. *Nouvelles Assyriologiques Brèves et Utilitaires* 2005/2: 43–6.

Holm, Tawny L.
   2007   'The Sheikh Faḍl Inscription in Its Literary and Historical Context'. *Aramaic Studies* 5: 193–224.

Houston, Stephen, John Baines, and Jerrold Cooper
   2003   'Last Writing: Script Obsolescence in Egypt, Mesopotamia, and Mesoamerica'. *Comparative Studies in Society and History* 45: 430–79.

Lindenberger, James
   1983   *The Aramaic Proverbs of Ahiqar*. Baltimore: The Johns Hopkins University Press.

Linssen, Marc J. H.
   2004   *The Cults of Uruk and Babylon: The Temple Ritual Texts as Evidence for Hellenistic Cult Practices*. Cuneiform Monographs 25. Leiden: Brill/Styx.

McEwen, Gilbert J. P.
   1981   *Priest and Temple in Hellenistic Babylonia*. Freiburger altorientalische Studien 4. Wiesbaden: Franz Steiner.

Oelsner, Joachim
   2002   'Sie ist gefallen, sie ist gefallen, Babylon die grosse Stadt'. *Vom Ende einer Kultur*. Sitzungsberichte der Sächsichen Akademie der Wissenschaften, Philologisch-historische Klasse 138/1. Stuttgart and Leipzig: S. Hirzel.
   2007   '30 Thesen zum Thema "Aramaisierung-Hellenisierung-Iranisierung Babyloniens"'. In Robert Rollinger, Andreas Luther, and Josef Wiesehöfer (eds), *Getrennte Wege? Kommunikation, Raum und Wahrnehmung in der alten Welt*. Oikumene 2. Frankfurt: Verlag Antike, 218–27.

Pongratz-Leisten, Beate
   1999   *Herrschaftswissen in Mesopotamien*. State Archives of Assyria 10. Helsinki: The Neo-Assyrian Text Corpus.

Sherwin-White, Susan
   1987   'Seleucid Babylonia: A Case for the Installation and Development of Greek Rule'. In Amélie Kuhrt and Susan Sherwin-White (eds), *Hellenism in the East*. Berkeley and Los Angeles: University of California Press, 1–31.

Spek, Robartus J. van der
   1985   'The Babylonian Temple during the Macedonian and Parthian Domination'. *Bibliotheca Orientalis* 42: 541–62.
   2003   'Darius III, Alexander the Great and Babylonian Scholarship'. In Wouter Henkelman and Amélie Kuhrt (eds), *A Persian Perspective: Essays in Memory of Heleen Sancisi-Weerdenburg*. Achaemenid History 13. Leiden: Nederlands Instituut voor het Nabije Oosten, 289–346.
   2004a 'Ruin of Esagila Chronicle'. http://www.livius.org/cg-cm/chronicles/bchp-ruin_esagila/ruin_esagila_01.html, last accessed 6 June 2008.
   2004b 'Chronicle Concerning Antiochus and Sin'. http://www.livius.org/cg-cm/chronicles/bchp-antiochus_sin/antiochus_sin_01.html, last accessed 6 June 2008.

Steiner, Richard C.
   1997   'The Aramaic Text in Demotic Script'. In William W. Hallo and K. Lawson Younger, Jr. (eds), The Context of Scripture I. Leiden: Brill, 309–27.

Taylor, David K.

   2002   'Bilingualism and Diglossia in Late Antique Syria and Mesopotamia'. In J. N. Adams, Mark Janse, and Simon Swain (eds), *Bilingualism in Ancient Society: Language Contact and the Written Text*. Oxford: Oxford University Press, 298–331.

Westenholz, Aage

   2007   'The Graeco-Babyloniaca Once Again'. *Zeitschrift für Assyriologie* 97: 262–313.

5

Script Obsolescence in Ancient Italy: From Pre-Roman to Roman Writing[1]

Kathryn Lomas

The disappearance of the indigenous writing systems of pre-Roman Italy is inextricably bound up with the Roman conquest of the peninsula in the fourth and third centuries BC, and the so-called 'Romanization' of Italy—the post-conquest process of acculturation.[2] Their demise cannot, however, be explained as a process of collapse resulting from the active suppression of indigenous cultures, but was the result of a far more complex and long-term interaction between competing cultures of writing, and of evolution within those cultures. It must also be examined in terms of the socio-political power relations between Rome and the rest of Italy and the ways in which these changed and developed between the third century BC and early first century AD. The disappearance of indigenous scripts and associated changes in the wider culture of writing is a valuable indicator of changes in elite culture and perceptions of group identity. However, it can only be a partial representation of the process, as all the surviving evidence of writing from ancient Italy takes the form of inscriptions on durable materials—documents which were intended to last and to be a formal and lasting representation of the writer's culture. The wider culture of literacy represented by writing on non-durable materials such as wooden tablets and papyrus is not recoverable, although it must be borne in mind that it certainly existed and that surviving documents do not represent the totality of ancient literacy (Cornell 1991).

The population of ancient Italy consisted of numerous linguistic and cultural communities (Figs 5.1 and 5.2), with their own forms of social and political organization and sense of their own ethnic and cultural identities (Dench 1995; Capuis 1993; Cornell 1997; Herring and Lomas 2000; Bradley 2000). These have traditionally been conceptualized as ethnic groups, partly because ancient Greek and Roman authors did so, assigning them ethnic names (e.g. *Samnitae* for the peoples of the Apennines, *Veneti* [Lat.] or *Henetoi* [Gk] for the peoples of north-east Italy, *Iapyges* or *Messapi* for the population of south-east Italy etc.) and ascribing languages and cultural characteristics to them, and partly because modern scholars have frequently seen the non-urbanized areas as 'tribal' or 'ethnic' in nature.[3] These definitions are, however, increasingly problematic in the light of research on ethnic identity and state development in pre-Roman Italy (Dench 1995; Herring and Lomas 2000; Herring 2000: 48–57). In most cases, there is very little evidence for what these populations called themselves or even whether they considered themselves to be an ethnic group. Where we have evidence for self-defined group identity, through collective names in inscriptions or on coinage, the principal form of group identity seems to be that of the individual state or community, not the *ethnos* (Bradley 2000: 19–28; Lomas 2000: 85–8). However, for the sake of simplicity, the traditional collective terms are used throughout this chapter, although with the caveat that they should not be understood as necessarily carrying an implication of ethnic or linguistic unity (Wilkins 1990: 58–9).

Archaeologically, from the sixth century BC onwards, many areas of Italy show a broadly similar trend towards enlarging settlement sizes, the emergence of dominant central places, and an increasingly steep social hierarchy characterized by a restricted and wealthy elite and strong kinship groups. The point at which urbanization or the development of complex non-urban states can be said to have taken place is currently a matter of debate, but there is little doubt that by the fourth century BC, most areas either had, or were in the process of acquiring, a complex state organization, in many cases of an urban nature (Barker and Rasmussen 1998; Lomas 1993b; Holloway 1994; Cornell 1995: 96–118). In particular, they developed distinctive scripts and their own cultures of writing and literacy from the sixth century onwards, which show considerable levels of regional variation in both the practices of literacy and the scripts used.[4]

The complex cultural and political relationship between Italy and Rome is an essential factor in the development of Italy in general, and for the process of script change and obsolescence in particular. At the beginning of the fifth century BC, Rome was just one of a considerable number of expanding states in central Italy but by its end, she dominated the surrounding region and was starting to move out significantly beyond it—firstly at the expense of immediate neighbours such as the Volsci to the south and the Etruscan city of Veii to the north and then into other areas of Italy (Cornell 1995: 293–326). During the fourth century, Rome came to dominate most of Italy, fighting off challenges from Capua, the central Apennine Samnite peoples, and the Greeks of southern Italy along the way (Fig. 5.1). By 270 BC, most of peninsular Italy (i.e. south of the River Po) was under direct or indirect Roman control (Cornell 1989: 351–91).

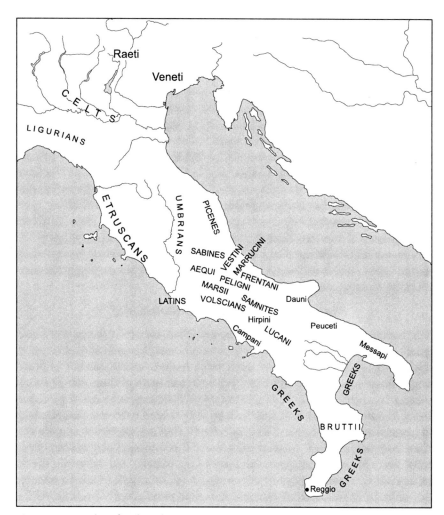

Figure 5.1 Peoples of early Italy.

Rome's *modus operandi*, since it remained a city-state with only rudimentary administrative capacity, was to tie other states to her by a series of exclusive alliances which left the other signatory in theory free and independent, but obliged to offer Rome diplomatic and military support (Sherwin-White 1973). This was backed up by a substantial number of colonies founded by Rome, which had a much more direct relationship with the mother city and a stronger impetus towards being culturally Roman (Homeyer 1957: 426–33; Sherwin-White 1973: 80–94; cf. Bradley 2006 and Bispham 2006 for a more nuanced view).

Until the first century BC, therefore, Italy was in theory a mosaic of autonomous states allied to Rome, but in practice, was subject to increasingly close

Roman supervision. Despite this apparently hands-off policy and respect for local culture and autonomy, there was some degree of cultural convergence between aspects of Roman culture and those of other Italian states during the third and second centuries BC, as both sides interacted with each other and other external influences came into play, such as growing contact with the Greek world. At the same time, Rome's relations with many Italian states became increasingly fraught as the empire expanded Mediterranean-wide and inequalities between the Roman and Italian elites became more apparent (Keaveney 1987: 21–44; Mouritsen 1998: 39–86). In 90 BC a mass revolt broke out in many areas of Italy and after a short and bitter war, Rome extended her own citizenship to all of Italy (initially south of the Po, then extended to continental Italy in 49 BC). This left Italian communities as locally self-administering parts of the Roman state, and with a much greater pre-supposition of adoption of certain key areas of Roman culture. It is against this background of growing Roman dominance and the integral role of the Latin language and script in expressing cultural *Romanitas* that changes to both script communities and linguistic communities must be considered.

Language and Script in Pre-Roman Italy

The number of script communities in any given society is frequently much smaller than the number of linguistic communities (Houston *et al.* 2003: 433), and this is demonstrably true of early Italy. A considerable number of broad linguistic groups can be pinpointed (Fig. 5.2), and some of these can be subdivided into several individual languages. Most Italic languages are regarded as being of Indo-European origin and are broadly related (with the exceptions of Etruscan and a related Alpine language, Raetic) but are nevertheless quite distinct from one another.[5] In addition, some of the languages originated outside Italy. Parts of coastal southern Italy were linguistically and culturally Greek, as a result of Greek settlement in the region in the eighth to sixth centuries BC, while Celtic was both written and spoken in parts of northern Italy: on the fringes of the Veneto, in parts of Lombardy and Piedmont, and around Lakes Como, Maggiore, and Garda.

In contrast, there were initially only two main script communities, although these also divided into several sub-groups (Fig. 5.3). The earliest inscription found in Italy, a graffito on a pottery vessel dated to c. 775 BC from the Latin settlement of Osteria dell'Osa, just south of Rome, is widely regarded as being in the Greek language but is written in an alphabet very similar to both Phoenician and Etruscan. This object and its interpretation are still very contentious, however, and it is difficult to draw too many conclusions from it (Ridgway 1996). After this point, all scripts used for epigraphic purposes in Italy are developed from either the Etruscan script (itself developed from Greek and Phoenician script) or from Greek script.

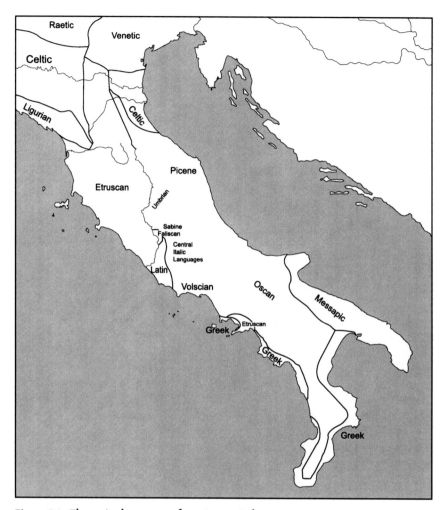

Figure 5.2 The major languages of pre-Roman Italy.

Scripts are not static, and we can see a rapid process of diversification and adaptation as they develop and subdivide. A major reason for this is the need to adapt scripts taken from elsewhere to the needs of other languages. The Etruscan language, for instance, lacks the vowel 'o', so those areas which were linguistically not Etruscan—such as the Veneto—but which adopted Etruscan script, had to adapt it by both local innovation and borrowings from other sources (principally the Greek alphabet) to accommodate this linguistic difference (Wallace 2004: 844–6). Similarly, Italic languages make frequent use of 'h', which is much less commonly used in Greek scripts, although it exists in south Italian Greek alphabets, and 'w' which is represented by the digamma in archaic Greek scripts

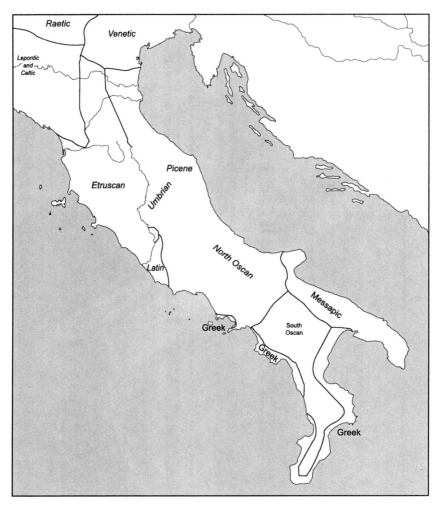

Figure 5.3 The scripts of pre-Roman Italy (names in ordinary type are derived from Greek script; names in italic type are derived from Etruscan script).

but which disappears from Greek at an early date. Italic scripts therefore had to develop ways of representing these by adding new characters (Lejeune 1970; Lazzeroni 1983; De Simone 1983; De Simone and Marchesini 2002: 7–12).

However, this diversification is not simply a result of a functionalist need to accommodate specific sounds and symbols. Scripts are cultural as well as linguistic artefacts, which have a strong connection to the social and political needs and power structures of particular societies (Keller-Cohen 1994; Gaur 2000), and numerous examples of script development seem to have little to do with linguistic needs. The Raetic language found in the Trentino and north-west Veneto is closely related to Etruscan, but the script in which it is written—although derived from Etruscan—develops clear regional characteristics and also subdivides into two subgroups within the region, the Magrè alphabet in the south of the area and the Sanzeno or Bolzano alphabet in the north (Morandi 1999; Rix 1996: 26–7). In the Veneto, a script which is closely based on the Etruscan alphabet is adapted to write a very different language by addition of extra letter-forms adopted from Greek script, but it also undergoes a complex process of chronological and geographical evolution. The earliest Venetic inscriptions date to the late seventh to sixth centuries BC (Pellegrini and Prosdocimi 1967: Pa1; Prosdocimi 1968–1969, 1972) and use a script closely based on Etruscan. After this date, inscriptions in the region develop a complex form of syllabic punctuation which is significantly different from that used in most parts of Etruria and northern Italy. It may be based on that used by some areas of southern Etruria, notably Veii, but it developed into a distinctive feature of the script of the Veneto (Pandolfini and Prosdocimi 1990: 183–7; Whitehouse and Wilkins 2006). At the same time, the Venetic alphabet begins to develop several regional sub-groups associated with the major settlements of Padua and Este and also with groups of inscriptions found in the northern Veneto (Pandolfini and Prosdocimi 1990: 245–58; Marinetti 2001: 61–72). Divergence into regional sub-groups has sometimes been identified as a sign of a script in decline (Houston *et al.* 2003: 432–4, 469), but in these instances, the culture of writing in the respective regions appears to be relatively strong, and the process of divergence takes place at a fairly early stage of development. The explanation for this development should probably be sought in the development of increasingly strong state or local identities in this part of Italy in the sixth to fourth centuries BC.

By the third century BC, the point at which Rome had come to dominate Italy politically and militarily, a considerable number of scripts have a strong claim to be regarded as separate alphabets, and there seems to be a relatively weak link between scripts and the languages they are used to transcribe. Many different languages use scripts derived from Etruscan, and several non-Greek languages in both Italy and Sicily (Messapic and Oscan in Italy, and Sikel and Elymnian in Sicily) adopt Greek script and modify it to their own needs (Agostiniani 1977; Lejeune 1970; De Simone and Marchesini 2002). In some areas, different scripts were used to write the same language. By the end of the fifth century BC, the language known as Oscan (or Sabellian) was used throughout large parts of the central and southern Apennines, Campania, Calabria, and Basilicata, and parts of northern Sicily (Fig. 5.3) but was written in both North Oscan script, which was derived from Etruscan, and South Oscan script, used in Basilicata, Calabria, and Sicily, which was adapted from Greek script (Lejeune 1970, 1972; Lazzeroni 1983; Del Tutto Palma 1990). At the point of Roman conquest, therefore, Italy has a high level of diversity of linguistic communities, scripts and cultures of writing.

	Writing/ language	Personal names	Onomastic formulae	Epigraphic form
Pre 100 BC	Mostly Etruscan lang. Mostly Etruscan script Small number of Latin inscriptions	Majority Etruscan names with some Roman or Romanized names	Mainly Etruscan form (name + filiation)	Mainly Etruscan
Early 1st cent. BC	Mostly Etruscan lang. Mostly Etruscan script Small number of Latin inscriptions	Some individuals have both Roman and Etruscan name	Roman and Etruscan forms co-exist, even within same families	Latin and Etruscan co-exist, sometimes in same tomb
Late 1st cent. BC	Latin more widespread; Etruscan used in limited areas	Use of Roman names increasing; Etruscan names confined mainly to Etruscan inscriptions.	Greater use of Roman name-forms Etruscan forms restricted to limited areas	Roman formulae increasing, but some Etruscan forms persist, even in Roman(ized) texts
Early 1st cent. AD	Mainly Latin	Name-stock mainly Romanized	Name-forms mainly Romanized	Epigraphic forms mainly Romanized

Table 5.1 Changes to language, script, and personal names at Chuisi, Perugia, and Arezzo. After Benelli 1994.

Cultures of Literacy in Early Italy

Although writing on durable materials is found in almost all areas of Italy from the sixth century onwards, each region has its own distinctive culture of writing, using it in different contexts and for different purposes (Lomas forthcoming). Any examination of script change must therefore be undertaken in the context of changes to the overall culture of literacy. In a multilingual, multiliterate, and also multicultural context, it is important to examine not just the transition from one script or language to another but also the cultural implications of all the cultural indicators contained in a particular inscription, such as script, language, form and content of personal names, form and content of epigraphic formulae, and the general inscriptional format (Cardona 1988: 9–12; Campanile 1988: 17–19; Benelli 1994). The disappearance of scripts must therefore be set in the context of the wider cultures of inscription and literacy in Italy.

Indigenous forms of writing start to develop in Italy in the seventh century BC, but there are variations between regions in date, and also regional variations in when and how writing was used, and for what purpose. In Etruria, for instance, writing begins in the seventh century BC and in its early phase (seventh to fifth centuries BC) it occurs mainly in funerary or ritual contexts, or as marks of ownership on portable objects (Stoddart and Whitley 1988; Bagnasco Gianni 1996: 357–63; see also Cornell 1991 for a critique of this view). In Umbria, in contrast, the oldest inscriptions date to the fifth century. Most of the earliest are votive, but by the third century BC, inscriptions are appearing on coinage and the epigraphic record includes inscriptions recording public documents or activity by the governing bodies of various communities (Bradley 2000: 23–6, 203–17, 282–93). In northern Italy, writing is focused on religious and ritual use, and is restricted in the settings and locations in which it occurs (Lomas 2007). Funerary inscriptions form a substantial minority, but there are few state or public inscriptions.

This situation is in marked contrast with what happens further south, where both the Oscan-speaking areas (which also adopted writing in the sixth century) and Rome produce a large number of state and public inscriptions as well as funerary and ritual ones. In Rome, in particular, an epigraphic culture developed in which inscriptions become a vehicle for recording public acts by both the state and by powerful individuals. Acts of the senate were inscribed and displayed both in Rome and elsewhere by the second century BC. Many public buildings carried monumental inscriptions recording the name of the builder and often details of his career. Statues and other monuments were set up to commemorate members of the elite, each carrying an inscription extolling his virtues and achievements. In all of these cases, writing is linked with symbols of identity and power, and by the second century BC they are highly politicized. The emergence of Roman as the dominant script in Italy during the course of the third to first centuries BC is, therefore, not just a matter of script change or of language change, but is also linked, in many regions, to potentially profound changes in the culture of public writing—the so-called 'epigraphic habit' of a region (Macmullen 1982; Woolf 1996; Häussler 2002).

Script change in central Italy: Etruria and Umbria

The Etruscans were the first peoples in Italy to produce written documents in quantity, inscribing on a huge range of objects and materials. They had a flourishing literature, although none has survived, and in the late fourth century, the Etruscan city of Caere was where aristocratic Roman youths were sent for their education (Livy 9.36.3; Bonfante and Bonfante 2002: 114–6). They also produced a wide range of inscribed documents. The earliest fall into three categories: funerary, ritual (ranging from simple votives to complex ritual texts), and marks of manufacture or ownership inscribed on portable objects (Bagnasco

Gianni 1996: 357–63); but relatively few public or state documents are known. From the fourth century BC, a greater number of state and public inscriptions, such as boundary markers and documents relating to land-ownership, appear but the emphasis is still on short funerary, votive, or ownership inscriptions (Bonfante and Bonfante 2002: 58–63). Nevertheless, there was a very well developed culture of literacy from an early date.

The large body of surviving evidence from Etruria has made it possible to study the cultural changes of the second and first century BC in some detail. A study of inscriptions from North Etruria (Benelli 1994), from the cities of Clusium, Arretium, and Perusia, has revealed a complex pattern of cultural change in practices of funerary commemoration (Table 5.1). Initially, all fields of cultural practice—script, language, onomastic form/content, and funerary formula—remain pretty much Etruscan in all aspects. By the middle of the first century BC, however, Etruscan language and script is being eroded. Latin script is widely used, and the Etruscan language becomes more restricted, and concentrated into smaller geographical areas. The Etruscan script falls out of use almost completely by the end of the first century BC, the latest inscription written in Etruscan script dating to c. AD 15–20 (Rix 1991, Ar 1.8; Benelli 1994: 15–16). During the second and early first centuries BC, however, there is considerable use of bilingual and biliterate inscriptions in the area. The epitaph of Lucius Cafatius, probably from Pisaurum and dating to the mid first century BC (TLE 697; Conway *et al.* 1933: No. 346; CIL I². 2127; Benelli 1994, 13–15), gives prominence to the Latin inscription in large monumental Roman capitals ('[L. Ca]fatius L. F. Ste. haruspex fulguriator'), but includes the same information in Etruscan language and script ('[c]afates. Lr. Lr. Netśvis. Trutnvt. Frontac'), placed in a subordinate position and in much smaller letters. Another example, an epitaph on an urn shaped like a temple, from Perugia and dating to the last decade of the first century BC (CIE 3763; CIL I² 2037; TLE 605; Rix 1991: Pe. 1.313; Benelli 1994, 18–20), separates the inscriptions and locates them so as to give increased prominence to the Latin version. The inscription in Latin script and language ('P. Volumnius A.f. Violens Cafatia natus') appears on the front of the urn, where it would be visible to all, whereas the Etruscan ('pup velimna au cahatial') is placed on the top in a position where it would be much less visible. Etruscan and Roman scripts and writing cultures seem to have co-existed but remained fairly separate until the first century BC, followed by a century of cultural amalgamation, with Etruscan script disappearing from widespread use significantly earlier than the language or other cultural indicators such as personal names or local funerary formulae.

In neighbouring Umbria, writing developed later than in Etruria, and used an alphabet adapted from the Etruscan script of Volsinii (Bradley 2000: 100). This was a region of intense Roman colonization in the third and second centuries BC (Livy 10.10.5; *Periochae* 15 and 20, 27.9; Velleius Paterculus 1.14.7–8; Harris

1971: 150–60; Bradley 2000: 128–39, 203–4), a factor which may have had a significant impact on the adoption of the Latin script and the abandonment of the indigenous one. There is a strong link between colonization and the adoption of Latin script and alphabet, as all colonies which had the status of citizen communities were probably expected to adopt Latin as their language for conducting and recording public business, and it is likely that colonies with Latin status did likewise (Homeyer 1957: 430–1; Dubuisson 1982; Crawford forthcoming). This phase of colonial settlement may have been a major factor in encouraging the early adoption of both the Latin language and the Latin alphabet in some parts of Umbria (Bradley 2000: 203–4). As in Etruria, language is more resilient than script. An Umbrian inscription dating to c. 250–150 BC has been found at the Roman colony of Fulginiae but was written in cursive Latin script not the Umbrian alphabet (Vetter 1953: No. 234). There was clearly a period of co-existence between the Umbrian and Roman traditions of writing until shortly after the Social War.

The best, but most problematic, evidence for Umbrian is provided by the Iguvine Tables, a long ritual inscription on a series of bronze tablets from Gubbio (Devoto 1975; Prosdocimi 1984). All the tablets are written in Umbrian language, but some use Umbrian script with letter-forms characteristic of the third to second centuries BC, while others use Latin script of the first century BC, the change occurring mid-tablet (Table V.b; Prosdocimi 1984: 192–3; Bradley 2000: 12–13, 76–8, 206).[6] Elsewhere, we can pinpoint the transition by examining inscriptions from the end of the second century, such as a sundial set up by a local notable of Bevagna (Poccetti 1979: No. 4), which is inscribed in Umbrian script, and a roughly contemporary boundary stone from Assisi set up by the local magistrates, which uses the Umbrian language but Roman script (Vetter 1953: No. 236). In general, the Umbrian language co-exists with Latin until the Social War of 90–89 BC, at which point it disappears within a period of ten years or so, but Umbrian script disappears considerably earlier. The Umbrian alphabet remains in use until c. 150 BC, but thereafter is eroded and most of the later Umbrian inscriptions are written in Latin script, sometimes of cursive type (Bradley 2000: 205–13).

Script change in northern Italy: The Celts and the Veneti

The use of writing in the Veneto is prominent and appears early, in the late seventh century BC, but was restricted in its field of usage. There is a significant minority of funerary inscriptions and marks of ownership on pottery or bronze items, but the majority of inscriptions are on votive objects from sanctuaries. The geographical distribution is also limited, with large concentrations of inscribed objects at two particular sites: the sanctuaries at Baratella, near Este, and at Lagole, in the upper Piave valley (Capuis and Chieco Bianchi 2002; Fogolari and Gambacurta 2001). Venetic script is derived from Etruscan, but it develops some very distinctive features of its own, notably a complex syllabic punctuation system (Prosdocimi 1983; Pandolfini and Prosdocimi 1990: 184–6). The complexity of the script and the very high quality of most of the inscriptions found has led to speculation that writing may have been taught at, and disseminated from, a single source—the sanctuary of the goddess Reitia at Baratella (Pandolfini and Prosdocimi 1990: 259–98). There was, therefore, a culture of writing which was deep-rooted but narrow, with strong elite connotations and a distinctive cultural identity of its own.

The pattern of script obsolescence is similar to that in Etruria, with disappearance of the script considerably before that of the language. There are a small number of bilingual inscriptions, many of them stamps on amphorae from Padua dating to the second century BC, and written in both Venetic and Latin language and script.[7] A longer bilingual inscription, probably also of the second century BC, is one of a sequence of votive bronze tablets from the sanctuary of Reitia. These are bronze replicas of writing tablets inscribed with a dedication to the goddess, and a grid containing a complicated alphabetic sequence, consisting of the consonants of the Venetic alphabet, a repeated sequence of letters which may represent the vowels, and a series of syllables and combinations of letters. They may have been used in the teaching of writing, giving the alphabet and a guide to the syllables (Frescura and Prosdocimi 1986; Marinetti 2003: 48–53). Most are early in date (fifth to third centuries BC), but two later examples dating to the first century BC show Roman influence. One is a bilingual dedication in Venetic by Voltiomnos (Pellegrini and Prosdocimi 1967: Es27), whose dedication is inscribed in Venetic language and script, with a short additional dedication—not a direct translation of the Venetic—in Latin.[8] Most of the tablet is laid out in the usual Venetic form, but the top line includes an additional Latin alphabet, and the punctuation of the Venetic dedication is irregular. This is also true of a second century BC example (Pellegrini and Prosdocimi 1967: Es28), which is written in Venetic script and language only, and this may suggest that writing skills in Venetic were in the process of being eroded (Langslow 2002: 34–5). The other Latin inscription on a votive writing tablet occurs in a much simplified version, with rudimentary lines embossed across the tablet but no proper grid, and a basic Latin alphabet but no Venetic characters. The inscription is in Venetic language but Latin script and gives only the basic dedicatory formula 'mego donasto' ('X dedicated me'), with neither dedicator's name nor name of deity (Pellegrini and Prosdocimi 1967: Es29). It may be unfinished, but it could also be a simplified pro forma, to which a dedicator's name could later be added.

Baratella continued to be an important religious site until well into the second century AD, but changes to the deities worshipped from Reitia to a number of Roman deities, and to the types of votives and votive inscriptions, indicate major cultural changes as a result of the foundation of a Roman colony at Este in reign of Augustus (Keppie 1983: 195–201; Lejeune 1978). Elsewhere in the Veneto, the pattern is consistent with this general trend towards the disappearance of Venetic script near the end of the second century BC, but continued persistence of the language and other aspects of indigenous epigraphic culture. A group of thirteen funerary inscriptions on pottery ossuaries from Este is written in Venetic language but Roman script, as are several examples from Montebelluna, while Venetic names, onomastic forms, and epigraphic formulae persist until the beginning of the first century AD.[9]

In contrast, the Lepontic inscriptions of north-west Italy show a remarkable resilience in script as well as language. Lepontic script developed early and was also derived from the Etruscan alphabet. The first Lepontic inscriptions date to the seventh to fifth centuries BC and comprise graffiti on pottery and some longer inscriptions on stone stelae. The content is usually brief and consists mainly of personal names (e.g. the stele of Vergiate, Lejeune 1971: 88–96). In the fourth century the number of Lepontic inscriptions drops, but revives in the late third to first centuries BC. These inscriptions, sometimes termed Gallo-Lepontic, had a wider distribution than the earlier inscriptions in Lepontic script, and represent a greater variety of epigraphic forms, including coin legends and longer inscriptions (Häussler 1997; Häussler and Pearce 2007, 221–4). Here, the Roman conquest is marked not by the demise of the local language and script but by its renewed lease of life. The process by which the script disappears is also rather different. In the second and early first centuries BC, Latin and Lepontic scripts co-exist. A Gallo-Lepontic public inscription from Briona of this date (Lejeune 1971: 39–47) contains some Roman cultural features. For instance, it features 'Kvintos lekatos', possibly a Lepontic version of the Roman name Quintus and his official rank, *legatus*, but is otherwise Lepontic in language and script. Another example of similar date from Vercelli is bilingual, with both Lepontic and Latin language and script (Lejeune 1988: 26–37; Häussler 2002: 149–50).[10] By the late first century BC, Latin language and script weres used for the majority for public and monumental inscriptions, as they were in other areas of Italy, but writing in Lepontic language and script continues in other, less monumental and elite-driven contexts. A cemetery from Oleggio in Piedmont, a small rural community, has produced a series of fifteen Lepontic graffiti dating from the second century BC to the first century AD (Gambari 1989: 195–7; Häussler and Pearce 2007, 223–4). In this region, therefore, we have a possible case of the use of script as well as language as a form of cultural resistance, although the indications of Roman influence on epigraphic formulae and personal names suggests a complex cultural interaction.

Script change in southern Italy: Greeks and Messapians

In southern Italy, the local scripts used were derived from Greek script rather than Etruscan. The south Oscan script used in Calabria and Basilicata was

	Writing	Personal names	Onomastic formulae	Epigraphic form
Pre 100 BC	Greek language and script	Mainly Greek and Oscan; some Etruscan	Greek	Greek
Early 1st cent. BC	Greek; few Latin inscriptions	Mainly Greek and/or Oscan; some Latin	Greek; small number of Latin forms	Greek; small number of Latin formulae
Late 1st cent. BC	Mainly Greek; small quantity of Latin inscriptions	Mainly Greek and/or Oscan; some Latin	Greek; small number of Latin forms	Greek; small number of Latin formulae; some Latin forms trans. into Greek
Early 1st cent. AD	Mainly Greek but Latin inscriptions increasing	Greek, and some Greek/Latin hybrids; Latin increasing but still a minority	Mix of Greek and Latin forms	Greek and Latin; some Latin forms trans. into Greek
Late 1st cent. AD	Mainly Greek but Latin inscriptions increasing	Greek and Latin	Mix of Greek and Latin forms	Greek and Latin; some Latin forms trans. into Greek
2nd cent. AD	Greek and Latin co-exist equally	Latin names increasing rapidly	More use of Latin name-forms	Latin and Greek; some Latin forms trans. into Greek
3rd cent. AD	Mainly Latin	Mainly Latin; Greek names mostly low-status	Mainly Latin; Greek names mostly low-status	Mainly Latin; some Greek

Table 5.2   Changes to language, script, and personal names at Naples.

adapted from Greek (Lejeune 1970, 1972), as was the script used in Puglia to write the language conventionally termed 'Messapic'.[11] The earliest Messapic inscriptions date to the sixth century BC, but occur in fairly small numbers and include a mixture of funerary and votive inscriptions (Marchesini 1999: 183–5). The frequency of Messapic inscriptions rises considerably in the fourth century and increases still more markedly in the third, the period of Roman conquest and the first years of alliance with Rome. Thereafter the number of inscriptions in Messapic script and language declines, although a small number date to the second to first century. The nature of inscriptions is also different throughout the period of writing in Messapic script, with fewer inscribed votives, a larger number of funerary inscriptions, and a small but significant number of longer inscriptions which appear to be civic or ritual documents (for instance, Parlangèli 1960: IM2.21, 5.21–4, 6.21, 9.19, 21.11, 22.21, 26.15). Unlike the areas already considered, there seems to be a much greater correlation between the disappearance of the local script and the disappearance of Messapic as a written language, although it is possible that it continued to be spoken. There are very few bilingual inscriptions in Latin and Messapic (Benelli 2001: 9; Parlangèli 1960: IM 2.22), and also little or no use of the Latin alphabet to write Messapic.[12] In this region, the apparent upsurge of inscriptions in Messapic script in the immediate aftermath of the Roman conquest is possibly an assertion of local identity in response to a loss of autonomy and contact with another, dominant culture, but both script and written language disappeared by the end of the first century BC.

The Greek communities of southern Italy provide a sharp contrast in their epigraphic habits. Although the Greek world had a strong culture of literacy and many states generated inscriptions by the thousand during the classical period and later, documenting both public and private life, the Greek colonies of the western Mediterranean did not have such a strong epigraphic culture, particularly in the archaic period. In comparison, they produced a relatively small number of inscriptions, and most have notable gaps in the epigraphic record coinciding with the immediate aftermath of Roman conquest, in the second and first centuries BC. Some evidence suggests that Greek continued to be spoken and written in some of them (Strabo *Geog.* 5.4.7, 6.1.2, 6.3.4), but the inscriptions of the first century BC and of the early Roman empire in some of these cities are entirely Roman, in script, language, epigraphic forms, and names of individuals (Lomas 1993a: 174–85). The reason is not hard to find. Punitive Roman reprisals against cities such as Tarentum, Croton, Metapontum, and Locri, which had revolted during Hannibal's invasion of Italy in 218–205 BC, involved colonization and land confiscations on a significant scale, introducing new, non-Greek population into the region (Livy 27.16.7–9, 34.45.4–5, 39.53.2; Appian *Hannibalic Wars* 8.49, 9.57; Velleius Paterculus 1.15.4; Lomas 1993a: 86–94, 172–5). However, the change of script and language cannot be entirely tied to demographic change, and there are some striking exceptions to this. At Naples,[13] and to a lesser extent at Rhegium and Velia, Greek script and language persist in inscriptions until the second century AD, but only in very restricted contexts. Public inscriptions, such as acts of the city council or records of certain cults, games, and festivals, are recorded in Greek, as are some elite epitaphs (Leiwo 1994; Lomas 1993a: 176–81; 1997: 118–20). Whereas in other parts of Italy, languages—and in many cases other cultural indicators such as non-Roman forms of personal name or epigraphic formulae—persist longer than scripts, language and script are closely linked in the Greek areas of Italy, and the Greek language is rarely written in Latin script.[14] In this case, the script and language also seem to persist more strongly than other cultural features (Table 5.2). It is not unusual at Naples, for instance, to find Romanized names, onomastic forms, or funerary or other epigraphic formulae inserted (often by means of literal translation) into inscriptions written in Greek script or language. In this case, the pattern found elsewhere of script disappearance, followed by language change and erosion of local onomastic and epigraphic practices, seems to be reversed. The timespan of the change is also much longer, with Greek persisting well into the first or even second century AD (Leiwo 1994; Lomas 1997: 118–20).

Co-existence of scripts: North and South Oscan

The inscriptions in the languages usually termed Oscan or Sabellian are found over a large area of central and southern Italy. A full discussion of Oscan inscriptions is well beyond the scope of this paper,[15] but they pose some interesting questions about the relation between script and language, because two distinct scripts were introduced to write this particular language. North Oscan (or Etrusco-Oscan) script was adopted in the fifth century BC from Campania, and consisted in the Etruscan alphabet with some modifications. It was used by most Oscan-speaking communities in Campania, and by the populations of the central and southern Apennines (Lazzeroni 1983: 171–3). South Oscan (or Graeco-Oscan) script, developed towards the end of the fifth century, was closely based on the Greek alphabet and was used by the Oscan-speaking populations of Lucania, Calabria, Basilicata and parts of Sicily (Lejeune 1970 and 1972; Lazzeroni 1983: 171–3). Both scripts show signs of interaction with each other and also undergo a phase of reform and change in the late fifth to early fourth centuries BC, after which the north Oscan script developed into a majority script often described as the Oscan 'national alphabet', while the south Oscan script remained pre-eminent in Oscan-speaking areas of southern Italy.[16]

The transition from Oscan to Roman epigraphic cultures was complex and highly politicized, as the Oscan-speaking Samnites were amongst Rome's fiercest opponents, fighting several bitter wars against Rome and forming the core of the anti-Roman alliance which revolted in 90 BC (Salmon 1967; Dench 1995). Language and script were powerful symbols of identity which could be—and were—used to demonstrate local identities in opposition to Rome. However, this was not a one-way linear process of change from Oscan to Roman script or from Oscan to Latin language. As in Umbria and parts of northern Italy, the local script disappears more rapidly than the language, but is still tenacious. By the middle of the second century BC, it is not uncommon for inscriptions—including those recording acts of state—to be written in Roman script, and an increasing number of inscriptions are written in the Latin language. Where the Oscan language continues to be used, there is evidence of an increasing influence of external factors in epigraphic practices. Inscriptions dating to the later second century BC and set up by local dignitaries at the major religious sanctuaries at Pietrabbondante and Rossano di Vaglio, for instance, are written in Oscan language and also, for the most part, in Oscan scripts, but use dedicatory formulae almost indistinguishable from those found on contemporary Roman inscriptions (cf. Poccetti 1979: Nos. 14–16, 167; Lejeune 1975).

Perhaps the most telling example of the transition is the Tabula Bantina, a bronze tablet from Bantia in Lucania which was re-used, having a Latin inscription on one side and an Oscan one, written in Roman script, on the other. There is some argument over the relative dating of the inscriptions, and of the identification of the Latin inscription, but it seems fairly certain that the Oscan text is the later of the two (Crawford 1996: 193–208, 271–92). The Latin inscription appears to be part of a copy of a Roman law dating to c. 100 BC, and its presence implies that the community of Bantia had adopted the Latin language and Roman script for at least part of its public business and public records by the late second century BC. The Oscan inscription, however, seems to date to the period immediately before the Social War, probably c. 100–90 BC. It records part of the constitution of the community, laying down regulations for the conduct of magistrates and the local town council. At one level, the re-adoption of Oscan as the official language of record at Bantia in the years before the Social War suggests that the Oscan language—but not necessarily the Oscan scripts—was a powerful symbol of local identity and anti-Roman feeling (however, cf. Dench 1995: 214, for an alternative view of language in the Social War). However, it should also be noted that much of the format and content of the document is very close to that of Latin municipal or colonial charters of the late second and first centuries BC, and it seems that, despite the symbolic choice of language, Roman influence on epigraphic culture in general was considerable.

The Oscan inscriptions of Pompeii indicate the full complexity of the interaction of Roman and indigenous inscribing practices. A number of fine stone-cut dedicatory inscriptions recording building by civic magistrates have survived. Most appear to date to the mid to late second century BC and are written in Oscan language and North Oscan script, but their content is very similar to that of contemporary Latin inscriptions elsewhere, suggesting a convergence between Roman and non-Roman epigraphic habits (Vetter 1953: Nos 8–20; Cooley 2002). Both Oscan language and script disappear from the epigraphic record after the foundation of a Roman colony at Pompeii in c. 80 BC, but Oscan *dipinti* and graffitti, some of them in Oscan script, are found in contexts which may postdate the founding of the colony, suggesting that the two languages and scripts may have co-existed for a time (Vetter 1953: 29–30; for problems of dating, see Cooley 2002: 82–3).

Script Obsolescence and the Culture of Writing in Early Roman Italy

In general, in most areas of Italy, indigenous scripts disappear before the non-Latin languages which they were used to write. Of all the cultural indicators which can be gleaned from inscriptions—language, script, personal names, and name-forms, and the general form and phraseology of the inscription—the script employed appears to be the weakest and the most likely to change first.

With the exception of Greek script in small parts of southern Italy and Lepontic in the north, Italian scripts seem to be vulnerable to cultural change to a greater degree than other aspects of linguistic and written culture. Non-Latin languages continued to be used epigraphically in most parts of Italy for up to a century after the disappearance of non-Roman scripts, but Roman script was increasingly adopted as the medium for writing in these languages. Except in areas where Greek is both the indigenous script and the indigenous language, where there is an exclusive connection between language and alphabet, the Latin alphabet is frequently used as a vehicle for non-Latin inscriptions after c. 150 BC. Non-Latin scripts, therefore, are already in the process of being eroded well before the Social War and the political and cultural upheavals which followed, and it is clear that the disappearance of both non-Latin scripts and non-Latin epigraphic cultures in the first century BC is the culmination of a long-term process of cultural interaction and exchange beginning in the third century BC and culminating in a more rapid phase of change in the late first century. There are, of course, significant regional variations. In some areas, such as south-east Italy, both the indigenous language and script disappear from the epigraphic record, whereas elsewhere—such as Etruria and the Veneto—the transition is documented by bilingual or biliterate inscriptions, or by bicultural inscriptions in which the indigenous language and formulae co-exist with Latin script.

The relationship between script and language is complicated by the exceptional status of Latin in Italy, and in particular by its links to the Roman state. Scripts, especially as used on public monuments, can be a powerful symbol of cultural identity, but the use of Latin language in a public or official context may have had a specific link to legal status as well as being a cultural indicator. However, there are considerable uncertainties about how far Rome actively sought to impose Latin as an official language in Italy. The adoption of the Latin language is linked to the acquisition of Roman citizenship and to mechanisms of Roman rule, as well as to cultural *Romanitas*. During the third and second centuries BC, Latin had already begun to spread throughout Italy, but it may have been disseminated principally by its growing prestige as an elite *lingua franca*, as well as by the effects of colonization (Homeyer 1957: 427–33, 437–40; Dubuisson 1982; Woolf 1998: 77–105). By the late second century, the rising tension between Rome and many of her Italian allies politicized the use of Latin, and it is possible that other languages such as Oscan were seen in some contexts as a potential symbol of resistance to Rome, but here again the issue is not clear cut (cf. Dench 1995: 182, for arguments against the use of Oscan as a political symbol). After 90 BC, however, the extension of Roman citizenship to the rest of Italy gave Latin a position of privilege in practical, if not formal, terms. The process of becoming a Roman community involved adopting Roman-style forms of government and public business, together with Roman law-codes, and most of these were recorded in Latin. Aspiring Italian aristocrats with ambitions to pursue a political career at Rome required good Latin in which to address the senate and conduct their election campaigns.[17] As the vehicle of both political and administrative dominance and social prestige, Latin had an overwhelmingly privileged position as a written language.[18] Equally, some other features of inscriptions such as onomastic forms have close links to the formal status of Roman citizen as well as to a more general cultural identity. By the early empire, the characteristic Roman name-form of personal name, family name, filiation and cognomen came to be restricted to use by Roman citizens (cf. Suetonius, *Claudius* 17, 25, for enforcement of dress-codes and onomastic forms for Roman citizens). Scripts notably do not fit into this pattern. Their early disappearance suggests that the process of script change is not as politicized as that of language change and less closely connected with the formalities of the transition to Roman citizenship.

There are a number of possible reasons behind these changes in the scripts used for inscriptions in the third to first centuries BC. One possibility, given that in some areas writing was closely linked with ritual activity at specific cult sites, is that the disappearance of scripts was the result of the disappearance of the cults with which they were associated or of major cultural changes to these cults (cf. Houston *et al.* 2003: 434–5). Scribal schools which may have been associated with various sanctuaries in Etruria and the Veneto, notably those at Veii and Este, may have been undermined by the weakening of their associated cults or changes to them, but it is difficult to extrapolate this explanation to other areas of Italy, or even to see how indigenous writing in a region with such a strong tradition of literacy as Etruria could be undermined fatally by this process. By the second century BC, the point at which the erosion of non-Latin scripts and languages gathered serious momentum, literacy, and the teaching of reading and writing, was a much more widespread phenomenon, and it seems unlikely that disappearance or change to a number of cult centres would be sufficient to undermine it.

Assessing the impact of teaching and transmission of pre-Roman scripts on the decline and disappearance of these scripts is in fact very difficult, as we know very little about teaching and education in any part of early Italy Harris 1989: 157–9). Early reading and writing was an elite-driven phenomenon, although writing was probably undertaken by specialist scribes or craftsmen, and it is much debated how widespread literacy skills and the use of writing actually were (Harris 1989: 157; Stoddart and Whitley 1988: 769; for arguments in favour of a less restricted literacy in early Italy, see Cornell 1991). The little evidence available suggests that aristocratic families educated their children within their own households, although there are references to youths from fourth-century Rome being sent to Etruscan Caere to learn their letters, and to the presence of a schoolmaster at Falerii (Livy 5.27, 9.36.3; Harris 1989: 158). By the second century BC, however, the teaching of letters by specialist schoolmasters was becoming a more widespread phenomenon at Rome, the first professional schoolmaster being a freed slave who began teaching c. 230 BC (Plutarch, *Moralia* 278e). The difficulty lies in assessing how far we can rely on later sources of this type, written long after the event, and how far we can extrapolate from Rome or various Etruscan cities to other areas of Italy.

The most likely factor underlying script change in Italy—and conversely, script survival in limited Greek-speaking areas—is the question of prestige. In ancient Italy writing was clearly an elite activity, linked with high craft skills and aristocratic activities, and therefore with high prestige. Houston, Baines, and Cooper (2003: 433–4) have noted that 'a subordinate script is a despised script', and while there is no direct evidence that the Romans actively imposed this view or discouraged indigenous scripts, there are plenty of reasons why the spread of Latin language and script, with their links to the dominant political power, might have resulted in the eclipse of non-Latin scripts. Ancient Italy comprised aristocratic societies, with a strong 'international' elite culture and a long tradition of friendships, intermarriage, and kinship links between leading families of different communities, crossing ethnic and state boundaries. Once Rome had established domination over the peninsula, it acted as a focal point for this sort of activity. Social integration with Roman aristocrats gave status and networking opportunities, and ultimately (after 90 BC) the opportunity to pursue a political career at Rome for those who wished to do so and could afford it. All this was predicated on the ability to communicate in Latin and to write in a script comprehensible to Romans. A pre-existing social structure therefore linked the various script and language communities of Italy at the upper levels of society, coupled with a strong social motivation for favouring Latin language and script over local equivalents. Although Romans did not actively suppress other languages and scripts, they could be unashamedly chauvinist about Latin in formal contexts (Dubuisson 1982). Latin was the language of business throughout Italy and the western provinces, and although Greek was the language of the eastern empire, some Roman officials in the second and first centuries BC refused to speak Greek in formal contexts (Cicero *de Finibus* 1.9 and 5.89, *Tusculan Disputations* 5.108, *Brutus* 131, *De Provinciis Consularibus* 15, *In Verrem* 2.4.147; Valerius Maximus 2.2.2–3; Wardman 1979: 41–50; on Romans and the Greek language more generally, see Kaimio 1979). The complexity of the issue, however, is demonstrated by examples of public inscriptions written in Latin language but Greek script. Greek is a special case, because it was regarded as a high-status language by the Roman elite, becoming an essential part of an elite education in the first century BC, but attitudes towards this were ambivalent, and Roman aristocrats who espoused Greek language and culture too wholeheartedly, such as Scipio Africanus, could find themselves attacked by their political enemies as anti-Roman (Plutarch, *Cato the Elder* 3.10; Wardman 1979: 41–50).

Although this ambivalence about use of other languages for official purposes explains why the ability to speak and read Latin was important when dealing with Romans, it does not answer the question of why Latin script was adopted so readily and so early within the other communities of Italy. The answer here may lie in the changing sense of what was most appropriate and effective as a means of elite status display. Italian societies—particularly at the elite level—were characterized by constant competition between leading men in a community for power, status, and dominance within the peer group. They were consequently under pressure to demonstrate their pre-eminence and social status in a wide variety of ways, and to advertise their achievements and generosity towards the community. At a regional level, similar patterns of competition for regional dominance existed between cities and communities. The growing pre-eminence of Roman culture means that by the end of the second century BC, indigenous scripts and epigraphic habits were no longer the best medium for elite status display. Symbols of Roman culture such as Latin script, Latin language, and Romanized idiom and epigraphic forms were adopted as the symbolic language in which members of the elite sought to establish their status *vis-à-vis* each other. A strong impetus followed for the adoption of Roman epigraphic practices and for Roman habits to be absorbed into indigenous traditions. The same process encouraged a more general Romanization of the types of inscriptions which were set up. By the end of the first century BC, there is a trend away from pre-Roman inscribing cultures and towards the type of large-scale inscriptions on public monuments which are characteristic of the late Republic and early Empire.

The pattern of adoption of Roman ways, whether in script, language, or general epigraphic culture, was complex, and the limitations of the evidence available mean that we can only have a partial understanding of it. Research on north-west Italy shows that in some areas, older scripts and epigraphic habits co-exist with the new Latinized ones (Häussler 2002; Häussler and Pearce 2007). Lepontic graffiti and votives continue for some time after the adoption of Latin language and script for monumental civic inscriptions. It is also possible that there were differences between public and 'private' spheres of display or activity, with a greater likelihood that indigenous languages and scripts would be used for more personal documents or inscriptions aimed at family and friends, while Latin script was used for more high-profile public documents. The persistence of Etruscan script in parallel with Latin in parts of Etruria indicates that local culture continued to be important to the processes of personal commemoration. Genders and social levels may have differed in choice of script, but this is an area in which more work needs to be done.

The processes of script change in Italy were, therefore, closely tied to issues of Roman power, culture, and citizenship, but were not directly dictated by Rome. Strong evidence suggests that the abandonment of local scripts in favour of the Latin alphabet was driven by local priorities and the cultural agenda of the local elites throughout Italy. It is also clear that this was a complex process with considerable local variations. Both the practice of writing in general, and the choice of script used in particular, sent out powerful cultural signals about a society and its sense of its own identity. In areas with a number of different traditions of writing, the choice of script employed at any particular time and for any particular purpose reflects a cultural choice on the part of the writer, commissioner, or manufacturer of the text. In Italy, changes in script, language, and the overall culture of writing are closely bound up with these processes of culture change resulting from the Roman conquest, and many factors, such as adoption of Latin script and language or of Romanized forms of personal name or epigraphic formulae, are closely linked with the encroachment of Roman power structures, the adoption of Roman culture, and ultimately the acquisition of Roman citizenship. This process is neither linear nor straightforward. Language, script, and the wider epigraphic culture of a region cannot be regarded as a 'cultural package', but as a group of cultural features, any element of which can be adopted, modified, or rejected, as part of a complex process of interaction between cultural groups or as part of internal changes within a cultural group. The disappearance of the pre-Roman scripts of Italy must therefore be considered within the wider context of a diverse and changing cultural climate and of the rise of Roman power.

Notes

1. I would like to thank John Baines for inviting me to contribute to this conference.

2. The processes of culture contact and exchange in Italy after the Roman conquest are much discussed and there is a vast body of literature on the subject which is too large to be reviewed here. For recent reviews of the subject see: Häussler 1997; Woolf 1998; Terrenato 1997 and 2001.

3. There are significant difficulties in this conceptualization of *ethnos* and state in pre-Roman Italy, and these categories are increasingly being problematized. In many parts of Italy—particularly Apennine Italy—forms of political and social organization suggest the emergence of complex state societies which are nevertheless not urban, while in other areas a sense of ethnic identity over and above the city-state seems to emerge as a response to Roman conquest (Bradley 2000).

4. Traditionally the inscriptions in the non-Latin languages of Italy have been collected in studies according to linguistic and regional groups. The principal publications are: Conway *et al.* 1933 (all Italic languages); Crawford, forthcoming, Vetter 1953, Poccetti 1979 (Oscan, Umbrian, and central Italian languages); Rix 1991 (Etruscan); Parlangèli 1960, Santoro 1982–84, De Simone and Marchesini 2002 (Messapic); Pellegrini and Prosdocimi 1967 (Venetic); Schumacher 1992 (Raetic); Lejeune 1971, 1988 (Lepontic).

5. Pulgram 1958, but see Wilkins 1990: 63–6 for a critique of the methodological problems involved in linking language, inscriptions, and ethnic groups.

6. There is considerable controversy about the dating of the Iguvine Tables. The surviving copy may represent a re-copying or codification of an earlier text (or texts), which would account for some of the peculiarities of the script. Most scholars date them to the second century BC (Prosdocimi 1984: 151–61), but the presence of Latin script has been used to argue for a first century BC date (cf. Bradley 2000: 74–8, 205–6 on the chronological problems of these inscriptions).

7. The stamps record the name Keutenis/Ceutenius in both Latin and Venetic. Pellegrini and Prosdocimi 1967: Pa 19; Marinetti 1999: Nos 4 and 5.

8. The Venetic text reads '[vda]n Vol[tion]mnos donasto Kelag[s S'ai]natei Reitiai op [vo]ltio le[no]', giving the dedication in the usual Venetic form, while the Latin, which is fragmentary, reads either 'dedit libens merito' (Lejeune 1953) or '[---] tio[--]o[-------] dedit' (Pellegrini and Prosdocimi 1967: Es 27).

9. Pellegrini and Prosdocimi 1967, Es104–Es112 (from Este) and Tr3–Tr5 are Venetic inscriptions written in the Latin alphabet. Even in Latin inscriptions, Venetic names and funerary formulae remain in use. Compare Pellegrini and Prosdocimi 1967: Pa6, a Latin epitaph for Manius Gallenius and Ostiala Gallenia which uses the Venetic funerary formula 'ekupetaris'.

10. '[F]inis campo quem dedit Acisius argantocomaterecus comunem deis et hominibus, ita ut lapide[s] III statute sunt. Akisios Arkatoko{k}materekos atom tenoctom koneu'.

11. In this chapter, this term is used to cover the whole of Puglia, although increasing evidence suggests that there were differences in both language and writing between Messapia proper (southern Puglia) and northern Puglia: De Simone 1990: 303–4.

12. Our understanding of the interaction between Latin and Messapic script and language may, however, be greatly enhanced by the inscriptions from a ritual site in the cave of Grotta della Poesia, near Rocavecchia, which are only partially published at the time of writing, but which contains Greek and Latin as well as Messapic inscriptions (see De Simone 1988 and De Simone and Marchesini 2002: 362–71 for the Messapic inscriptions).

13. Naples is a particularly complex case. It was originally a Greek settlement, but by the end of the fifth century it had acquired a substantial minority of Oscan-speaking Campanians, and there many also have been a smaller minority of Etruscans there. All three groups are attested in the onomastics of the city down to the early Roman Empire.

14. See also the Greek inscriptions of Rome, in which Greek script is sometimes used to write Latin, but rarely the other way around. Adams and Swain 2002: 5–6.

15. Such a study would be premature at this stage, as a new edition of Oscan inscriptions (the *Imagines Italicae* research project) is currently in preparation.

16. There is strong evidence both for interaction between North and South Oscan scripts and for divergence. North Oscan, for instance, does not use the well-attested Etruscan character 8 to transcribe an F, but a modified form of the Greek Θ. After the reforms of the late fifth and early fourth centuries BC, the two scripts develop very different conventions for transcribing long and short vowels, again in a way which suggests interaction between them. See also Lazzeroni 1983.

17. There is some debate, however, as to how far Latin was formally imposed on a community by Rome as part of the colonization process or acquisition of municipal status, and how far its adoption was a matter of choice by the local elite. See also Dubuisson 1982.

18. Despite the fact that Latin predominates in inscribed documents by the middle of the first century BC, due to lack of evidence it is impossible to draw any firm conclusions about the survival of local languages as spoken languages, or even as written languages in less formal contexts and on perishable media. It is quite possible that languages other than Latin survived in speech—particularly for informal communication or in isolated and rural areas—well after they ceased to be used for formal inscribed records (Wilkins 1990: 82–5; Bradley 2000: 212–7; Cooley 2002: 77–86).

References

Adams, James, and Simon Swain
2002 'Introduction'. In J. Adams, M. Janse, and S. Swain (eds), *Bilingualism in Ancient Society: Language Contact and the Written Word*. Oxford: Oxford University Press.

Agostiniani, Luciano
1977 *Iscrizioni anelleniche di Sicilia: le iscrizioni elime*. Florence: Olschki.

Bagnasco Gianni, Giovanna
1996 *Oggetti iscritti di epoca orientalizzante in Etruria*. Florence: Olschki.

Barker, Graeme, and Tom Rasmussen
1998 *The Etruscans*. Oxford: Blackwell Publishing.

Benelli, Enrico
1994 *Le iscrizioni bilingui etrusco-latine*. Florence: Olschki.
2001 'The Romanization of Italy through the Epigraphic Record'. In S. Keay and N. Terrenato (eds), *Italy and the West: Comparative Issues in Romanization*. Oxford: Oxbow, 7–16.

Bispham, Edward
2006 '*Coloniam deducere*: How Roman was Roman colonization during the Middle Republic?' In Guy J. Bradley and John-Paul Wilson (eds), *Greek and Roman Colonization: Origins, Ideologies and Interactions*. Swansea: The Classical Press of Wales, 73–160.

Bonfante, Giulio, and Larissa Bonfante
    2002   *The Etruscan Language: An Introduction*, second ed. Manchester: Manchester University Press.

Bradley, Guy
    2000   *Ancient Umbria: State, Culture and Identity in Central Italy from the Iron Age to the Augustan Era*. Oxford: Oxford University Press.
    2006   'Colonization and identity in Republican Italy'. In Guy J. Bradley and John-Paul Wilson (eds), *Greek and Roman Colonization. Origins, Ideologies and Interactions*. Swansea: The Classical Press of Wales, 161–88.

Campanile, Enrico
    1988   'Per una definizione del testo epigrafico bilingue'. In E. Campanile, G. Cardona, and R. Lazzeroni (eds), *Bilingualismo e biculturalismo nel mondo antico*. Pisa: Giardini, 17–21.

Capuis, Loredana
    1993   *I Veneti*. Milan: Longanesi.

Capuis, Loredana, and Anna Maria Chieco Bianchi
    2002   'Il santuario sud-orientale: Reitia e i suoi devoti'. In A. Ruta Serafini (ed.), *Este preromana: una città e i suoi santuari*. Treviso: Canova, 233–47.

Cardona, Giorgio
    1988   'Considerazioni sui documenti plurilingui'. In E. Campanile, G. Cardona, and R. Lazzeroni (eds), *Bilingualismo e biculturalismo nel mondo antico*. Pisa: Giardini, 9–15.

Conway, Robert, Joshua Whatmough, and Sarah Elizabeth Jackson Johnson
    1933   *The Prae-Italic Dialects of Italy*. Cambridge, MA: Harvard University Press.

Cooley, Alison
    2002   'The Survival of Oscan in Roman Pompeii'. In A. Cooley (ed.), *Becoming Roman, Writing Latin? Literacy and Epigraphy in the Roman West*. Portsmouth, RI: Journal of Roman Archaeology, 77–86.

Cornell, Tim
    1989   'The Conquest of Italy'. *Cambridge Ancient History*, 2nd ed. VII.2: 351–419. Cambridge: Cambridge University Press.
    1991   'The Tyranny of the Evidence: A Discussion of the Possible Uses of Literacy in Etruria and Latium in the Archaic Age'. In *Literacy in the Roman World*. Journal of Roman Archaeology, Supplementary Series 3. Ann Arbor: Journal of Roman Archaeology, 7–33.
    1995   *The Beginnings of Rome*. London: Routledge.
    1997   'Ethnicity in Early Roman History'. In T. J. Cornell and K. Lomas (eds), *Gender and Ethnicity in Ancient Italy*. London: Accordia Research Institute, 9–21.

Crawford, Michael H.
    1996   *Roman Statutes*. London: Institute of Classical Studies.
    forthcoming. *Imagines Italicae*. London: Institute of Classical Studies.

Del Tutto Palma, Lauretta
    1990   *Le iscrizioni della Lucania preromana*. Padua: Unipress.

Dench, Emma
    1995   *From Barbarians to New Men: Greek, Roman, and Modern Perceptions of Peoples from the Central Apennines*. Oxford: Clarendon Press.

De Simone, Carlo
    1983   'L'evidenza messapica: tra grafematica e fonologia'. *AION (Ling)* 5: 183–95.

De Simone, Carlo, and Simona Marchesini
    2002   *Monumenta linguae Messapicae*. Wiesbaden: Reichert.

Devoto, Giacomo
    1975   *Le Tavole di Gubbio*, second ed. Florence: Sansoni.

Dubuisson, Michel
    1982   'Y a-t-il une politique linguistique romaine'? *Ktema* 7: 187–210.

Fogolari, Giulia, and Giovanna Gambacurta
    2001   *Materiali veneti preromani e romani del santuario di Lagole di Calalzo al Museo di Pieve di Cadore*. Rome: Giorgio Bretschneider.

Frescura, Giovanni, and Aldo L. Prosdocimi
    1986   'Tavolette alfabetiche atestine: revisoni ed acquisizioni. Appendice: placchetta bronzea iscritta in vda-, fraten-, donasa-'. *Aquileia Nostra* 57: 353–84.

Gambari, Filippo M.
    1989   'L'iscrizione vascolare della T.53 di Oleggio-Loreto'. In G. Amoretti (ed.), *Il Ticino. Strutture, storia e società nel territorio tra Oleggio e Lonate-Pozzolo*. Turin: Nicolini, 195–7.

Gaur, Albertine
    2000   *Literacy and the Politics of Writing*. Bristol: Intellect.

Harris, William V.
    1971   *Rome in Etruria and Umbria*. Oxford: Clarendon Press.
    1989   *Ancient Literacy*. Cambridge, MA: Harvard University Press.

Häussler, Ralph
    1997   'The Romanization of Liguria and Piedmont'. PhD Diss. University of London.
    2002   'Writing Latin—From Resistance to Assimilation: Language, Culture and Society in N. Italy and S. Gaul'. In A. Cooley (ed.), *Becoming Roman, Writing Latin: Literacy and Epigraphy in the Roman West*. Portsmouth, RI: Journal of Roman Archaeology, 61–75.

Häussler, Ralph, and John Pearce
    2007   'Towards an Archaeology of Literacy'. In K. Lomas, J. Wilkins, and R. Whitehouse (eds), *Literacy and State Societies in the Ancient Mediterranean*. London: Accordia Research Institute, 219–36.

Herring, Edward
    2000   ' "To See Oursels as Others See Us!". The Construction of Native Identities in Southern Italy'. In E. Herring and K. Lomas (eds), *The Emergence of State Identities in Italy in the First Millennium BC*. London: Accordia Research Institute, 45–78.

Herring, Edward, and Kathryn Lomas
    2000   *The Emergence of State Identities in Italy in the First Millennium BC*. London: Accordia Research Institute.

Holloway, Ross R.
    1994   *The Archaeology of Rome and Latium*. London: Routledge.

Homeyer, Helen
    1957   'Some Observations on Bilingualism and Language Shift in Italy from the Sixth to the Third Century BC'. *Word* 13: 415–34.

Houston, Stephen, John Baines, and Jerrold Cooper
    2003   'Last Writing: Script Obsolescence in Egypt, Mesopotamia and Mesoamerica'. *Comparative Studies in Society and History* 45: 430–79.

Kaimio, Jorma
    1979   *The Romans and the Greek Language*. Helsinki: Societas Scientiarum Fennica.

Keaveney, Arthur
    1987   *Rome and the Unification of Italy*. London: Croom Helm.

Keller-Cohen, D. (ed.)
    1994   *Literacy: Interdisciplinary Conversations*. Cresskill, NJ: Hampton Press.

Keppie, Laurence
    1983   *Colonisation and Veteran Settlement in Italy, 47-14 BC*. London: British School at Rome.

Langslow, David
    2002   'Approaching Bilingualism in Corpus Languages'. In J. N. Adams, M. Janse, and S. Swain (eds), *Bilingualism in Ancient Society*. Oxford: Oxford University Press, 23–51.

Lazzeroni, Renato
    1983   'Contatti di lingue e di culture nell'Italia antica. Modelli egemoni e modelli subordinate nelle iscrizioni osche in grafie greche'. *AION (Ling)* 5: 171–82.

Leiwo, Martti
    1994   *Neapolitana*. Helsinki: Societas Scientiarum Fennica.

Lejeune, Michel
    1953   'Les plaques de bronze votives de sanctuaire Venète d'Este'. *Revue des études anciennes* 55: 58–112.
    1970   'Phonologie osque et graphie grecque, I'. *Revue des études anciennes* 72: 271–316.
    1971   *Lepontica*. Paris: Les Belles Lettres.
    1972   'Phonologie osque et graphie grecque, II'. *Revue des études anciennes* 74: 5–13.
    1975   'Inscriptions de Rossano di Vaglio'. *Rendiconti di Lincei*, ser. 8, 30: 319–39.
    1978   *Ateste à l'heure de la romanisation: Etude anthroponymique*. Florence: Olschki.
    1988   *Recueil des inscriptions gauloises*, vol. 2.1. Paris: CNRS.

Lomas, Kathryn
    1993a   *Rome and the Western Greeks: Conquest and Acculturation in Southern Italy*. London: Routledge.

1993b 'The City in South-East Italy. Ancient Topography and the Evolution of Urban Settlement, 600-300 BC'. *Accordia Research Papers* 4: 63–77.

1997 'Graeca urbs? Ethnicity and Culture in Early Imperial Naples'. *Accordia Research Papers* 7 (1997-1998): 113–30.

2000 'Cities, States and Ethnic Identity in South-East Italy'. In E. Herring and K. Lomas (eds), *The Emergence of State Identities in Italy in the First Millennium BC*. London: Accordia Research Institute.

2007 'Writing boundaries: Literacy and Identity in the Ancient Veneto, 600–300 BC'. In K. Lomas, R. Whitehouse, and J. B. Wilkins (eds), *Literacy and the State in the Ancient Mediterranean*. London: Accordia Research Institute, 149–70.

forthcoming. *Literacy in Ancient Italy: New Approaches to the Development of Writing in Society*. London: Institute of Classical Studies.

Macmullen, Ramsay

1982 'The Epigraphic Habit in the Roman Empire'. *American Journal of Philology* 103: 233–46.

Marchesini, Simona

1999 'Confini e frontiera nella Grecità d'occidente: la situazione alfabetica'. In *Confini e frontiera nella Grecità d'occidente. Atti di XXVII° convegno di studi sulla Magna Grecia*. Taranto: Istituto per la Storia e l'Archeologia della Magna Grecia, 173–212.

Marinetti, Anna

1999 'Venetico 1976–1996. Acquisizioni e prospettive'. In O. Paoletti (ed.), *Protostoria e storia del 'Venetorum Angulus'. Atti del XX Convegno di Studi Etruschi ed Italici*. Pisa and Rome: Istituti Editoriale e poligrafici internazionali, 377–90.

2001 'Il venetico di Lagole'. In G. Fogolari and G. Gambacurta (eds), *Materiali veneti preromani e romani del santuario di Lagole di Calalzo*. Rome: Giorgio Bretschneider, 61–72.

2003 'Caratteri e diffusione dell'alfabeto venetico'. In AAVV *AKEO. I tempi della scrittura*. Montebelluna: Museo di Storia Naturale e Archeologia du Montebelluna, 39–54.

Morandi, Alessandro

1999 *Il cippo di Castelciès nell'epigrafia retica*. Rome: L''Erma' di Bretschneider.

Mouritsen, Henrik

1998 *Italian Unification: A Study in Ancient and Modern Historiography*. London: Institute of Classical Studies.

Pandolfini, Maristella, and Aldo L. Prosdocimi

1990 *Alfabetari dell'Italia antica*. Florence: Olschki.

Parlangèli, Oronzo

1960 *Studi Messapici*. Milan: Istituto Lombardo di Scienze e Lettere.

Pellegrini, Giovanni B., and Aldo L. Prosdocimi

1967 *La Lingua Venetica*. 2 vols. Padua: Istituto di Glottologia dell'Università di Padova.

Poccetti, Paolo

1979 *Nuovi documenti italici: a complemento del Manuale di E. Vetter*. Pisa: Giardini.

Prosdocimi, Aldo L.
1968–69 'Una iscrizione inedita dal territorio atestino. Nuovi aspetti epigrafici linguistici culturali dell'area paleoveneta'. *Atti dell'Istituto Veneto di scienze lettere ed arti, classe di scienze morali e lettere* 127: 123–83.
1972 'Venetico'. *Studi Etruschi*, 40: 193–245.
1983 'Puntuazione sillabica e insegnamento della scrittura nel venetico e nelle fonti etrusche'. *AION (Ling)* 5: 75–126.
1984 *Le Tavole Iguvini: I.* Florence: Olschki.

Pulgram, Ernst
1958 *The Tongues of Italy: Prehistory and History.* Cambridge, MA: Harvard University Press.

Ridgway, David
1996 'Greek letters at Osteria dell'Osa'. *Opuscula Romana* 20: 87–97.

Rix, Helmut
1991 *Etruskishe Texte: Editio Minor.* Tübingen: Narr.
1996 'Il problema di retico'. In A. Marinetti, M. T. Vigolo, and A. Zamboni (eds.), *Varietà e continuità nella storia linguistica del Veneto: atti del Convegno della Società Italiana di Glottologia.* Rome: Il Calamo, 25–48.

Salmon, Edward Togo
1967 *Samnium and the Samnites.* Cambridge: Cambridge University Press.

Santoro, Ciro
1982–84 *Nuovi Studi Messapici.* 3 vols. Galatina: Congedo editore.

Schumacher, Stefan
1992 *Die Rätischen Inschriften. Geschichte und heutiger Stand der Forschung.* Archaeolingua—Innsbrucker Beiträge zur Kulturwissenschaft. Budapest: Archaeolingua Alapítvány.

Sherwin-White, Adrian Nicholas
1973 *The Roman Citizenship.* Oxford: Clarendon Press.

Stoddart, Simon and James Whitley
1988 'The Social Context of Literacy in Archaic Greece and Etruria'. *Antiquity* 62: 761–72.

Terrenato, Nicola
1997 'The Romanisation of Italy: Global Acculturation or Cultural *Bricolage*'? In *TRAC 97: Proceedings of the Seventh Theoretical Roman Archaeology Conference.* Oxford: Oxbow, 20–7.
2001 'Introduction'. In S. Keay and N. Terrenato (eds), *Italy and the West: Comparative Issues in Romanization.* Oxford: Oxbow, 1–7.

Vetter, Emil
1953 *Handbuch der Italische Dialekte.* Heidelberg: Carl Winter.

Wallace, Rex T.
2004 'Venetic'. In Roger D. Woodard (ed.), *The Cambridge Encyclopaedia of the World's Ancient Languages.* Cambridge: Cambridge University Press.

Wardman, Alan
    1979   *Rome's Debt to Greece*. London: Elek.

Wilkins, John B.
    1990   'Nation and Language in Ancient Italy: Problems of the Linguistic Evidence'. *Accordia Research Papers* 1: 53–72.

Woolf, Greg
    1996   'Monumental Writing and the Expansion of Roman Society in the Early Empire'. *Journal of Roman Studies* 86: 22–39.
    1998   *Becoming Roman: The Origins of Provincial Civilisation in Gaul*. Cambridge: Cambridge University Press.

6

Whatever Happened to Kharoṣṭhī?
The Fate of a Forgotten Indic Script

Richard Salomon

The Kharoṣṭhī Script

The Kharoṣṭhī script tends to be viewed as a minor node on the family tree of Indian scripts; a sort of stepsister to the much better known and more influential complex of scripts that are conventionally grouped under the name 'Brāhmī'. For whereas Kharoṣṭhī died out some fifteen centuries ago, leaving no descendents, Brāhmī lived on to become the parent of nearly all of the modern scripts of India as well as of many other parts of Southeast and Central Asia. Kharoṣṭhī, moreover, was always geographically circumscribed, restricted for the most part to the northwestern region of the Indian subcontinent (modern northern Pakistan and eastern Afghanistan; see Fig. 6.1), while Brāhmī predominated everywhere else in the Indian world.

Nonetheless, the Kharoṣṭhī script in its time was considerably more widespread and influential than is usually realized, and had the winds of history blown in different directions at certain critical junctures, Kharoṣṭhī might well have had a much happier fate. I refer here in particular to the period around the first two centuries AD, when the northwestern region in question, known in traditional geography as Gandhāra, was the centre of political power in northern India under a series of dynasties founded by Greek, Scythian, Parthian, and other invaders from the west, with their capitals at Taxila and Peshawar. Particularly under the last of these dynasties, that of the Kuṣāṇas, which in the late first and throughout most of the second century covered a vast area in modern India, Pakistan, Afghanistan, and Central Asia, the Kharoṣṭhī

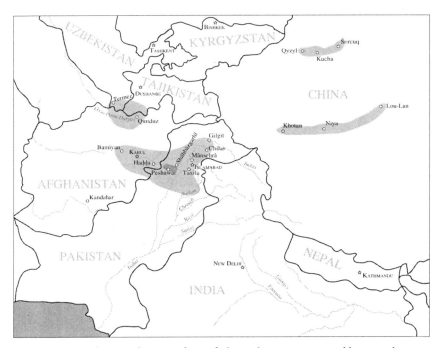

Figure 6.1   Map showing the area of use of Kharoṣṭhī script. Prepared by Timothy Lenz and Andrew Glass.

script was for a time one of the major forms of writing in Asia, with examples being found as far afield as Uzbekistan, Tajikistan, the Tarim Basin in the modern Xinjiang-Uighur Autonomous Region of China, and even Luoyang and Changan in China proper (Salomon 1998a: 43–6, 160).

This situation has become much clearer within the last decade with the discovery, not only of many new inscriptions, but also of large numbers of Buddhist manuscripts written in Kharoṣṭhī on birch bark and palm leaf, found in areas around Haḍḍa and Bamiyan in eastern Afghanistan (see summaries in Salomon 2002; 2003). This material (to be further discussed in the next section) confirms what had long been suspected on the basis of various clues, namely that Kharoṣṭhī was the medium of a Buddhist literature, probably a very voluminous one, besides serving as a bureaucratic script.

Prior to these recent discoveries, Kharoṣṭhī had been known from three main bodies of material:

1. Inscriptions, primarily Buddhist dedicatory or ritual records on stone or metal surfaces, many hundreds of which are now known (Fig. 6.2);

2. Coin legends, often in biscript combination with Greek, which provided the main keys to the decipherment of Kharoṣṭhī around the

middle of the nineteenth century (Fig. 6.3; on the history of decipherment, see Salomon 1998a: 209–15);

3. A large corpus of legal and administrative documents, of which about a thousand are now known, from the kingdom of Shanshan (鄯善) or Kroraina in the southwestern quadrant of the Tarim Basin, in modern Xinjiang (Fig. 6.4).

With the addition of the new corpus of manuscript materials, which now number in the hundreds if small fragments are included in the count, the Kharoṣṭhī script is gradually becoming better understood, both with regard to the details of its structure and to its historical and cultural role. Systemically, Kharoṣṭhī is a vocalically modified syllabary or *abugida* script according to the typology proposed by Peter Daniels (in Daniels and Bright 1996:

Figure 6.2   Tīrath footprint inscription (Swat Valley, Pakistan).

Figure 6.3 Coin of Apollodotus I with legends in Greek and Kharoṣṭhī.

4), of the type that is characteristic of Indic scripts (Table 6.1). The repertoire of the oldest form of the script consists of thirty-one consonantal symbols plus five vowels, with two types of sign for each vowel. The basic vowels are *a, i, u, e,* and *o*. Some later texts also have a vowel sign for 'vocalic' or 'syllabic' *r*. According to the *abugida* system, an unmodified consonant is understood to represent that consonant with the 'neutral' or 'inherent' vowel *a* following; for example, ꢪ = *ka*. Other post-consonantal vowels are indicated by an additional diacritic stroke added to the consonant, as in ꢪ = *ki* or ꢪ = *ku*. Vowels which are in word-initial position or are preceded by another vowel are marked by a separate set of independent vocalic characters: *a* is represented by the basic sign ꢪ, while other initial vowels are indicated by adding to this vowel base the same diacritic marks that are applied to the consonants, for instance, ꢪ *i* and ꢪ *u*.[1] (For an example of an inscriptional text in Kharoṣṭhī script, see Table 6.2.)

In these regards, Kharoṣṭhī is systemically and typologically similar, though not identical, to Brāhmī and its many derivatives. Both systems share the basic features of the inherent post-consonantal vowel *a* and the marking of other post-consonantal vowels by diacritics attached to the consonant, as well as the dual sets of independent and post-consonantal vowel graphs. They differ, however, in that in Brāhmī each of the independent vowel signs is a distinct charac-

Figure 6.4 Wedge-shaped wooden document in Kharoṣṭhī from Niya: document no. 523.

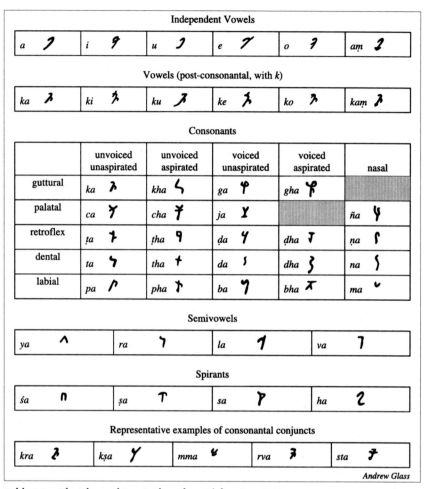

Table 6.1 The Kharoṣṭhī script based on Aśokan inscriptions.

ter (e.g. ૪ = *a*, ∴ = *i*), whereas in Kharoṣṭhī, as described above, they are variants of a single basic character. Another important difference is that Kharoṣṭhī does not distinguish vowel quantity (⁊ = *a* or *ā*; ᚦ = *ki* or *kī*), while Brāhmī does (૪ = *a* v. ⊦ = *ā*; ⨍ = *ki* v. ⨍ = *kī*).

Brāhmī and Kharoṣṭhī also share the system of consonantal conjuncts or ligatures used to indicate consonant clusters in the graphic syllable types CCV (for example ჳ = *rva*), although they differ in the exact manner of formation of such conjuncts (see further Salomon 1998a: 48–9). They also differ with regard to their direction of writing: right to left for Kharoṣṭhī; left to right for Brāhmī.

Kharoṣṭhī script is first attested in the northwestern versions of the rock edicts of King Aśoka, at Shāhbāzgaṛhī and Mānsehra in the Northwest Frontier

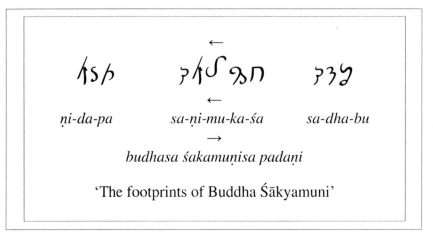

←

𝄐 ni-da-pa   sa-ni-mu-ka-śa   sa-dha-bu

←

→

budhasa śakamuṇisa padaṇi

'The footprints of Buddha Śākyamuni'

Table 6.2   The Tīrath Kharoṣṭhī inscription (compare Figure 6.2).

Province of Pakistan, which date from around the middle of the third century BC. However, most authorities agree that Kharoṣṭhī is likely to have existed before the time of Aśoka, perhaps originating as early as the fourth or even the fifth century BC, and many though not all specialists now consider it likely that Kharoṣṭhī predated Brāhmī.[2] It is also generally agreed that Kharoṣṭhī came into being as an adaptation to an Indian language of the Aramaic script, which had been used in northwestern India when that area was part of the Achaemenid Empire, and which was still in use there at the time of Aśoka (Salomon 1998a: 107).

From the very beginning, Kharoṣṭhī was intimately associated with the local Middle Indo-Aryan vernacular language of the northwest, generally known as Gāndhārī, that is, the language of Gandhāra. This language has been revealed by the recent manuscript discoveries to have been, in its time, one of the major literary languages of the Buddhist tradition. Later in its history, however, Kharoṣṭhī was also sometimes used to represent Sanskrit, in Central Asia as well as, probably, in its Indian homeland (Salomon 1998b: 133–5). Although the number of Kharoṣṭhī-Sanskrit documents is still small, they may well represent the surviving remnants of a once-large literature of this type. This shows that, contrary to what had previously been assumed, Kharoṣṭhī script was capable, with a few modifications and adaptations such as the introduction of a long vowel indicator, of representing Sanskrit adequately, and that it could in theory have fulfilled the role of a pan-Indian script that, as the accidents of history had it, actually fell to Brāhmī and its derivatives.

Since its first attested appearance in the third century BC, Kharoṣṭhī remained the dominant script of the northwest for the next four to five centuries. But around the first half of the third century AD it fell out of use, apparently quite suddenly, in its northwestern homeland, although it continued to be employed in some outlying areas for a few more centuries. The question of how and why Kharoṣṭhī declined, apparently so rapidly and completely, is the principal topic of this chapter.

The Decline and Disappearance of Kharoṣṭhī Script

Our best sources of evidence for the date of the disappearance of Kharoṣṭhī are dated Buddhist inscriptions from northwestern India. The chronology of this material, however, is by no means simple, mainly because at least three different chronological systems were in use simultaneously, and more often than not the inscriptions do not specify to which system their date refers. Moreover, the absolute chronological values of these eras are subject to various degrees of doubt. However, the recent discovery of an inscription which provides a value for the oldest of these eras, namely the Indo-Greek era of 186/185 BC (Salomon 2005), enables us to fix, with much greater precision and certainty than before, the absolute dates of some of the latest Kharoṣṭhī inscriptions.

The highest known date in a Kharoṣṭhī inscription is probably the year 399 in the Skārah Ḍherī image inscription (Konow 1929: no. LX). It is generally agreed that this and a few other Kharoṣṭhī inscriptions dated in years in the two- and three-hundreds are to be attributed to the oldest of the eras in question, namely the newly identified Indo-Greek era of 186/185 BC. This would yield a date of about AD 213 for the inscription in question. However, the reading and interpretation of this date[3] are difficult and by no means certain. Other than this questionable one, the highest definite date in a Kharoṣṭhī inscription is the year 384 in the Hashtnagar pedestal inscription (Konow 1929: no. LIII), which according to the Indo-Greek era would correspond to AD 198; and the next latest inscriptional date is 359, or AD 173, in the Jamālgaṛhī stone inscription (Konow 1929: no. XLV).

Another relatively late date is the year 89 of the Mamāne Ḍherī pedestal inscription, which according to Konow (1929: no. LXXXVIII) can be attributed to the era of Kaniṣka on the grounds of its late palaeography. The date of the commencement of the era of Kaniṣka is still a highly controversial issue, but a consensus seems to be emerging in favour of the first half of the second century, perhaps in or around AD 127 (Falk 2001). If this is correct, and if the year 89 of the Mamāne Ḍherī inscription is in fact a Kaniṣka-era date, it would correspond to sometime early in the third century AD, possibly about AD 216. Other than the uncertain Mamāne Ḍherī date, the latest definite Kaniṣka-era year in a Kharoṣṭhī inscription is 51 in the Wardak inscription (Konow 1929: no. LXXXVI), which would correspond to the second half of the second century, perhaps c. AD 178.[4]

Thus, to judge from the epigraphic record, the Kharoṣṭhī script seems to have fallen out of use quite abruptly sometime around the early third century AD, at least in its Indian homeland and in adjoining regions of Afghanistan.[5] The newly discovered manuscript material agrees with, or at least does not contradict, this picture. Among the three large groups of manuscripts in Kharoṣṭhī that have been discovered within the last decade, the oldest seems to be the British Library collection, which can be dated, mainly on the basis of historical references in the manuscripts and in associated inscriptions, to about the first half of the first century AD, although a later date in the second half of the first century, or possibly even in the early second century is not ruled out (Salomon 1999: 141–55).

The second group of manuscripts, namely the Senior scrolls, is more firmly and precisely datable on the basis of an inscription dated in the year 12, attributable to the Kaniṣka era, on the pot in which the scrolls were found. Although, as noted above, the exact date of Kaniṣka is uncertain, this means that the pot itself dates from the first half of the second century, and the manuscripts contained in it are probably contemporary with it, or slightly but not very much earlier (Salomon 2003: 74–8).

This dating for the Senior scrolls is consistent with the results of radiocarbon tests which have been carried out on two fragments from this collection (details in Allon *et al.* 2006). These tests have yielded date ranges (2σ) of AD 129–263 (74.5% probability) or AD 273–339 (25.5%) for the first fragment, and AD 81–244 (98.5%) or AD 305–315 (1.5%) for the second. Although these ranges are too broad to provide precise answers, the most probable date ranges for the two fragments, namely AD 129–263 and AD 81–244, are consistent both with the proposed dating of the Senior scrolls on epigraphic grounds and with the estimated date of the disappearance of Kharoṣṭhī script in general.

The third large group of Kharoṣṭhī manuscripts, which comprises part of the Martin Schøyen collection in Oslo, does not have any epigraphic or historical correlations like those of the British Library and Senior collections, but approximate dates can be attributed to them on the basis of their palaeographic and linguistic features. In these respects the Schøyen Kharoṣṭhī manuscripts are distinctly later than the British Library and Senior groups. The language of many of the fragments is strongly Sanskritized, which we know from inscriptions to be a characteristic of the later phase of Gāndhārī, appearing from the time of Kaniṣka onwards. Their script is similarly advanced, showing innovative letter forms and ligatures that are clearly later developments, many of them unknown from other Kharoṣṭhī inscriptions or manuscripts. We can therefore safely conclude that the Schøyen Kharoṣṭhī manuscripts represent the late phase of Kharoṣṭhī script, and that they should date, at the earliest, from the second century AD, and could be later than this, perhaps from the third century (Allon and Salomon 2000: 266–7).

This palaeographic and linguistic estimate for the dating of the Schøyen Kharoṣṭhī manuscripts is also supported by the results of radiocarbon tests performed on three fragments. The 2σ date ranges for these three fragments are AD 72–245; AD 34–35 (0.3% probability) or AD 53–234 (99.7%); and AD 140–153 (1.3%), AD 168–194 (2.9%) or AD 210–417 (95.8%). As in the case of the Senior scrolls, these ranges are too wide to give specific answers, but once again the most likely dates for each fragment, namely AD 72–245, AD 53–234, and AD 210–417, all fall within the predicted period of use of Kharoṣṭhī script. Particularly interesting is the last result, AD 210–417, which, assuming that it is accurate, confirms that Kharoṣṭhī was still in use in the early third century. This range also leaves open the possibility that Kharoṣṭhī was still being used in the fourth century or even later, but in light of the epigraphic and other evidence that is currently available, this seems unlikely. In any case, it is hoped that in the future further radiocarbon tests can be carried out on other Kharoṣṭhī manuscripts, which may provide more precise dates for late Kharoṣṭhī documents.

The Schøyen Kharoṣṭhī fragments, however, comprise only a small portion of a very large group of manuscripts found at or near Bamiyan, Afghanistan, the majority of which are written in local varieties of Brāhmī script and its derivatives. The Brāhmī manuscripts are datable, on palaeographical grounds, to a period ranging from about the second (Braarvig 2002: 249) to the seventh centuries AD. This does not mean that Brāhmī replaced Kharoṣṭhī as the literary script at Bamiyan during the second century, but rather that there was a transitional period, perhaps a lengthy one, during which Kharoṣṭhī and Brāhmī were in use side by side. This is supported, not only by the radiocarbon dates of the Kharoṣṭhī manuscripts,[6] but also by the evidence of extensive biscript activity in the Kharoṣṭhī throughout its history (see 'The Death of Kharoṣṭhī and the Principles of Script Disappearance' below), as well as by the fact that Brāhmī manuscripts of the earliest period among the Schøyen collection are quite few in number, suggesting that Brāhmī was not the exclusive or even the dominant script at that time.

Thus the material from Gandhāra proper and from neighbouring regions of Afghanistan points clearly towards some time around the early third century AD for the disappearance of Kharoṣṭhī script. The situation is quite different, however, when we look further afield, to the more distant regions where Kharoṣṭhī had been established, presumably as a result of the conquests or influence of the Kuṣāṇa Empire. There, Kharoṣṭhī script remained in use for at least a century more, and quite possibly much longer. The clearest and most copious evidence of this is the enormous corpus of secular documents from Shanshan or Kroraina (mentioned above in 'The Kharoṣṭhī Script'), most of which can be fairly securely dated to the latter half of the third century and the early part of the fourth. Excavations at Kara-tepe and Fayaz-tepe near Termez in southern Uzbekistan have yielded numerous Kharoṣṭhī inscriptions as well as biscripts (Kharoṣṭhī/Brāhmī) and triscripts (Kharoṣṭhī/Brāhmī/Bactrian) on pottery which according to their editor (Vertogradova 1995: 28) may be dated as late as the fifth century AD. This dating however seems improbably late, and other than palaeographic estimate there are no firm grounds for dating the Termez inscriptions, although they could conceivably be as late as the third century. Finally, the oasis cities on the northern rim of the Tarim Basin in Xinjiang have yielded some biscript documents in Brāhmī (in Tocharian language) and late local varieties of Kharoṣṭhī. Although these scripts and documents are as yet poorly understand and mostly unpublished,[7] some of them have been ascribed a date possibly as late as the seventh century (Bailey 1950: 121).

Causes of the Disappearance of Kharoṣṭhī Script

Despite its survival in outlying regions, all indications are that in its original homeland the Kharoṣṭhī script fell out of use, apparently quite abruptly, sometime in or soon after the early third century AD. The evidence of dated inscriptions shows that it was definitely still in use at the end of the second century, and apparently also in the early third. The manuscripts point in the same direction, providing corroboration of the general timeframe but no greater precision. The question then becomes: What political, cultural, or other forces were at work around this period that might have led to the rapid disappearance of Kharoṣṭhī? The obvious—and I think probably correct—answer is that this is just about the time when the Kuṣāṇa Empire underwent a rapid decline, losing its position as a vast intraregional empire and contracting into a set of small local kingdoms.

The history and chronology of the later Kuṣāṇa period is highly problematic, but it is fairly clear that the decline of the Kuṣāṇas began soon after the reign of Huviṣka, the successor of the great Kaniṣka. Huviṣka's latest inscriptional date (in a Brāhmī inscription) is the year 60 of Kaniṣka's era, which most likely corresponds to a date late in the second century, perhaps about AD 187. From external sources, principally the Arab historian Ṭabarī and the Naqsh-i-rustam inscription of the Sassanian king Shāpūr I, it appears that Ardashīr I, founder of the Sassanian dynasty, conquered the territories of the old Kuṣāṇa Empire soon after AD 225 (Bivar 1983: 203). Thus the various indications of the time of the collapse of the Kuṣāṇa Empire, uncertain though they are, show a good correlation with the dates of the latest Kharoṣṭhī inscriptions.

From this time on, for many centuries, the northwest ceased to be the politically dominant region of the Indian subcontinent, while the kingdoms of the Gangetic region, where Brāhmī-based scripts had always been used, began to grow in power and extent, eventually to be consolidated into the great pan-north-Indian Gupta dynasty in the fourth century. But the history of north India in the third and early fourth centuries AD is very much a dark period during which dedicatory and donative inscriptions, usually our main source of historical information in the Indian world, suddenly become very scarce. This development presumably reflects an economic decline that went hand in hand with the prevailing political disorder, so that the sources of patronage for the donations which such inscriptions recorded dried up. This is probably why the epigraphic record in the northwestern region with which we are primarily concerned here is virtually a blank after the early third century, which has the unfortunate effect of obscuring the exact date of the disappearance of Kharoṣṭhī. But the evidence of the Schøyen manuscripts, as discussed in 'The Decline and Disappearance of the Kharoṣṭhī Script', above, tends to confirm that Kharoṣṭhī did in fact decline, if not disappear entirely, early in the third century, and the circumstantial evidence argues compellingly that this development must have been linked to the collapse of the Kuṣāṇa Empire. In any case, when substantial numbers of inscriptions do begin to come to light again in the northwest—not until about the fourth or even fifth centuries AD—they are, without exception, in Brāhmī-derived scripts.

Kharoṣṭhī's survival for some time longer, perhaps as much as several centuries, in areas far to the north and northeast of its original territories, is presumably to be explained on the grounds of their remoteness and isolation from the central area, and to the cultural conservatism that is often characteristic of frontier areas. As such, it does not disprove the hypothesis that the decline of the Kharoṣṭhī in its homeland was closely connected with, if not directly caused by, the collapse of the Kuṣāṇa dynasty.

The Death of Kharoṣṭhī and the Principles of Script Disappearance

Most of the examples of the obsolescence or disappearance of scripts discussed in Houston *et al.* (2003) can be divided into two types: those caused by what I propose to call 'civilizational shifts', in which a radically different culture is adopted or imposed, as in the case of the Egyptian and cuneiform scripts, and those which were conditioned by a general collapse of the society which used them, as in the case of Mayan, Cretan Linear B, and the Indus Valley script (Houston *et al.* 2003: 461, 467). Cases of script disappearance that are directly attributable to dynastic changes or declines are generally less common and less well-attested; among the few examples mentioned there are Hieroglyphic Luwian, the Mormon Deseret alphabet, and, most prominently, Kharoṣṭhī (Houston *et al.* 2003: 432, 467), to which may also be added Old Persian.

It was presumably the loss of Kharoṣṭhī's niche as the bureaucratic script of the Kuṣāṇa Empire that was the principal factor behind its demise in the Gandhāran heartland around the beginning of the third century AD. Still, it might seem surprising that its demise was apparently—as far as we can tell from the admittedly rather opaque evidence—so rapid and so complete. One might expect Kharoṣṭhī to have remained in use in its homeland, at least as a subsidiary script, even for some time after it ceased to be the script of officialdom. And yet this seems not to have happened, or at least, if it did happen, it was only to a minimal degree.[8]

If this rapid and nearly total disappearance of Kharoṣṭhī is not an illusion caused by the paucity of evidence for the period in question—and this cannot be ruled out—we need to seek an explanation for the phenomenon. Here, I would point out that the attitudes towards scripts which prevailed in the ancient Indian world were quite different from those of the ancient (and modern world) in general. The 'identification of writing with language, religion and civilization' that is cited by Houston *et al.* (2003: 450) in connection with Egyptian writing and culture, and which could equally well be applied to the other script domains discussed in their article, was evidently not so powerful a force in the traditional Indian world. For although language and religion certainly were primary determinants of identity there, script was apparently not nearly so important in this regard. One index of this fact is that the classical and elite languages in traditional India were typically not linked to single scripts, so that, for example, Sanskrit could (and still can) be written in any number of regional scripts, such as Bengali, Oriya, Grantha (Tamil), Malayalam, and many others, besides the north Indian Devanāgarī script which is usually associated with it. Similarly, Pāli can be written in Sinhalese, Thai, Burmese, Khmer, or other scripts, according to the writer's own education and background. Thus although high-caste Hindus feel a strong sense of identity with the Sanskrit language, and although followers of Theravāda Buddhism in South and Southeast Asia revere the Pāli language, the vehicle for the *writing* of these languages is only secondarily, if at all, an article of cultural identity. In traditional India it was oral tradition that tended to be most highly valued, while written documents, though often also revered, tended to be perceived as secondary to the spoken word; writing was typically felt to be the reflection of language, not its reality or essence.

In light of this cultural background, it is easier to see how the substitution of Brāhmī for Kharoṣṭhī, conditioned by political developments, could have taken place so quickly and thoroughly. We have no reason to think that the Kharoṣṭhī script was a prominent object of cultural identity among the people of the northwest, and the shift may have been merely a practical one: it was not at all a 'civilizational' change, like the replacement of the Egyptian scripts by the Greek alphabet, but merely an adjustment. The overall systemic similarity between the two scripts, despite superficial differences such as the direction of writing, would have made it quite easy for scribes accustomed to writing Kharoṣṭhī to learn Brāhmī—if indeed they did not already know it. For in fact we have extensive evidence of biscript usages throughout the history of Kharoṣṭhī, manifested in numerous bilingual inscriptions, coins, and seals (Salomon 1998a: 70–1). Among the newly discovered manuscript collections too, we find similar indications that scribes and scholars were comfortable with both scripts; the Schøyen collection consists of an extensive mixture of fragments, some of them apparently contemporary, in both scripts, while the British Library collection of Kharoṣṭhī manuscripts also contains one scroll written in Brāhmī.[9]

As far as we can reconstruct it from the documents which happen to have survived, the Kharoṣṭhī script community in the northwestern borderlands of the Indian subcontinent in the late second century AD seems to have consisted primarily of government bureaucrats on the one hand and Buddhist monastic scholars on the other. There must also have been a contingent of ordinary citizens—private clerks, businessmen, and the like—who used Kharoṣṭhī for everyday documents. Although none of their ephemera have survived, their existence is attested by numerous graffiti inscriptions in Kharoṣṭhī (and Brāhmī) left by merchants along the trade routes of northern Pakistan (e.g. Neelis 2000 with references, esp. 923). Many if not most members of this script community would have been at least familiar with, and perhaps even able to read and write, the contemporary forms of north Indian Brāhmī script (Neelis 2000: 906). We cannot know for sure whether they felt the Kharoṣṭhī script to be an element of their cultural or personal identity, but there is no evidence of this, and from what we know of the typical Indian attitudes toward script and writing, it is more likely that they did not. When the ruling Kuṣāṇa dynasty, which used Kharoṣṭhī as its local administrative script, collapsed and Brāhmī-using polities based further to the east become dominant in the region, the Kharoṣṭhī script community presumably found it easy to adopt Brāhmī—although, admittedly, we have virtually no direct evidence of the historical situation at this critical period.

Therefore, unlike the cases of the three major script groups discussed by Houston *et al.* (2003), namely Egyptian, cuneiform, and Mayan, the disappearance of Kharoṣṭhī was probably not a result of the decline of a script community as such. We have no reason to think that the scribes and scholars who used Kharoṣṭhī ceased to exist as a community; rather, they seem to have adapted, easily and quickly, to a new practical reality. The change from Kharoṣṭhī to Brāhmī involved no traumatic or fundamental shift in culture, and the types, contents, and cultural orientations of the documents in the two scripts from around the period in question are quite similar. The change in script was primarily one of outward form, conditioned and facilitated by the casual attitude toward script that prevailed in ancient India.

This is not to say, however, that other explanations of the disappearance of Kharoṣṭhī should be ruled out entirely. One could, for example, posit a scenario in which the abandonment of Kharoṣṭhī was caused or at least promoted by its association with rulers of non-Indian origins. But this is not likely, since we know from a great many dedicatory inscriptions that the Kharoṣṭhī script community was patronized by, and to a large extent ethnically affiliated with, these non-Indian elites, so that it would hardly be inclined to have viewed them negatively.

It could be countered that some Buddhists, at least, had a complex and ambi—valent attitude towards the 'foreign' dynasts of the late BC—early AD period. Although some of them, such as the Indo-Greek Menander and the Kuṣāṇa Kaniṣka, are revered as sympathizers or patrons in later Buddhist literature, elsewhere in Buddhist tradition one can find negative descriptions of the Greek, Scythian, and Parthian kings of the northwest as 'enemies of the Dharma' (Nattier 1991: 154–7). In light of this one might speculate that at least some members of the Buddhist community felt that Kharoṣṭhī was somehow tainted. But in fact I know of no direct statement or implication, anywhere in Buddhist tradition, that Kharoṣṭhī script was ever viewed in a negative light.

Thus there is simply no evidence to show that Kharoṣṭhī was rejected on grounds of negative cultural connotations. Therefore it seems more reasonable to revert to the explanation proposed above, namely that the death of the Kharoṣṭhī script was no more than an incidental artefact of shifting centres of power in the Indian world.

Notes

1. Thus the basic independent vowel *a* is formally (and also historically, being derived from the Aramaic *alif*) a consonant, but practically and linguistically, with regard to the Gāndhārī language, a vowel.

2. See the discussion of the various views on this topic, especially those of Falk, Fussman, and von Hinüber, in Salomon 1995: 273–5, 278.

3. *Vaṣ(*e) ek[u]na[ca]duśatimae*, 'in the four-hundredth-less-one year', according to Konow (1929: 127).

4. A possible complication arises in connection with the 'theory of omitted hundreds', according to which some inscriptions with dates in the era of Kaniṣka under 100 may actually represent years of the second century of the era. If this is correct, some Kharoṣṭhī inscriptions might have to be dated a full century later than is usually thought, which would have a drastic effect on the date of the disappearance of the script. However, as pointed out in Fussman (1987: 72 and 84 n. 24), it is unlikely that any of the Kaniṣka-era dates in Kharoṣṭhī inscriptions are really 'omitted hundred' dates.

5. One possible exception to this pattern is the six Kharoṣṭhī inscriptions on a stūpa at Jaulian (one of the sites of the Taxila complex in northern Pakistan), which on archaeological and art-historical grounds is thought to date from as late as the fifth century AD. However, Konow comments that '[i]t is perhaps unsafe to infer too much from the occurrence of Kharoshthī votive inscriptions in the beginning of the fifth century' (1929: 92), since 'such ex-voto inscriptions might have been written in Kharoshthī even after that alphabet had ceased to be the common one in Taxila, in imitation of older inscriptions of the same kind [...]. It is even conceivable that some of the inscriptions are copies of older ones, executed when the old images and decorations were restored or repaired' (1929: 93). Konow further notes (1929: 93) that the apparently archaizing use of Kharoṣṭhī in the Jaulian inscriptions reflected a sense that 'Kharoshthī was more efficacious than Brāhmī in such inscriptions, which were more or less some kind of charms'. If his speculation is correct, this would imply that Kharoṣṭhī retained a vestigial function as a 'display script', as did hieroglyphic

Egyptian (Houston *et al.* 2003: 444–5), or as a cultic icon as in the case of the Cypriot syllabary (Houston *et al.* 2003: 434).

6. To date no radiocarbon tests have been reported for the Brāhmī fragments in the Schøyen collection.

7. For an important recent exception, see Schmidt 2001. Schmidt (2001: 13) however declines to attribute a date to the specimens that he has published.

8. See, for example, the comments in note 5 above on the anomalous and apparently isolated example of the Jaulian Kharoṣṭhī inscriptions.

9. Salomon 1998a: 39. The description there of the manuscript in question as a medical text has subsequently proven to be incorrect. It is rather a Buddhist text of some sort, as yet unidentified.

References

Allon, Mark, and Richard Salomon
  2000 'Fragments of a Gāndhārī Version of the Mahāparinirvāṇa-sūtra in the Schøyen Collection'. In Jens Braarvig (ed.), *Buddhist Manuscripts in the Schøyen Collection* I. Manuscripts in the Schøyen Collection I. Oslo: Hermes Publishing, 243–73.

Allon, Mark, Richard Salomon, Geraldine Jacobsen, and Ugo Zoppi
  2006 'Radiocarbon Dating of Kharoṣṭhī Fragments from the Schøyen and Senior Manuscript Collections'. In Jens Braarvig (ed.), *Buddhist Manuscripts in the Schøyen Collection* III. Oslo: Hermes Publishing, 279–91.

Bailey, H. W.
  1950 'A Problem of the Kharoṣṭhī Script'. In D.W. Thomas (ed.), *Essays and Studies Presented to Stanley Arthur Cook.* London: Taylor's Foreign Press, 121–3.

Bivar, A. D. H.
  1983 'The History of Eastern Iran'. In Ehsan Yarshater (ed.), *The Cambridge History of Iran* III.1: *The Seleucid, Parthian and Sasanian Periods.* Cambridge: Cambridge University Press, 181–231 (chapter 5).

Braarvig, Jens
  2002 *Buddhist Manuscripts in the Schøyen Collection* II. Manuscripts in the Schøyen Collection III. Oslo: Hermes Publishing.

Daniels, Peter T., and William Bright (eds)
  1996 *The World's Writing Systems.* New York: Oxford University Press.

Falk, Harry
  2001 'The *Yuga* of Sphujiddhvaja and the Era of the Kuṣāṇas'. *Silk Road Art and Archaeology* 7: 121–36.

Fussman, Gérard
  1987 'Numismatic and Epigraphic Evidence for the Chronology of Early Gandharan

Art'. In Marianne Yaldiz and Wibke Lobo (eds), *Investigating Indian Art: Proceedings of a Symposium on the Development of Early Buddhist and Hindu Iconography held at the Museum of Indian Art Berlin in May 1986.* Berlin: Museum für Indische Kunst, 67–88.

Houston, Stephen, John Baines, and Jerrold Cooper
    2003   'Last Writing: Script Obsolescence in Egypt, Mesopotamia, and Mesoamerica'. *Comparative Studies in Society and History* 45: 430–79.

Konow, Sten
    1929   *Kharoṣṭhī Inscriptions with the Exception of Those of Aśoka.* Corpus Inscriptionum Indicarum 2.1. Calcutta: Government of India, Central Publication Branch.

Nattier, Jan
    1991   *Once Upon a Future Time: Studies in a Buddhist Prophecy of Decline.* Nanzan Studies in Asian Religions 1. Berkeley, CA: Asian Humanities Press.

Neelis, Jason
    2000   'Kharoṣṭhī and Brāhmī Inscriptions from Hunza-Haldeikish: Sources for the Study of Long-Distance Trade and Transmission of Buddhism'. In Maurizio Taddei and Giuseppe De Marco (eds), *South Asian Archaeology 1997: Proceedings of the Fourteenth International Conference of the European Association of South Asian Archaeologists.* Serie Orientale Roma 90. Rome: Istituto Italiano per l'Africa et l'Oriente 2: 903–23.

Salomon, Richard
    1995   'On the Origin of the Early Indian Scripts'. *Journal of the American Oriental Society* 115: 271–9.
    1998a   *Indian Epigraphy: A Guide to the Study of Inscriptions in Sanskrit, Prakrit, and the Other Indo-Aryan Languages.* South Asia Research. New York: Oxford University Press.
    1998b   'Kharoṣṭhī Manuscript Fragments in the Pelliot Collection, Bibliothèque nationale de France'. *Bulletin d'Études Indiennes* 16: 123–60.
    1999   *Ancient Buddhist Scrolls from Gandhāra: The British Library Kharoṣṭhī Fragments.* Seattle: University of Washington Press; London: British Library.
    2002   'Gāndhārī and the Other Indo-Aryan Languages in Light of Newly-discovered Kharoṣṭhī Manuscripts'. In Nicholas Sims-Williams (ed.), *Indo-Iranian Languages and Peoples* [H. W. Bailey Centennial Volume]. *Proceedings of the British Academy* 116. Oxford: Oxford University Press, 119–34.
    2003   'The Senior Manuscripts: A Second Collection of Gandhāran Buddhist Scrolls'. *Journal of the American Oriental Society* 123: 73–92.
    2005   'The Indo-Greek Era of 186/5 BC in a Buddhist Reliquary Inscription'. In Osmund Bopearachchi and Marie-Françoise Boussac (eds), *Afghanistan: Ancien Carrefour entre l'Est et l'Ouest.* Indicopleustoi: Archaeologies of the Indian Ocean 3. Turnhout: Brepols, 359–401.

Schmidt, Klaus T.
    2001   'Entzifferung verschollener Schriften und Sprachen dargestellt am Beispiel der Kučā-Kharoṣṭhī Typ B und des Kučā-Prākrits'. *Göttinger Beiträge zur Asienforschung* 1: 7–27.

Tanabe, Katsumi
   1993   *Silk Road Coins in the Hiryama Collection.* Kamakura: Institute of Silk Road Studies.
Vertogradova, V. V.
   1995   *Indijskaja Epigrafika iz Kara-tepe v Starom Termeze: Problemy Dešifrovki i Interpretacii.* Moscow: Vostočnaja Literatura.

7

On the Demise of Egyptian Writing:
Working with a Problematic Source Basis

Martin Andreas Stadler

For the study of the end of Egyptian writing systems, demotic is of special relevance, because Egyptian texts continued to be notated in demotic long after
other Egyptian scripts were abandoned ('Demotic' refers to the Egyptian language of 650 BC onwards and 'demotic' to the script). The demotic Philae graffiti are the latest of all Egyptian inscriptions. Therefore the focus should lie on
demotic, which underwent dramatic changes from being originally an everyday
script to one that became perfectly acceptable for religious texts. However, the
case of hieroglyphic and its demise is also revealing and should be compared to
the end of demotic. I therefore discuss the following topics: After summarizing
the models that Egyptologists have proposed for interpreting the disappearance
of Egyptian scripts and culture, I discuss briefly the ups and downs of Egyptian
writing competence throughout Egyptian history. I then ask whether available sources and data allow us to draw definite conclusions. I explore in some
detail the impact of increasing complexity in hieroglyphic temple inscriptions
in the Ptolemaic and Roman periods in the wider context of the development of
intellectual trends in that epoch. Finally, I reflect on whether demotic followed
the same trajectory as hieroglyphic when it applied so-called unetymological or
phonetic writings, which turned demotic into a script of restricted knowledge.

    At the outset I should address one point of terminology. To speak of 'Egyp-
tian writing' is vague because it does not specify to which script I refer: writing
has never ceased in Egypt since late predynastic times, when the first hieroglyphs are found in Egypt (Dreyer 1998; cf. Breyer 2002; Morenz 2004a), but the
vernacular Egyptian scripts (for the triscript system in Egypt see Houston *et*

al. 2003: 440)—were replaced by the Greek alphabet writing Coptic and by the Arabic script in Islamic times; and all texts notated in Coptic and Arabic within the geographical area of Egypt may be called 'Egyptian writing(s)'. However, as an Egyptologist I use 'Egyptian writing', 'Egyptian script', or the like, for purposes of convenience, to refer to the indigenous scripts. This usage also encompasses the triscript system, which underwent changes in its historical development as described by John Baines (Houston *et al.* 2003: 439–42), and should be perceived as a unity, since certain basic features are shared by hieroglyphs, hieratic, and demotic. All Egyptian scripts (hieroglyphic, hieratic, and demotic) use a complex combination of one, two, and three consonant signs, ideograms, and determinatives; all are interrelated, for all are more or less descendants of hieroglyphs.

Script and Civilization in Roman Egypt:
A Review of Previous Research

The article by Houston *et al.* (2003) is not the only indicator of a reawakened scholarly interest in the end of Egyptian writing. Research on Roman Egypt is also increasing and beginning to reach the general public (e.g. Lembke 2004, including a descriptive chapter on writing and administration by Günter Vittmann, 85–98). At about the same time, and independently from Houston *et al.*, Eugene Cruz-Uribe (2002) published a study on the end of demotic in Philae in which he uses the word 'death', which Houston *et al.* found inadequate to describe script obsolescence because of its biological metaphor. Contrary to the Egyptological section in Houston *et al.* 2003, which prudently concentrates on describing phenomena pertaining to the end of Egyptian writing rather than offering a full explanation, Cruz-Uribe explores the possibility of identifying the causes of the end of demotic in Philae. He is able to do this by focusing on a single script (demotic) and a single place (Philae). Of course the island of Philae is of particular interest, because the latest demotic inscriptions, that is, the latest Egyptian writings, consist of graffiti in its temple of Isis. Cruz-Uribe identifies various factors concerning the death of demotic there, of which he believes the most important to be the role of the Nubian peoples and the idea of the 'state' in Nubia. He emphasizes how sacred the island was to the Nubians who were virtually the last worshippers of Isis, whereas Egypt had mostly converted to Christianity. The absence of Nubian support for the island, together with the imperial intervention in AD 536, put an end to the Isis cult.

Consideration of the end of Egyptian writing always touches upon the quest for the causes of the demise of ancient Egyptian civilization in general. Some scholars tend to blame the loss of state support for the temples and their priesthood, coupled with a shift from the vernacular language to Greek as the language of administration already in the Ptolemaic period. The former measure deprived the population of the means of expressing themselves in their traditional cult, while the latter left the Egyptians without the possibility of undertaking legal actions in their own language. This process would have been reinforced by the introduction of Coptic, which Roger Bagnall (1993: 235–40, 261–8) sees as a deliberate invention for the translation of the Bible. All three factors, however, are problematic. The focus on the financial state support for the temples disregards the private aspect of Egyptian religion and the local level, that is, private worship and local support for the temples. Greek was not the only language used for higher- and middle-level administration during the Ptolemaic period: demotic documents had full legal validity if officially registered (Lewis 1993). The role of demotic in the Roman period is not yet fully understood—a point to which I return in more detail below. Finally, Coptic could not be seen as an invented language. Bagnall's incorrect statement (1993: 238) is based on a misunderstanding of an article by Quaegebeur (1982: 132), who was writing about the invention of the Coptic script, not language. Demotic—a term that does not mean just a script, but also the stage of the Egyptian language from 650 BC until the fifth century AD—shows a clear development from a proto-demotic idiom in the latest phase of Late Egyptian (Quack 1995) to an idiom very close to Coptic (Johnson 1976: 2). Thus we must assume a gradual progression from Demotic to Coptic, rather than the introduction of an invented Esperanto-like language.

Both Frankfurter (1998: 249–50) and Bagnall (1993: 237–8) stress the linguistic isolation of demotic texts and the social isolation of those who used the script, the priests. Frankfurter's theory of Greek as a widely used conversational language already in the Ptolemaic period must be modified if not rejected, as he illustrates it with the *Oracle*, or rather *Apology of the Potter*, which he interprets as 'militantly anti-Greek yet composed in Greek'. The anti-Greekness of the text, however, is not so clear and indeed questionable, while the Greek texts moreover claim to be translations from an Egyptian original (Koenen 2002: esp. 172–83). It is not unlikely that an Egyptian, demotic version will come to light, as it did for *Nectanebo's Dream* (Gauger 2002; Ryholt 2002), another literary text that earlier scholars had seen as nationalist propaganda, but for which more differentiated interpretations have recently been proposed (Blasius and Schipper 2002). This is not the place to discuss in depth the intentions and direct relationship of the Greek and demotic versions of *Nectanebo's Dream*, still less the so-called apocalyptic and prophetic texts in general, but it cannot be overstressed that our knowledge of demotic literature is still very imperfect and any new fragment that is published can shatter current views. Kim Ryholt, for instance, advocates a much more direct relationship between the demotic and the Greek versions of *Nectanebo's Dream* than Jörg-D. Gauger does. Ryholt (2002: 232) even argues that the newly discovered demotic fragments support the postulation of an Egyptian original of the *Apology of the Potter*, because the two texts are very similar. Finally, it is not the case that demotic texts of the Roman period were 'in a state of sacred isolation from common tongue that was steeped in Greek loanwords' (Frankfurter 1998: 249). This implication that demotic was unable to adjust to the current language is problematic, because the demotic magical papyri of the second or third centuries AD (Fig. 7.1) exhibit a mixture of Greek and demotic spells, with Greek transcribed into demotic and vice versa (Johnson 1986; Dieleman 2005). Furthermore, these texts contain a considerable number of Greek words, names of demons, nouns, and even verbal forms which are transcribed into demotic (Quack 2004).

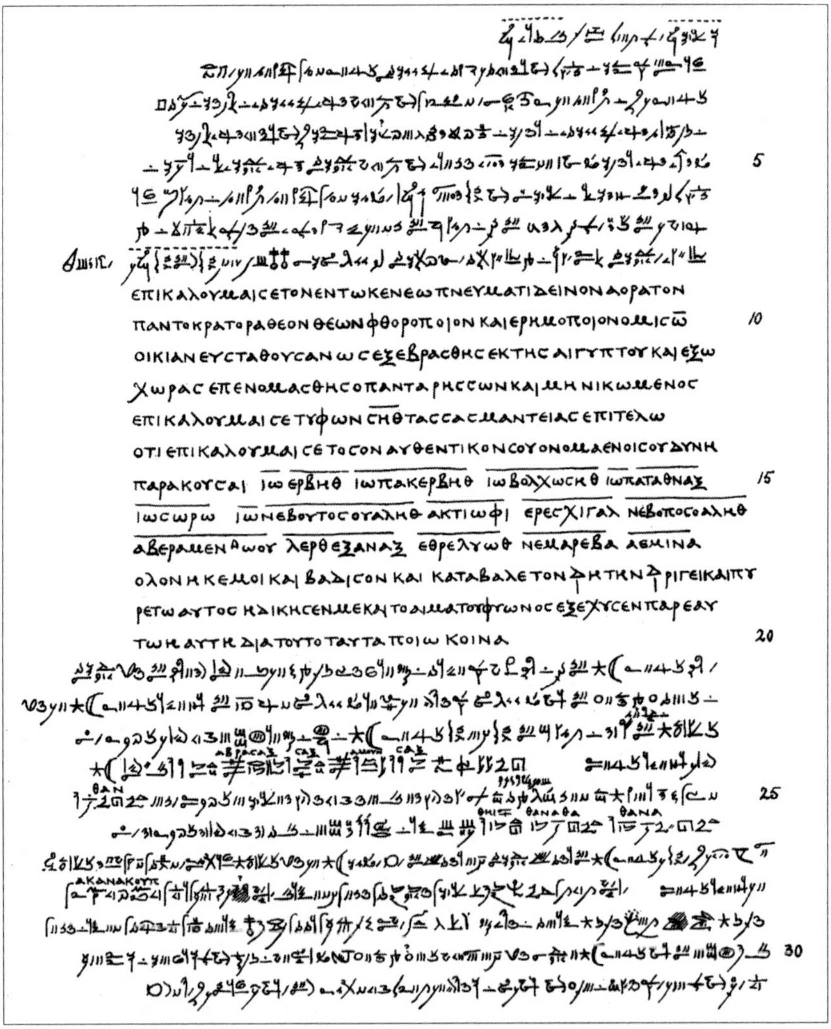

ΕΠΙΚΑΛΟΥΜΑΙϹΕΤΟΝΕΝΤΩΚΕΝΕΩΠΝΕΥΜΑΤΙΔΕΙΝΟΝΑΟΡΑΤΟΝ
ΠΑΝΤΟΚΡΑΤΟΡΑΘΕΟΝΘΕΩΝΦΘΟΡΟΠΟΙΟΝΚΑΙΕΡΗΜΟΠΟΙΟΝΟΜΙϹΩ
ΟΙΚΙΑΝΕΥϹΤΑΘΟΥϹΑΝΩϹΕΧΕΒΡΑϹΘΗϹΕΚΤΗϹΑΙΓΥΠΤΟΥΚΑΙΕΧΩ
ΧΩΡΑϹΕΠΕΝΟΜΑϹΘΗϹΟΠΑΝΤΑΡΗϹϹΩΝΚΑΙΜΗΝΙΚΩΜΕΝΟϹ
ΕΠΙΚΑΛΟΥΜΑΙϹΕΤΥΦΩΝϹΗΘΤΑϹϹΑϹΜΑΝΤΕΙΑϹΕΠΙΤΕΛΩ
ΟΤΙΕΠΙΚΑΛΟΥΜΑΙϹΕΤΟϹΟΝΑΥΘΕΝΤΙΚΟΝϹΟΥΟΝΟΜΑΕΝΟΙϹΟΥΔΥΝΗ
ΠΑΡΑΚΟΥϹΑΙΙΩΕΡΒΗΘΙΩΠΑΚΕΡΒΗΘΙΩΒΟΛΧΩϹΗΘΙΩΠΑΤΑΘΝΑΞ
ΙΩϹΩΡΩΙΩΝΕΒΟΥΤΟϹΟΥΑΛΗΘΑΚΤΙΩΦΙΕΡΕϹΧΙΓΑΛΝΕΒΟΠΟϹΟΑΛΗΘ
ΑΒΕΡΑΜΕΝΘΩΟΥΛΕΡΘΕΞΑΝΑΞΕΘΡΕΛΥΩΘΝΕΜΑΡΕΒΑΛΕΜΙΝΑ
ΟΛΟΝΗΚΕΜΟΙΚΑΙΒΑΔΙϹΟΝΚΑΙΚΑΤΑΒΑΛΕΤΟΝΔΗΚΤΗΝΡΙΓΕΙΚΑΙΠΥ
ΡΕΤΩΑΥΤΟϹΚΑΙΚΗϹΕΝΜΕΚΑΤΟΔΙΜΑΤΟΠΟΡΩΝΟϹΕΞΕΧΥϹΕΝΠΑΡΕΑΥ
ΤΩΚΑΥΤΗΔΙΑΤΟΥΤΟΤΑΥΤΑΠΟΙΩ ΚΟΙΝΑ

Figure 7.1 A column from the London–Leiden magical papyrus showing the mixture of demotic (lines 1–8, 21–31) and Greek (lines 9–20) scripts, with foreign words transcribed into demotic and accompanying glosses in Greek letters (lines 24, 26, 28) in order to safeguard the correct pronunciation.

It becomes evident that the quest for the reasons for Egyptian writing's demise is interwoven with matters of the Egyptian history of thought in Ptolemaic and Roman times, as well as Egyptian identity during times of foreign rule. Religion plays a crucial role here, as religion provides imagery, rhetoric, and definitions of identity. Searching for the causes of the Egyptian religion's extinction, Peter Hubai (2003) has suggested that the focus of Egyptian religion on the Egyptian nation (whereby one becomes a member of this religious community and its soteriological conceptions through birth and not initiation) did not fit the new circumstances of Egypt as a multi-cultural society. According to Hubai, the new conceptions of human beings that Christianity brought to Egypt could not be expressed in the Egyptian language, which had developed during Pharaonic times for a very different conception. This difficulty is reflected in the high proportion of loan-words in Coptic. The Isis religion that spread all over the Roman Empire could not counteract the trend and give new vigour to the dying Egyptian religion, because its deity was not an Egyptian Isis but a universal goddess worshipped as Isis. This approach too is unconvincing, for it is doubtful whether the Isis religion was Hellenistic rather than Egyptian. Several Egyptologists have recognized Isis as Egyptian outside Egypt even in Late Antiquity (e.g. Junge 1979, cf. Schulz 2000). The iconography of the Iseum Campense, the major Isis temple in Rome, as well as the Greek Isis aretalogies, for instance, how a quite detailed knowledge of the Egyptian myth of Isis and Osiris, and of the Egyptian cult pertaining to it (Quack 2003a). The aretalogies may indeed be Greek translations of Egyptian originals (Quack 2003b). Apart from the tendency of Egyptologists to defend 'their' Egyptians against classicists (Stadler 2005a) and to emphasize the Egyptian nature of Isis, the case of the Iseum Campense indicates that Isis can be more Egyptian outside Egypt than classicists are inclined to acknowledge. In general the question why people turned to Christianity with its new conceptions of human beings, and why they ceased to adhere to their traditional cults, remains open.

Robert K. Ritner's answer (1989) to this question is surprisingly simple and at first sight very attractive: It is not that Egyptian religion dissolved 'in a debased cult and foreign-inspired magic of Greco-Roman eras, a collection of moribund superstitions which readily collapsed before a vigorous Christianity', but that late Egyptian religion became too complex: 'the latest Egyptian theologians [...] seem to have produced a religion too intellectually sophisticated for general understanding. The contrasting simplicity of Christianity was undoubtedly a factor in its success'. While Ritner concedes it may have been very significant, one might argue that many Church fathers developed a complex theology. In favour of his hypothesis, however, Ritner could cite a sermon of the fifth century Coptic monk Apa Shenoute, an abbot of the White Monastery in Akhmim (Emmel 2002), who saw hieroglyphs as 'nonsense and humbug'. Hieroglyphic texts are 'prescriptions for murdering man's soul that are therein, written with blood and not with ink alone'. Shenoute contrasts this symbol of pagan magic and evil with Christianity: Christian writings on the other hand come with *logos* and save souls (Young 1981; cf. Morenz 2002). It may be inferred that for Shenoute this logical clarity finds its graphic expression in the new script, the Greek alphabet. Since the latest attested Egyptian writing is contemporary with Shenoute's life (c. 361/2–441/51; see Behlmer 1996: LV–LX), his sermon is a direct source about the discourse on religion of the century that witnessed the final extinction of Egyptian writing.

Recent research exemplifies how the end of Egyptian scripts should be studied together with the demise of Egyptian civilization (with religion as its defining framework), because all Egyptian scripts (hieroglyphic, hieratic, and demotic) were national scripts. General factors favouring the rise and final victory of Christianity in Egypt have been identified, whereas scholars who concentrate on the specific phenomenon of script obsolescence have introduced as additional factors the lack of financial support from Roman officials and, for the temple of Isis on Philae island, from the Meroites who had come to Philae to worship and now stayed away, in combination with particular political events of the East Roman Empire.

Scholarly Presuppositions, Cultural Context of Sources, and the State of Publication

I now turn to Heike Sternberg-el Hotabi's contributions to the study of the decay of Egyptian writing. The issues she has raised relate to how we should interpret the sources and whether it is possible to draw unambiguous conclusions from them. This reflection is the principal focus of my chapter and raises methodological issues rather than pointing to reasons for the script obsolescence. Sternberg-el Hotabi (1994) studied the decay and the death of writing in Egypt ('Schriftverfall und Schrifttod'), using as her point of departure the Horus cippi (see also Sternberg-el Hotabi 1999; Gasse 2004). The Horus cippi are stelae which show Horus as a child, usually standing on crocodiles and seizing snakes, scorpions, and other wild animals. On the more elaborate specimens of the group, this symbol for the young god's victory over evil is accompanied by magical spells against evil in all its manifestations. The smaller pieces are designed as apotropaic amulets and some contain inscriptions that are illegible or rather pretend to be inscriptions. Looking at the Horus cippi Sternberg-el Hotabi dates the beginning of the decay of Egyptian writing as early as the mid Ptolemaic period (second century BC). This dating has been rejected for three reasons. First, the Horus cippi are as a special, private group of monuments an inadequate source basis to postulate a general decay, while both hieratic papyri and temple inscriptions are written for at least another 400 years (Houston *et al.* 2003: 445). Second, some forgeries have been included in her discussion and weaken her argument (Quack 2002: 725–6). Third pseudo-hieroglyphs can be found as early as the early dynastic period (late fourth millennium BC, Houston *et al.* 2003: 444) and then again, for example, in the eighth century BC (Raven 1991: 29, pl. 25). Many later copies of the Egyptian Book of the Dead in the late first millennium BC are often corrupt. No one would argue that the decay of Egyptian writing started as early as that. Other explanations must be sought for the writing on the Horus cippi, including their owners' social status, the prestige of writing as a magical instrument, and the sacredness of hieroglyphs that prompted the craftsmen's customers or—if coffins and other funerary objects were made for a market—the craftsmen themselves to fashion objects with pseudo-hieroglyphic inscriptions to enhance their ritual value (Houston *et al.* 2003: 444–5). It is therefore doubtful whether the Horus cippi suffice by themselves to postulate a decay or decline of Egyptian writing at any period. As private religious monuments the stelae might be compared to short formulaic mortuary texts that were written in demotic and designed to accompany the deceased as a sort of passport on his or her way to the netherworld. One of these has a line of hieroglyphs that yield no sense, but precede a perfectly comprehensible demotic composition (Fig. 7.2). This is a further example of the magical and ritual prestige that was accorded to hieroglyphs.

Scholars should also bear in mind the limitations of knowledge: the ancient writer or carver of an inscription is not necessarily to be blamed for an apparent illegibility. Egyptologists did not succeed in deciphering the two well-known hymns in the temple of Esna that were basically written with ram-signs in one case and crocodile-signs in the other case until Christian Leitz (2001) and Ludwig Morenz (2002) independently proposed readings. The graphic form of the two texts contains a pictorial dimension that contributes to the textual message and vice versa—visual poetry, as Morenz (2002) terms it—demonstrating the author's magisterial command of principles of the hieroglyphic script (Figs. 7.3). It could hardly be doubted that the hymns were meaningful, because of their context in a temple and the (in this case correct) presupposition that a temple's priesthood would not allow gibberish to be carved into its walls. It turns out that both hymns are very conventional, and Leitz (2001: 252) argues that if that had not been the case and unique texts had been encoded cryptographically in this way, then even learned Egyptians would have had no prospect of reading them.

The example of Esna is instructive in different ways. Esna is the apogee of a priestly practice of enriching religious texts with an extra dimension by exploiting the pictorial aspect of hieroglyphs and/or incorporating mythological symbolism pictorially (cf. Kurth 1983). Thus, hieroglyphs could be distanced from their standard phonetic values by the mythological reinterpretation. Three examples can illustrate these principles: Before the Ptolemaic period the hieroglyph of a beetle 🪲 normally encoded the three consonants *ḫpr*.

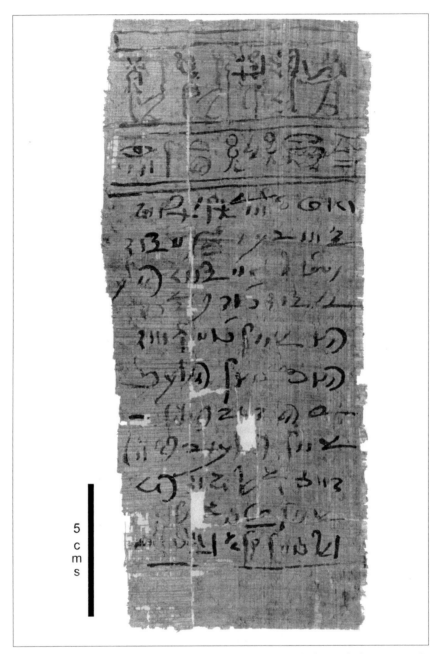

5
c
m
s

Figure 7.2 Papyrus British Museum EA 10415: the hieroglyphs beneath the vignette do not form a legible text, whereas the following demotic section is perfectly comprehensible (Stadler 2004b).

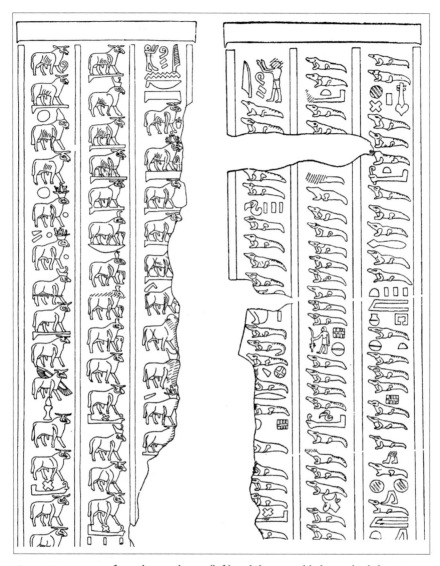

Figure 7.3 Excerpts from the ram hymn (left) and the crocodile hymn (right) at Esna.

The scarab that the hieroglyph represents emerges from the earth and that is probably why it acquired the new phonetic value *t3* 'earth' (Daumas 1988: 389). The traditional value *ḫpr*, meaning 'to come into being', remained valid, and the reader would have retained an awareness of it, so that text writing *t3* 'earth' with the scarab operates on at least two levels. Similarly, but more theologically, the djed-pillar 𓊽 usually read *ḏd* (hence its name) can have the value *psḏ* 'to shine' in

Ptolemaic-Roman temple inscriptions (Daumas 1990: 599). As *ḏd* the sign writes 'to endure', and in Egyptian theology the djed-pillar was the backbone of the god Osiris. The Egyptian word for 'backbone' is *psḏ* which provides the sign's new phonetic value, because *psḏ* 'backbone' and *psḏ* 'to shine' have the same consonantal structure and a similar sound. Here again, two dimensions are mobilized, in addition to the reading *psḏ* 'to shine' that is required in the particular context: an Osirian dimension and the association of duration. My last example is a word written with a combination of signs: ⌒〰️🏛️ looks like *iri mw* 'to create water' plus the determinative for people. This group has been plausibly explained as writing *rmṯ* 'people' by disregarding the weak consonants *i* in *iri* and *w* in *mw*, leaving *r* and *m* for *rm*. By that date when the word was written in this manner the final consonant in *rmṯ* was lost, as Coptic ⲢⲰⲘⲈ (rōme) shows. This analysis is partly in terms of the history of Egyptian language, but in mythical terms the combination of signs is also meaningful, because there was an Egyptian mythical conception that humanity came into being as the tears of the creator god. Thus the grapho-phonetic value—what Morenz (2002: 82) terms 'graphonetics'—in alluding to 'to make water (that is, tears)' refers to the mythical origin of the beings referred to.

The two Esna hymns fit logically and consistently into this development. The anonymous author (or authors) displayed piety towards the deity he wished to praise. Since Khnum, lord of Esna, is a ram-headed god, the ram hymn is the highest possible graphic realization of the god within a text. The crocodile hymn may address the special form of Khnum-Re, the lord of the field, who is manifest as a crocodile, or it could be for the crocodile god Sobek himself. The inscription itself is not specific and a reading has to be based on the temple's theology, in which both Khnum-Re and Sobek are important (Leitz 2001: 252–4, 262–73; Morenz 2002: 92). Thus cryptography forces the author(s) and later the readers to reflect and meditate the implications of the text, and this seems to be the intention: to stimulate engagement with the sacred writings (cf. Stadler 2004: 275). The particular copies of the hymns can hardly be read without binoculars in their position on the walls of the temple in Esna. So the main purpose of these inscriptions themselves was simply their presence through which the god was eternally celebrated. The pious work with the texts was already achieved at the moment of their grapho-phonetic composition. It is not unlikely that a copy on papyrus existed which did not survive.

It has been argued that fewer and fewer people were able to tackle such compositions, because on a generous estimate only a few hundred priests knew hieroglyphs and demotic in Roman Egypt (Bagnall 1993: 237–8). Thus the general tendency of Egyptian religion to keep sacred writings secret (cf. Morenz 1996: 78–87) was an internal factor that provided a trigger for the religion's obsolescence and was connected with that for the obsolescence of the writing system which encoded the religion's compositions. When the number of priests initiated to the sacred writings fell below the mark of critical mass that is necessary to sustain the institution of writing (Houston *et al.* 2003: 432–3), the seclusion that was expressed in the text's grapho-phonetical and intellectual complexity would cause it to die. However, the demise of Egyptian religion does not provide a fully satisfying model to explain why hieroglyphs ceased to be used, because demotic was also used for writing religious texts. Furthermore, Egyptian religion did not absolutely require any use of writing (Traunecker 1991), nor did it exclude non-Egyptian writing, as is demonstrated by stelae combining Egyptian iconography for example with Aramaic inscriptions (Vittmann 2003: 106–7). Nor was the end of Egyptian writing contemporaneous with that of Egyptian religion: at Philae the cult continued for another eighty years after the last Egyptian, more precisely demotic, graffito had been inscribed on the temple's walls (Cruz-Uribe 2002). In search of other approaches to an explanation I turn now to demotic, and look at its development in more detail.

Demotic came into use around 650 BC, presumably as a further graphical abstraction of the Lower Egyptian cursive hieratic (Fig. 7.4), and was used at first for documentary texts. Demotic spread from Lower Egypt southwards, replacing Abnormal Hieratic, which had been in use in Upper Egypt. In extension of a proposal by Anthony Leahy (1985), Günter Vittmann (2003: 10) has suggested that, just as in the seventh century BC the ethnically Libyan elite in Lower Egypt preferred to write hieroglyphs phonetically rather than in traditional Egyptian etymological writing, demotic could be seen within this framework in view of the demotic tendency towards phonetic spelling. Vittmann concedes that he cannot prove the hypothesis, but it is an attractive suggestion. Unless a literary text from the seventh to fifth century BC in demotic comes to light, it seems that demotic was not used for literary compositions until the fourth century BC. The earliest unquestionable literary compositions in demotic date to the fourth century BC (Smith and Tait 1983), and it was another 200 years or more before religious compositions were written in demotic (Smith 1978: 17). Apart from the song inspired by Amun in Papyrus Rylands 9 (sixth century BC: Vittmann 1998: 198–203, 639–43; Hoffmann and Quack 2007: 51–4), the first more or less isolated examples of religious texts in demotic are three hymns, two of which come from a private priestly archive (Ray 1976: 46–8, 66–73), and may therefore belong in a documentary context. Another unedited text of the second century BC seems to be literary with a mythological topic, rather than religious in a narrower sense (cf. Smith 1978: 17). In any case, hymns are documents of private or personal religiosity of people who might have wished to write them down in the most current script, which was certainly demotic for Egyptians of the second century BC. Thus hymns are examples of the use of demotic as an everyday script in the second century BC, while they also broke new ground for religious texts, especially mortuary compositions which became more common from the first century BC onwards (e.g. Smith 1987, 1993), whereas the first century AD

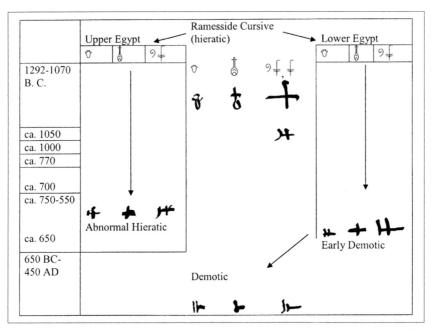

Figure 7.4 The development from hieroglyphs to demotic illustrated by three examples. For some characters, including those in the example, graphic abstraction results in almost identical shapes in demotic despite different phonetic
values and hieroglyphic origins.

witnessed a further increase in their currency (e.g. Widmer 1998; Stadler 2003,
2004a, and forthcoming b).

Alongside this considerable extension of text genres, demotic underwent
significant changes in its orthography to accommodate religious texts, which
belong to a conservative sphere, in a development that is paralleled by hieratic
in earlier periods. Demotic religious texts are in three forms of the language
(Smith 1987: 28): texts in pure Classical Egyptian, a stage of Egyptian that was
some 1700 years older than the current language; texts with traces of Classical
Egyptian; texts entirely written in Demotic language. This required that grammatical and lexical archaisms had to be represented in writing (Smith 1978,
1979) and may have been the point of departure for the phenomenon known as
unetymological writing.

Before tackling this I should give an impression of the high proportion of
demotic texts that is still unpublished (Fig. 7.5; for progress since this figure was
compiled, see Lippert and Schentuleit 2006a, 2006b). One demotist has stated
within the context of discussing demotic inscription on stone: 'demotic inscriptions should die out with demotic scribal praxis in the 1st cent. AD' (Vleeming 2001: 250). Naphtali Lewis (1993)—who states that demotic is not his field—

argues from published demotic texts. In so doing he adds to the hazards of phys-ical survival those of publication (cf. Zauzich 1983: 78–9), which are particularly severe: scholars have preferred to study and edit the generally better pre-served, formulaic, and therefore less difficult documentary texts of the Ptole-maic period such as contracts and receipts (letters, by contrast, pose extreme difficulties). Ptolemaic demotic also tends to be more accessible for modern scholars than Roman demotic. On the other hand, apart from a few well-known exceptions, many literary and religious texts have tended to be disregarded. This may be exemplified by Richard Holton Pierce's ironical statement, at the first conference of demotic studies in Berlin 1978, in response to the question as to the kind of demotic texts in which people would like to specialize, that unpublished, well-preserved, and easily decipherable demotic papyri were his favourite area of research.

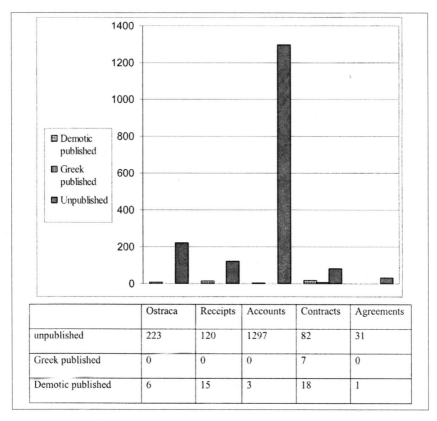

	Ostraca	Receipts	Accounts	Contracts	Agreements
unpublished	223	120	1297	82	31
Greek published	0	0	0	7	0
Demotic published	6	15	3	18	1

Figure 7.5 Unpublished versus published demotic material from Soknopaiou Nesos in the Fayyum: documentary texts (as of August 2004, courtesy Sandra L. Lippert and Maren Schentuleit).

The intensive study of Roman demotic texts—documentary, literary, and religious—began with serious effort just over thirty years ago in works by Karl-Theodor Zauzich (e.g., 1971, 1972, 1974, 1977—ground-breaking for the study of demotic in Sokonopaiou Nesos), Mark Smith (e.g. 1987, 1993), and Friedhelm Hoffmann (1995, 1996). Younger scholars such as Ghislaine Widmer (1998, 2002) and myself (2003, 2004a, b) continue to work in the field of demotic religious compositions. A Würzburg research project with Sandra Lippert and Maren Schentuleit, under Zauzich, to study the documentary texts from Roman period Soknopaiou Nesos in the Fayyum has significantly changed the figures cited by Lewis (1993: 276). Lewis counted 600 published papyrus documents in demotic dating to the Ptolemaic period, but fewer than sixty from the Roman period even including Greek documents with brief demotic notations or signatures. Roger Bagnall (1993: 237), referring to Zauzich (1983), has stated that the range of demotic texts is 'geographically narrow: after Augustus not a single published Demotic documentary papyrus comes from anywhere except Tebtunis or Soknopaiou Nesos, both in the Fayum'. This assertion, however, is based on an argument from silence and the hazards of preservation and modern fieldwork at particular sites. At Soknopaiou Nesos, for instance, conditions favour the survival of papyrus, because the village was abandoned around AD 250 for unknown reasons probably including desertification, and the site has never since been inhabited (Hagedorn 1975). One cannot then be completely sure that demotic gradually became obsolescent during the third century AD with just a few exceptions, such as some magical papyri (Johnson 1986) and the *Myth of the Sun's Eye* in Leiden (Cenival 1988; Jasnow 1991; Smith 1992). A statement like that of Vleeming on the death of demotic in the first century AD cited above is far too absolute.

From Simplification to Complexity:
The Impact of Religious Compositions on Demotic

Why have demotists been so reluctant to study Roman demotic texts in general and religious compositions in particular? Apart from the intellectual complexity of the non-documentary sources, the palaeography of late demotic is a factor even where the orthography is clear. But religious texts display an additional un- or non-etymological writing style: a word is 'unetymologically' written when the writing combines groups that usually express other lexemes. These lexemes are phonetically similar to syllables or the whole of the word but have another meaning by themselves. This is best presented through some examples.

The earliest known papyrus that is entirely notated in this sort of writing is the Papyrus Vienna D 6951, which is securely dated by the colophon to 8 BC (Hoffmann 2002).

Ex. No.	Papyrus Vienna D. 6951 (handcopies not facsimiles)	literal reading	intended reading
1	*(demotic handcopy)*	*ptḥ i.ir snfy*, 'Ptah who created blood'	*ptḥ rsy inb=f*, 'Ptah south of his wall'
2	*(demotic handcopy)*	*tš*, 'nome, province'	*tȝ š*, 'land of the lake' (= Fayyum)
3	*(demotic handcopy)*	*ḥr-ry.t ḥr-ib-tp*, 'under the room in the middle of the first'	*ḥry-ḥb.t ḥry-tp*, 'chief lector priest'

Example 1 is a current writing of an ancient epithet of Ptah (Quaegebeur 1980; Devauchelle 1998: 591–2), whereas, for example 2, a standard demotic writing could be: *(demotic)*. Example 3 would not yield any sense in context if it were taken literally.

Published examples of unetymological writing in Papyrus Berlin P 6750 of the later first century AD include the following (Widmer 1998, 2002, 2005):

Ex. No.	Papyrus Berlin 6750 (handcopies not facsimiles)	literal reading	intended reading
4	*(demotic handcopy)*	*ḫnt šy*, 'the foremost of the lake'	*ḫnṯš*, 'to rejoice'
5	*(demotic handcopy)*	*pȝ wt*, 'the offspring' or 'the fresh one'	*pȝ wt*, 'the embalmer'
6	*(demotic handcopy)*	*ḥsm(n) mr.w*, 'mr-natron'	*ḥs.wy mr.wy*, 'how praised, how loved'

A ritual text for entering the temple of Soknopaiou Nesos survives in at least five manuscripts. The grammar seems to be Classical Egyptian with a few Demoticisms (Stadler 2005b, 2007, and forthcoming a):

Ex. No.	Papyrus Berlin P 15652	literal reading	intended reading
7	*(demotic handcopy)*	*ḥtp-tȝ-nsw* 'The (fem.) king rests'.	*ḥtp di nsw* 'an offering which the king gives'
8	*(demotic handcopy)*	*nṯr-ḥnꜥ-tw=tn* 'god with you'	*ind-ḥr=tn* 'Hail to you!'
9	*(demotic handcopy)*	*wp w* 'to open the bark' or 'open the bark'	*wp-wȝ.wt* 'Upuaut' (name of a god, literally 'opener of the ways'

In example 7 the syntax is awkward, because it combines a masculine noun with the feminine definite article. While example 8 sounds familiar to Christians, it is not an Egyptian phrase, is ungrammatical at least in a pre-demotic form, and again does not yield sense in context.

These unetymological writings can be divided into two categories: phonetic writings, and visually poetic writings. Phonetic writings are cases when ancient words would not be properly rendered in demotic either because there was no demotic standard spelling for the word, or the pronunciation would be best notated by using other words as components that language change had brought close to a current phonetic form (cf. Smith 1977: 118). By visually poetic writings I mean ones that deliberately use other words as components, even though standard demotic spellings were available, to add a further dimension to the written word (for the term 'visual poetry' see Morenz 2002, 2004b). Words in the second category are mainly religious terms, names of gods, and other sacred matters in particular. On the other hand, one could argue that unetymological writings should be seen within the context of changes in the language that would make it impossible to notate an ancient or archaizing form in proper demotic, so that it would be necessary to use other words as components to indicate the vocalization. Most examples in papyrus Vienna D 6951 (examples 1 and 2 of the list above) favour such an interpretation (Hoffmann 2002).

Why, however, should the scribe choose to write a potentially misleading *tš* 'nome, province' in order to encode a normal *tꜣ šy*? The glosses in other texts, such as the manuals of priestly wisdom from Tebtunis (Osing 1998) or the London–Leiden magical papyrus (Griffith and Thompson 1904–9), show that to ensure a proper pronunciation, which would be particularly necessary in ritual texts, other means could be used, either demotic alphabetic writings, that is, use of uniconsonantal signs, or Greek letters.

Many unetymological writings in Berlin papyri P 6750 and P 15652r seem to exhibit the intent to add another layer of meaning to the words, as the contemporary priests designing hieroglyphic inscriptions did. Example 4 would evoke the crocodile god Sobek who is the foremost of the lake, that is, the Fayyum, and is the god a Fayyumic worshipper might think of when rejoicing, whereas in example 5 the writing of *pꜣ wt* 'offspring' or 'the fresh one' would imply the embalmer's rejuvenation of a corpse; similarly the graphic reference to embalming substances in example 6 actually encodes words of praise. While *nṯr-ḥnꜥ-tw=tn* in example 8 is to be explained by phonetic change, *wp-w* 'open the bark' for Upuaut, a god for whom demotic provides a conventional writing (ʃ·ⵊ or similar, Erichsen 1954: 87), again has a twofold meaning: the 'opener of ways' is also the god who helps to clear the way for the solar bark. Therefore the editor of an unetymological demotic text should not discard too readily the possibility that its writings may convey two or more layers of meaning. Demotic seems to follow the same lines of development as hieroglyphs took some 400 years earlier, reaching a stage at which it was fully effective for encoding priestly wisdom alongside hieroglyphs and hieratic. Hieratic, however, barely partook in this development and usually kept the traditional orthography. The unetymologically written demotic texts ceased to be easy to compose and quick to read.

I propose the analysis that demotic was fully functioning in the Roman period for both documentary and religious texts. Furthermore, new graphic, visually poetic options were developed for religious compositions through unetymological writings; this development was the beginning of the end of demotic. Yet such analyses face three serious objections. The first is that only a few of the known religious texts are consistently written unetymologically, whereas most other texts have only a smattering of unetymological words. Second, all known entirely unetymologically written texts come from a single site: Soknopaiou Nesos in the Fayyum. Third, all documentary sources of the period—again mostly from Tebtunis or Soknopaiou Nesos—originated in the administration and economy of the temples: in other words demotic did cease to be an official script of the Roman administration. This latter point is supported by the rich Greek documentation from Soknopaiou Nesos (e.g. Jördens 1998), which clearly demonstrates that economic and legal transactions outside the temple or between the temple and the Roman administration had to be written down in Greek.

The first and second objections might be disproved over time with new discoveries, but for now they remain valid and should caution us from generalizing. The third objection concerns the theory of the full functioning of demotic in Roman times and points to the diminution in the use of Egyptian writing, from a broad range of contexts to very restricted priestly circles, whereby demotic abandoned, or was forced to abandon, its character as an everyday script. However, study of the temple's economic documentation from Soknopaiou Nesos shows that this particular institution remained a regional economic centre (Lippert and Schentuleit 2005a).

There were too few people still using Egyptian scripts to keep them alive forever. Although the priests did not abstain from interaction with non-priestly contemporaries in everyday life, they appear to have cultivated an intellectual and religious exclusivity. This in itself would not be a problem, if the cultural environment had not changed, but in Roman Egypt it did so at an accelerating pace. The absence of a king was an initial blow for the temples, but one that they learned to remedy (Hölbl 2000: 9–46). A second-century-AD demotic ostrakon from Medinet Madi seems to indicate that the only way to earn one's living with Egyptian scripts outside the temple was to be an astrologer or fortune-teller (Hoffmann 2000: 45–7), although Jacco Dieleman (2003) suggests that the piece must be seen as belonging in a temple milieu. It might be inferred that, similarly to the situation of cuneiform (see David Brown, 'Increasingly Redundant: The Growing Obsolescence of the Cuneiform Script in Babylonia from 539 BC', in this volume), the shift to scripts that were easier to write and more widely understood demolished the last strongholds of Egyptian writing outside the temples. Greek certainly played a major part as sole official language for legal transactions that the Roman administration recognized, together with the decrease in financial support of the temples, but these pressures were complemented by the exclusivist attitude, expressed in an intellectual complexity that the common worshippers could not follow. A new religion, which was propagated as clear, logical, and accessible to everyone, found fertile ground on which to grow.

Conclusions

It is difficult to interpret the source material, as it is diverse, complex, and little explored. Philae, and the death of demotic there, offers a very special case, because it seems to be the last flicker of a candle. Egyptian culture at Philae was finally snuffed out by vigorous imperial military intervention: the imperial commander of the Thebaid Narses closed the temple and converted it into a Christian church in 536. Yet demotic had ceased to exist more than two generations earlier, and the last demotic inscriptions, from 452, were left by a Meroite, not an Egyptian. One might conclude that Egyptian culture and religion could indeed exist without Egyptian writing. The inverse is in fact impossible: Egyptian writing makes no sense without its cultural and religious background and backbone. It is therefore doubtful whether general conclusions may be drawn from the situation at Philae in the fifth century AD, because it only explains the cultural, political, and historical environment in which Egyptian culture could survive for a relatively short period; the abrupt end of the Egyptian cult at Philae cannot be expanded to account for Egypt as a whole. In my opinion, the end of demotic in Philae can easily be described and explained. For the rest of Egypt, however, the picture is far more colourful and it is impossible to specify any one factor that would account for the beginning of its demise. Some factors emerge as significant, such as religious development, economic circumstances, and political events. We may add to these the attitude of Egyptian priests in Roman Egypt responsible for the traditional pagan cult. They became culturally and religiously isolated, and supported that development by composing both hieroglyphic and demotic texts encoded in a most difficult system. Texts written in that manner required some effort to be understood and were regarded as obsolete, because they did not respond to the contemporary social environment.

References

Bagnall, Roger
  1993   *Egypt in Late Antiquity*. Princeton, NJ: Princeton University Press.
Behlmer, Heike
  1996   *Shenoute von Atripe De Iudicio*. Catalogo del Museo Egizio di Torino. Serie Prima—Monumenti e Testi 7. Turin: Ministero per i Beni Culturali e Ambientali—Soprintendenza al Museo delle Antichità Egizie.
Blasius, Andreas, and Bernd Ulrich Schipper (eds)
  2002   *Apokalyptik und Ägypten. Eine kritische Analyse der relevanten Texte aus dem griechisch-römischen Ägypten*. Orientalia Lovaniensia Analecta 107. Leuven: Peeters.

Breyer, Francis A. K.
2002 'Die Schriftzeugnisse des prädynastischen Königsgrabes U-j in Umm el-Qaab: Versuch einer Neuinterpretation'. *Journal of Egyptian Archaeology* 88: 53–65.

Cenival, Françoise de
1988 *Le Mythe de l'œil du soleil*. Demotische Studien 9. Sommerhausen: Gisela Zauzich.

Cruz-Uribe, Eugene
2002 'The Death of Demotic at Philae, a Study in Pilgrimage and Politics'. In Tamás A. Bács (ed.), *A Tribute to Excellence: Studies offered in Honor of Ernő Gaál, Ulrich Luft and László Török*. Studia Aegyptiaca 17. Budapest: La Chaire d'Égyptologie: 163–84.

Daumas, François (ed.)
1988 *Valeurs phonétiques des signes hiéroglyphiques d'époque gréco-romaine* vol. 2. Montpellier: Université de Montpellier.
1990 *Valeurs phonétiques des signes hiéroglyphiques d'époque gréco-romaine* vol. 3. Montpellier: Université de Montpellier.

Devauchelle, Didier
1998 'Une invocation aux dieux du Sérapéum de Memphis'. In Willy Clarysse, A. Schoors, and Harco Willems (eds), *Egyptian Religion: The Last Thousand Years. Studies Dedicated to the Memory of J. Quaegebeur*. Orientalia Lovanensia Analecta 84. Leuven: Peeters, vol. 1: 589–611.

Dieleman, Jacco
2003 'Claiming the Stars: Egyptian Priests Facing the Sky'. In Susanne Bickel and Antonio Loprieno (eds), *Basel Egyptology Prize: Junior Research in Egyptian History, Archaeology, and Philology*. Aegyptiaca Helvetica 17. Basel: Schwabe, 277–89.
2005 *Priests, Tongues, and Rites: The London-Leiden Magical Manuscripts and Translation in Egyptian Ritual (100–300 CE)*. Religions in the Graeco-Roman World 153. Leiden/Boston: Brill.

Dreyer, Günter, Ulrich Hartung, and Frauke Pumpenmeier
1998 *Umm el-Qaab* vol. 1. *Das prädynastische Königsgrab U-j und seine frühen Schriftzeugnisse*. Deutsches Archäologisches Institut, Abteilung Kairo, Archäologische Veröffentlichungen 89. Mainz: Philipp von Zabern.

el-Aguizy, Ola
1998 *A Palaeographical Study of Demotic Papyri in the Cairo Museum from the Reign of Taharka to the End of the Ptolemaic Period (684–30 BC)*. Mémoires publiées par les membres de l'Institut français d'archéologie orientale 113. Cairo: Institut français d'archéologie orientale.

Emmel, Stephen
2002 'From the Other Side of the Nile: Shenute and Panopolis'. In Arno Egberts, Brian R. Muhs, and Jan van der Vliet (eds), *Perspectives on Panopolis: An Egyptian Town from Alexander the Great to the Arab Conquest*. Leiden: Brill, 95–113.

Erichsen, Wolja
1954 *Demotisches Glossar*. Copenhagen: Einar Munksgaard.

Frankfurter, David
   1998   *Religion in Roman Egypt: Assimilation and Resistance.* Princeton, NJ: Princeton University Press.

Gasse, Annie
   2004   *Le stèles d'Horus sur les crocodiles.* Paris: Editions de la Réunion des musées nationaux.

Gauger, Jörg-D.
   2002   'Der "Traum des Nektanebos"—die griechische Fassung'. In Blasius and Schipper 2002, 189–219.

Griffith, Francis Ll., and H. Thompson
   1904-9   *The Demotic Magical Papyrus of London and Leiden.* London: Grevel.

Hagedorn, Dieter
   1975   'Dimeh.' In Wolfgang Helck and Eberhard Otto (eds), *Lexikon der Ägyptologie* vol. 1. Wiesbaden: Harrassowitz, 1094.

Hölbl, Günter
   2000   *Altägypten im Römischen Reich. Der römische Pharao und seine Tempel.* Mainz: Philipp von Zabern.

Hoffmann, Friedhelm
   1995   *Ägypter und Amazonen. Neubearbeitung zweier demotischer Papyri. P. Vindob. D 6165 und P. Vindob. D 6165 A.* Mitteilungen aus der Papyrussammlung Erzherzog Rainer 24. Vienna: Gebrüder Hollinek.
   1996   *Der Kampf um den Panzer des Inaros. Studien zum P. Krall und seiner Stellung innerhalb des Inaros-Petubastis-Zyklus.* Mitteilungen aus der Papyrussammlung Erzherzog Rainer 26. Vienna: Gebrüder Hollinek.
   2000   *Ägypten. Kultur und Lebenswelt in griechisch-römischer Zeit. Eine Darstellung nach den demotischen Quellen.* Berlin: Akademie Verlag.
   2002   'Die Hymnensammlung des P. Wien D6951.' In Kim Ryholt (ed.), *Acts of the Seventh International Conference of Demotic Studies, Copenhagen, 23–27 August 1999.* CNI Publications 27. Copenhagen: Museum Tusculanum Press, 219–28.

Hoffmann, Friedhelm, and Joachim Friedrich Quack
   2007   *Anthologie der demotischen Literatur.* Einführungen und Quellentexte zur Ägyptologie 4. Berlin: Lit.

Houston, Stephen, John Baines, and Jerrold Cooper
   2003   'Last Writing: Script Obsolescence in Egypt, Mesopotamia, and Mesoamerica.' *Comparative Studies in Society and History* 45: 430–79.

Hubai, Peter
   2003   'Religionswechsel im Ägypten der Römerzeit.' In Zahi Hawass (ed.), *Egyptology at the Dawn of the Twenty-First Century: Proceedings of the Eighth Congress of Egyptologists Cairo, 2000.* Cairo and New York: The American University in Cairo Press, vol. 2, 316–23.

Jasnow, Richard
   1991   Review of Cenival 1992. *Enchoria* 18: 205–15.

Jördens, Andrea
1998   *Griechische Papyri aus Soknopaiu Nesos (P. Louvre I).* Papyrologische Texte und Abhandlungen 43. Bonn: Dr Rudolf Habelt.

Johnson, Janet H.
1976   *The Demotic Verbal System.* Studies in Ancient Oriental Civilization 38. Chicago: The Oriental Institute of the University of Chicago.
1986   'Introduction to the Demotic Magical Papyri.' In Hans D. Betz (ed.), *The Greek Magical Papyri in Translation Including the Demotic Spells.* Chicago and London: University of Chicago Press, lv–lviii.

Junge, Friedrich
1979   'Isis und die ägyptischen Mysterien.' In Wolfhart Westendorf (ed.), *Aspekte der spätägyptischen Religion.* Göttinger Orientforschungen IV: 9. Wiesbaden: Harrassowitz, 93–115.

Koenen, Ludwig
2002   'Die Apologie des Töpfers an König Amenophis oder das Töpferorakel.' In Blasius and Schipper 2002: 139–87.

Kurth, Dieter
1983   'Die Lautwerte der Hieroglyphen in den Tempelinschriften der griechisch-römischen Zeit—zur Systematik ihrer Herleitungsprinzipien.' *Annales du Service des Antiquités de l'Égypte* 69: 287–309.

Leahy, Anthony
1985   'The Libyan Period in Egypt: An Essay in Interpretation.' *Libyan Studies* 16: 51–65.

Leitz, Christian
2001   'Die beiden kryptographischen Inschriften aus Esna mit den Widdern und Krokodilen.' *Studien zur Altägyptischen Kultur* 29: 251–76.

Lembke, Katja
2004   *Ägyptens späte Blüte. Die Römer am Nil.* Mainz: Philipp von Zabern.

Lewis, Naphtali
1993   'The Demise of Demotic: When and Why.' *Journal of Egyptian Archaeology* 79: 276–81.

Lippert, Sandra L., and Maren Schentuleit (eds)
2005a   *Tebtynis und Soknopaiu Nesos. Leben im römerzeitlichen Fajum. Akten des interdisziplinären Symposions in Sommerhausen bei Würzburg vom 11. bis zum 13.12.2003.* Demotische Dokumente aus Dime Sonderband. Wiesbaden: Harrassowitz.

Lippert, Sandra L., and Maren Schentuleit
2005b   'Die Tempelökonomie nach den demotischen Texten aus Soknopaiou Nesos.' In Lippert and Schentuleit 2005a, 71–8.
2006a   *Ostraka.* Demotische Dokumente aus Dime 1. Wiesbaden: Harrassowitz.
2006b   *Quittungen.* Demotische Dokumente aus Dime 2. Wiesbaden: Harrassowitz.

Morenz, Ludwig
1996   *Beiträge zur Schriftlichkeitskultur im Mittleren Reich und in der 2. Zwischenzeit.* Ägypten und Altes Testament 29. Wiesbaden: Harrassowitz.

2002   'Schrift-Mysterium. Gottes-Schau in der visuellen Poesie von Esna—Insbesondere zu den omnipotenten Widder-Zeichen zwischen Symbolik und Lesbarkeit.' In Jan Assmann and Martin Bommas (eds), *Ägyptische Mysterien?* Munich: Wilhelm Fink, 77–94.

2004a   *Bild-Buchstaben und symbolische Zeichen. Die Herausbildung der Schrift in der hohen Kultur Altägyptens.* Orbis Biblicus et Orientalis 205. Fribourg and Göttingen: Academic Press/Paulusverlag/Vandenhoeck & Ruprecht.

2004b   'Visuelle Poesie als eine sakrale Zeichen-Kunst der altägyptischen *hohen Kultur*'. *Studien zur Altägyptischen Kultur* 32: 311–26.

Osing, Jürgen
1998   *Hieratische Papyri aus Tebtunis I.* Carlsberg Papyri 2 = CNI Publications 17. Copenhagen: Museum Tusculanum Press.

Quack, Joachim F.
1995   'Notes en marge du Papyrus Vandier.' *Revue d'Égyptologie* 46: 163–70.

2002   Review of Sternberg-el Hotabi 1999. *Orientalistische Literaturzeitung* 97: 713–39.

2003a   'Zum ägyptischen Ritual im Iseum Campense in Rom.' In C. Metzner-Nebelsick *et al.* (eds) *Rituale in der Vorgeschichte, Antike und Gegenwart. Studien zur Vorderasiatischen, Prähistorischen und Klassischen Archäologie, Ägyptologie, Alten Geschichte, Theologie und Religionswissenschaft.* Interdisziplinäre Tagung vom 1.–2. Februar 2002 an der Freien Universität. Berlin and Rahden/Westfalen: Leidorf, 57–66.

2003b   '"Ich bin Isis, die Herrin der beiden Länder"—Versuch zum demotischen Hintergrund der memphitischen Isisaretalogie.' In Sibylle Meyer (ed.), *Egypt—Temple of the Whole World. Ägypten—Tempel der Gesamten Welt. Studies in Honour of Jan Assmann.* Leiden and Boston: Brill, 319–65.

2004   'Griechische und andere Dämonen in den spätdemotischen magischen Texten.' In Thomas Schneider (ed.), *Das Ägyptische und die Sprachen Vorderasiens, Nordafrikas und der Ägäis.* Akten des Basler Kolloquiums zum ägyptisch-nichtsemitischen Sprachkontakt Basel 9.–11. Juli 2003. Münster: Ugarit-Verlag, 427–507.

Quaegebeur, Jan
1980   'Une épithète méconnaissable de Ptah.' In Jean Vercoutter (ed.), *Livre du centenaire, 1880–1980.* Mémoires publiés par les membres de l'Institut français d'archéologie orientale du Caire 104. Cairo: Institut français d'archéologie orientale, 61–71.

1982   'De la préhistoire de l'écriture copte.' *Orientalia Lovanensia Periodica* 13: 125–36.

Raven, Maarten J.
1991   *The Tomb of Iurudef: A Memphite Official in the Reign of Ramesses II.* Excavation Memoir 57. London: Egypt Exploration Society.

Ray, John D.
1976   *The Archive of Hor.* Texts from Excavations 2. London: Egypt Exploration Society.

Ritner, Robert K.
1989   'Horus on the Crocodiles: A Juncture of Religion and Magic in Late Dynastic Egypt.' In James P. Allen *et al.*, *Religion and Philosophy in Ancient Egypt.* Yale Egyptological Studies 3. New Haven, CT: Egyptological Seminar, Department of Near Eastern Languages and Civilizations, 103–16.

Ryholt, Kim
  2002   'Nectanebo's Dream or The Prophecy of Petesis.' In Blasius and Schipper
          2002: 221–41.

Sauneron, Serge
  1963   *Le Temple d'Esna* II. Cairo: Institut français d'archéologie orientale.

Schulz, Regine
  2000   'Warum Isis?' In Manfred Görg and Günter Hölbl (eds), *Ägypten und der östli-
          che Mittelmeerraum im 1. Jahrtausend v. Chr.* Ägypten und Altes Testament 44.
          Wiesbaden: Harrassowitz, 251–79.

Smith, Harry S., and William J. Tait
  1983   *Saqqâra Demotic Papyri* vol. 1. Texts from Excavations 7. London: Egypt
          Exploration Society.

Smith, Mark
  1977   'A New Version of a Well-Known Egyptian Hymn.' *Enchoria* 7: 115–49.
  1978   'Remarks on the Orthography of Some Archaisms in Demotic Religious Texts.'
          Enchoria 8/2: 17–27.
  1979   'The Demotic Mortuary Papyrus Louvre E. 3452.' Unpublished PhD disserta-
          tion, University of Chicago.
  1987   *The Mortuary Texts of Papyrus British Museum 10507.* Catalogue of Demotic
          Papyri in the British Museum. London: British Museum Publications.
  1992   Review of Cenival 1992. *Bibliotheca Orientalis* 39: 80–95.
  1993   *The Liturgy of Opening the Mouth for Breathing.* Oxford: Griffith Institute.

Stadler, Martin A.
  2003   *Der Totenpapyrus des Pa-Month (P. Bibl. nat. 149).* Studien zum altägyptischen
          Totenbuch 6. Wiesbaden: Harrassowitz.
  2004a   *Isis, das göttliche Kind und die Weltordnung. Neue religiöse Texte nach dem Papyrus
          Wien D. 12006 recto.* Mitteilungen aus der Papyrussammlung Erzherzog Rainer.
          Vienna: Gebrüder Hollinek.
  2004b   'Fünf neue funeräre Kurztexte (Papyri Britisches Museum EA 10121, 10198,
          10415, 10421a, b, 10426a) und eine Zwischenbilanz zu dieser Textgruppe'.
          In Friedhelm Hoffmann and Heinz-Josef Thissen (eds), *Res severa verum Gau-
          dium. Festschrift Karl-Theodor Zauzich zum 65. Geburtstag am 8. Juni 2004.* Studia
          Demotica 6. Leuven: Peeters, 551–72.
  2005a   'Zur ägyptischen Vorlage der memphitischen Isisaretalogie.' *Göttinger Miszel-
          len* 204: 7–9.
  2005b   'Das Ritual, den Tempel des Sobek, des Herren von Pai, zu betreten. Ein Ritu-
          altext aus dem römischen Fayum'. In Burckhard Dücker and Hubert Roeder
          (eds), *Text und Ritual. Essays und kulturwissenschaftliche Studien von Sesostris bis
          zu den Dadaisten,* Hermeia 8. Heidelberg: Synchron, 150–63.
  2007   'Zwischen Philologie und Archäologie: Das Tägliche Ritual des Tempels in
          Soknopaiou Nesos'. In Mario Capasso and Paola Davoli (eds), *New Archaeologi-
          cal Researches on the Fayyum. Proceedings of the International Meeting of Egyptol-
          ogy and Papyrology, Lecce, June 8th–10th 2005.* Papyrologica Lupiensia 14/2005.
          Lecce: Congedo, 283–302.
  forthcoming a 'Drei Textzeugen eines neuen magisch-religiösen Textes (Berlin P 8043
          verso, P 15799+23538, P 15652 recto).' In Karl-Theodor Zauzich (ed.), *Akten*

der 8. Internationalen Konferenz für demotische Studien, 27.-30. August 2002. Wiesbaden: Harrassowitz.

forthcoming b *Einführung in die demotische religiöse Literatur.* Berlin: Lit.

Sternberg-el Hotabi, Heike
   1994   'Der Untergang der Hieroglyphenschrift. Schriftverfall und Schrifttod im
           Ägypten der griechisch-römischen Zeit'. *Chronique d'Égypte* 69: 218–54.
   1999   *Untersuchungen zur Überlieferungsgeschichte der Horusstelen. Ein Beitrag zur Reli-
           gionsgeschichte Ägyptens im 1. Jahrtausend v. Chr.* 2 vols. Ägyptologische Abhand-
           lungen 62. Wiesbaden: Harrassowitz.

Traunecker, Claude
   1991   'Observations sur le décor des temples égyptiens.' In Françoise Dunand, Jean-
           Michel Spieser, and Jean Wirth (eds), *L'Image et la production du sacré.* Paris:
           Méridiens Klincksieck, 77–101.

Verhoeven, Ursula
   2001   *Untersuchungen zur späthieratischen Buchschrift.* Orientalia Lovanensia Anal-
           ecta 99. Leuven: Peeters.

Vittmann, Günter
   1998   *Der demotische Papyrus Rylands 9,* 2 vols. Ägypten und Altes Testament 38.
           Wiesbaden: Harrassowitz.
   2003   *Ägypten und die Fremden im ersten vorchristlichen Jahrtausend.* Mainz: Philipp
           von Zabern.

Vleeming, Sven P.
   1991   *The Gooseherds of Hou (Pap. Hou): A Dossier Relating to Various Agricultural Affairs
           from Provincial Egypt of the Early Fifth Century B.C.* Studia Demotica 3. Leuven:
           Peeters.
   2001   *Some Coins of Artaxerxes and Other Short Texts in the Demotic Script Found on Vari-
           ous Objects and Gathered from Many Publications.* Studia Demotica 5. Leuven,
           Paris, and Sterling, VA: Peeters.

Widmer, Ghislaine
   1998   'Un papyrus démotique religieux du Fayoum: P. Berlin 6750.' *Bulletin, Société
           d'Égyptologie Genève* 22: 83–91.
   2002   'Pharaoh Maâ-Rê, Pharaoh Amenemhat and Sesostris: Three Figures from
           Egypt's Past as Seen in Sources of the Graeco-Roman Period.' In Kim Ryholt
           (ed.), *Acts of the Seventh International Conference of Demotic Studies, Copenhagen,
           23-27 August 1999.* CNI Publications 27. Copenhagen: Museum Tusculanum
           Press, 377–93.
   2005   'P. Berlin P 6750: On Egyptian Religion in Soknopaiou Nesos during Roman
           Times.' In Lippert and Schentuleit 2005a, 171–84.

Young, Dwight W.
   1981   'A Monastic Invective against Egyptian Hieroglyphs.' In Dwight W. Young
           (ed.), *Studies Presented to Hans Jakob Polotsky.* East Gloucester, MA: Pirtle and
           Polson, 348–60.

Zauzich, Karl-Theodor
   1971   'Spätdemotische Papyrusurkunden.' *Enchoria* 1: 29–42.

1972 'Spätdemotische Papyrusurkunden II.' *Enchoria* 2: 83–6.

1974 'Spätdemotische Papyrusurkunden III.' *Enchoria* 4: 71–82.

1977 'Spätdemotische Papyrusurkunden IV.' *Enchoria* 7: 151–80.

1983 'Demotische Texte römischer Zeit.' In Günter Grimm, Heinz Heinen, and Erich Winter (eds), *Das römisch-byzantinische Ägypten. Akten des internationalen Symposions 26–30 September 1978 in Trier*. Aegyptiaca Treverensia 2. Mainz: Philipp von Zabern, 77–83.

8

The Last Traces of Meroitic? A Tentative Scenario for the Disappearance of the Meroitic Script

Claude Rilly

Meroitic Language: Presentation and General Issues

Meroitic was the language of the successive kingdoms of Kush, the Ancient Sudan, along the Middle Nile, roughly from the first Cataract upstream to the Khartoum Reach (see Fig. 8.1). Although this language was not written with a script of its own before its latest stage, in the Kingdom of Meroe (c. 300 BC–AD 350), I have presented evidence for its having appeared altogether earlier in the Nile Valley (Rilly 2001). The Egyptian Papyrus Golenischeff,[1] written in hieratic script at the end of the Hyksos period (first part of the sixteenth century BC) includes a list of carefully written foreign names, forming a secondary inscription on the blank area of the document. It is possible to demonstrate that the names include some Proto-Meroitic elements and are those of officials or members of a delegation sent from the king of Kerma, the earliest Kushite state, to the Hyksos king who was then ruling in Lower and Middle Egypt. According to the most recent archaeological work (Bonnet 2001; Honegger 2002), Kerma was founded around 2400 BC and did not undergo any important ethnic or cultural change until it was finally destroyed by the Egyptian forces around 1450 BC. In addition, some of the names listed in Pap. Golenischeff can be convincingly connected with the names of the rulers of Kush and their relatives that appear in the Egyptian 'execration texts' of the Twelfth Dynasty (around 2000 BC). Consequently, the origin of the Meroitic language in a specific society can now be placed around the middle of the third millennium or probably a little earlier.

The Meroitic scripts (hieroglyphic and cursive) were deciphered from 1907 to 1911 by the British Egyptologist Francis Llewellyn Griffith (1911). But this

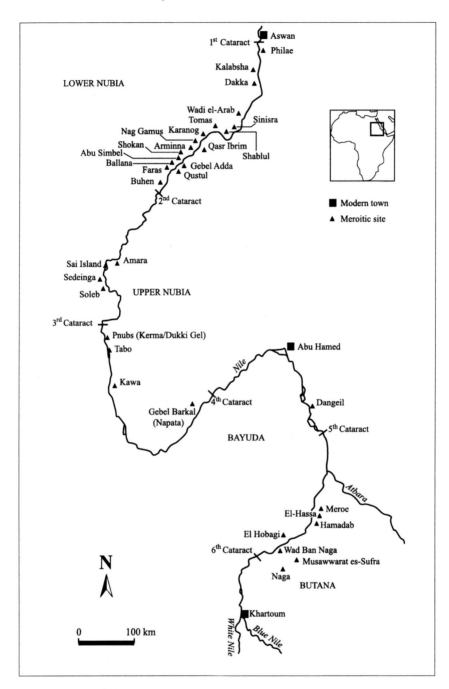

Figure 8.1 Map of the main Meroitic sites.

decipherment did not provide a key to translating the texts, because the language appeared very remote from any known language of the region. Although Nubian, the language that replaced Meroitic in the Middle Nile Valley after the fall of Meroe, seemed to share many features with Meroitic, Griffith's efforts to link the two languages proved fruitless. Apart from some names of places, kings, and gods, and from such rare Egyptian loanwords as titles for 'priest', 'envoy', or 'general', no more than three dozens of indigenous words could be translated with certainty. Meroitic seemed to be 'the Etruscan of Africa'. Several types of texts, especially funerary inscriptions, are well understood, but their stereotyped content provides little information about Meroitic civilization, whereas the long inscriptions of the kings of Meroe, which could potentially tell us so much on the kingdom's history, remain impenetrable. Scholars such as Fritz Hintze, the greatest German specialist in Meroitic, tended to believe that the language was an isolate and therefore unlikely ever to be translated (Hintze 1955: 372; 1989).

The situation has changed recently, although it is still impossible to know how far the changes will open the way to a complete understanding of the texts. New morphological and lexical identifications provide evidence that Meroitic belonged to a specific linguistic family within the Nilo-Saharan phylum, Northern East Sudanic (NES), which groups several languages extending from the border between Chad and Sudan to Western Eritrea and including Nubian (Rilly 2003b; 2004). Bruce G. Trigger (1964) suggested already a similar hypothesis some forty years ago, but at that time the known Meroitic lexical stock was too scanty, the data for the related languages insufficient, and the methods employed, which were based on phonetic resemblance, unreliable (see Hintze 1973, for a ruthless review of Trigger). The next step is now to reconstruct a proto-language, since the present linguistic distance within the NES family is as great as that between remote Indo-European languages. This is a major undertaking, involving long and arduous work on various very poorly known African languages. Initial results are, however, encouraging, since it has been possible to clarify some aspects of Meroitic morphology and to increase the number of verbs for which a translation can now be established.

The Meroitic Script

When and how did the script appear?

Meroitic, although the language of the indigenous elite during the two kingdoms of Kerma (c. 2400–1450 BC) and Napata (c. 800–300 BC), was not written before the third century BC. Evidence of its existence and status can be firmly identified in transcriptions in Egyptian hieroglyphs of the indigenous names of kings, queens, and important officials. No native written document has so far been discovered in excavations of sites of the Kerma culture, and it has been concluded that writing was unknown then (Valbelle 2004: 177). Much later, in the kingdom of Napata, Egyptian was the sole written language: funerary texts as well as royal inscriptions were in Egyptian script and language, the use of which was a consequence of six centuries of Egyptian colonization, but also ironically, of the power of the early kings of Napata over Egypt, during the famous period of the Black Pharaohs (Twenty-Fifth Dynasty) who ruled fifty years (715–664 BC) over both kingdoms.

From the fourth century onwards, Napatan texts show a rapidly diminishing knowledge of standard Egyptian, with increasing numbers of misspellings and grammatical errors (Schäfer 1901: 72–5). In my opinion, these mistakes are not indices of a specific Egyptian dialect (*contra* Peust 1999), but are simply due to a widening separation from Egyptian culture. It became necessary, particularly for administrative and religious purposes, to develop a script that made it possible to record the spoken language of the kingdom. The first traces of the cursive Meroitic script, used for graffiti of pilgrims in the temples of Dukki Gel (Rilly 2003a) and Kawa (Macadam 1949), can be dated to the beginning of the second century, but it is likely that the script was invented some decades earlier. In these early inscriptions, Meroitic is sometimes mixed with Egyptian demotic signs in the names of deities. This detail, together with the general resemblance of the signs of the two scripts, shows that Meroitic cursive was largely adapted from demotic (Griffith 1911: 11; Millet 1974: 50; Rilly 2007: 241–60).[2]

Principles of the graphic system

The Meroites, however, did not copy the complex writing system of their pres-tigious neighbours, but developed a purely phonetic system, maybe originating in the style of transcription of indigenous names into Egyptian hieroglyphs used in the kingdom of Napata. Fritz Hintze (1973: 322–3; 1987) established firmly that the Meroitic script is not alphabetical or consonantal, but constitutes an 'alphasyllabary' similar in its principles to Indian scripts (see Fig. 8.2). Unfor-tunately, the standard transliteration from Meroitic in Latin script, which con-tinues to be used as much for convenience as for respect for scholarly tradition, obscures the nature of the Meroitic script. Each basic sign represents a syllable with the vowel /a/ and accordingly, *Npte* 'Napata' (the religious capital) was pronounced /napate/, or more likely /nabate/ (Greek Ναπατα or Ναβατα). If the vowel is different, a special sign, more a vocalic modifier than a true vowel-sign, accompanies the basic sign: for instance, *nob* 'Nubian, slave' was realized /noba/ or /nuba/ (Greek Νουβα). Contrary to Indian scripts, this modifier is not written above or below the line, but simply follows to the left of the basic sign, the direction of writing being right to left as in demotic. If a bare conso-nant is required, particularly in consonant clusters, the basic sign is followed by the modifier *e*, which writes both /e/ and /ə/ (schwa); thus *Qoreti* 'Qurta' (a place-name) was realized /k(ʷ)urti/, compare Greek Κορτη.

A rather variable system was created for initial vowels. Some complicated phonetic features such as diphthongs or double consonants were left unrecorded: diphthongs were notated defectively with the second element (*Kisri* 'Caesar', for /kaisari/, Greek Καισαρ), while doubling was graphically avoided by haplography (e.g. *Amnpte* 'Amun of Napata' for /amannabatte/). Although the Meroitic script was developed through a process of simplification in relation to its demotic source, it nonetheless required from the Meroitic readers some knowledge of traditional orthography. Moreover, as the language underwent phonetic shifts (particularly loss of initial vowels and assimilations), a double standard came into use, sometimes within a single text: a conservative practice, faithful to old syllabic boundaries, and a phonetic one, favouring current pro-

hieroglyphic	cursive	transliteration	values
𓋴	5₹	*a*	Initial /a/ or /u/
𓃟	↙	*b*	/ba/
𓄿	ᴎ	*d*	/da/
ß	ς	*e*	/e/, /ə/ , or no vowel
●	⊂	*ḫ*	/ḫa/
℧	ʒ	*h*	/ẖa/
𓏏	4	*i*	modifier /i/
𓃭	₹	*k*	/ka/
𓊃	ʒ	*l*	/la/
𓂝	ʒ	*m*	/ma/
∿	ℛ	*n*	/na/
ꝗꝗ	⅄	*ne*	/ne/, /nə/ or /n/
ℵ	/	*o*	modifier /u/
⊕	⟨	*p*	/pa/
Δ	/ʔ	*q*	/qa/
▫	ɯ	*r*	/ra/
𓏲	3	*s*	/sa/
⧺	⋃//	*se*	/se/, /sə/ or /s/
⌐♀	ʒ	*t*	/ta/
⊓	/ɬ	*te*	/te/, /tə/ or /t/
☞	╰	*to*	/tu/
𓎡	ʒ	*w*	/wa/
𓏹𓏹	///	*y*	/ya/
⋮	∶	∶	word-divider

Figure 8.2 Meroitic syllabary.

nunciation. So the sentence 'he is the ruler' could be spelled *qorelo* /kʷurlau/ (REM 1089)[3] in the old-fashioned orthography, or *qoro* /kʷurrau/ (REM 1294) in the modernized spelling. In spite of these variations, the Meroitic script is a remarkable achievement, especially since foreign influence on its elaboration can now be ruled out: since the system is syllabic, it cannot have been influenced by Greek (*contra* Griffith 1909: 50–1; Houston *et al.* 2003: 443), while chronology excludes the possibility of Persian influence (Priese 1997: 253).

Hieroglyphic and cursive Meroitic scripts

About a thousand Meroitic documents, many of which are short or fragmentary texts, have been found so far in excavations in Egyptian Nubia and Northern Sudan; nine tenths of these are written in cursive. The hieroglyphic script was used exclusively by rulers, in captions of scenes depicting the royal family in state temples, particularly at Naga (Zibelius 1983) or carved on some funerary objects, offering-tables, bowls, etc. The writing system of both scripts is the same, consisting of an alphasyllabary of twenty-three signs plus a word-divider. The earliest inscription in Meroitic hieroglyphic now known is a double cartouche with the name of Queen Shanakdakhete (REM 0039), for whom a dating in the last decades of the second century BC is now suggested (Török, in Eide *et al.* 1996: 661). Some inscriptions in Temple M260 at Meroe (REM 0401) could be earlier, since they include some purely Egyptian signs that were subsequently excluded from the 'classical' set. There is no reason to think that Meroitic hieroglyphic script antedated the cursive script. On the contrary, it is plausible that the cursive script was introduced first for requirements of everyday life, while the hieroglyphic script was developed later for prestige purposes and because of the magical power connected with its iconicity. The cursive script derived naturally from a judicious adaptation of Egyptian demotic, whereas the hieroglyphic signs seem to have been chosen rather arbitrarily inside the vast stock of Egyptian signs. It is moreover evident that some hieroglyphic signs were selected because they resembled the corresponding cursive sign graphically, even though their Meroitic value was unrelated to the original Egyptian value. An example is the eye of Horus, hieroglyphic 𓂀, corresponding to cursive ⵒ *d*.

Literacy in the kingdom of Meroe

Although we know very little about the sociological aspects of literacy in the Meroitic kingdom (but see Millet 1974: 49, 52–3), it seems that, as in later Egypt, the art of writing was in the hands of the priests. But contrary to the situation which prevailed in late Egyptian society (Houston *et al.* 2003: 443–4), the Meroitic priesthood was deeply involved in royal administration (Török 1979). The numerous funerary texts from Lower Nubia, in which the titles of the deceased are proudly enumerated, show this intertwining of temple and state structures.

Most priests (Meroitic *ant*) also held offices connected with local or central administration. Conversely, the highest officials of the royal administration in Nubia, at least nominally, held many cult offices. Abratoye, 'viceroy'[4] of Nubia (*peseto Akine-te*) around AD 260, was in addition 'priest of Amun of Primis' and 'priest from Quban all the way to Primis' (Carrier 2001: 26). Interestingly, he held the further office of '*qorene* of Isis of Philae': *qorene* is traditionally translated 'royal scribe' (Millet 1974: 53), although the evidence for this is scarce. The overall picture we obtain of the Meroitic civilization displays a situation very similar to that of Egypt before the foreign invasions, where administration, priesthood, and literacy were in the hands of the same group of people. The special connection of literacy with religious centres is obvious from the fact that most non-funerary Meroitic texts have been found in association with the main sanctuaries of the kingdom, such as the temples of Amun at Qasr Ibrim, Kawa, Napata, and Meroe or the temple of Apedemak at Naga. Although several scholars have suggested that literacy was widespread in the Meroitic population (Millet 1974: 52), the available Meroitic corpus of a thousand texts, is much smaller than the corpora available for other ancient languages that are attested over a comparable span of time and territory.

The palaeographical development of the cursive script during the six centuries of its existence displays the influence of professional scribes on the writing techniques and on the spread of literacy. The main changes in the script are the following:

1. The squat shape of many archaic signs became progressively more slender;
2. The signs which were originally upright came to slant more and more to the left;
3. The tails of the signs *a*, *k*, *n*, and *p* grew longer, running under the line in the Late period;
4. Many originally distinct signs became increasingly similar.[5]

All these developments point towards a close relationship between the lost genres of writing on perishable media and the epigraphic texts which mostly form the surviving corpus.

1. Slender signs could be written closer together and allowed the scribes to save precious material such as papyrus.
2. Slanted handwriting is characteristic of people who are used to writing often and quickly.
3. The long tails of some signs, which would take a little longer to write, exhibit a tendency toward calligraphic quality that probably imitated official documents written in ink. These three features suggest that the teaching of writing was in the hands of professional scribes whose techniques were increasingly reflected in the handwriting of the rest of the population.

4. Finally, weakly differentiated signs may make reading difficult, but only for those people who have to read letter by letter, not for fluent readers who can instantly identify a word just from its overall appearance.

This last feature shows that speed reading was common in the late period: contrary to what is generally assumed, it seems that the last centuries of the kingdom of Meroe (AD 150–350) were by no means a period of intellectual decline, but on the contrary the golden age of Meroitic literacy.

Disappearance of the Meroitic Script: A State of the Art

The disappearance of the Meroitic script has never been studied as a specific issue. As with other scripts, scholars have almost always been more interested in its origins and first appearance (Priese 1973). While a few scattered comments can be found (Griffith 1911: 21 with n. 2; Millet 1974: 54–6; Priese 1997: 255), there is no detailed analysis of the problem. The scarcity of evidence is one of the main reasons for this apparent lack of interest. The following overview is in no way a final approach to the issue, but must be viewed as an initial sketch. Similarly, an in-depth theoretical analysis of the reasons that caused the disappearance of the Meroitic script would be premature. Therefore, unlike colleagues dealing with more favoured fields, I will have to limit the following study largely to factual matter.

The end of Meroe is itself a much debated question.[6] Scholars disagree particularly about the ethnic and cultural character—Late Meroitic or Pre-Nubian?—of the states that emerged after the disintegration of the central Meroitic power. The city of Meroe was undoubtedly seized by King Ezana of Aksum around AD 350, as emerges from his stelae and other inscriptions (Eide *et al.* 1998: 1094–1103). But these documents report also how the king had to fight against the *Noba* (Nubian)[7] tribes that had settled in large parts of the dying Meroitic empire (Hintze 1967). In addition, Ezana's direct predecessor(s) had already fought victoriously against the kings of Meroe in the first part of the fourth century or still earlier (Eide *et al.* 1998: 1066–72). The disappearance of the central administration in Meroe, due to the simultaneous assault of Noba tribes and the Aksumite empire, resulted in an economic and cultural collapse in this part of the kingdom (Török 1997: 481; Hinkel and Sieversten 2002: 64; Shinnie and Anderson 2004: 128–31), although it is not clear how long Meroitic royal power survived.[8] In the north of the Meroitic kingdom, the situation was comparable, but with different actors. Another Nubian tribe, the Noubades, and the Blemmyan kinglets, who originated in the Eastern desert,[9] shared the spoils of Meroitic Nubia. Around the beginning of the fifth century, rulers of presumably Noubadian origin founded a powerful dynasty known as the Ballana kingdom, from the name of its rich necropolis at Ballana. Meroitic influence on this state is still obvious from the style of the material excavated in the royal tombs, particularly jewels and crowns, although no Meroitic inscription was found there. By the beginning of the sixth century, the Middle Nile valley was divided into three Nubian kingdoms: Nobatia with its capital at Faras, Makuria with its capital at Dongola and Alodia with its capital at Soba. Significantly, Dongola and Soba were new towns built far away from any previous Meroitic settlement, whereas the main cities of Nobatia, Faras and Primis (modern Qasr Ibrim), were ancient Meroitic settlements.

Earlier scholars generally accepted Griffith's suggestion that Meroitic script and language vanished soon after the kingdom of Meroe disintegrated, in the fourth century AD. Old Nubian superseded Meroitic as the dominant spoken language and Greek became the main vehicle of literacy. We know that the royal cemetery in Meroe (Begrawwiya North) was abandoned around AD 350. This date fits with king Ezana's invasion of what remained of the Meroitic empire (Eide *et al.* 1998). Thus the latest Meroitic text now known, the cursive inscription of King Kharamadoye on a column in the temple of Kalabsha in Lower Nubia (REM 0094, see Fig. 8.3), was traditionally dated to the mid-fourth century, and Kharamadoye himself was regarded as a Meroitic king, although no trace of his reign has been found in the south of the kingdom.

Fifty years after Griffith's publication of the text, Nicholas Millet restudied the inscription of Kharamadoye. He suggested that the sequence *Yismeniye* in lines 8 and 15 was the Meroitic transcription of the name of a Blemmyan ruler recorded as 'Isemne' in a Greek inscription in the same temple of Kalabsha (Millet 1973: 33). The Blemmyan occupation of Kalabsha can be dated from Latin and Greek sources to AD 394–453 (Eide *et al.* 1998: 1115–23). So Kharamadoye's inscription had to be redated some decades later than originally suggested, and at all events later than the disintegration of the Meroitic empire. This text therefore demonstrates that the Meroitic script survived the fall of the southern metropolis.

A final point of great importance was noticed by Griffith and his successors, but without further comment (Griffith 1911: 14; 1913: 73; Hofmann, 1981: 3; Hintze, 1987: 43–4). The Old Nubian alphabet (example in Fig. 8.4), which was based on a mixture of Greek and Coptic signs, also incorporates three Meroitic signs for sounds unknown to the other two scripts, namely /ñ/, /ng/, and /w/, the last of these however being notated more frequently by the digraph OY. But the earliest documents in Old Nubian that can be dated with certainty were written at the end of the eighth century AD. There is a gap of three centuries between the latest known Meroitic text and the earliest Old Nubian inscriptions, yet it is necessary to assume that the two scripts overlapped in use, at least for a short period. If this were not so, how could one account for signs passing from Meroitic into Old Nubian script?

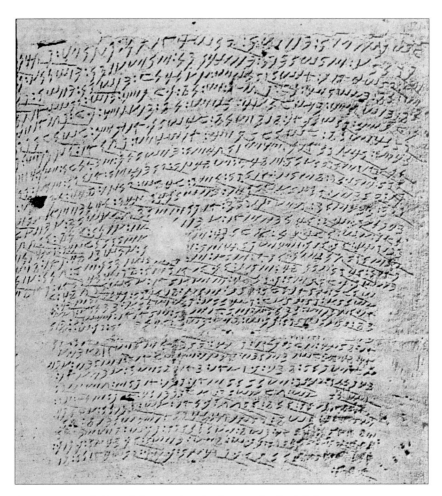

Figure 8.3   Inscription of Kharamadoye in the Temple of Kalabsha.

Late Meroitic Texts

The inscription of Kharamadoye

It is now established that Meroitic was used as a written language at least until the fifth century AD. Török has restudied the historical context of the inscription of Kharamadoye (REM 0094, see Fig. 8.3) and suggests a date around AD 420 (Eide *et al.* 1998: 1103–7). He proposes that Kharamadoye was one of the earliest Noubadian kings buried in the Ballana cemetery with royal artefacts such as silver crowns. If so, he must be regarded as a member of the new Nubian-speaking elite and no longer a 'pure' Meroitic king. However, the name 'Kharamadoye'

Figure 8.4   Old Nubian text: pages of the lectionary.

does not fit with what we know of Nubian languages. None of them, including Old Nubian, uses the velar fricative consonant /x/, which is transcribed Kh- in the royal name. In addition, several Blemmyan names known from Greek or Coptic transcriptions contain a first element *khara-*.[10] So it is conceivable that Kharamadoye was of Blemmyan extraction.[11] But the fact that he chose Meroitic in order to inscribe what seems to be a list of his military campaigns and political deeds (Millet 1973; 2003) is by no means insignificant: it is obviously a claim to legitimacy in a formerly Meroitic territory. Evidence for such a purpose can be found in the long initial protocol, which is copied from an earlier Meroitic royal inscription. A fragment of the original text, which can be dated palaeographically to the early fourth century AD, was found in 1984 in excavations at Qasr Ibrim (REM 1228, cf. Edwards 1994). Around the same date, at the beginning of the fifth century, the Blemmyan king Isemne, whose name is quoted in Kharamadoye's inscription, but whose precise connection with Kharamadoye cannot yet be established,[12] used Greek for a short graffito recording his pious deeds in the temple of Kalabsha (Eide *et al.* 1998: 1131–2). It is possible that the use of Meroitic in Kharamadoye's text was intended to present the ruler as the keeper of the old traditions, as opposed to rival Blemmyan kings who yielded to the more fashionable use of Greek in display inscriptions.

Yet the inscription of Kharamadoye includes some unusual spellings that indicate the intrusion of a late or provincial pronunciation into traditional Meroitic orthography. Three examples are:

ፍ𝘂𝘂 / /⁊ *qore* /kwurrə/ 'the king' (with article), for the usual 𝘂𝘂 / /⁊ *qor* /kʷurra/ (l.1)

⁊𝘂𝘂 / /⁊ *qorh* / k ʷurraxʷ a / 'great king', for the usual ⁊ϟፍ𝘂𝘂 / /⁊ *qore lh* /kʷur laxʷa/ (l.18)

𝘓// Ծ *wse* /was/ or perhaps /us/ 'his, her', for the usual 𝘓// ፍ /⁊ *qese* /kʷəs/ (ll.15, 17)

The first and second examples show the increasing tendency to vocalic neutralization and assimilation which is attested in Meroitic as known from the first century AD onward. While the former writing is not unprecedented in late Meroitic texts, the latter is especially surprising since it hampers the understanding of the text by reducing the adjective to a single sign. Moreover, the fact that the usual spelling occurs in line 8 of the same text, shows that the scribe's orthography was inconsistent. The third example is typical of the northern pronunciation /w/ of the initial labiovelar consonant /kʷ/, which is known from other contexts where variant spellings were accepted (Rilly 1999: 102). Nevertheless, such a provincialism in the spelling of the possessive is unique in Meroitic texts.

Ironically, these misspellings show that Meroitic was still a living language at the beginning of the fifth century. But they also reveal the decay of the norms of writing and the decreasing competence of the scribes, even those directly connected with the royal administration of late Nubia. In this respect, late Meroitic writing exhibits the same symptoms of decline as late Egyptian hieroglyphic script or Mayan writing (Houston *et al.* 2003: 445, 458).

Post-Meroitic texts from Qasr Ibrim

Qasr Ibrim (Meroitic *Pedeme*, Greek *Primis*) is a significant site because it is the only settlement in Nubia that was inhabited continuously from the earliest Kushite dynasties to post-medieval times. In addition, it is the only Meroitic urban centre where thorough excavations have been conducted for decades. In the 1976 season there, the British archaeologists found no fewer than 113 cursive Meroitic inscriptions, most of which still await publication (Adams 1982: 202–13). Many of them were discovered in strata that can be dated on the basis of ceramics to the post-Meroitic period (c. AD 350–550) and later, that is after Lower Nubia was converted to Christianity (AD 543–546). Their distribution is of great interest, as can be seen in the chart opposite (Adams 1982: 212, fig. 1, still using the term X-Group for the post-Meroitic period).

However, the connection of these texts with their ceramic contexts is not unambiguous. Apart from the ostraka (potsherds), for which the ceramic context is precisely the material on which the text is written, re-use, or simply later clearance of old material must be allowed for as possibilities. Unfortunately,

Ceramic contexts

	Definitely Meroitic	Meroitic or X-Group	Definitely X-Group	Late X-Group	X-Group or Early Christian	Christian and later	Uncertain or unrecorded	Totals
Stelae	–	–	1	–	–	8	2	11
Ostraka	2	15	14	–	2	4	4	41
Papyri	1	7	29	3	6	–	4	50
Wooden tablets	–	–	7	–	–	–	2	9
Other	–	1	1	–	–	–	–	2
Totals	3	23	52	3	8	12	12	113

only two of these 113 documents, both wooden tablets,[13] have been published so far, but no ostrakon. Meroitic stelae found in Christian period strata had been removed from their original locations and re-used as building material in houses and churches (Adams 1982: 212; Plumley 1971: 19–20). Although Adams' chart shows the wooden tablets as having been discovered only in post-Meroitic ceramic contexts, one of them (REM 1324) can be dated by palaeography and textual typology to the end of the third century AD, that is in the last decades of the Meroitic period (Rilly 2000: 114, 117–18). Moreover, this text, probably an oracular amuletic decree enacted by the priesthood of the temple of Amun, was addressed to a *peseto*, that is to the highest official of Meroitic Nubia, second only to the king. The text definitely could not have been written after the collapse of the Meroitic administration. Its presence in post-Meroitic refuse deposits can only be explained as the result of a later clearing-out of obsolete archives from the temple. Some of the documents listed in Adams' chart must therefore be dated to earlier periods. However, it is very improbable that the Meroitic texts found in the Christian strata were written during the Meroitic period—that is some two centuries earlier—and kept in their original locations for such a long time. These texts were doubtlessly written during the post-Meroitic times, and could be contemporary with the Kharamadoye's inscription.

Moreover, even if some texts in Adams' chart must be redated to earlier periods, a progressive decrease in the range of text types can be observed: this is particularly evident for ostraka, the usual medium for texts relating to everyday life, and for papyri, which were often used for religious and perhaps administrative purposes. Stelae, used in funerary contexts, and wooden tablets, which are only known in connection with temples (Driskell *et al.* 1989: 20), went out of use after the Meroitic period. A comparable decline in the use of writing in religious and funerary contexts is attested in other parts of the former Meroitic empire: several post-Meroitic burials around the city of Meroe contained many offering-tables—twelve of different periods in the single Tomb 307—that had been removed from earlier graves, with unaltered inscriptions commemorating their original owners (Hofmann 1981: 57). This decline in the functions of writing can of course be paralleled in many other cases of script obsolescence (Houston *et al.* 2003: 467).

The el-Hobagi bowl

Finally, further south, at el-Hobagi, 100 km upstream from Meroe, a French team excavating a royal post-Meroitic tumulus in 1992, under the direction of Patrice Lenoble, found a bronze bowl with a Meroitic hieroglyphic inscription (REM 1222, Leclant *et al.* 2000: 1832–3). Török (1996: 111) suggested that this bowl could have been re-used. However, the ductus of the signs is still later than in another hieroglyphic inscription engraved on the mane of a sandstone lion found at Qasr Ibrim (Hallof 2003) that bears the name of king Yesbokhe-Amani, the latest known king of Meroe (between AD 300 and 350). The offering table of King Yesbokhe-Amani has now been identified and published by Paola Davoli and Michael H. Zach (2003). Its palaeographical features are very close to those of the inscription of King Kharamadoye, so that a dating around AD 350 is by no means too early. Yesbokhe-Amani was presumably the last king buried in the royal cemetery at Begrawwiya North, just before or after the Ezana's campaign.

A radiocarbon date around AD 350 ± 50 has been established for the tumulus where the bronze bowl was found (Lenoble, personal communication); re-use of the object can therefore be ruled out. Consequently, it seems that not only the cursive, but also the hieroglyphic, script survived the collapse of the centralized Meroitic state.

Silko's Triumphal Inscription and Related Texts from Kalabsha and Qasr Ibrim: Greek as a *Lingua Franca* in Post-Meroitic Lower Nubia?

One of the enemies of the Blemmyan kings was Silko (c. AD 450), a Noubadian king well known from his inscription engraved in twenty-two lines on a wall of the same temple of Kalabsha (Burstein 1998: No. 21), which he seized after he repelled the Blemmyes. In this inscription (Fig. 8.5), he introduces himself explicitly as 'King of the Noubades and of all the Ethiopians', reasserting Kharamadoye's claim to the legacy of the Meroitic ('Ethiopian') rulers. But he did not use Meroitic script: this time, the text was written in Greek. Barely a generation after Kharamadoye, this choice showed that Meroitic had lost its prestige once and for all, and had been superseded by the language of Byzantium. I have noted above that some Blemmyan kinglets of the early fifth century AD already used Greek for their inscriptions, particularly at Kalabsha (Eide *et al.* 1998: 1128–32).

Greek also became the official language of diplomacy in Lower Nubia. A letter on papyrus from Phonen, king of the Blemmyes, to Abourni, king of the Noubades and probably Silko's successor, was found at Qasr Ibrim in 1976 (Skeat 1977, Rea 1979; Hägg 1986; Eide *et al.* 1998: 1158–65). The letter includes a quotation from an earlier message sent by Abourni, which was therefore also written in Greek. However, the content is obscured by the faulty syntax and morphology used by the presumably Blemmyan scribe. Not only did he mix up most of the Greek case endings, he also made more awkward confusions between the first, the second, and sometimes even the third person, so that it is very difficult to know to whom is being referred: the addresser, namely Phonen; or the addressee, namely Abourni. The three modern scholars who have dealt successively with this letter, Theodore Skeat, John Rea, and Tomas Hägg, published three divergent translations. As Skeat rightly suggested (1977: 159–60), the letter in itself was of no use if the messenger sent by Phonen did not explain to the Nubian king, preferably in his language, the content of the message. Hence the question can be raised as to what was the use of this letter. Skeat suggested that it was an *aide-mémoire*. It seems more probable that the letter in Greek, whatever its grammatical correctness might be, was simply a prestige object intended to show the high status of the Blemmyan king in a context of difficult diplomatic relations. Greek was therefore less a *lingua franca* than a display script. The status of Greek as a prestige language among the Blemmyes and the Noubades is easily explained by their frequent relations with the Greek-speaking Roman administration in Egypt, for which the presence of these restless neighbours on the southern border was a constant concern (Eide *et al.* 1998: 1138–41, 1153–8, 1188–93).

Old Nubian Script: The Meroitic Legacy

In the Greek-based alphabet used by Nubian scribes of the sixth to fifteenth century Christian kingdom of Nobatia to notate their language, Old Nubian, three signs are generally assumed to have been borrowed from the Meroitic syllabary: ⲛ̄ *ñ* (palatal nasal), from Meroitic ⲛ *ne*; ⲱ *w*, from Meroitic ⲃ *w*; ⲅ *ng* (velar nasal) from Meroitic ⊂ *ḫ*. Only the first and second signs are certainly of Meroitic origin. It cannot be ruled out that the third was originally a Greek Γ with a diacritic lower stroke, a suggestion that can account more easily for its Old Nubian phonemic value (Peust 1999: 78, n. 58). So the evidence would be weak if there were not some southern inscriptions, recorded by Richard Lepsius (1849–58: VI, 11) from Wadi es-Sebua to Soba, south to Khartoum. These short texts, rarely quoted and difficult to understand, seem to write a southern

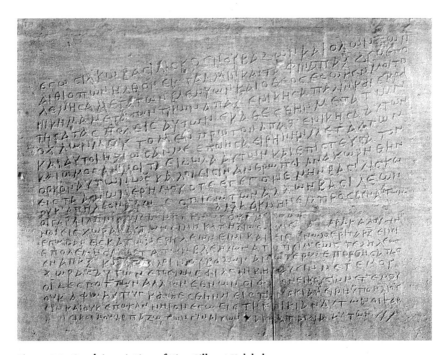

Figure 8.5 Greek inscription of King Silko at Kalabsha.

dialect of Old Nubian with a similar Greek-like alphabet (Zyhlarz 1928: 190–1). But this alphabet includes more Meroitic signs, especially specific signs for /kw/ and for /j/ which seem to be descendants of very late Meroitic characters.

The earliest datable text in Old Nubian is from AD 797 (Łatjar 1997: 117), although another document, a Coptic/Old Nubian papyrus, seems older on palaeographical grounds (Browne 1993).[14] But it is certain that the Greek (and in part the Coptic) alphabets were adapted much earlier for Old Nubian, even if evidence has not yet been found. In the excavations of Qasr Ibrim, Coptic letters addressed to a Noubadian tribal chief were found (Pierce in Eide *et al.* 1998: 1165–75). They can be dated around AD 450 and are therefore contemporary with the latest Meroitic inscriptions from the same site. It would not be surprising that some Noubadian scribes should lay the foundations of what would become later the Old Nubian script in such a multicultural and multilingual context. Perhaps a date close to the Christianization of Nubia, around AD 550, would be a plausible suggestion for the appearance of the Old Nubian alphabet. A clerical invention is actually very probable. But we still do not know the names of these Nubian counterparts of SS. Cyril and Methodius, who adapted the Greek alphabet to translate the Bible into Old Slavic.

Reconstructing a Scenario for the Disappearance of Meroitic Script

In conclusion, it is possible to suggest a general and very tentative outline of the disappearance of Meroitic script. Until the fall of Meroe (c. AD 350), Meroitic was the dominant language throughout the kingdom and the only one which could be written. Literacy was connected mainly with the royal and religious administrations. Temples were the main centres where the art of writing was practised and taught.

With the collapse of the central power of Meroe, Blemmyan and Nubian-speaking tribes—Noubades in Lower Nubia, Makurites in Upper Nubia, 'Red Nobas' in Central Sudan—replaced the Meroitic elites. These new rulers deprived the Meroitic temples of their influence and economic support, either because they had their own cults or because, by doing this, they wished to suppress any possible opposition to their power. The disappearance of Meroitic priesthood resulted in the decline of the Meroitic script, which however retained some prestige in the north (Lower Nubia) for two or three further generations, as is shown by the inscription of Kharamadoye at Kalabsha. As in Roman and Byzantine Egypt, Greek also became the written language of prestige in Nubia. Although the Meroitic script probably remained in use for some decades longer, it had lost its former prestige. One century later, it probably received its final death blow with the conversion of the Nubian kingdoms to Christianity. It is, however, very likely that the invention of the Old Nubian script, traditionally dated to the eighth century, must be placed two centuries earlier, at a time when Meroitic signs were still known and could provide characters that were otherwise lacking for the notation of Old Nubian in a Greek-derived alphabet.

If this scenario is accurate, nearly all the factors which can cause obsolescence of a writing system were present: a radical political shift, with the collapse of the central power in Meroe; socio-linguistic change, with the emergence of a new Nubian-speaking elite; importance of a new prestige written language, Greek; and finally, religious upheaval, leading to the elimination of the institutional structures of the temples that had supported Meroitic literacy. Faced with all these lethal forces, Meroitic had not the slightest chance of survival.

Notes

1. The only extant publication is Erman (1911), which does not include the hieratic text, but only a hieroglyphic transcription. Later studies of the document have all been based on Erman's work. The list was transliterated anew and briefly studied by Vernus (1984).

2. A connection with abnormal hieratic, a script used in the Theban region during the seventh and sixth centuries BC), as was assumed by Priese (1973: 281 and passim), can now be ruled out. This hypothesis was based mainly on the puzzling shape of the numeral 20, but cannot be sustained for the rest of the signs.

3. REM: texts numbered according to the *Répertoire d'épigraphie méroïtique* (Leclant *et al.* 2000).

4. On this much discussed title, see Yoyotte 1987: 84-6; Török 2002: 464-7.

5. Compare for instance in Fig. 8.2 the signs ẖ / m / s ; e / t ; l / t.

6. On this issue, which was the main topic of the Eighth Conference for Meroitic Studies, held in London in 1996, see the conference proceedings (Welsby 1999).

7. The ethnic term 'Noba' or 'Nubians' must not be confused with the geographical term Nubia. 'Nubia' is generally used for all periods to designate the part of the Nile Valley extending from the First to the Fourth Cataract. 'Nubians' were tribes inhabiting the western part of Sudan until some of them—called *Noba* or *Nuba* in Meroitic, Greek, and Ge'ez texts—invaded the Meroitic kingdom from the fourth century onward.

8. The rich tumuli at el-Hobagi (60 km upstream from Meroe), excavated in the 1990s by a French archaeological team, are dated to the middle of the fourth century. According to Patrice Lenoble, they may demonstrate the persistence of Meroitic regalia in central Sudan (Lenoble and Sharif 1992). László Török (1997: 482), by contrast, assumes that the el-Hobagi burials were made for Nubian rulers.

9. The Blemmyes were presumably the ancestors of the modern Beja, a northern Cushitic people now scattered along the Red Sea shore from the south of Egypt to the north of Eritrea. However this identification is not absolutely certain (for discussion, see Satzinger 1992).

10. Kharakhen 'King of the Blemmyes', Kharapatkhour, and Kharahiet, his sons, are quoted in a royal decree written in Coptic (early sixth century?) and allegedly originating from Gebelein, in Upper Egypt. Cf. Eide *et al.* 1998: 1209–10.

11. That is also Millet's assumption (2003: 59), based on the second part of the royal name (*mdo-ye*) which he considered to be the Meroitic name of the allegedly Blemmyan God Mandulis, who was particularly venerated at Kalabsha.

12. Isemne's inscription mentions another king, named Degou or Derou. As Török points out Eide *et al.* 1998: 1132), it seems that 'the Blemmyan state was an association of tribal units, the chiefs of which termed themselves Βασιλευς, "king", in Greek [...]. It remains obscure whether they were equal in rank or there was a hierarchy of Blemmyan kings'.

13. REM 1158 (Leclant *et al.* 2000: 1704–5), REM 1324 (Edwards and Fuller 2000: 85–6.)

14. Griffith (1913: Graffito No. 4) assumed that a graffito at Wadi es-Sebua contained the mention 'year 511 of the Martyrs', corresponding to AD 795. Gerald Browne (1996: 1) has shown that Griffith's reading of the abbreviation that supposedly gave the date was wrong.

References

Adams, William Y.
    1982   'Meroitic Textual Material from Qasr Ibrîm'. In Nicholas B. Millet and Allyn
            L. Kelley, (eds), *Meroitic Studies: Proceedings of the Third International Meroitic
            Conference, Toronto 1977*. Meroitica 6. Berlin: Akademie Verlag, 211–16.
Bonnet, Charles
    2001   'Kerma. Rapport préliminaire sur les campagnes de 1999–2000 et 2000–2001'.
            Genava 48: 199–218.
Browne, Gerald M.
    1993   'A Papyrus Document in Coptic and Old Nubian'. *Journal of Juristic Papyrology*
            23: 29–32.
    1996   *Old Nubian Dictionary*. Leuven: Peeters.
Burstein, Samuel
    1998   *Ancient African Civilizations: Kush and Axum*. Princeton, NJ: Princeton University Press.
Carrier, Claude
    2001   'La stèle méroïtique d'Abratoye (Caire, J.E. n° 90008)'. *Meroitic Newsletter* 28:
            21–53.
Davoli, Paola, and Michael H. Zach
    2003   'A Meroitic Offering Table in the Museo Civico Archeologico di Bologna'.
            Beiträge zur Sudanforschung 8: 21–30.
Driskell, Boyce N., Nettie K. Adams, and Peter J. French
    1989   'A Newly Discovered Temple at Qasr Ibrim: Preliminary Report'. *Archéologie
            du Nil Moyen* 3: 11–54.
Edwards, David N.
    1994   'A New Meroitic Inscription from Qasr Ibrim and a Tentative Reconstruction'. *Meroitic Newsletter* 25: 21–5.
Edwards, David N., and Dorian Q. Fuller
    2000   'Notes on the Meroitic "Epistolary" Tradition: New Texts from Arminna West
            and Qasr Ibrim'. *Meroitic Newsletter* 27: 77–98.
Eide, Tormod, Tomas Hägg, Richard Holton Pierce, and László Török
    1996   *Fontes Historiae Nubiorum, II. From the Mid-Fifth to the First Century BC. Textual
            Sources for the History of the Middle Nile between the 8th Century BC and the 6th AD.*
            Bergen: University of Bergen, Department of Classics.
    1998   *Fontes Historiae Nubiorum, III. From the First to the Sixth Century AD. Textual Sources
            for the History of the Middle Nile between the 8th Century BC and the 6th AD.*
            Bergen: University of Bergen, Department of Classics.
Erman, Adolf
    1911   *Hymnen an das Diadem der Pharaonen aus einem Papyrus der Sammlung Gole-
            nischeff*. Abhandlungen der Königlich Preussischen Akademie der Wissen-
            schaften, phil.-hist. Klasse 1911: 1. Berlin: Georg Reimer.

Gauthier, Henri
    1911   *Le temple de Kalabchah*. Les Temples Immergés de la Nubie. Cairo: Imprimerie de l'Institut Français d'Archéologie Orientale.

Griffith, Francis Llewelyn
    1909   'Meroitic Inscriptions'. In David Randall-Maclver, and Leonard Wooley, Areika. Eckley B. Coxe Junior Expedition to Nubia, vol. 1. Oxford: Oxford University Press, 43–54.
    1911   *The Meroitic Inscriptions of Shablûl and Karanog*. Eckley B. Coxe, Jr., Expedition to Nubia 6. Philadelphia: Philadelphia University Museum.
    1913   *The Nubian Texts of the Christian Period*. Berlin: Abhandlungen der Königlich Preussischen Akademie der Wissenschaften, phil.-hist. Klasse 1913. Berlin: Georg Reimer.

Hägg, Tomas
    1986   'Blemmyan Greek and the Letter of Phonen'. In Martin Krause, (ed.), *Nubische Studien; Tagungsakten der 5. Internationalen Konferenz der International Society for Nubian Studies. Heidelberg, 22.-25. September 1982*. Mainz: Philipp von Zabern, 281–6.

Hallof, Jochen
    2003   'Yesbokheamani—der Löwe von Qasr Ibrim'. *Journal of Egyptian Archaelogy* 89: 251–4.

Hinkel, Friedrich Wilhelm, and Uwe Sieversten
    2002   *Die Royal City von Meroe und die repräsentative Profanarchitktur in Kusch*. Archaeological Map of the Sudan, Suppl. 4. Berlin: Verlag Monumenta Sudanica.

Hintze, Fritz
    1955   'Die Sprachliche Stellung des Meroitischen'. *Afrikanische Studien* 26: 355–72.
    1967   'Meroe und die Noba'. *Zeitschrift für Ägyptische Sprache* 94: 79–86.
    1973   'Some Problems of Meroitic Philology'. In Fritz Hintze, (ed.), *1. Internationale Tagung für meroitistische Forschungen in Berlin 1971*, Meroitica 1. Berlin: Akademie Verlag, 321–36.
    1987   'Zur Interpretation des meroitischen Schriftsystems'. *Beiträge zur Sudanforschung* 2: 41–50.
    1989   'Meroitisch und Nubisch, eine vergleichende Studie'. *Beiträge zur Sudanforschung* 4: 95–106.

Hofmann, Inge
    1981   *Material für eine meroitische Grammatik*. Veröffentlichungen der Institute für Afrikanistik und Ägyptologie der Universität Wien 16. Vienna: Afro-Pub.

Honegger, Mathieu
    2002   'Evolution de la société dans le bassin de Kerma (Soudan), des derniers chasseurs aux premiers royaumes de Nubie'. *Bulletin de la Société française d'égyptologie* 53: 12–27.

Houston, Stephen, John Baines, and Jerrold Cooper
    2003   'Last Writing: Script Obsolescence in Egypt, Mesopotamia and Mesoamerica'. *Comparative Studies in Society and History* 45: 430–79.

Łatjar, Adam
    1997   'Greek Funerary Inscriptions from Old Dongola: General Notes'. *Oriens Christianus* 81: 107–26.

Leclant, Jean, André Heyler, Catherine Berger-El Naggar, Claude Carrier, and Claude Rilly
    2000   *Répertoire d'épigraphie méroïtique: Corpus des inscriptions publiées.* 3 vols. Académie des Inscriptions et Belles-Lettres. Paris: De Boccard.

Lenoble, Patrice, and Nigm-el-Din Mahmoud Sharif
    1992   'Barbarians at the Gates? The Royal Mounds of el-Hobagi and the End of Meroe'. *Antiquity* 66: 626–35.

Lepsius, Carl Richard
    1849–58   *Denkmaeler aus Aegypten und Aethiopien,* 6 parts. Berlin: Nicolai.

Macadam, M. F. Laming
    1949   *The Temples of Kawa. The Inscriptions.* 2 vols. Oxford University Excavations in Nubia. London: Oxford University Press for Griffith Institute.

Millet, Nicholas B.
    1973   'The Kharmadoye Inscription'. *Meroitic Newsletter* 13: 31–49.
    1974   'Writing and Literacy in Ancient Sudan'. In Abdelgadir M. Abdalla, (ed.), *Studies in Ancient Languages of the Sudan: Papers Presented at the Second International Colloquium on Language and Literature in the Sudan Sponsored by the Sudan Research Unit, 7–12 December 1970.* Khartoum: Khartoum University Press, 49–57.
    2003   'The Kharamandoye Inscription (MI 94) revisited'. *Meroitic Newsletter* 30: 57–72.

Peust, Carsten
    1999   *Das Napatanische: ein ägyptischer Dialekt aus dem Nubien des späten ersten vorchristlichen Jahrtausends. Texte, Glossar, Grammatik.* Monographien zur Ägyptischen Sprache 3. Göttingen: Peust und Gutschmidt.

Plumley, J. Martin
    1971   'Pre-Christian Nubia (23 BC–535 AD). Evidence from Qasr-Ibrîm'. *Etudes et travaux* 5: 7–24.

Priese, Karl-Heinz
    1973   'Zur Entstehung der meroitischen Schrift'. In Fritz Hintze, (ed.), *1. Internationale Tagung für meroitistische Forschungen in Berlin 1971.* Meroitica 1. Berlin: Akademie-Verlag, 273–306.
    1997   'La langue et l'écriture méroïtiques'. In D. Wildung, (ed.), *Soudan: royaumes sur le Nil.* Paris: Institut du monde arabe, 251–64.

Rea, John R.
    1979   'The Letter of Phonen to Aburni'. *Zeitschrift für Papyrologie und Epigraphik* 34: 147–62.

Rilly, Claude
    2000   'Deux exemples de décrets amulétiques oraculaires en méroïtique: les ostraca REM 1317/1168 et REM 1319 de Shokan'. *Meroitic Newsletter* 27: 99–118.
    2001   'The Earliest Traces of Meroitic'. In Mechthild Reh, (ed.), *Eighth Nilo-Saharan*

Linguistics Colloquium, Hamburg, 21-25 August 2001, abstracts of papers, Hamburg, 38-9. (Final version in the Proceedings, forthcoming.)

2003a 'Récents progrès dans le domaine de la philologie méroïtique'. *Meroitic Newsletter* 30: 73-7.

2003b 'Les graffiti archaïques de Doukki Gel et l'apparition de l'écriture méroïtique'. *Meroitic Newsletter* 30: 41-55.

2004 'The Linguistic Position of Meroitic'. *Arkamani* (www.arkamani.org/arkamani-library/meroitic/rilly.htm). Accessed 29 May 2008.

2007 *La Langue du royaume de Méroé: un panorama de la plus ancienne culture écrite d'Afrique subsaharienne*. Bibliothèque de l'Ecole des Hautes Etudes, IVe section, Sciences Historiques et Philologiques 344. Paris: Champion.

Satzinger, Helmut
1992 'Die Personennamen von Blemmyern in koptischen und griechischen Texten: orthographische und phonetische Analyse'. In Erwin Ebermann, Erich R. Sommerauer, and Karl E. Thomanek, (ed.), *Komparative Afrikanistik: Sprach-, geschichts- und literaturwissenschafliche Aufsätze zu Ehren von Hans G. Mukarovsky anlässlich seines 70. Geburtstag*. Veröffentlichungen der Institut für Afrikanistik und Ägyptologie 61; Beiträge zur Afrikanistik 44. Vienna: 313-24.

Schäfer, Heinrich
1901 *Die aethiopische Königsinschrift des Berliner Museums: Regierungsbericht des Königs Nastesen, des Gegners des Kambyses*. Leipzig: J. C. Hinrichs.

Shinnie, Peter L., and Julie R. Anderson
2004 *The Capital of Kush II: Meroe Excavations 1973-1984*. Meroitica 20. Wiesbaden: Harrassowitz.

Skeat, Theodore C.
1977 'A Letter from the King of the Blemmyes to the King of the Noubades'. *Journal of Egyptian Archaeology* 63: 169-78.

Török, László
1979 *Economic Offices and Officials in Meroitic Nubia: A Study in Territorial Administration of the Late Meroitic Kingdom*. Studia Aegyptiaca 5. Budapest: ELTE.

1996 'The End of Meroe'. In Derek Welsby, (ed.), *Eighth International Conference for Meroitic Studies. London, 1996. Pre-prints of the Main Papers and Abstract*. London: British Museum Press.

1997 *The Kingdom of Kush: Handbook of the Napatan-Meroitic Civilization*. Handbook of Oriental Studies I. The Near and Middle East. Leiden: E. J. Brill.

2002 *The Image of the Ordered World in Ancient Nubian Art: The Construction of the Kushite Mind, 800 BC-AD 300*. Leiden, Boston, MA, Cologne: E. J. Brill.

Trigger, Bruce G.
1964 'Meroitic and Eastern Sudanic: A Linguistic Relationship?' *Kush* 12: 188-94.

Valbelle, Dominique
2004 'The Cultural Significance of Iconographic and Epigraphic Data Found in the Kingdom of Kerma'. In Timothy Kendall, (ed.), *Nubian Studies: Proceedings of the Ninth Conference of the International Society of Nubian Studies, August 21-26, 1998*. Boston, MA: Department of African-American Studies, Northeastern University, 176-83.

Vernus, Pascal
  1984 'Vestiges de langues chamito-sémitiques dans des sources égyptiennes méconnues'. In James Bynon, ed., *Current Progress in Afro-Asiatic Linguistics: Papers of the Third International Hamito-Semitic Congress, London, 1978*. Amsterdam and Philadelphia, PA: John Benjamins, 477–81.

Welsby, Derek (ed.)
  1999 *Recent Research in Kushite History and Archaeology: Proceedings of the Eighth International Conference for Meroitic Studies (London, 1996)*. London: British Museum Press.

Yoyotte, Jean
  1989 'Le nom égyptien du "ministre de l'économie"—de Saïs à Méroé'. *Comptes rendus de l'Académie des Inscriptions et Belles-Lettres* janvier.–mars 1989: 73–88.

Zibelius, Karola
  1983 *Der Löwentempel von Naq'a in der Butana (Sudan) IV: Die Inschriften*. Beihefte zum Tübingen Atlas des vorderen Orients B 48: 4. Wiesbaden: Dr Ludwig Reichert.

Zyhlarz, Ernst
  1928 *Grundzüge der nubischen Grammatik im christlichen Frühmittelalter (Altnubisch)*. Abhandlungen für die Kunde des Morgenlandes 18: 1. Leipzig: Deutsche Morgenländische Gesellschaft.
  1930 'Das Meroïtische Sprachproblem'. *Anthropos* 25: 409–63.

9

The Phoenix of Phoinikēia:
Alphabetic Reincarnation in Arabia

M. C. A. Macdonald

The Two Alphabetic Traditions

Shortly after its invention in the second millennium BC, the alphabet split into two traditions. One of these—the Phoenico-Aramaic—spread both west to the Greeks[1] and beyond, and east, across Asia as far as Manchuria (Stary, in this volume), becoming the ancestor of all but one of the traditional alphabets in use today.[2] By contrast, the other—South Semitic—alphabetic tradition was used almost exclusively within the Arabian Peninsula[3] in antiquity, and only one of its descendants has survived into the modern world (Fig. 9.1).

Neither tradition had dedicated signs for representing vowels and neither showed doubled letters. Moreover, it was singularly unfortunate that the first widely used linear alphabet was designed to express Phoenician, which had one of the smallest repertoires of consonantal phonemes of any Semitic language.[4] Alas, the twenty-two letters of the Phoenician alphabet were treated as sacrosanct within the Near East, and the non-Phoenician Near Eastern languages which came to be written in it were squeezed into this rigid frame, regardless of the resulting ambiguities.[5]

By contrast, the South Semitic scripts had a fluid number of letters which represented far more effectively the consonantal repertoires of the languages they were transcribing. When a South Semitic script was used to write a previously unrecorded language, users simply took the letters needed to express its consonantal phonemes, and ignored those which were irrelevant, or changed the value of a letter to represent a different sound.[6] The result is that letters of

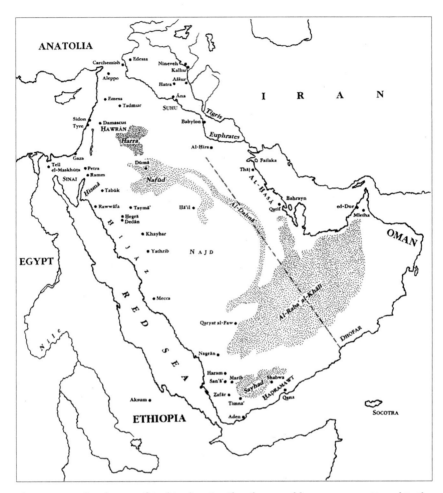

Figure 9.1 A sketch map of Arabia showing the places and languages mentioned in the text, and the rough geographical division between the west, where languages were written, and the east where they were not.

the same, or similar, form can represent unrelated sounds in different South Semitic alphabets, but within a particular script there is little if any ambiguity as to the phonemes represented (see Fig. 9.2), because—apart from the rare use of matres lectionis[7]—one sign represented only one phoneme. In this, the users of the South Semitic alphabets showed the same spirit as the archaic Greeks, who had no qualms about adapting the letters of the Phoenician alphabet, and inventing new signs, to express their local dialects and local tastes (see Sherratt 2003 and Luraghi forthcoming).

The South Semitic alphabetic tradition consisted of two major groups, the

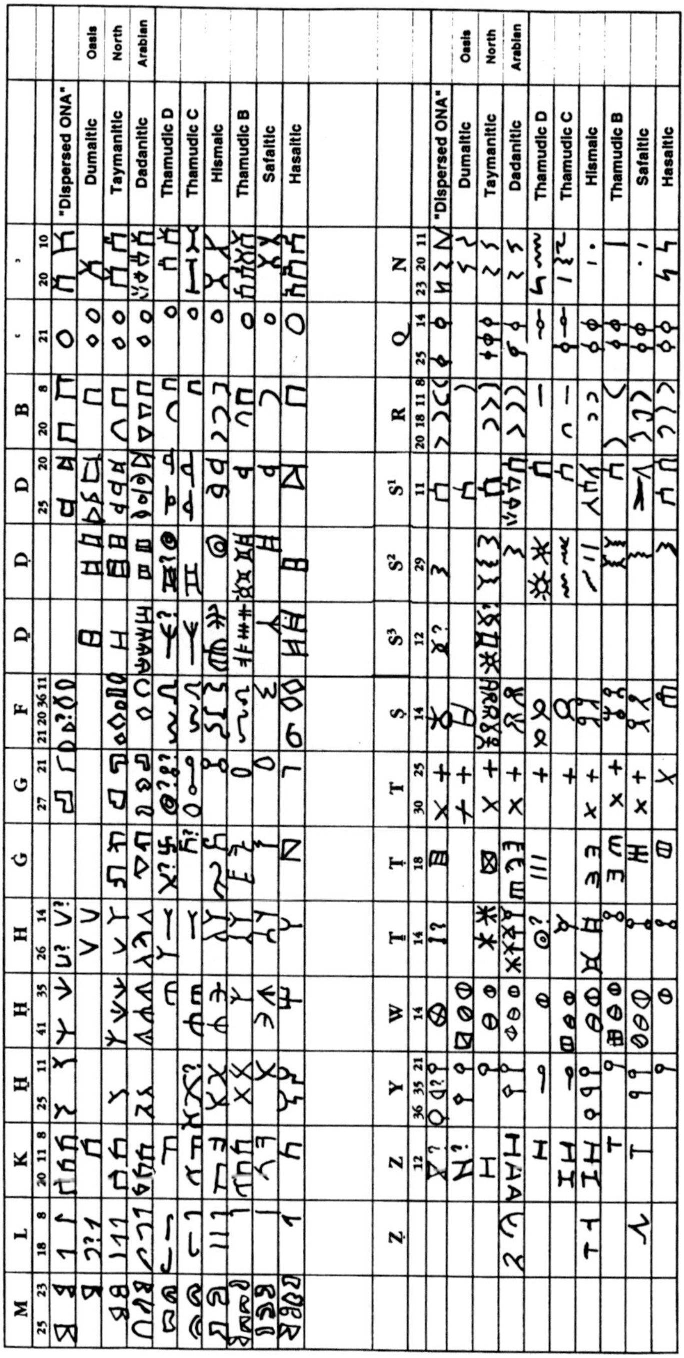

Figure 9.2 Script table of the Ancient North Arabian [ANA] alphabets.

Ancient North Arabian [ANA][8] alphabets and the South Arabian. Each of these groups was made up of a number of different scripts, and from the South Arabian monumental script developed the one modern survivor of this tradition: the Ethiopic vocalized alphabet.[9]

Written and Unwritten Languages in Ancient Arabia (Fig. 9.3)

In the Arabian Peninsula, north of Yemen, two groups of North Arabian dialects[10] were spoken. One group consisted of what is now generally called 'Old Arabic', that is, dialects which later developed into the written and spoken forms of Arabic which we know from the seventh century AD onwards (Macdonald 2000: 29–30, 48–57; 2008). Until the late pre-Islamic period, Arabic was a purely spoken tongue, co-existing with numerous written languages in the Arabian Peninsula, Mesopotamia, the Levant, and Egypt.[11] Before the sixth century AD, it was written only exceptionally, in scripts which usually expressed other languages. It was only shortly before the rise of Islam (seventh century AD) that it became associated with a particular alphabet, and only with the Islamic conquests that writing in Arabic became widespread. The other subgroup of 'North Arabian' is known as 'Ancient North Arabian' and consists of a collection of dialects which were spoken and written in the oases of central and north-west Arabia, and by nomads in the western two-thirds of the Peninsula from the borders of Yemen to Palmyra (Macdonald 2000: 29–30, 41–6). The Ancient North Arabian dialects and Old Arabic are very closely related and would certainly have been mutually comprehensible. Indeed, in the unvocalized ANA and South Arabian scripts they are sometimes difficult to distinguish.[12]

Languages used in Pre-Islamic Arabia				
South Arabia		**North and Central Arabia**		
INDIGENOUS	IMPORTED	INDIGENOUS	INDIGENOUS	IMPORTED
ANCIENT SOUTH ARABIAN	ARABIC	ANCIENT NORTH ARABIAN	ARABIC	
(Written languages)	*(Normally unwritten)*	(All written languages)	*(Normally unwritten)*	(All written languages)
		Languages of the oases		
Sabaic }	*Old Arabic*	Dumaitic	*Old Arabic*	Akkadian
Madhabic }		Taymanitic		Imperial Aramaic
} Sayhadic				
Qatabanic } group		Dadanitic		Nabataean Aramaic
}				
Hadramitic }		Hasaitic (?)		Greek
		Languages of the nomads		
		Hismaic		
		Safaitic		
		'Thamudic' dialects		
	Normally <u>written</u> languages, in Roman type		*Normally <u>unwritten</u> languages, in italics*	

Figure 9.3 A list of the principal written and unwritten languages in ancient Arabia.

However, as far as we can tell, Arabic speakers rarely used the ANA and South Arabian alphabets,[13] and at present it is difficult to explain why.

The oasis scripts of north-west Arabia

In north-west Arabia (Fig. 9.1), from perhaps as early as the eighth century BC, the inhabitants of each of the large oases, at Dadan (Biblical Dedān, modern al-ʿUlā), Taymāʾ, and Dūma (modern al-Jawf), developed their own forms of the South Semitic alphabet,[14] in which they wrote the Ancient North Arabian dialects spoken in these towns. The caravans of the frankincense trade had to pass through these oases on their way from the producers in South Arabia to the consumers in Mesopotamia, the Levant, Egypt, and the Mediterranean, and the oases grew rich on the profits (Macdonald 1997).

The coming of Aramaic

The desire to control this lucrative trade, soon aroused the greed of neighbouring empires and, in the mid-sixth century BC, the last king of Babylon, Nabonidus, conquered the major North Arabian oases and settled for ten years in Taymāʾ (Ephʿal 1982: 179–91; Beaulieu 1989: 149–85). He brought with him a bureaucracy which introduced Aramaic to Taymāʾ as the language of administration and this must have continued under the Persian empire, which conquered Babylon shortly afterwards. Under this pressure, the local ANA alphabet (Taymanitic) apparently soon fell out of use (though dating is a problem), and the Aramaic script in Taymāʾ followed a local development until the turn of the era when northern Arabia was absorbed into the Nabataean kingdom.

The Nabataeans were a nomadic tribe which, some time in the third century BC, settled down in what is now southern Jordan. They founded a kingdom which eventually stretched from southern Syria to northern Arabia. It is not absolutely certain what language they spoke, though for some, at least, it was probably a dialect of Old Arabic. However, they used as their written language a dialect of Aramaic expressed in a particular version of the Aramaic script.

Under the Babylonian and Persian empires, Aramaic had been the written language of government administration and the vehicle of international communication, from Egypt to Iran. Even after the conquests of Alexander the Great (333–323 BC), when Aramaic ceased to be the language of government, it remained the most common vehicle of written communication throughout the Levant and Mesopotamia. Under the Nabataeans, Aramaic became the new written language of prestige in the north-west Arabian oases of Ḥegrā (modern Madāʾin Ṣāliḥ), Dadan, Dūma, and Taymāʾ. The local ANA alphabets of northwest Arabia no doubt co-existed with Aramaic for a generation or two, before gradually falling into disuse, while in Taymāʾ—whose native ANA script had already disappeared in the Persian period—the local Aramaic script became 'regularized' to the Nabataean model. Thus, by the end of the first century AD, if not earlier, Aramaic had become the written language of the region, used both by speakers of Old Arabic—which had always been unwritten—and by those oasis-dwellers who spoke Ancient North Arabian dialects, which had now ceased to be written.

In AD 106, the Nabataean kingdom was annexed by the Romans and became the Province of Arabia. After the annexation, the language of official documents was changed to Greek. However, Nabataean Aramaic naturally continued to be used as a written language among many of the kingdom's former subjects. In the 'Nabataean heartland' of southern Jordan and the Negev, the epigraphic use of the Nabataean script gradually declined over the next century and a half, though there is no way of telling whether, or for how long, it continued to be used on perishable materials.

Understandably, it lingered on most successfully in peripheral areas, like north-west Arabia. The Romans recognized this and when, between AD 166 and 169, two successive governors of the Province of Arabia erected a Roman-style temple in the desert there, for a military unit levied from a local tribe,[15] the beautifully carved dedication to the emperors Marcus Aurelius and Lucius Verus was written in Greek (for the Roman side) and Nabataean Aramaic as the 'local' written language. The transformation was now complete. The local oasis scripts of the South Semitic family, expressing local languages, had been superseded by an imported alphabet from the Phoenico-Aramaic tradition, expressing a 'foreign' written language, which had to be learned by those who wished to write.

Literate nomads and the South Semitic script

One of the unexpected features of Arabian history is that, from the early first millennium BC until, say, the fourth century AD, literacy was widespread throughout the western two-thirds of the Peninsula, not only in the settled areas of Yemen, and the oasis towns of north-west Arabia, but also among huge numbers of nomads, whose graffiti, in their scores of thousands, cover the desert rocks from the borders of Yemen right up into southern Syria.

Like most nomads, they did not need writing for communicating or recording information, for which they used word-of-mouth and highly developed memories. Their way of life was not suited to the preservation of texts on perishable materials, and reference documents on non-portable surfaces, such as stelae or cliff faces, are of little use to those of no fixed abode (see Macdonald 1993: 382–8, and Macdonald 2005: 75). However, writing did have one practical use for nomads. The life of a pastoralist involves long periods of enforced, usually solitary, idleness: guarding and tending the flocks while they pasture all day, or keeping watch for game or for enemies. In these situations anything which can relieve boredom is welcome. For thousands of years, these nomads had carved their tribal marks or drawn pictures on the rocks, sometimes with great skill.

When some nomads—probably out of curiosity while visiting an oasis—learnt the principle of writing, and the letters of one of the South Semitic alphabets, they must have returned to their encampments and demonstrated their new-found skills to their friends and relations.[16] With the powerful memories of the non-literate it would have taken very little time for the skill to have been learnt and passed on, and now those out with the flocks could pass the time by carving their names and genealogies, descriptions of what they were doing or would like to be doing, their thoughts, feelings, and prayers. Needless to say, they did not stop drawing, but now they signed their work—and sometimes other people's.[17]

Given that this was an endlessly entertaining way of banishing boredom, it is difficult to understand why, having used it for hundreds of years, the nomads stopped writing by the mid-fourth century AD.[18] One can speculate on the reasons for this, though I should make it clear that there is simply no evidence for any particular hypothesis. One possibility is that the literate nomads settled down and became farmers or town-dwellers. By the third century AD, Aramaic and Greek were the written languages in the settled areas of Arabia and Syria respectively. Thus, the ANA alphabets these nomads had used in the desert would have been incomprehensible in the towns and, apart perhaps from the desert's edge, in the countryside, and so would have been of no practical use to them. Nor would they now have needed their literacy in the ANA scripts to banish boredom, since as agricultural labourers and workers in towns they would no longer have been afflicted by the long periods of enforced solitary idleness characteristic of the life of the nomadic pastoralist.

The world of farmers and townsmen in Syria and Arabia in the fourth century AD—unlike that of earlier centuries in north-west Arabia—was apparently one in which literacy was largely unnecessary, except for the patrician class, bureaucrats and scribes, and possibly some merchants. Ironically, the 'literate nomads' who may have settled in the fourth century AD, would have come from a non-literate society,[19] where memory and oral communication had not been ousted by the advent of writing (see Macdonald 2005: 78). Looked at from this point of view, the nomad who settled was moving from a non-literate society to a non-literate enclave within a literate society, the only difference being that whereas he had used writing as a pastime in the desert, he no longer needed it in his new life as a townsman or farmer. The literate culture of the upper echelons of his new society, which was conducted in languages and scripts which were unknown to him, would have passed him by, and writing in his own script, which had never been used for communication and record but had only ever been a pastime, would rapidly fall into disuse. However, as I emphasized above, this can be no more than speculation, and all we can be sure of is that these desert alphabets ceased to be used.

Southern Arabia

Ancient Yemen was dominated by powerful states of which the most famous were Saba⁾ (Biblical Sheba), Qatabān, Maʿīn, and Ḥaḍramawt. Their written languages are known collectively as Ancient (or Epigraphic) South Arabian, or Sayhadic, and belong to the South Semitic linguistic group. The languages used by these four states were all written in the same monumental South Arabian alphabet. Both the script of the monumental inscriptions and the minuscule used for everyday documents incised on sticks, are now known to have been used from at least the tenth century BC, until the sixth century AD.[20]

There may also have been unwritten languages in South Arabia. Christian Robin has suggested that the Minaeans, when they settled in the Yemeni Jawf, took over a pre-existing written language, which he has called 'Madhabic', that was quite different from their spoken tongue (1991: 98). He has also suggested that the Himyarites, who ruled southern Arabia from the fourth to late sixth centuries, spoke a normally unwritten language but used Sabaic for their written documents (see Robin 1991: 96; 2001: 522–8); but recently this view has been questioned by Peter Stein (2003: 6–7; 2004: 229–32, 235–40) who has proposed a more convincing interpretation of the evidence (see Macdonald forthcoming c). However, one thing is certain: from about the turn of the era onwards, increasing numbers of Arabic-speakers gradually settled in Yemen.

By the first century AD, the kingdom of Saba⁾ had enjoyed a long period of political and cultural hegemony, during which time the Sabaic language, and the South Arabian script in which it was written, had become the prestige means of written communication and record in the southern half of the Peninsula.

This can be seen at a site called Qaryat al-Fāw, on the north-western edge of the Empty Quarter (see Fig. 9.1), where there are reportedly large numbers of Sabaic inscriptions. Qaryat al-Fāw (known in antiquity as Qaryat Dhāt Kahil) was a staging post on one of the routes of the frankincense caravans and had grown rich on the proceeds (al-Ansary 1982). It also became the 'capital' of a number of Arab tribes, Qaḥṭān, Madhḥij, and Kinda. The members of these tribes spoke Arabic, but, because it was not written, would normally have used Sabaic as their written language (if necessary through translators and scribes). However, there are some inscriptions at Fāw which are in the Arabic language written in the Sabaic script (Beeston 1979: 1–2; Macdonald 2000: 49–50; Robin 1991: 115–16; 2001: 549), and others where the author appears to have been trying to use correct Sabaic, but has filled in the gaps in his knowledge with Arabic words and phrases—a situation parallel to that in Ḥegrā described below. However, this brief experiment in writing Arabic in the South Arabian script appears to have came to nothing. This is a pity since the South Arabian alphabet had more than enough letters to express the full consonantal repertoire of Arabic, whereas the Aramaic alphabet, which was eventually used to write Arabic, did not.

In the early centuries AD, three major processes began in South Arabia. Firstly, the trickle of Arabic-speaking immigrants into Yemen from the north, became a stream and then a flood, making Arabic, for the first time, one of the most widely spoken languages in south-west Arabia, though one with no prestige there. Secondly, from the mid-fourth century AD, when the Himyarites conquered Ḥaḍramawt, until the mid-sixth century, Sabaic became the only habitually written language in South Arabia. Thirdly, during the same period, the number of inscriptions in Yemen declines dramatically, and after the Iranian conquest in the late sixth century, dated monumental inscriptions disappear altogether.

Thus, from the fourth century onwards, the balance of written and unwritten languages in South Arabia underwent a massive shift. In the past, Sabaic, Qatabanic, and Hadramatic had been the spoken and written languages of the kingdoms of Sabaʾ, Qatabān, and Ḥaḍramawt respectively, and only perhaps in Maʿīn were these different functions fulfilled by different languages. Now, there was only one written language, Sabaic, and ever-increasing numbers of people spoke an unwritten tongue, Arabic. The decline in numbers of inscriptions (and documents on sticks) between the fourth and late sixth centuries does not necessarily mean a decline in literacy or in the use of the Sabaic language, but it suggests that the publicly visible written word was less important in the societies of this period than in those of previous generations (see Macdonald forthcoming c). This was, after all, a period of religious and political turmoil in Yemen with rapid changes from paganism to Judaism to Christianity, and invasions by the Ethiopians and the Iranians. Whatever the reasons, by the mid-sixth century AD, there are no more datable monumental inscriptions and documents on sticks in the Sabaic language and South Arabian alphabet (Robin 1991: 19), and by the rise of Islam, in the early seventh, Arabia's last alphabet of the South Semitic tradition was terminally obsolescent, if not actually dead.[21]

The Reincarnation of a South Semitic Alphabet

Yet, from the fourth century AD onwards, at the very time the South Arabian alphabet in Yemen was beginning its slow drift towards oblivion, a new shoot was springing up on the other side of the Red Sea. By the turn of the era, Sabaean colonists had brought their alphabet to Ethiopia, and in the fourth century AD it was adapted in a way which is unique among the alphabets used by Semitic languages.

Both the Phoenico-Aramaic tradition (as used in the Near East) and the South Semitic produced purely consonantal alphabets, though the Aramaic alphabet and its descendants adopted the system of matres lectionis by which some letters representing consonants (ʾālaph, hē, waw, yūdh) could, in certain circumstances, represent a long vowel. Among the South Semitic alphabets, only Dadanitic regularly used matres lectionis, and, for the most part, the other alphabets of this family remained severely consonantal (though for possible exceptions see Robin 2001: 570–7).

In Ethiopia, however, a novel approach was adopted. The obsolescent South Arabian consonantal alphabet was reincarnated as a vocalized one, not with dedicated vowel letters, as in Greek, nor with matres lectionis, but by modifying the shape of each letter in a largely consistent manner to indicate the vowel which follows it (cf. Kharoṣṭhī). At the same time, some of the twenty-nine letters of the Sabaic alphabet were eliminated because they did not represent Ethiopic phonemes; one letter was re-assigned to an Ethiopic sound which had not existed in Sabaic; and a new letter was invented: the final product being a vocalized alphabet in which each of the twenty-six letters has seven different forms indicating the consonant, plus the vowel which follows it.[22] This reincarnation was very much in the tradition of the South Semitic family of alphabets, which were adapted more or less to fit the languages they expressed.

Arabic and the Reincarnation of a Phoenico-Aramaic Alphabet

As pointed out above, the Phoenico-Aramaic alphabet, in the Near East, appears to have been treated as a 'fixed system': users were unwilling to add to or to subtract from the original twenty-two letters. Any changes or improvements had to be made within the existing system. This was done either by giving some letters multiple values (e.g. by making a letter a mater lectionis or by making it represent more than one consonant), or by using discrete diacritical points and other marks as clues to the correct reading of the text.[23] These points and marks were not considered to be essential elements of the script and so could be—and usually were—omitted, without in any way changing the meaning of what was written. This, if not apparent from prior knowledge, had to be divined from the context.

Nor were these the only obstacles to reading. In many Middle Eastern alphabets of the Phoenico-Aramaic tradition, the forms of two or more letters had become identical. From an early stage in Aramaic, d and r were indistinguishable and remained so in many of its offshoots: e.g. early and 'Classical' Nabataean, Palmyrene, and Syriac.[24] At various times, in different forms of the Aramaic alphabet, other letters developed identical forms. In an Aramaic text from the Arabian/Persian Gulf the letters d, k, ʿ, and r have an identical shape; as do ḥ and m; l and n; and q and t (Teixidor 1992: 696, and see Puech 1998: 37–48, copy and script table on 54–5). As a result, the number of distinct letter-forms in this text was reduced from twenty-two to thirteen. This, combined with an inability to show short vowels, medial [aː], or doubled consonants; an inability to distinguish between [iː] and [eː], or between [oː] and [uː]; and no division between words, makes one wonder why anybody bothered to write in such a script! Yet, clearly they did. Indeed, the Pahlavi script—a form of the Aramaic alphabet, used to write an Indo-European language of Iran—achieved even greater levels of ambiguity and confusion, and yet was used for the administrative and religious records of the Parthian empire. Interpreting ambiguity was accepted as one of the skills of literacy, and one scholar has remarked of Pahlavi that 'in practice, remarkably, the many ambiguities rarely impede interpretation' (Hale 2004: 764).

In the case of the late Nabataean script, the individual development of a number of letters had produced several with shapes that were more or less indistinguishable from others. Thus, of the original twenty-two letters of the Phoenico-Aramaic alphabet, one, samekh, was seldom used since it represented a sound, [s], which was not in the Nabataean or Old Arabic phonemic repertoire (Beeston 1962; Macdonald 2000: 45, fig. 5; Macdonald 2008: 465) while /š/ and /ś/ were represented by a single letter š. Moreover, in certain positions, the forms of: b and n; l and n; y and t; g and ḥ; z and r, and in badly written texts sometimes even f and q, and d and k, were indistinguishable (Fig. 9.4). This made the Nabataean alphabet an unsatisfactory vehicle for expressing the twenty-two consonantal phonemes of the Aramaic language, let alone Arabic's repertoire of twenty-eight.

Nevertheless, suitability is seldom considered when a particular script is used to express a particular language, and so it was with Arabic. From the fourth century AD onwards, the Nabataean form of the Aramaic alphabet was no longer used exclusively to write the Aramaic language. This change can be seen in southern Syria and northern Arabia, and may well have also been happening in southern Mesopotamia at the court of the Lakhmids, an Arab dynasty which had settled there, though as yet we have only hearsay evidence for this.

One sign of change is a graffito in Nabataean Aramaic found near ʿĒn ʿAvdat, in the Negev, in which the author included a possible quotation in Arabic, which he wrote in the Nabataean script.[25] This shows that the conceptual shift which allowed a purely spoken language to be written in a 'borrowed' script, had been made, at an individual level, though it was to be some time before this realization would become widespread.[26] Indeed, so strong was the prestige of the Aramaic language, or so fixed its association with the Nabataean alphabet, that Arabic speakers went on trying to write in Aramaic long after the language was beginning to fade from common memory in the areas around them. Thus, in the third century AD, at Umm al-Jimāl, Jordan, the tombstone of the former tutor of the king of the Arab tribe of Tanūkh was carved in bad Nabataean Aramaic and bad Greek (Littmann 1914: 37–40, No. 41; Littmann et al. 1913: 138–9, No. 238[1]), while in Ḥegrā at about the same period, another epitaph was written in the equivalent of franglais, that is, Aramaic helped out with Arabic words, phrases and syntax (Jaussen and Savignac 1909–1922, vol.1: 172–6, No. Nab 17; Healey 2002; Macdonald 2008: 471).

However, in the early fourth century in southern Syria, the Nabataean script was used to write a text completely in the Arabic language: the famous Namārah epitaph of King Marʾ l-qays (see most recently Bordreuil *et al.* 1997; and Macdonald 2008: 469). Yet in North Arabia, a couple of decades later, an epitaph

	Late Nabataean	Early Arabic	Modern Arabic		Late Nabataean	Early Arabic	Modern Arabic
ʾ			١	z			ز
h			ه	r			ر
w			ﯰ				
m			ﻢ	ṭ			ط
				ẓ			ظ
b			ﺒ				
y			ﯿ	ṣ			ﺻ
t			ﺘ	ḍ			ﺿ
th			ﺜ				
n			ﻨ	ʿ			ﻋ
l			ﻟ	gh			ﻏ
				f			ﻓ
g			ﺠ	q			ﻗ
ḥ			ﺤ				
kh			ﺨ	sh			ﺴ
				ś			ﺸ
d			ﺪ				
dh			ﺬ	s	Not used		
k			ﻚ				

Figure 9.4 Late Nabataean and Early Arabic letter-forms.

also in the late Nabataean script, but this time in good Aramaic, was set up for the wife of the ruler of Ḥegrā (Stiehl 1970), though, on current evidence, this appears to be the swansong of Aramaic in Arabia. We have no more monumental inscriptions in the Aramaic language and the Nabataean script. The Aramaic language probably disappeared from the 'Nabataean heartland' some time in the third century AD, having been replaced by Greek as a written language, and gradually by Arabic as the spoken vernacular.[27] The Namārah epitaph of AD 328, is already in the Arabic language and is the last text in the Nabataean script in Syria until the early sixth century. Then this alphabet reappears in a developed form—as the Arabic script [28]—and, with the rise of Islam a century later, takes on an extraordinary new life.

We have no evidence of how, or even whether, this process took place in Syria and in southern Mesopotamia. However, recent discoveries by Saudi Arabian scholars in the regions of al-Jawf (ancient Dūma) and al-ʿUlā (ancient Dadan), have illuminated the development. They have discovered a number of graffiti, some dated to the fifth century AD, in scripts which are clearly transitional between what we call 'Late Nabataean' and 'Early Arabic'. Some of these texts use the Aramaic 'talismanic' expressions so common in Nabataean graffiti (šlm 'May he be safe and sound', dkyr 'may he be remembered', etc.), but are otherwise in the Arabic language. These rough graffiti are extremely important for they show us the process of reincarnation of the Nabataean Aramaic alphabet, as a vehicle for a previously unwritten language (Macdonald forthcoming d).

Unlike the systematic transformation of the South Arabian alphabet into the Ethiopic, the reincarnation of the Nabataean script appears to have been messy and haphazard. In its earliest form, the Arabic script was just another example of a language squeezed into the straitjacket of the Phoenico-Aramaic alphabet: twenty-eight phonemes represented by the sixteen or so different letter-forms to which the Nabataean alphabet had by this time been reduced (Fig. 9.4), with no way of showing short vowels, medial [aː], or doubled letters, and only the ambiguous system of matres lectionis to represent [uː], [iː], and final [aː]. If the Pahlavi script was 'one of the most imperfect and ambiguous ever known' (Hosking and Meredith-Owens 1966: 10), the Late Nabataean-Early Arabic script must have been a close second.

Yet, already in the earliest Arabic papyri (AD 643, see Grohmann 1966: pl. 2) dots were being used to distinguish letters with identical forms but different values, and by the eighth century AD, a series of adjustments typical of the South Semitic, rather than the Phoenico-Aramaic, tradition had been made to what was now truly the 'Arabic alphabet'. First, a more-or-less consistent system of diacritical points had been developed at an early stage, which increased the number of letters to the twenty-eight needed to express the consonantal phonemic repertoire of Written Arabic (Revell 1975). Although, at first, these were used sparingly and usually only where there was a danger of serious ambiguity, they relatively soon became essential elements of the letters to which they were attached. Naturally, in a script used by vast numbers of people from the Atlantic to Indonesia, there were considerable variations in practice, and careless scribes often omitted points at random. Equally, the unpointed angular ('Kufic') form of the script continued to be used for inscriptions, particularly graffiti, long after it had been abandoned on other media.

However, this does not take away from the fact that the Arabic alphabet is the only Near Eastern form of the Phoenico-Aramaic script, to have expanded the number of letters to fit the consonantal phonemic repertoire of the language. On the other hand, it remained typical of the Phoenico-Aramaic tradition in that although unambiguous systems of marking short vowels, no vowel (sukūn), and doubled letters (shadda) were developed, they are only used systematically in the text of the Qurᵓān, and, elsewhere, are introduced individually only when a serious ambiguity might arise.[29] For, as with Pahlavi, readers take a perverse pride in the ambiguity of the script, and in the skill required to interpret it— or so it appears to those brought up on the descendants of the Greek alphabet. Nabia Abbott (1939: 41) cites ᶜAbdallāh ibn Ṭāhir, governor of Khurāsān, (died AD 844/845) who, 'when presented with a piece of elaborate penmanship exclaimed "How beautiful this would be if there were not so much coriander seed [diacritical dots] scattered over it"', while as late as the seventeenth century, Ḥājī Khalīfah 'advised omitting vowels and diacritical points, especially in addressing persons of consequence and refinement, in regard to whom it would be impolite to suppose that they did not have a perfect knowledge of the written language' (Abbott 1939: 41). Even today, while diacritical points are employed in all careful writing, it would be considered a slur on the reader's intelligence and education to use the signs marking short vowels when writing to an adult.

With the spread of Islam, the Arabic script became (until the twentieth century) one of the most widely used alphabets in the world. By the end of the seventh century AD, the Arabian Peninsula was united under one rule for the first time in its history. In the past, South Semitic alphabets had been widely used to record the many different languages and dialects of Arabia. Now, Arabic, a language which in those days had normally been unwritten, had spread throughout the Peninsula and a reborn and remodelled version of the Phoenico-Aramaic alphabet, was carrying the language, with the Islamic faith, to a wider world. Meanwhile, across the Red Sea, in Ethiopia, the last scion of the South Semitic tradition, reborn as a vocalized alphabet, was flourishing as the vehicle of another language and another faith.

At the conference, Stephen Houston began his paper with the opening line from T. S. Eliot's *East Coker*, 'In my beginning is my end'. It seems appropriate that this tale of alphabetic reincarnation should conclude with the poem's final line: 'In my end is my beginning'.[30]

Notes

1. According to Herodotus (*Histories* V.58), the first Greeks to borrow the alphabet from the Phoenicians 'gave to these characters ... the name phoinikēia', i.e. 'Phoenician [letter]s'. Indeed, a Cretan document of c. 500 BC contains a verb poinikázen 'to use phoinikēia' [i.e. letters], to write', and a noun of agent poinikastás '[official] scribe' (Jeffery and Morpurgo-Davies 1970: 132–3, 152–3). The 'Phoenix' of my title—symbol of the cycle of life, death, and rebirth, which Herodotus (II.73) and later tradition placed in Arabia—takes its name from a homonymous Greek root.

2. By 'traditional' alphabets, I mean those derived from other alphabets, rather than those—such as Braille or semaphore—whose signs were invented ex nihilo.

3. The Arabian Peninsula is clearly defined on three sides by its coastline, but its northern limits have always been vague (Fig. 9.1). For the sake of brevity, when referring to the 'Arabian Peninsula' here I shall include modern Jordan and southern Syria, which geographically form part of the same land mass and, in antiquity at least, part of a cultural continuum which ran south to north through the western two-thirds of the Peninsula.

4. Phoenician has twenty-two consonants, and only Akkadian, with twenty consonants, appears to have had a smaller repertoire. For a recent description of Phoenician see Hackett (2004).

5. Thus, Hebrew had twenty-three consonants, and so š had to represent [ʃ] and /ś/ (a phoneme whose realization is disputed but which may have been something like [ɬ]). Only more than 1500 years later did the Masoretes (see Revell 1992) create a diacritical dot to distinguish when this letter represented etymological /ś/ and when /š/. Ironically, by this time /ś/ had long since ceased to represent a separate phoneme in Hebrew, having fallen under /s/, which was represented by a different letter (same-kh). For a brief summary see McCarter 2004: 324. Old Aramaic may have had as many as twenty-seven consonantal phonemes. When it was written in the alphabet inherited from Phoenician, z had to represent both [z] and [ð], ṣ had to represent both [s'] and [θ'], q had to represent both [k'] and the phoneme /ḍ/ (which was probably realized as [ɬ'] or [ð']), while š had to represent three consonants: [ʃ], /ś/, and [θ]. See Creason 2004: 396 for a brief description of the phonemes of Old Aramaic.

6. Thus, the Ancient South Arabian written languages (Sabaic, Madhabic, Qatabanic, and Hadramitic) used a maximum of twenty-nine consonants, though in some languages, or at particular stages of a language, some sounds fell together, e.g., /s³/ and /t/ in Hadramitic or /s¹/ and /s³/ in late Sabaic. Some of the Ancient North Arabian dialects had twenty-eight consonants (Dadanitic, Safaitic, Hismaic), others fewer (e.g., Taymanitic). Dadanitic, Safaitic, and Hismaic appear to have had a similar consonantal phonemic repertoire to Arabic (Macdonald 2004: 497–502). Taymanitic, however, apparently had no equivalent to Arabic /ẓ/ and the use of the same sign for /ḍ/ and /z/ suggests that [ð] and [z] had fallen together. On the other hand, unlike Arabic and all the other Ancient North Arabian dialects, it appears to have used a letter to represent /s³/, at least in loan names containing [s]. See Macdonald 2004: 499–500.

7. Matres lectionis are letters representing consonants which, in certain circumstances, are also used to represent a long vowel. Dadanitic (see below) is the only South Semitic alphabet to use matres lectionis systematically, and even here the practice is restricted to the final long vowels [a:] and [u:], represented by -h and -w respectively, and the diphthong [ai] represented by y. In the orthography of the South Arabian alphabet (see below) -y and -w are used regularly in certain positions, and sporadically elsewhere, to represent [i:] and [u:] respectively. See the excellent treatment in Stein 2003: 41–7, and the radical suggestions in Robin 2001: 570–7.

8. Since the term 'Ancient North Arabian' describes both a group of alphabets and the dialects they normally expressed, for the sake of clarity I will use the abbreviation 'ANA' to refer to the alphabets and the full title 'Ancient North Arabian' to refer to the dialects.

9. This is used to write Geꜥez, Amharic, and other Semitic languages of Ethiopia. See Gragg 2004: 431–3; and below.

10. 'North Arabian' is a subgroup of Central Semitic: see Macdonald 2000: 29, fig. 1; 2004: 488–93.

11. There were populations which their contemporaries called 'Arabs' in all these areas from at least the fifth century BC onwards, and in Mesopotamia considerably earlier. See Macdonald 2001 and 2003.

12. I have called the texts in which this is so 'Undifferentiated North Arabian'. See Macdonald 2000: 54–7.

13. It is possible that they used them more often than we realise, for if they confined themselves to writing their names, we cannot tell which language they spoke. For some of the very few examples where Arabic speakers appear to have used the Safaitic and Dadanitic scripts, see Macdonald 2000: 51–3 and 2008: 467–8.

14. I have called these scripts 'Taymanitic', 'Dumaitic', and 'Dadanitic' after the oases in which they were used (Fig. 9.3). 'Dadanitic' was formally called 'Dedanite' and 'Lihyanite'. On the new terminology see Macdonald 2000: 33 and for the different letter-forms in these alphabets see Fig 9.2 above.

15. This, at least, is the interpretation of the inscription put forward in Macdonald (1995) and a revised and expanded English version in Macdonald forthcoming b, though it differs from that of the editio princeps (Milik 1971).

16. The various forms of the South Semitic script used by the nomads are known today as 'Safaitic', 'Hismaic', and 'Thamudic'. For more detail see Macdonald 2000: 29, fig. 1, 43–6; 2004: 492.

17. There are several examples of a single drawing being claimed by two different people, e.g. Winnett and Harding 1978, nos 767/768, 3502/3503, and possibly Oxtoby 1968, nos 425/426, though the latter are known only from a copy and a second drawing may have been missed. In one case, from al-ꜥĪsāwī in southern Syria, a Safaitic inscription lays claim to what is clearly a prehistoric drawing.

18. Note, however, that this dating is based simply on the facts that the last datable inscriptions are from the mid-third century AD and that there is no reference in any

of the graffiti to the existence of Christianity. This is not a satisfactory basis for a terminus ad quem, but it is all we have.

19. In Macdonald 2005: 49–50, I have defined what I mean by the terms used here, as follows: 'I would define a literate society as one in which reading and writing have become essential to its functioning, either throughout the society (as in the modern West) or in certain vital aspects, such as the bureaucracy, economic and commercial activities, or religious life'. 'I would regard a non-literate ... society as one in which literacy is not essential to any of its activities, and memory and oral communication perform the functions which reading and writing have within a literate society. Pre-historic and—at least until very recently—most nomadic societies were of this sort'. 'When large sections of the population of a literate society cannot read and/or write, they inhabit [a non-literate] enclave within that literate society, since their daily lives are usually touched by reading and writing only when they come into contact with the authorities, or when, in relatively rare cases, they need to use long-distance written communication'.

20. For the monumental script see Robin 2001: 512 and references there for the earliest examples. For the latest Sabaic inscription, see Robin 1991: 19, 134. Thirty-six docu-ments on sticks in the minuscule script have recently been radiocarbon dated. The earliest has a range between 1055 and 901 BC, and the most recent in the late fourth century AD. See Drewes et al. forthcoming. However, in another collection, there are a number of sticks dated on internal evidence to the fifth and early sixth centuries AD. See Stein forthcoming. Two sticks inscribed in the Arabic script have been pub-lished, but their authenticity has been questioned (see Robin 2001: 536–7).

21. However, knowledge of the script appears to have lingered on for several centuries. Al-Ḥasan al-Hamdānī, a Yemeni antiquary of the tenth century AD, still knew the values of the Sabaic letters even though he could not understand the language (Rob-in 1991: 134). There are also two graffiti by men whose names and whose fathers' names are Islamic, both of which begin with an Arabic verb (Robin 1976: 188–92; 1991: 134). The texts are clearly not by habitual users of the South Arabian script, nor are they transcriptions of spoken Arabic into the South Arabian alphabet. Instead, they are calques of Written Arabic, copying its orthographic conventions in every detail save one, and totally ignoring those of the South Arabian script. Is it possible that they are not ancient, but were perhaps produced by modern Yemeni villagers who had learnt the South Arabian alphabet, but not its orthographic conventions? I have myself come across such people in relatively remote parts of Yemen.

22. Thus, for instance, those letters representing [θ] and [ɣ] were eliminated; s³ which represented [s] in the South Arabian alphabet, was re-assigned to represent emphat-ic p [p]; and the letter pa was invented to represent [pˢ].

23. These points could represent vowels, accents, the pronunciation of certain allo-phones, doubled letters, guides for chanting, etc. See, for instance, Revell (1992) for Hebrew, and Segal (1953) for Syriac. In Hebrew, even the dot distinguishing /š/ from /ś/ (see n.5, above) is not considered part of the letter and, in most texts, is omitted along with the other diacritical marks.

24. In Syriac the letters d and r were regularly distinguished by a diacritical dot. In Palmyrene, the use of the distinguishing dot is sporadic, but consistent (dot over r and under d, as in Syriac). In Nabataean, it is sporadic. Ironically, the dot over the d is mainly used in later inscriptions in which the shapes of the two letters have anyway grown distinct.

25. The inscription is alas undated (the dating offered in the editio princeps [Negev *et al.* 1986: 60] is extremely speculative). The exact reading and interpretation of the Arabic part of the text are disputed, see Lacerenza (2000) for most of the bibliography.

26. If one is not used to writing one's spoken language, it requires something of a 'mental leap' to realize that it is possible to do so, and, until that change in attitude becomes habitual and widespread, it seems more 'natural' to use a language that is normally written. Thus, many Arabs today will say that it is 'impossible' to write colloquial Arabic and that only the literary language (which has to be learnt) can be written. Similarly, most speakers of Modern South Arabian languages (Jibbāli, Mahri, Soqoṭri, etc.) do not consider transcribing them in the Arabic script, but instead, if they need to record something or communicate in writing, will do so in Arabic (if necessary through a scribe) even if the recipient is a speaker of the same Modern South Arabian language.

27. If, indeed, Aramaic had ever been the principal spoken language in this region. Note that, in AD 374–376, Epiphanius of Eleutheropolis records that the people of Petra, and Elusa in the Negev, sang hymns in the Arabic language (Panarion 51.22.11), while in the sixth-century Greek papyri recently discovered at Petra there are large numbers of Arabic toponyms and names of buildings (Daniel 2001).

28. See the Zebed inscription (Grohmann 1971: pl. II; Gruendler 1993: 13–14; Robin 2006: 336–8), the Jabal Usays graffito (most recently Robin and Gorea 2002), and the Harrān inscription (Gruendler 1993: 14; Robin 2006: 332–6).

29. This is no doubt a major reason why during the twentieth century such languages as Turkish, Bahasa Indonesian, and Malay abandoned the Arabic script in favour of the Roman. It is interesting to note that in 1981 a fully vocalized text of the great medieval Arabic-Arabic dictionary, Lisān al-ᶜarab, was published in Beirut, possibly a sign of decreasing tolerance of traditional adherence to the somewhat hermetic principles of the Phoenico-Aramaic script. In the thirteenth century AD, Bar Hebraeus had already bewailed the lot of those who had to read the Hebrew, Syriac, and Arabic alphabets (all descendants of the Phoenico-Aramaic script) in comparison to 'those who have perfect alphabets (... for example, Greek, Latin, Coptic, or Armenian). Without the labour of artificial devices and (simply by looking at) their letters they can fly unburdened over passages they have never known (before), that are not marked by symbols, and that they have never previously heard' (translation from Segal 1953: 8).

30. Eliot was quoting Mary, Queen of Scots (1542–1587), who is said to have embroidered the motto 'En ma fin gît mon commencement' together with an emblem of her mother, Marie de Guise.

References

Abbott, Nabia
  1939   *The Rise of the North Arabic Script and its Ḳurʾānic Development, with a Full Description of the Ḳurʾān Manuscripts in the Oriental Institute.* Oriental Institute Publications 50. Chicago: University of Chicago Press.

al-Ansary, Abdul Rahman T.
  1982   *Qaryat al-Fau: A Portrait of Pre-Islamic Civilisation in Saudi Arabia.* London: Croom Helm.

Beaulieu, Paul-Alain
  1989   *The Reign of Nabonidus King of Babylon 553–534 BC.* New Haven, CT: Yale University Press.

Beeston, Alfred F. L.
  1962   'Arabian Sibilants'. *Journal of Semitic Studies* 7: 222–33.
  1979   'Nemara and Faw'. *Bulletin of the School of Oriental and African Studies* 42: 1–6.

Bordreuil, Pierre, Alain Desreumaux, Christian J. Robin, and Javier Teixidor
  1997   '205. Linteau inscrit: AO 4083'. In Yves Calvet and C.J. Robin, *Arabie heureuse Arabie déserte. Les antiquités arabiques du Musée du Louvre.* Notes et documents des musées de France 31. Paris: Éditions de la Réunion des musées nationaux, 265–9.

Creason, Stuart
  2004   'Aramaic'. In Roger D. Woodard, ed., *The Cambridge Encyclopedia of the World's Ancient Languages.* Cambridge: Cambridge University Press, 391–426.

Daniel, Robert W.
  2001   '*P.Petra* Inv. 10 and its Arabic'. In Isabella Andorlini, G. Bastianini, M. Manfredi, and G. Menci, (eds), *Atti del XXII Congresso Internazionale di Papirologia, Firenze, 23–29 agosto 1998.* Florence: Istituto Papirologico 'G. Vitelli', 331–41.

Drewes, A. J., Thomas F. G. Higham, Michael C. A. Macdonald and Christopher Bronk Ramsey
  forthcoming. 'A first dating sequence for the documents on wood in the South Arabian minuscule script'.

Ephʿal, Israel
  1982   *The Ancient Arabs: Nomads on the Borders of the Fertile Crescent 9th–5th Centuries BC.* Jerusalem: Magnes; Leiden: Brill.

Gragg, Gene
  2004   'Geʿez (Aksum)'. In Roger D. Woodard, ed., *The Cambridge Encyclopedia of the World's Ancient Languages.* Cambridge: Cambridge University Press, 427–33.

Grohmann, Adolph
  1966   I. *Arabische Chronologie.* II. *Arabische Papyruskunde.* Handbuch der Orientalistik. I. Abteilung. Der Nahe und der Mittlere Osten. Ergänzungsband II. 1. Halbband. Leiden: Brill.
  1971   *Arabische Paläographie*, vol.2: Denkschriften. Österreichische Akademie der Wissenschaften in Wien. Philosophisch-historische Klasse 94.2. Vienna: Böhlaus.

Gruendler, Beatrice
  1993 *The Development of the Arabic Scripts. From the Nabatean Era to the First Islamic Century According to Dated Texts.* Harvard Semitic Studies 43. Atlanta, GA: Scholars Press.

Hackett, Jo Ann
  2004 'Phoenician and Punic'. In Roger D. Woodard, (ed.), *The Cambridge Encyclopedia of the World's Ancient Languages.* Cambridge: Cambridge University Press, 365–85.

Hale, Mark
  2004 'Pahlavi'. In Roger D. Woodard, (ed.), *The Cambridge Encyclopedia of the World's Ancient Languages.* Cambridge: Cambridge University Press, 764–76.

Healey, John F.
  2002 'Nabataeao-Arabic: Jaussen–Savignac nab. 17 and 18'. In John F. Healey and V. Porter (eds), *Studies on Arabia in Honour of Professor G. Rex Smith.* Journal of Semitic Studies Supplement 14. Oxford: Oxford University Press, 81–90.

Hosking, Richard F., and Glyn M. Meredith-Owens
  1966 *A Handbook of Asian Scripts.* London: British Museum.

Jaussen, Antonin, and M. Raphaël Savignac
  1909–22 *Mission archéologique en Arabie.* 5 vols. Paris: Leroux; Geuthner.

Jeffery, Lilian H., and Anna Morpurgo-Davies
  1970 'ΠΟΙΝΙΚΑΣΤΑΣ and ΠΟΙΝΙΚΑΖΕΝ: BM 1969. 4–2. 1, a new archaic inscription from Crete'. *Kadmos* 9: 118–54.

Lacerenza, Giancarlo
  2000 'Appunti sull'iscrizione nabateo-araba di ʿAyn ʿAvdat'. *Studi epigrafici e linguistici sul vicino oriente antico* 17: 105–14.

Littmann, Enno
  1914 *Nabataean Inscriptions from the Southern Ḥaurân.* Publications of the Princeton University Archaeological Expeditions to Syria in 1904–1905 and 1909. Division IV. Section A. Leiden: Brill.

Littmann, Enno, David Magie, Jr, and Duane R. Stuart
  1913 *Publications of the Princeton University Archaeological Expeditions to Syria in 1904–1905 and 1909.* Division III. *Greek and Latin Inscriptions in Syria.* Section A. *Southern Syria.* Part 3. *Umm idj-Djimâl.* Leiden: Brill.

Luraghi, Nino
  Forthcoming 'Local Scripts from Nature to Culture'. In Peter Haarer (ed.), *Alphabetic Writing in the Mediterranean in the First Millennium B.C.* Oxford: Oxford University Press.

McCarter, P. Kyle
  2004 'Hebrew'. In Roger D. Woodard, (ed.), *The Cambridge Encyclopedia of the World's Ancient Languages.* Cambridge: Cambridge University Press, 319–64.

Macdonald, Michael C. A.
  1993 'Nomads and the Ḥawrān in the Late Hellenistic and Roman Periods: A Reassessment of the Epigraphic Evidence'. *Syria* 70 : 303–413.

1995   'Quelques réflexions sur les Saracènes, l'inscription de Rawwāfa et l'armée romaine'. In Hélène Lozachmeur (ed.), *Présence arabe dans le Croissant fertile avant l'Hégire.* Actes de la Table ronde internationale ... au Collège de France, le 13 novembre 1993. Paris: Éditions Recherche sur les Civilisations, 93–101.

1997   'Trade Routes and Trade Goods at the Northern End of the "Incense Road" in the First Millennium B.C'. In Alessandra Avanzini (ed.), *Profumi d'Arabia.* Atti del Convegno. Saggi di Storia Antica 11. Rome: 'L'Erma' di Bretschneider, 333–49.

2000   'Reflections on the Linguistic Map of Pre-Islamic Arabia'. *Arabian Archaeology and Epigraphy* 11: 28–79.

2001   'Arabi, Arabie e Greci. Forme di contatto e percezione'. In Salvatore Settis (ed.), *I Greci. Storia Cultura Arte Società.* 3. *I Greci oltre la Grecia.* Turin: Einaudi, 231–66.

2003   '"Les Arabes en Syrie" or "La pénétration des Arabes en Syrie". A question of perceptions'. In *La Syrie hellénistique.* Topoi Supplément, 4. Paris: Boccard, 303–18.

2004   'Ancient North Arabian'. In Roger D. Woodard, (ed.), *The Cambridge Encyclopedia of the World's Ancient Languages.* Cambridge: Cambridge University Press, 488–533.

2005   'Literacy in an Oral Environment'. In Piotr Bienkowski, C. B. Mee and E. A. Slater (eds), *Writing and Ancient Near Eastern Society: Papers in Honour of Alan R. Millard.* New York/London: T. and T. Clark Library of Biblical Studies, 49–118.

2008   'Old Arabic, epigraphic'. In Kees Versteegh (ed.), *Encyclopedia of Arabic Language and Linguistics,* vol. 3. Leiden: Brill, 464–77.

forthcoming a. *Old Arabic and its Legacy in the Later Language. Texts, Linguistic Features, Scripts and Letter-Orders.*

forthcoming b. 'On Saracens, the Rawwāfah Inscription, and the Roman Army'. In M. C. A. Macdonald, *Literacy and Identity in Pre-Islamic Arabia.* Aldershot: Ashgate.

forthcoming c. 'The Decline of the "Epigraphic Habit" in Late Antique Arabia: Some Questions'. In Christian J. Robin and J. Schiettecatte (eds), *L'Arabie à la veille de l'Islam.* Bibliothèque de l'Antiquité tardive. Turnhout: Brepols, 2008 (in press).

forthcoming d. 'ARNA Nab 17 and the Transition from the Nabataean to the Arabic Script'. In Werner Arnold, M. Jursa, W. W. Müller, and S. Prochazka (eds), *Semitica In Memoriam Alexandri.* Wiesbaden: Harassowitz.

Milik, Josef T.
1971   'Inscriptions grecques et nabatéennes de Rawwafah'. In Peter J. Parr, G. L. Harding, and J. E. Dayton, 'Preliminary Survey in N.W. Arabia, 1968, Part II: Epigraphy'. *Bulletin of the Institute of Archaeology, University of London* 10: 54–8, pl. 26–31.

Negev, Avraham, Joseph Naveh, and Shaul Shaked
1986   'Obodas the God'. *Israel Exploration Journal* 36: 56–60, pl. 11B.

Oxtoby, Willard G.
    1968   *Some Inscriptions of the Safaic Bedouin.* American Oriental Series 50. New Haven, CT: American Oriental Society.

Puech, Émile
    1998   'Inscriptions araméennes du Golfe: Failaka, Qalaᶜat al-Baḥreïn et Mulayḥa (ÉAU)'. *Transeuphratène* 16: 31–55.

Revell, E. J.
    1975   'The Diacritical Dots and the Development of the Arabic Alphabet'. *Journal of Semitic Studies* 20: 178–90.
    1992   'Masorah,' 'Masoretes,' 'Masoretic Accents,' 'Masoretic Studies,' and 'Masoretic Text'. In D.N. Freedman (ed.), *The Anchor Bible Dictionary*, vol. 4. New York: Doubleday, 592–9.

Robin, Christian J.
    1976   'Résultats épigraphiques et archéologiques de deux brefs séjours en République Arabe du Yémen'. *Semitica* 26: 167–93.
    1991   'L'Arabie antique de Karibʾîl à Mahomet. Nouvelles données sur l'histoire des Arabes grâce aux inscriptions'. *Revue du monde Musulman et de la Méditerranée* 61/3.
    2001   'Les inscriptions de l'Arabie antique et les études arabes'. *Arabica* 48: 509–77.
    2006   'La réforme de l'écriture arabe à l'époque du califat médinois'. In François Déroche, (ed.), Procedings of the International Conference on the Manuscripts of the Qurʾān, Università di Bologna, Centro interdipartimentale di Scienze del Islam, 28–29 September 2002. *Mélanges de l'Université Saint-Joseph,* 59: 319–64.

Robin, Christian J., and Maria Gorea
    2002   'Un réexamen de l'inscription arabe préislamique du Ǧabal Usays (528–529 è. chr.)'. *Arabica* 49: 505–10.

Segal, J. B.
    1953   *The Diacritical Point and the Accents in Syriac.* London Oriental Series 2. London: Oxford University Press.

Sherratt, Susan
    2003   'Visible Writing: Questions of Script and Identity in Early Iron Age Greece and Cyprus'. *Oxford Journal of Archaeology* 22: 225–42.

Stein, Peter
    2003   *Untersuchungen zur Phonologie und Morphologie des Sabäischen.* Epigraphische Forschungen auf der Arabischen Halbinsel 3. Rahden: Leidorf.
    2004   'Zur Dialektgeographie des Sabäischen'. *Journal of Semitic Studies* 49: 225–45.
    forthcoming. *Die altsüdarabischen Minuskelinschriften auf Holzstäbchen aus der Bayerischen Staatsbibliothek in München*, vol. 1: *Die Inschriften der mittel- und spätsabäischen Periode.*

Stiehl, Ruth
    1970   'A New Nabataean Inscription'. In Ruth Stiehl and H. E. Stier (eds.), *Beiträge zur alten Geschichte und deRen Nachleben. Festschrift für Franz Altheim zum 6.10.1968*, vol. 2. Berlin: de Gruyter, 87–90.

Teixidor, Javier
    1992   'Une inscription araméenne provenant de l'Émirat de Sharjah (Émirats Arabes Unis)'. *Comptes Rendus de l'Académie des Inscriptions et Belles-Lettres*: 695–707.

Winnett, Frederick V., and Gerald Lankester Harding
    1978   *Inscriptions from Fifty Safaitic Cairns*. Near and Middle East Series 9. Toronto: University of Toronto Press.

10

The Small Deaths of Maya Writing[1]

Stephen D. Houston

Death happens once to any organism, which lives and expires, not to be reborn unless by miracle. Whether writing systems 'die', finally so, was the question posed from various angles in a recent paper by the author and two colleagues, John Baines and Jerrold Cooper (Houston *et al.* 2003). The topic had seemed over-looked, so our essay probed the twisting fate of writing systems *in extremis*. We came to the conclusion that diminished functions of script, linkages to obsolete knowledge with which a script had become identified, and the physical expira-tion of script-users from the effects of war or disease led systematically to the obsolescence of certain writing systems. Most defunct scripts were replaced by writing systems regarded—at least at the time—as facilitators of a wider variety of uses. Histories differed: a few scripts, such as cuneiform and Egyptian hiero-glyphs, enjoyed long 'lives', decrepit only after three millennia; others, such as Rongorongo, travelled along much shorter paths.

Our paper mentioned several problems with respect to Maya script, in use throughout eastern Mexico and northern Central America over a period of at least 1600 years, from the time of Christ until (or perhaps shortly before) AD 1600. The puzzle was the turbulent and unclear history of Maya writing at the end of the Classic period (c. AD 250 to AD 800), by a magnitude the time of peak production for Maya writing. This chapter attempts to untangle that puzzle by favouring an unconventional view over an obvious one. Without question, Maya writing continued in use for over a millennium—so much is plain. But from an historical, even sociological point of view, the perception of continuity and resilience is illusory. A second approach is to examine the use of script at the level of individual communities that employed and, ultimately, discarded the skills of reading and writing. This perspective avoids what might be called the 'synoptic fallacy', the notion that any one writing system equates to a single, timeless entity. Any one script is malleable in response to changing needs, with the logical consequence that it must mutate, Lamarckian fashion, over the long term. A biological metaphor, used here with some diffidence, would liken this process to the continuance of 'Life' over generations in contrast to the abbreviated life of a single human being. Trilobites were our ancestors but that does not mean we exist in the same environment or issue the same appendages and exhibit the same scaly exterior.

The Script Community

A key concept in understanding the extinction of writing is that of the 'script community'. Some years ago Brian Stock (1996: 23, 150) developed a similar notion, that of 'textual communities', which were 'microsocieties organized around the common understanding of a script'. For Stock (1996: 23), such communities might include non-literates but required at least 'one literate', an *interpretes* who could analyse texts and disseminate textual content to others. The texts created a sense of community among those who read and listened, an impression of 'solidarity' within and 'separation' outside (Stock 1996: 150). Stock's main goal was to understand the interaction of literacy and orality in medieval Europe. Sacred texts, such as the Torah or Scriptures, were only the foundation. What came thereafter, indispensably so, were the rules of behaviour extracted from texts, the Mishnah from the Torah, the Rule of St Benedict from Christian Scripture.

The idea of a 'textual community' focuses on the content of texts, which Stock perceives as actual things, a scroll and book, or mental pictures of their substance. But there are other ways of understanding the relation between texts and social groups. I term one alternative the 'script community'. The script community exists in relation to a writing system; it survives because the system is used and transmitted across generations. The contents recorded by script are undeniably important. Yet a sense of shared identity can also result from the use of a writing system or witnessing that system in a less active capacity. The actual members of the script community differ in skill. For the purposes of this essay, the common distinction between literates and non-literates is insufficient. As a concept, 'literacy' consists of two distinct components, the ability to produce a text and the faculty of responding to it. The first is 'writing', the second 'reading' (Houston 1994: 28–9). These are not absolute skills that are merely there or not-there. In reality, they exist in a fluid relationship that floats on a chart showing one axis as 'production' ('writing'), the other as 'response' ('reading', Fig. 10.1). Dictation represents a special case in such a scheme: until recorded, the uttered and received statement remains in the domain of oral transmission.

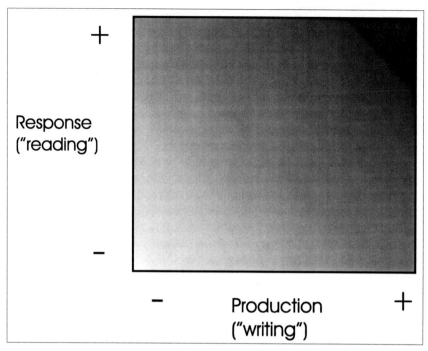

Figure 10.1 The fluid relationship between 'production' and 'response'.

'Perfunctory literacy', a condition of low-response and low-production, describes those who can sign their names but little more than that. An educated person with poor motor skills and illegible scrawl would fit into the category of high-response/low-production. Illiterate or barely literate copyists, such as those in Roman Egypt, fit within the sector of low-response/high-production, the Mandarin exegete and calligrapher within high-response/high-production. No one is born to write or read. In any one lifetime, as knowledge accumulates, a person's abilities tend to shift upwards, to higher levels of response. Practice and repetition improve 'production', and the plain objective of pedagogy is to deliver a person efficiently from the lower left of the chart to the upper right.[2] Where the scribe ends up depends on other sociological matters, such as the desired professional niche or target: few academics need to be calligraphers, and the intercession of technical aids, such as computers, vaults production skills higher than they would ordinarily be. Biographies also move in other directions. Great age and manual decrepitude would lead to where we all began as newborns, in a condition of low-response/low-production. Still, it would be misleading to believe that these stations of life are quantifiable. In large part, aesthetic judgments of varying and arbitrary nature may determine relative position on the chart, one external judge perceiving more elevated position than another.

In Stock's formulation, literacy has a necessary relationship to orality. Non-literates feel a sense of belonging to a script community by receiving meaningful statements from a text. Since they have no direct access to sacred documents, communications must be broadcast by speech or other forms of signalling, such as imagery and ritual. What Stock does not say, although it results logically from his statements, is that a 'text' could just as well be an orally transmitted scripture like the Rig-Veda. The medium of writing has no inherent role in his 'text-community', only a set of organized and potently phrased narratives that present sacred propositions. In contrast, the script community involves a more restricted focus on who used a writing system, how the system was employed, and how the script was taught, learned, and practised. At the same time response seldom occurred in silent or private acts, as shown by numerous studies of ancient scripts that reveal the enduring role of oral performance in reading (e.g. Civil 1972; King 1994; Monaghan 1990). As a result, it becomes difficult to accept the claim that literacy and orality are mutually exclusive, the former steadily usurping the latter (McKitterick 1989: 273, argues for the centrality of texts in Carolingian society, but more in Stock's sense that they 'were essential elements of a civilized Christian society'. This is not the same as suggesting

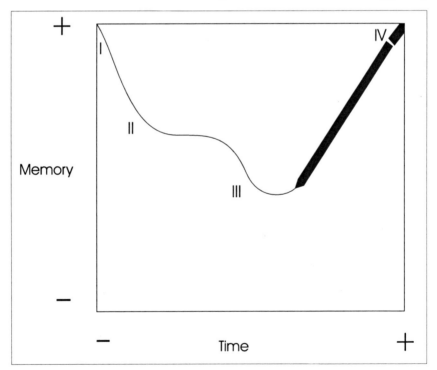

Figure 10.2 The stations of script use in relation to forms of memory 'storage'.

high rates of production and response.) Rather, we can speak of both as extending the arts of 'memory' in the settings that continue to require a heavy dose of oral disquisition (Robb 1994: 35; R. Thomas 1992: 50–1, 70–1). After all, even prodigious acts of memory in oral traditions require a variety of cues for 'serial recall', in which long texts are memorized in fixed sequence (Rubin 1995: 190–2). Full, grammaticalized writing, which contains something more than lexemes doing business as *aides-mémoire*, is the logical augmentation of cues to their greatest possible extent. The memory required is that of knowing how to access text, not supplying portions of it.

The extinction of writing involves exactly the reverse: relinquishing the content of script back to memory in a process by which 'back-up' storage in script is gradually eliminated. This is illustrated in Fig. 10.2. Station I is when memory is relieved by the instrument of script, which achieves a plateau at Station II. Here is the environment of many early texts, with markedly impoverished grammar and syntax. Station III is the shift found in most early scripts in which texts introduce grammaticalization. Station IV is the moment of script extinction, when memory-as-storage takes over once again, and the last producer stops working. It is useful to recognize that 'script obsolescence' is not necessarily the extinction of knowledge but its partial transfer to, or duplication by, organic storage within the brain—note in this formulation that 'memory' is not the same as 'orality', as the first relates to storage, the second to expression and modes of thought (e.g. Goody 1977; Ong 1988). At Station IV, however, such knowledge does lose a means of self-stabilization. As a result, gaps and reconfiguration of meaning begin to take place. In the terminology of David Rubin (1995: 190–2), 'serial recall' has now become more challenging and prone to misprision.

Several variables shape the script community. One divides people into convenient categories (see key in Fig. 10.3): (1) those who cannot respond; (2) those who respond passively; (3) those who produce and respond; and (4) those who produce and respond with high skill, as indicated in the diagram by a 'plus' sign. These are rough categories. Individual accomplishment varies along a continuum and over the lifetime of a user. The relations between the categories are just as important. For example, the number of people in each category has direct bearing on the resilience of a script community. A set of highly skilled producers and responders will have a different status depending on whether they are surrounded by a relatively large or small group of low-level producers and responders. To be non-literate is the natural human condition; to be literate is not, as it requires individual effort and societal investment. The marked nature of literacy and of those who master its arcane skills means that literacy will always carry a higher perception of value and prestige than the unmarked condition of non-literacy. Whether that prestige is equivalent to separate levels of rank and elite status depends entirely on historical and cultural circumstances. In some settings, response and production were seen as skilful crafts but crafts nonetheless; in others, they indicated social distinction. Eric Havelock (1982: 187-8) detected the craft model in much of the Mediterranean and beyond, courtly societies such as those of Heiian Japan placed response and production among the attributes of elite accomplishment (Morris 1964: 212).

Finally, and perhaps most important, 'script community' is a term that can be broadly and narrowly construed. A broad definition would embrace all users of, for example, Maya writing. At any one time, users of Maya glyphs compose an overall 'script community'; over a longer span, they participate in a 'script tradition'. But this definition misses the subtleties offered by a narrower definition, in which individual centres of response and production, often divided by political frontiers, form separate script communities with distinct histories. It is at this intermediate level—between the individual user and all conceivable users of writing across the Maya region—that this chapter addresses the biographies of 'script communities'.

What remains to be discussed in general terms is the effect over time of productions—i.e. materialized texts, a book, inscription or other object—on subsequent efforts. This process can be envisioned within a phenomenological framework (Fig. 10.4; Gell 1998: 23–36, fig. 9.4/1). Circles represent actual productions, texts materialized as documents or inscriptions, and the arrows indicate recollections of past productions or anticipations of future ones that

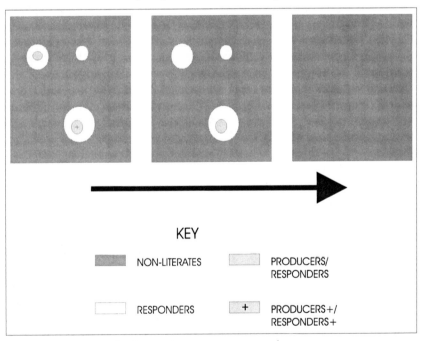

KEY

▨ NON-LITERATES		▨ PRODUCERS/ RESPONDERS	
☐ RESPONDERS		▨ + PRODUCERS+/ RESPONDERS+	

Figure 10.3 A changing landscape of script use.

connect them.[3] The agent is the 'producer', the creator of texts. A text partly modelled on an earlier production follows an arrow that shoots backwards in time. This recollection is a 'retention' that looks back—it copies or recapitulates. But an absolutely faithful copy is always impossible, in that the material for the materialized text may differ ever so slightly, as would the style of writing or carving. There may also be shifts in the setting of the text, its intended place of use and display. The arrows can be understood more accurately as transformations that are never complete replication of earlier productions. A persistent textual format at a Classic Maya site, such as the linkage of stone-erection to royal accession at Tikal, recurs through the process of 'retention'. In the same way, a text can operate as a source for later efforts, so that the arrow leading forwards represents an act of 'protention'. At first glance, this would seem an absurdity, time travel not yet being perfected. However, the fact that the Maya regarded calendrical celebrations as marking multiple, predictable cycles suggests some degree of self-conscious protention in the production of script. The abundance of arrows, one object likely to be pierced by many retentive and protentive 'darts', expresses the complexity of memory and anticipation. The edges of a script community would be those in which acts of retention and protention diminish appreciably. A literate person may move, although not often, or a portable text on a book or jade object may travel away from its point of origin. These are the occasions when retention and protention pass through the boundary of the script community. A robust script in 'equilibrium' is much like a stable language, without large divergence from earlier forms (Dixon 1997: 68–73). The truncation of this process, when all arrows cease and final productions appear, is when a script goes extinct.

The Shape of Script Communities

A possible imprecision in studies of ancient scripts is to see them as continuously spread across a landscape, for instance, seeing the southern Maya Lowlands as 'literate' (responsive/productive) during the Classic period. This is surely wrong and refers more to the broad definition of 'script community' as opposed to the narrower meaning favoured here. For the Classic Maya, large areas of rural hinterland show little to no evidence of script use: finds of pottery with glyphs tell us only about places of pottery production, most likely larger settlements, and, in any case, indicate nothing direct about the capacities of the buyers. Nor is the number of apparent literates, principally carvers who were named, much greater at large settlements. Several sites, such as those under Ruler III of Dos Pilas, Guatemala, have sculptures that, to judge from idiosyncratic details, were made by a single sculptor. The well-documented record of glyph-making sculptors at Piedras Negras, Guatemala, is better populated, if only slightly so, with a handful of artists working under the tutelage of a 'head

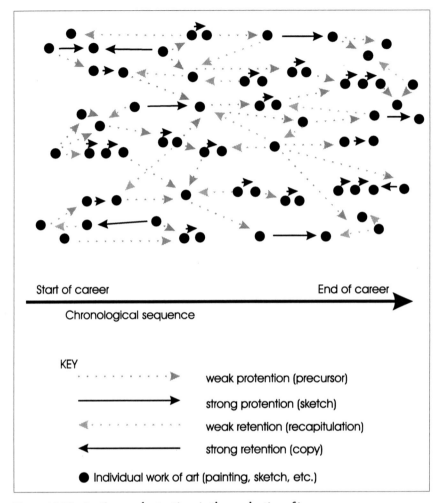

Figure 10.4 Protentions and retentions in the production of images.

sculptor', perhaps something like the 'master' found in ateliers elsewhere in the world (Houston 2000: 152–4).

The more probable pattern is one in which there were two kinds of settlements with literati: (1) those with a small number of masters who were likely to have been trained at (2) communities with better-organized centres of pedagogy and more extensive, many-authored cycles of production. The ability of masters to move freely from one site to another after fulfilling contractual obligations—the 'free-agent' model—is made less probable by the strong odds that most masters worked within 'court societies', the social groupings of the Classic Maya that attended to the needs and directives of a royal family or the co-residential kin and servants of a magnate (Houston 2004). In such systems literati could move from place to place, but mainly at the behest of their lords. This practice is well-documented in a textual description of 'loans'. The first was intangible, in what might be called the 'loan of graphically stabilized memory'. In this, masters hewed glyphically inscribed panels for shipment to subsidiary sites. Those who controlled such literati meted out small favours indeed, in the form of dynastic displays that could be admired but not reproduced locally or independently (Houston 1993: 135). The other system was overt, in that the masters themselves (*anab*) were sent to sites of equivalent status, both lender and recipient often being 'sacred lords' (*k'uhul ajaw*, Houston 2000: 154). At this level there must have been sustained negotiations for such services, considerations of alliance and regional politics, and, above all, a pronounced sense that the relationship between sculptor and king was highly personal. The recipient sites are careful to mention such continuing relationships within authorial statements.

If transported monuments and masters were the 'tendrils' between script communities, what did the sources, the origin of such 'shoots', look like? Two graphs assist the process of conceptualization. Fig. 10.5 shows four of many alternatives. In each there is 'width', which indicates a relative number of producers—the non-literates and passive responders reside outside this shape. (A full diagram, although impossible to create on present evidence, would display the sum total of population with respect to the number of direct users.) The vertical scale is time. Over time, indicated here by a vertical arrow, both may remain stable in number, diminish gradually or, as usually happens, undulate in quantity. The gradient within the low-level producers hints at unravelling ability, and, in some contexts, the same might be shown among high-level producers. The undulating 'script community' (Fig. 10.5, second from left), for example, loses such producers before production ceases entirely. Note also a singular feature of this variant, in that high-level producers can disappear and reappear. It is at such moments that ruptures of esoteric knowledge may occur. Hypothetically, some sites may lose production entirely, only to receive it again from other sources at a later date.

Script extinction corresponds to the top end of the first three variants. One extinction is 'radical', a dramatic breakdown in production and response. The second has low-level production but in relatively large numbers; the third shows gradually attenuating low-level production but sustained high-level production to the end. The three variants experience extinction at different times, but contrast with the fourth variant, in which the script community remains intact all the way to and beyond the Spanish conquest. It is in such communities that Maya writing survives, albeit with the possibility of high-production ruptures.

Another figure (Fig. 10.3, see above) situates the script communities in space and charts them through time, as shown by the arrow. To the left side, at the beginning of the sequence, are three script communities separated by areas of non-responders and non-literates—this tends to be the rural landscape. The width of the circles reflects the number of responders (shown in white), low-level producers (in grey), and high-level producers (marked by the 'plus' sign). Over time—the implication is that these planar view represent cross-sections of the shapes in Fig. 10.5—some circles disappear, being replaced by responders, and, in final extinction, witness the transfer of memory back to organic, cerebral storage. Nonetheless, it should be understood that this diagram can be misleading: memory cues exist anywhere, even in features of landscape, as shown by Chris Gosden in this volume and as widely noted by ethnographers and students of the materialization of memory (e.g. Basso 1996; see also Alcock 2002; Barton 2001; Mack 2003). The essential observation to be gleaned from the diagram is that production and response are spatially restricted, that they involve finite numbers of people, that those spaces of production and response potentially disappear at a variable rate, contingent on local circumstances. To use a biological metaphor, the 'biography' of a script can embrace three, nested levels: (1) that of an individual user; (2) that of a local script community; and (3) that of all users, regardless of site: thus, *the* Script Community vs *a* script community. Yet such charts are fundamentally descriptive rather than explanatory. Why cross-generational transmission and maintenance of standards break down; why, in a phrase, the 'script community' expires—these matters require a look at function and 'ecological niche', the circumstances that favour or discourage the continued use of script.

Unravelling Script Communities: The Terminal Classic Maya

The Maya collapse is a renowned event in world history, one of several instances in which a literate civilization disintegrated, for reasons that remain obscure and multifarious (Demarest *et al.* 2003; Webster 2002). Whether that disintegration was complete, spanning the Maya Lowlands, can now be answered in the negative; whether a catastrophic decline occurred in some areas receives an affirmative response. What is sometimes overlooked, however, is that there were at least two collapses, the well-known example that characterized the Terminal Classic period (c. AD 800 to 900), and an earlier one at the end of the Preclassic period (c. AD 200 [Webster 2002: 189–90]).

There are a small number of Preclassic Maya texts, but it is noteworthy how opaque they are in comparison to, for us, the summit of legibility, the texts of the Late Classic period (c. AD 550–800). Most of the Preclassic texts cannot be read, although certain sequences of signs are discernable. They appear to issue from a script community—here understood in the broadest possible terms—in which production continued, but with a perceptible rupture in pedagogy and, perhaps, high levels of production. This was most extreme in the Maya Highlands, as at Kaminaljuyu, Guatemala, where all signs of literacy disappear at the

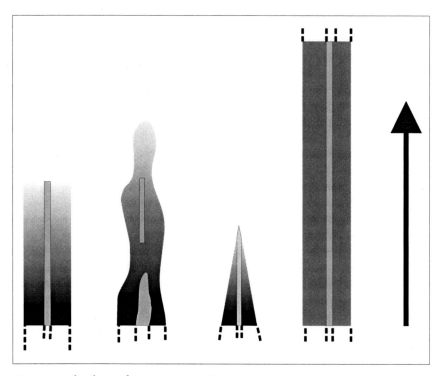

Figure 10.5 The shape of script communities over time.

end of this time. Still, Maya writing remained more or less intact as a recording mechanism, yet it had also gone through a dramatic attenuation that it seems barely to have survived. A second rupture can be detected between the Early and Late Classic periods, a time of dynastic interruption or dynastic inception, if not quite a 'collapse'. David Stuart and I have observed a break between the two periods that is reflected in systematic 're-interpretation' of signs: iconic referents of Early Classic glyphs have become unclear and new forms, formally disconnected from the original source, comprehensively replace them. In our judgment, 're-interpretation' points to a partial break in pedagogic transmission, although not so severe as that taking place between the Preclassic and Classic periods. The essential detail is that the Maya script community, as defined broadly, went through stresses and distortions, but it did not go 'extinct'.

So far, the argument has been that intermediate levels reveal more about script than regional or pan-regional scales of study. First a banality: Maya writing lasted from the time of Christ until a century or so after the Spanish conquest but this observation offers none of the subtleties needed to understand the Terminal Classic period. It is at the level of individual script communities, in dynastic centres such as Piedras Negras, Yaxchilan, Tikal, Calakmul, and others, that script use comes into focus. A review of the final texts at two centres helps us sketch examples of two trajectories of script death, abrupt and gradual (Houston *et al.* 2003: 434). The comparison begins around 11 March 830, or 10.1.0.0.0 in the Maya Long Count. This then leads to a discussion of two recently documented monuments of late date.

Tikal, Guatemala

The final dated text at Tikal is Stela 11, from 13 August 869 (Jones and Satterthwaite 1982: 29–31, fig. 16). It is a strong retention of earlier sculptures marking the end of twenty-year spans, an important cycle for the Maya. Unusually tall (at 3.41 m), and, in comparison to other inscriptions at Tikal, proportionally small glyphs, the stela presents highly accomplished calendrical notations, including lunar information and an enigmatic cycle known as the '819-day' count that involves the placement of ritual objects. It also mentions the name of a war captive. There are, in sum, no tinges of scriptural decay. Tikal, like a number of other sites, such as Piedras Negras, Guatemala, Copan, Honduras, and Palenque, Chiapas, ends its textual record with productions that display extensive knowledge of Maya script. It is only at small sites near Tikal, such as Jimbal and Ixlu (Jones and Satterthwaite 1982: figs. 78, 79, 81), that epigraphers see suggestions of aberrant (or innovative) reading order, as on Jimbal Stela 2 (dating to 30 April 889), and, in the same text, simplified verbs that have been stripped of necessary suffixes and numbers with peculiar space-fillers. Unfortunately, the published drawings are inadequate—in part because of the aberrancy, which tends to baffle the modern draftsman. However, enough is visible in these renderings to discern the weakening of retention and a fraying of traditions that had remained intact at Tikal until the very end.

Seibal, Guatemala

A problem in charting changes over time at Seibal is the difficulty of dating monuments: some provide sufficient clues to chronology, others have, at the risk of seeming to impart volition and action to objects, begun to transfer that memory load to storage in the mind of responders. John Graham (1990: 43), divides the final set of inscriptions into 'Group III' and 'Group IV,' respectively, the first dating to the span between AD 869 and 889, the second presumably to a span some decades thereafter. The ceramicist of the Harvard Seibal project, Jeremy Sabloff (1975: 238), feels that 'a termination date of AD 930 for Seibal definitely is a conservative figure', so AD 950 is a plausible cut-off for these late sculptures. Group III continues to present explicit dates, along with fully grammaticalized statements. Stela 1 (I. Graham 1996: 13), erected on 13 August AD 869, shows a transitive verb with correct affixation. Within twenty years, on 30 April 889 (I. Graham 1996: 51), Stela 20 records a text that is increasingly difficult to read, with legible calendrical notation but an apparent confusion between two similar signs, one read [ji], the other [BAAH]. A roughly contemporary monument, Stela 19 (I. Graham 1996: 49), has a series of day names in its first two columns, none with any explicit rooting in longer cycles that can be linked to the Maya Long Count. The principal figure is a god-impersonator, a relatively common occurrence in Maya texts of the Late Classic period, yet the final element in the text refers to a deity—probably the wind-deity—and does not, in what remains of the inscription, advert openly to an historical figure. An undated sculpture from this general time, Stela 14 (I. Graham 1996: 39), presents information that is consistent with earlier preoccupations at the site, including a patron deity, or set of deities, linked to an earlier dynasty at the site, and a statement of agency by a figure whose name is spelled [wo-ko-lo-?].[4] This would appear to form an effective, literate display, but for two problems: firstly, there are at least two misspellings or instances of transposed signs (a reverse [ni] and [TUUN], [wo-ko-lo] instead of the more likely, and locally attested [wo-lo-ko], 'lizard'), and secondly, the absence of required suffixes, [ji] and [ya] under the statement of agency. Thus, calendrical notations have begun to deviate from long-standing patterns, without clear linkage to longer cycles that can fix a date to longer periods. Certain glyphs merge incorrectly with others, as though the signary has become confused in the mind of the sculptor. Misspellings and incorrect transpositions occur alongside the elision of obligatory elements.

The texts of Group IV are even further from Classic-period norms. On some sculptures, such as Stela 3 (I. Graham 1996: 17), new forms of writing, especially foreign day-names functioning as godly epithets, begin to appear. Narrative is displaced with increasing force to images, so that, for example, Stela 3 has no verb in its text. The name of the patron gods occurs just after a calendrical notation, in violation of all former practice in glyphic syntax. On Seibal Stela 18 (I. Graham 1996: 47), there is not even a subject after the date, only an image that covers the surface of the sculpture. The Maya day sign Ajaw has adopted the square shape of introduced calendrical glyphs. What may be the final monument in Group IV, dating to the first decades of the tenth century AD, is Stela 13 (I. Graham 1996: 37). The text consists of three segments: a non-Maya day-sign in square cartouche, not easily linked to any longer cycle of time (such dates repeat every 260 days); a long string of syllables in Maya writing ([t'u?-pu-?-?-ba-e-he?-ke-ni-ta]), and a final title that seems to be a 'retention', an explicit copying from an earlier text, as it combines logographic and one syllabic element in a more supple way than appears in other parts of the inscription. The fact that this name was used at Terminal Classic Machaquila, a site up-river from Seibal, suggests some late connection to that city (e.g., I. Graham 1967: fig. 44). The string of syllables is, on present knowledge, incomprehensible, perhaps because foreign terms are being transcribed, as proposed by some (Mathews and Willey 1991: 58; cf. Stuart 1993: 339), but more likely from deepening scribal ineptitude. In these final texts is a pronounced pattern of script loss: dates that can only be understood with ancillary information not provided to the reader (or responder); the blurring of distinct glyphs; transpositions and misspellings; the elision of syntactically necessary elements, such as verbs; the seepage into Maya writing of non-local calendrical signs, displacing elements that had formed a central focus of Classic Maya script; and, finally, imagery that stood on its own, with little more than an abbreviated calendrical notation. Final loss is not attested in this record, other than in the cessation of monument erection. There is not, as at Yaxhom, Mexico, the 'retentions' of 'rememberers', who knew that glyphs existed and that they adopted a particular form, but little else (Houston *et al.* 2003: fig. 8). At Seibal, the script community became attenuated in competence, shifted memory to the brain of responders, yet probably suffered a firm and rapid truncation by about AD 950. The parallels with language death are striking. At Seibal, there are hints of 'simplifications' in the loss of complexity, examples of grammatical and substantive elision, blurring of signs, and 'reductions' or 'defectiveness' expressed as errors (Andersen 1982: 95). The drastic brevity of such texts is exemplified by another late text from the northern part of Guatemala, on Xultun Stela 10, dating to 30 April 889 (Von Euw 1978: 37). This text is a strong retention of Xultun Stela 3 (Von Euw 1978: 15), dating to thirty years before, which supplies the missing format—a reference to birth—that would have made clear sense of Stela 10. The slavishness of such retentions suggests a marked conservatism or, at this time, an impoverishment of inspiration that reflects the beginnings of script death.

Two recently documented texts

The final years of Maya script in the Terminal Classic period are now documented more fully because scholars have been able to access two texts: one in private hands in Switzerland (Fig. 10.6), the other, according to rumour, in a Spanish collection (Fig. 10.7). Original provenance is unclear, but some clues hint at northern Guatemala or an area over towards the Usumacinta River—the personage shown in Fig. 10.7 bears a headdress that may contain the name of the patron deity of Yaxchilan, a site just across the river from Guatemalan territory. The final dates are, respectively, 8 September 864 and 30 April 889 (Miller and Martin 2004: 191, pl. 107). Both inscriptions are worth mentioning because of their late date and unusual qualities of text. The sculpture in Fig. 10.6 has an ambitious text of twelve columns and thirteen rows, but with peculiarities of spacing. To maintain a curving outline, the sculptor, a youth (*ch'ok*), had to make awkward adjustments to the upper right, crimping the number of columns. The number of syllabic spellings is striking. Many of the names are rendered phonetically (positions E1–F1, J9–I10 [BAHLAM ~ ba-la-ma chi-ji U?-yu] or, H3-G4 [CHAK-wa-si-ki YAX-chi-ta-ma]). Even a glyph that usually occurs as a logograph, [TS'AK], appears here in syllabic form, [ts'a-ka], also an indication of late date. The phonetic spelling of the word is a hallmark of the latest Maya inscriptions in the southern Maya Lowlands, as at Piedras Negras and Naranjo, Guatemala, and another text now on display in the De Young Museum of San Francisco; this last has dates that appear far too early for the style of the monument, which has a text carved by two distinct and mutually inconsistent hands, one strongly calligraphic in orientation, the other not (Miller and Martin 2004: 102–3, pl. 46).

The sign shapes on the sculpture have become unclear or confused, such as the 'pedestals' of day-signs, here rendered in highly stylized form (e.g., D2 or I8). This is also evident in the blurring to two distinct syllables [la] and [ma] (J9, G4), which share one feature, a small 'face,' that has in this context come to dominate the sculptor's understanding of the sign. The sculptor has not been shy about advertising himself. His signature, at K1-L3, is almost as large as other glyphs on the monument, a flamboyant and aberrant self-projection that differs from the delicate backgrounding of most such names. Whimsically, one could even ask, 'Are there any adults in charge?' The text refers to a deceased lord, his grandfather and grandmother, a great-grandfather from whom the patron's father probably inherited the title, and, at the end, his own name and that of his mother. Like the sculptor, the patron was a youth. The line of lords is long on this monument. The authority of the final lord appears to have diminished, however: recall the small size of the sculpture, the immaturity of the patron, and the relative foregrounding of the sculptor.

The skill on the inscription is undeniable. The other text, in a collection rumoured to be in Barcelona, is among the latest known in Classic Maya style. It falls far short of the other in its textual ambition. Regrettably, available images are poor. The rendering presented in Fig. 10.7 is defective yet the best that can be obtained at this time. The first point to be made about the sculpture is that it highlights a woman, who unusually undertakes an incense-scattering ritual, a domain more often of male celebrants. In Maya sculpture, women play a more prominent role in moments of dynastic rupture, as at Palenque and Naranjo. The text is highly abbreviated. The reader must know that a calendrical celebration is intended from context, and even here might be misled by a highly aberrant day-sign. In other words, the meaning is to be inferred contextually; it is not explicitly registered on the text. The verb is confused as well, in that the direct object (*ch'aaj*, incense pellets) has, it seems, been semantically conflated with the indirect object (flames that receive the pellets). The background of the image extends out to an unclear boundary, in vivid contrast to the borders found on most Maya stelae. The longest texts may, in fact, be those of sculptors, whose names can be dimly spied to viewer's left. The fullest information, therefore, does not even pertain to the royal image but to the sculptors commissioned to carve the monument. The paucity of text bespeaks a reduced need to 'back-up' and 'broadcast' that which had formerly been available in inscribed form.

Figure 10.6 Miniature stela in private collection. Drawing by Simon Martin.

Figure 10.7 Stela fragment in private collection.

Conclusions

The script communities of the Terminal Classic Maya experienced two patterns, an abrupt extinction or at least one that left no vestige of gradual decline, and a second process that shares some characteristics of language death, namely, simplification and reduction or defectiveness. In loose, even misleading understanding, Maya writing 'survived' for another 700 years or so, but the contention here is that this supra-regional perspective misses the many small deaths of Maya writing at the time of their collapse—a collapse that, at some sites, Maya civilization did not overcome, unlike the rupture occurring at the end of the Preclassic period. (A pattern of more restricted literacy was likely then, to judge from surviving productions; this means that the dynamics would have been quite different from later developments.) Nonetheless, a crucial feature in considering the demise of Maya script communities—and the capacity to produce and respond to writing—is its relation to a changing language (Houston *et al.* 2000). By the Terminal Classic period, the elite language had, it appears, gone extinct as a living language. Presumably, a series of antiquarian measures—indeed, large intellectual investments—were needed to preserve knowledge of speech that had disappeared from most mouths. If the courtly societies of the Classic Maya crumbled, and this they certainly did, that investment would no longer be possible. The shift of written record from publicly visible inscriptions to handheld documents containing centimetre-high glyphs brings Maya literacy up to the 1600s. At that time, the script communities were not those of the southern Lowlands but those, probably from the northern part of Yucatan, that had somehow managed to traverse the shambles of the Collapse.

Notes

1. Many thanks to John Baines and John Bennet for their hospitable kindnesses at Oxford, and to Karl Taube and Marc Zender for commenting on this paper; Marc was especially helpful in elucidating a detail in the Josefiwitz Panel. Zachary Nelson afforded great assistance with the figures, for which my gratitude as well. As of July 2006, the stela fragment illustrated in Fig. 10.7 is on display in the Museu Barbier-Mueller, Barcelona.

2. Models of appropriate and efficacious learning have changed over time. Teaching that emphasizes gentle 'evaluation' and 'feedback' finds only a slight echo in the mechanical repetitions and brutal corrections among ancient scribes (Tinney 1998; Williams 1972). An alternative, 'Legitimate Peripheral Participation' (LPP), stresses the direct collaboration of apprentices in works supervised by 'masters' (Ames-Lewis 2000:34–46; Grimm 2000:63–4; Lave and Wenger 1991:34–6). As expertise increases, apprentices move slowly from peripheral to overall control of production, depending on the object—the master often handles the final touches and approves the overall effort. In such settings, learning can be improvised and

ad hoc, with little formal pedagogy (A. Thomas 1995: 1–2). In fact, in many aristo-cratic or exclusive practices, as in Early Modern France, there was an emphasis on grouping the socially like-with-like, with consequences for imitative speech and conduct (Motley 1990: 73–4). The likelihood is high among the ancient Maya that LPP characterized sculpting and mural painting. Smaller objects were more likely to be individual efforts rather than collaborative ones.

3. However, Alfred Gell's diagrams (1998: fig. 9.4/1) oversimplify the entities repre-sented by circles, 'individual work[s] of art (painting, sketch, etc.)'. They are not instantaneous productions but efforts that involve days, months, or years of la-bour. Consider a Maya stela: the master and his apprentices may duplicate the pat-tern of cloth selvage or the shape of a human foot on another part of the sculpture. But that duplication is a retention that is internal to the work. The same might be said of letter forms within an illuminated manuscript from the Middle Ages (Pächt 1987).

4. This set of deities ('GI', who was a version of Chahk, the storm god, and the enig-matic being known as K'awiil), is of long-standing interest to a neighbouring pol-ity centred on Dos Pilas, Guatemala (Houston and Stuart 1996: 301–2; fig. 14). The supposition is that these were supernatural beings connected to the royal family of Dos Pilas. What has not been stressed before is that mention of these deities at Seibal correlates negatively with use of the local 'Emblem glyph,' or 'holy lord' title. (The one exception, Hieroglyphic Stairway 1, tablet 4: U2-V2, is on a text appar-ently commissioned by the ruler of Dos Pilas: I. Graham 1996: 59.) In other words, when the lords of Seibal use the Seibal 'holy lord' title, the deities do not appear in local inscriptions (e.g. Seibal Stelae 8, 9, 10, 11, 12). When they do, different, supreme epithets are used, as on Seibal Stela 6: B7. My suspicion is that Seibal expe-rienced a dynastic break and that the sculptures erected at about AD 849 and those thereafter were commissioned by very different groups. In fact, a later sculpture from Seibal, Stela 2, exhibits one of the gods in rare frontal pose (I. Graham 1996: 15). A comparable shift in exalted titles can be seen at the nearby site of Altar de Sacrificios, in which an earlier title disappears in later texts, to be replaced by a dif-ferent epithet in Late Classic times (cf. J. Graham 1972: fig. 14, Stela 5: C12, and fig. 29, Stela 10: D9, and fig. 32, B11-C11).

References

Alcock, Susan E.
  2002 *Archaeologies of the Greek Past: Landscape, Monuments, and Memories.* Cambridge: Cambridge University Press.

Ames-Lewis, Francis
  2000 *The Intellectual Life of the Early Renaissance Artist.* New Haven, CT: Yale Univer-sity Press.

Andersen, R. W.
  1982 'Determining the Linguistic Attributes of Language Attrition'. In Richard D. Lambert and Barbara F. Freed (ed.), *The Loss of Language Skills.* Rowley, MA: Newbury House, 83–118.

Barton, Craig E. ed.
  2001   *Sites of Memory: Perspectives on Architecture and Race.* New York: Princeton Architectural Press.

Basso, Keith
  1996   *Wisdom Sits in Places: Landscape and Language among the Western Apache.* Albuquerque: University of New Mexico Press.

Civil, Miguel
  1972   'The Sumerian Writing System: Some Problems'. *Orientalia* 42: 21–34.

Demarest, Arthur A., Prudence Rice, and Don Rice (eds)
  2003   *The Terminal Classic in the Maya Lowlands: Collapse, Transition, and Transformation.* Niwot: University Press of Colorado.

Dixon, Robert M. W.
  1997   *The Rise and Fall of Languages.* Cambridge: Cambridge University Press.

Gell, Alfred
  1998   *Art and Agency: An Anthropology Theory.* Oxford: Clarendon Press.

Goody, Jack
  1977   *The Domestication of the Savage Mind.* Cambridge: Cambridge University Press.

Graham, John
  1972   *The Hieroglyphic Inscriptions and Monumental Art of Altar de Sacrificios.* Papers of the Peabody Museum of Archaeology and Ethnology 64(2). Cambridge, MA: Peabody Museum of Archaeology and Ethnology, Harvard University.
  1990   *Excavations at Seibal, Department of Peten, Guatemala: Monumental Sculpture and Hieroglyphic Inscriptions.* Memoirs of the Peabody Museum of Archaeology and Ethnology 17(1). Cambridge, MA: Peabody Museum of Archaeology and Ethnology, Harvard University.

Graham, Ian
  1967   *Archaeological Explorations in El Peten, Guatemala.* Middle American Research Institute Pub. 33. New Orleans, LA: Tulane University.
  1996   *Corpus of Maya Hieroglyphic Inscriptions,* vol. 7, part 1: *Seibal.* Cambridge, MA: Peabody Museum of Archaeology and Ethnology, Harvard University.

Grimm, Linda
  2000   'Apprentice Flintknapping: Relating Material Culture and Social Practice in the Upper Paleolithic'. In Joanna S. Derevenski (ed.), *Children and Material Culture.* London: Routledge, 53–71.

Havelock, Eric
  1982   *The Literate Revolution in Greece and its Cultural Consequences.* Princeton, NJ: Princeton University Press.

Houston, Stephen.
  1993   *Hieroglyphs and History at Dos Pilas: Dynastic Politics of the Classic Maya.* Austin: University of Texas Press.
  1994   'Literacy among the Pre-Columbian Maya: A Comparative Perspective'. In Elizabeth H. Boone and Walter Mignolo (eds), *Writing Without Words: Alternative Literacies in Mesoamerican and the Andes.* Durham, NC: Duke University Press, 27–49.

2000 'Into the Minds of Ancients: Advances in Maya Glyph Studies'. *Journal of World Prehistory* 14(2): 121–201.

2004 'The Acropolis of Piedras Negras: Portrait of a Court System'. In Mary Miller and Simon Martin (eds), *Courtly Art of the Ancient Maya*. Washington, DC: National Gallery of Art, 271–6.

Houston, Stephen, John Baines, and Jerrold Cooper

2003 'Last Writing: Script Obsolescence in Egypt, Mesopotamia, and Mesoamerica'. *Comparative Studies in Society and History* 45(3): 430–80.

Houston, Stephen, John Robertson, and David Stuart

2000 'The Language of Classic Maya Inscriptions'. *Current Anthropology* 41(3): 321–56.

Houston, Stephen, and David Stuart

1996 'Of Gods, Glyphs, and Kings: Divinity and Rulership Among the Classic Maya'. *Antiquity* 70: 289–312.

Jones, Christopher, and Linton Satterthwaite

1982 *Tikal Report No. 33, Part A: The Monuments and Inscriptions of Tikal, The Carved Monuments*. University Museum Monograph 44. Philadelphia: University Museum, University of Pennsylvania.

King, Mark B.

1994 'Hearing the Echoes of Verbal Art in Mixtec Writing'. In Elizabeth H. Boone and Walter Mignolo (eds), *Writing Without Words: Alternative Literacies in Mesoamerican and the Andes*. Durham, NC: Duke University Press, 102–36.

Lave, Jean, and Etienne Wenger

1991 *Situated Learning: Legitimate Peripheral Participation*. Cambridge: Cambridge University Press.

Mack, John.

2003 *The Museum of the Mind: Art and Memory in World Cultures*. London: British Museum Press.

McKitterick, Rosamund

1989 *The Carolingians and the Written Word*. Cambridge: Cambridge University Press.

Mathews, Peter, and Gordon R. Willey

1991 'Prehistoric Polities of the Pasion Region: Hieroglyphic Texts and their Archaeological Settings'. In T. Patrick Culbert (ed.), *Classic Maya Political History*. Cambridge: Cambridge University Press, 30–71.

Miller, Mary, and Simon Martin

2004 *Courtly Art of the Ancient Maya*. London: Thames and Hudson.

Monaghan, John

1990 'Performance and the Structure of the Mixtec Codices'. *Ancient Mesoamerica* 1: 133–40.

Morris, Ian

1964 *The World of the Shining Prince: Court Life in Ancient Japan*. Oxford: Oxford University Press.

Motley, Mark
  1990   *Becoming a French Aristocrat: The Education of the Court Nobility, 1580–1715*. Princeton, NJ: Princeton University Press.

Ong, Walter J.
  1988   *Orality and Literacy: The Technologizing of the Word*. New York: Methuen.

Pächt, Otto
  1987   *Book Illumination in the Middle Ages: An Introduction*. Oxford: Oxford University Press.

Robb, Kevin
  1994   *Literacy and Paideia in Ancient Greece*. Oxford: Oxford University Press.

Rubin, David C.
  1995   *Memory in Oral Traditions: The Cognitive Psychology of Epic, Ballads, and Counting-Out Rhymes*. Oxford: Oxford University Press.

Sabloff, Jeremy. A.
  1975   *Excavations at Seibal, Department of Peten, Guatemala: Ceramics*. Memoirs of the Peabody Museum of Archaeology and Ethnology 13(2). Cambridge, MA: Peabody Museum of Archaeology and Ethnology, Harvard University.

Stock, Brian
  1996   *Listening for the Text: On the Uses of the Past*. Philadelphia: University of Pennsylvania Press.

Stuart, David
  1993   'Historical Inscriptions and the Maya Collapse'. In Jeremy A. Sabloff and John S. Henderson (eds), *Lowland Maya Civilization in the Eighth Century AD: A Symposium at Dumbarton Oaks*. Washington, DC: Dumbarton Oaks Research Library and Collection.

Thomas, Anabel
  1995   *The Painter's Practice in Renaissance Tuscany*. Cambridge: Cambridge University Press.

Thomas, Rosalind
  1992   *Literacy and Orality in Ancient Greece*. Cambridge: Cambridge University Press.

Tinney, Steve J.
  1998   'Texts, Tablets, and Teaching: Scribal Education in Nippur and Ur'. *Expedition* 40: 40–50.

Von Euw, Eric
  1978   *Corpus of Maya Hieroglyphic Inscriptions*, vol. 5, part 1: *Xultun*. Cambridge, MA: Peabody Museum of Archaeology and Ethnology, Harvard University.

Webster, David
  2002   *The Fall of the Ancient Maya: Solving the Mystery of the Maya Collapse*. London: Thames and Hudson.

Williams, Ronald J.
  1972   'Scribal Training in Ancient Egypt.' *Journal of the American Oriental Society* 92: 214–21.

11

The Death of Mexican Pictography

Elizabeth Hill Boone

Mexican pictography—the graphic system of communication used by the Aztecs, Mixtecs, and their neighbours in central and southern Mexico c. AD 1300–1600—is not usually embraced within the term 'writing' by specialists in writing systems. This is because, as Houston *et al.* (2003: 430) have recently noted, Mexican pictography does not have as its goal the recording of speech or 'meaningful sound' and thus 'depart[s] from the linguistic underpinnings that characterize the writing systems of the world'. These scholars further assert that the study of Mexican pictography 'is not very helpful in understanding heavily phonic systems'. As a specialist in Mexican pictography, I am compelled to argue to the contrary.

Pictography for the Aztecs and their neighbours fulfilled all the requirements of the cultural category that is 'writing', and it fulfils these requirements for us today, with the exception of a close and direct link to spoken language. If we take the description of writing used by Houston *et al.* (2003: 430), but omit the requirement that writing must '[bridge] visual and auditory worlds by linking icons with meaningful sound,' we see that pictography fits all the other characteristics: 'It allowed writers to communicate with readers who were distant in time and space, extended the storage capacity of human knowledge, including information that ranged from mundane accounting to sacred narrative, [...] and offered an enduring means of displaying and manipulating assertions about a wide variety of matters.' Although the study of pictography does not necessarily help us understand the link between icon and sound, it can help us understand other phenomena of writings, such as how and why writing systems come into being, how they function within a culture, and how they finally expire.

This chapter intends to contribute to our understanding of the extinction of writing systems by analyzing the process by which Aztec pictography changed, endured, and ultimately expired under the domination of European alphabetic writing. Several transmutations contributed to the shifting nature of pictography in the colonial period: its pictorial vocabulary and even its structure changed. First, pictography added new imagery to accommodate the new colonial reality. Then, pictography began to mimic some of the glottographic and linear characteristics of European script. Pictography also bifurcated, moving from a figural and heavily iconic script toward the dual graphic code (script and artistic figuration) of the European tradition. Some pictographic genres became obsolete and were quickly extinguished; others lingered because they remained socially useful.

Characteristics of Preconquest Mexican Pictography

Prior to the Spanish invasion of Mexico, the goal of Mexican pictography was visually to record ideas, concepts, and facts. The latter usually were manifest as identities, places, times, quantities, relationships (temporal, spatial, social), and events. Only rarely did pictography record meaningful sound. Based on the evidence we now have, pure glottography seems only to have been employed when sound was required to signal a correct meaning that could not otherwise be indicated symbolically: it appears only in appellatives. In other semantic realms, meaning is achieved by figural images put into spatial association with each other; usually this association is tightly structured as in a grammar. The images range from pictorial representations of items, beings, and events to abstract symbols standing conventionally for concepts and phenomena.

The figural elements often stand simply for what they represent, and their meaning is usually straightforward once the conventions are understood. They are simplified in order to highlight salient features and reduce confusing elements. The physical features, hair, clothing, accoutrements, and posture of humans, for example, indicate their gender, age, occupation, and states of being (living/dead). Scenes of action or stasis tell of events and relationships. Landscape elements qualify place.[1]

Pictorial representations such as these are accompanied by other figural elements that symbolize concepts and phenomena that are not so easily portrayed. Most of these symbols are seemingly motivated, in that they picture items that stand in metonymic relation to what they signify. A round shield paired with an obsidian-edged club or a cluster of arrows thus stands for war between one polity and another (Fig. 11.1a). Other ideograms or symbols are unmotivated or arbitrary and must simply be learned. A band of chevrons signals the path to the enemy and implies warfare (Fig. 11.1b) (Smith 1973: 33). Twenty distinct images—of animals, plants, and phenomena (e.g. wind, water)—signify the twenty days of the principal day count, and disks numbering between one and thirteen signify the coefficients that accompany these day signs to yield specific days and years.

Appellatives appear both as distinct glyphic name signs and as adjectival elements added to nominal images. Humans have calendrical names, which are the day on which they are born, as well as personal names, which are given to them sometime after birth. The Mixtecs recorded both names pictographically in preconquest documents, but they may have primarily valued the calendrical names, because these appellatives endured longer in the colonial period than did personal names. The Aztecs, however, generally used only personal names on public monuments and in historical documents, although calendrical names occasionally appear as well in colonial period histories (e.g. Tira de Tepechpan 14, 15; Codex Xolotl 6; Codex en Cruz; Boone 2003: 255 n. 48). Calendrical names are always glyphic; personal names often are, but they can also be incorporated into the human's form or costume. For example, the Aztec ruler Moctezuma, or Angry Lord, is identified by the glyph of the royal diadem, often accompanied by a turquoise nose stud; both elements signify lordship (Fig. 11.1c). The Mixtec Lady 6 Monkey is identified by her calendrical name, 6 Monkey—which is rendered glyphically by six disks and the head of a monkey, and is attached to her body by a line—and also by her personal name, Serpent Quechquemitl, indicated by the serpent along her chest cape (Fig. 11.1d). Her ancestor, Lord 10 Flint, Earth Lord, is so named by the 10 Flint calendrical glyph and by the open jaw of the earth lord (in a conventional presentation) that replaces much of his face (Fig. 11.1e).

Places are also named both glyphically and adjectivally.[2] As glyphic compositions, place signs are usually composed of a topographic element (often a hill) that is qualified by another image (Smith 1973: 36–83; Boone 2000: 49–55). The sign for Coatepec, or Serpent Hill, for example, is composed of a conventionalized hill glyph and a serpent head (Fig. 11.1f); Tula or Tollan, Place of Reeds, is simply a short strip of reeds (Fig. 11.1g). Although these signs yield words, they can be (and were) voiced in many languages and thus do not operate phonically.

Phonography appears in appellatives when meaning can not easily be signified in other ways. Culhuacan (Place of the Culhua or Place of Those with Ancestors) is named by a hill sign that has a long peak that curves over on itself (Fig. 11.1h). The curved peak yields the Nahuatl (Aztec) word *coltic* ('curved'), which effectively delivers the *cul* sound in Culhuacan. From the Mixtec realm, the place sign of Teozacoalco, or Chiyo Ca'nu (Great Foundation) in Mixtec, is a human in the act of bending (*canu*) a platform (*chiyo*) (Fig. 11.1i). Before the Spanish invasion, phoneticism or phonetic transfer was clearly an acceptable if less common way of configuring appellatives.

These individual figural elements—signifying persons, places, times, phenomena, and concepts—yield more complex meanings when they are put into spatial association with each other, usually in compositions structured generally as diagrams or lists. Diagrammatic structures govern maps, cartographic histories, and some almanacs, in which images are bound into mutual relation-

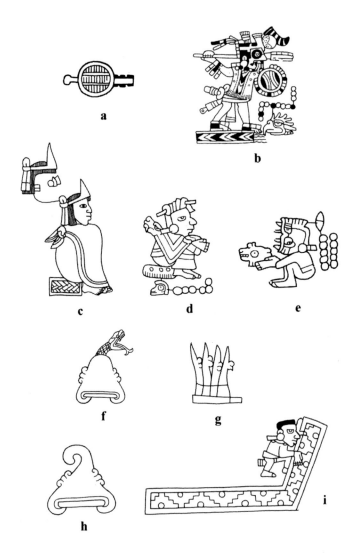

Figure 11.1 Symbols and appellatives in Mexican pictography: a, shield-and-club symbol for war; b, an armed Lord 13 Eagle standing on the chevron path (war path); c, Moctezuma (Angry Lord) with his personal name sign; d, Lady 6 Monkey, Serpent Quechquemitl; e, Lord 10 Flint, Earth Monster; f, place sign of Coatepec (Serpent Hill); g, place sign of Tollan (Place of Reeds); h, place sign of Culhuacan; i, place sign of Teozacoalco or Chiyo Ca'nu (Great Foundation). Drawing of c, after Berdan and Anawalt 1992: fol.15v. Sources: a, f, h, Codex Boturini 19, 5, 20; b, Bodley 28b; d, e, C. Selden 6c, 1c; g, C. Mendoza 8r; i, C. Bodley 15c.

ships according to their relative position over a two-dimensional area. In cartographic histories, for example, the events of the past are revealed in connection with the places where they occurred; these intersections of event and place are then arranged geographically or topologically. List structures, on the other hand, string together self sufficient units of meaning as a linear sequence, and the units take meaning from their place within the sequence. Such are annals histories, *res gestae* (event-oriented) histories, and some almanacs. In *res gestae* histories, for example, the story progresses as a sequence of events; these events can be assigned dates in real time and located geographically by the use of place signs (Fig. 11.2). In annals histories, events are organized and dated according to their placement next to the list of sequent year dates (e.g. Fig. 11.3b).

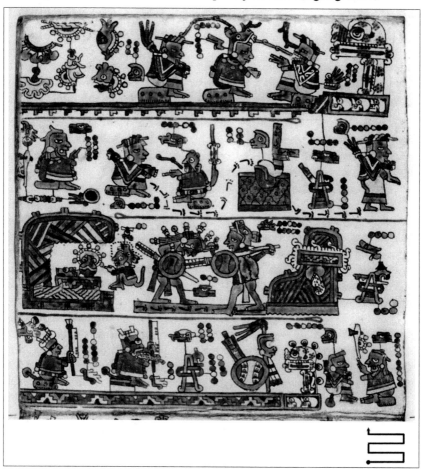

Figure 11.2 Codex Selden, a Mixtec *res gestae* history recording the life of Lady 6 Monkey. The page reads from bottom left to top in a boustrophedon pattern; it traces her story from her birth (lower right) to her betrothal to Lord 11 Wind (top).

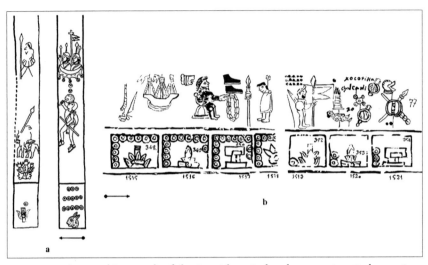

Figure 11.3 Pictographic records of the Spanish arrival and conquest: a, Codex en Cruz 3a–b (after Dibble 1981, atlas); b, Codex Mexicanus 76–77.

The two-dimensional space that surrounds these images can be inactive and empty or active and meaningful. In its inactive state, space serves merely to separate elements and thereby distinguish them from one another. In contrast, active space is employed in the pictorial histories to signify geographic location, temporality, or the unity of interacting figures. In an annals history, travel itinerary, or other series of sequent events, active space records temporal priority; the location of a pictorial element signifies whether it comes before or after other elements. In a map or tableau, active space locates elements according to a real or conceptual topography. Experiential space, the space that creates a scene and thereby unites participants in a mutual activity, can then be inserted into the surrounding space that otherwise is empty or active with temporal or topographic meaning (e.g. Figs. 11.2, 11.3).

The Aztecs and their neighbours found this kind of pictography well suited to their record-keeping needs. It often operated across linguistic borders and was therefore particularly adapted to the multilingual world of Postclassic central Mexico. On long strips and sheets of bark paper or hide and on great cotton sheets (*lienzos*) pictography was the graphic vehicle for treatises, protocols for ritual, and divinatory almanacs. It recorded history and genealogy, and it documented the practical side of life: as in maps, property plans, tax and tribute rolls, census records, business records, and court testimonies.

Essential knowledge that was not painted in these manuscripts could be found in sacred and secular acts of speech, in songs, and especially in the *huehuetlatolli* ('old, old speeches'), the long recitations that elders orated as prayers to the gods and admonitions to humans at major life events. Those *huehuetlatolli* directed to humans seem to have focused largely on social comport, containing instructions for correct living (e.g. Sahagún 1950–1982, bk. 6). These learned and recited speeches complemented the documentary base of pictography.

Colonization by European Script

The Spanish invasion and conquest introduced a different conception of visual communication and record-keeping. The Spaniards did not just bring alphabetic script to record spoken language; they also brought a rich tradition of figuration—an art tradition with a complex iconography that complemented, extended, and sometimes replaced the lettered texts. Cortés and his men may have carried books as they marched inland to Mexico-Tenochtitlan (the Aztec capital), but they travelled under a banner bearing the cross and the royal arms of Charles V, and their books were embellished with woodcuts and engravings (Díaz del Castillo 1956: 33; Sahagún 1952–1980, bk 12: Figs. 33, 34; Leonard 1949). In Europe these two graphic codes (script and figuration) had developed as separate systems. In Mexico, however, they remained united in pictography. Almost as soon as the Europeans and Mexicans came into contact, it became a project on both sides to understand the graphic systems of the other.

Mexican pictography remained a viable graphic system for several generations after the conquest largely because of European attitudes and needs. Europeans saw truth value in the Mexican painted books and records, and, needing precise and sure information about native culture, they looked to the indigenous records. From the beginning the conquerors relied on the accuracy of Aztec maps and remarked on native histories and tribute lists. Mendicant friars proselytizing in Mexico sought Aztec books to inform them about the indigenous calendar and religious system. Administrators gathered up practical documents that contained economic and political data on the empire. Desiring to set tax and service requirements, the Spanish Crown specifically ordered authorities in Mexico to gather and send painted tribute records, maps, and other native documents; the Crown continued to do so over a thirty-year period. One such request led to the creation in 1541 of the Codex Mendoza, which records Aztec imperial conquests and Aztec ways of life, as well as the tribute received by Moctezuma. Spanish administrators also accepted Aztec pictorials as valid documentary evidence in court cases, Inquisition trials, and petitions to Spanish and colonial authorities (Boone 1998: 155–8).

When pictography came under the social domination of European culture and alphabetic script, it adjusted to the new reality and changed internally. It did so in several ways: it developed a new colonial vocabulary to embrace European phenomena and to translate European facts and ideas into pictorial images (the graphic equivalent of loan words); it became more glottographic; and it began to mimic the linear properties of the new script.

A Colonial Vocabulary

The Spanish presence required a new graphic vocabulary, which pictography was quick to develop. Just as preconquest painters had identified foreigners by their distinctive dress and appearance, the early colonial painters signalled the Spaniards conventionally by their difference. They consistently characterized Spaniards as having beards and wearing tunics and trousers or leggings, brimmed hats, and leather shoes (usually coloured red, which signified leather to indigenous eyes). They represented Spaniards carrying lances with diamond-shaped points, riding horses, and sitting in a hip-chair. This hip-chair, a symbol of royal authority in Europe, itself then became a icon of political authority in Mexico, such that many colonial histories record the accession of indigenous rulers by picturing them seated in the hip-chair rather than the indigenous *icpalli* or reed throne (Boone 2000: 235–6; Diel 2005). Concurrently, the European crown replaced the indigenous turquoise diadem as the symbol of rulership. The cross and the pointed banner were introduced as symbols of Christianity and secular authority, respectively (Boone 2000: 229–36).

One sees this glyphic record of Spanish actions in the Codex en Cruz, an annals history painted in the 1550s (Fig. 11.3a).[3] It records that in the year 13 Rabbit (1518), a long distance merchant spotted a ship carrying Spaniards (this would have been the Grijalva expedition). The merchant is canonically identified by his fan and walking stick. The two Spaniards are also canonically identified: by their hats, spears, and the cross and banner combination representing the dual authority of the Church and Crown. Their ship is reduced to a lunette that floats in water rendered in the indigenous manner. Two circular eyes that lead from the merchant to the ship convey the act of sighting. The next year, 1 Reed (1519), records the arrival of the Spaniards in the Aztec capital: signified by the place sign of Tenochtitlan (a nopal cactus on a rock), an equestrian (again with brimmed hat and lance), and a Spanish soldier.

The Codex Mexicanus, an annals history painted probably 1571, uses the same conventions (Fig. 11.3b).[4] Above the year count, but linked to the year date 1 Reed (1519) by a line (and reading left to right), the Spanish arrival is represented by a ship, a place sign (probably for the arrival location), Cortés seated in the chair of authority, his gifts, and the Aztec lord (identified by his name sign) who was given these items. The gifts are leather shoes, a beaded necklace, and a lance, all things of interest to the native painter as items that were just then introduced. Directly above the year date 1 Reed, a Spanish soldier with lance and banner records the Spanish invasion proper. Above 2 Flint (1520) a prone spotted human represents the devastating smallpox epidemic of that year, and a temple in flames marks the destruction of the Aztec Templo Mayor. The final conquest is recorded above 3 House (1521) by the indigenous convention of a shield and spears, but this ancient symbol has been rendered as a European shield, spear, and sword, plus a European helmet, which together signal the Spanish conquest of Mexico-Tenochtitlan. The painter has reconfigured the indigenous convention, following all the principles of his pictographic system, to record this novel event (Mengin 1952: 463–71; Boone 2000: 232–4).

The new vocabulary embraced Catholicism also. Native historians signalled the coming of Christianity with the dove and cross. They used a bishop's mitre to signify the actions of Juan de Zumárraga and other bishops who followed him (e.g. Codex Mexicanus 78, 79, 83; Mengin 1952: 472, 475, 479). They used black, the colour of body paint that distinguished preconquest Aztec priests, for Spanish friars, and generally extended blackness to others in authority (e.g. Tira de Tepechpan 15; Boone 2000: 232). They developed new name signs to record the new Spanish names, as explained more fully below.

European script in indigenous terms

The cultural realm of alphabetic writing and European books and records also entered the graphic vocabulary. Colonial native scribes seem to have had a particular fascination with European books and alphabetic script, which they understood to be like but unlike their own. Books and alphabetic writing appear often in the painted records of the sixteenth century, where they have a glyphic, almost fetishistic quality. In keeping with the principles of indigenous pictography, the manuscript painters reduced the European graphic code to a cluster of basic conventionalized images, which are employed in the pictorial histories to signify royal and viceregal decrees, tax records, census reports, and religious texts. In painted court records conventional images of books and written documents stand for written evidence, and in pictorial catechisms they represent a range of concepts associated with 'writing' and 'veracity'. The contexts and appearance of these European documents in pictography tells us that the Nahuas understood alphabetic writing to convey authority and record truth.

A record of a property dispute involving the city and royal palace of Texcoco may be the earliest pictographic depiction of alphabetic writing to have survived (Seler 1904: 190–6) (Fig. 11.4). The dispute involved six Spaniards and the Texcocan ruler Tlauitoltzin (or Don Antonio Pimentel Tlauitoltzin, as he was baptized), who ruled c. 1540–1545 (Seler 1904: 194). Pimentel Tlauitoltzin is identified in the lower left of the document by his indigenous cloak, his name glyph (a bow or *tlauitolli*), and the high-backed woven reed throne (*icpalli*) of indigenous rulership. He and two Spanish witnesses or colleagues are shown seated on the left side of a large plan of the Texcocan palace, facing the defendant on the other side, who has turned away. The small scrolls in front of their mouths signal their animated speech. Presiding over the case, and pictured at the top of the document, are the president and two other judges of the Royal Audiencia, whose authority is conveyed by their staffs and the hip-chairs in which they sit. All three voice opinions over the plan and the four European

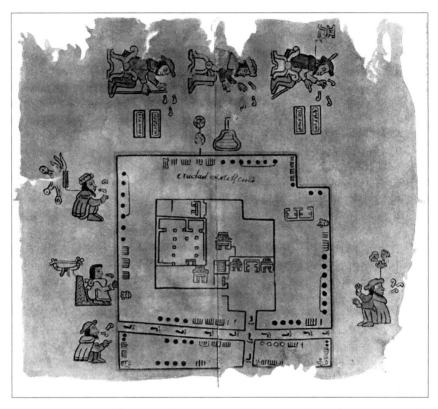

Figure 11.4 Litigation document for a property dispute involving the Texcocan ruler Tlauitoltzin. Humboldt Fragment 6.

documents that have been placed in front of them. The indigenous painter has not rendered these European documents faithfully but has instead reconfigured them to fit the appearance of indigenous written records. Accordingly, the papers are long strips, as are indigenous *tiras* (rolls) and screenfolds, and their alphabetic content is conveyed by a sequence of glyphs that runs the width of the document. As sources of authority, these European documents were central to the dispute being argued, but they have been Mexicanized to fit the indigenous understanding of what physically constitutes a written record.

European documents figure sporadically in the painted and scripted histories of the sixteenth century, where they take the form of sheets of paper and bound books. In the annals history of the Codex Aubin, for example, they function glyphically to signify royal, viceregal, or local authority. Normally, in such annals histories, events are recorded by conventionalized images that reference the happenings themselves, but in two cases, the Aubin historian used the image of a book to signal the announcement of an important event.

One of the seven events recorded for the year 13 House (1557) is a Spaniard reading an open book before the heads of four native rulers, who are so identified by their pointed turquoise diadems (Fig. 11.5a). The event refers to the accession of Philip II as king of Spain after the abdication of Emperor Charles V. One might expect that the native historian would have recorded the actuality of Philip II's accession; and it might have been rendered in the indigenous manner by showing Philip II enthroned. Instead, however, the annalist depicted the

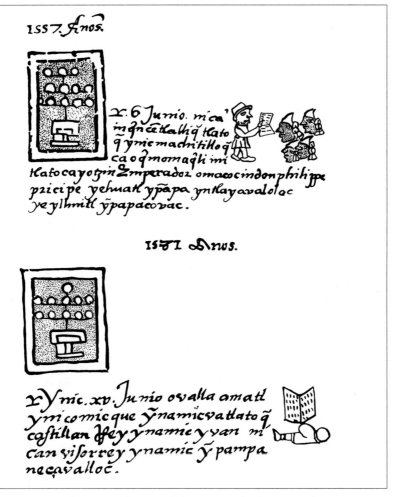

Figure 11.5 Images of books used to signal the arrival of information about important events external to the indigenous community: a, the accession of Philip II to the Spanish throne in 1557, Codex Aubin 50v; b, the deaths of the Spanish queen and the wife of the Viceroy in 1581, Codex Aubin 62v.

reading of the announcement of this event. The printed announcement, which must have come in the form of a royal proclamation, is the event that carries the import. The Nahuatl gloss to the left and below the images elaborates that the native rulers were assembled to hear the announcement that Philip II was their new sovereign; for this they held a procession and celebrated three days of festival (Dibble 1963: 70–1; Lehmann and Kutscher 1981: 39, 167 n. 3, 4). By depicting this glyphic reading of a book, the historian is informing us that it was the physical document (which carried the distant news), and its reading, that had a direct impact on the local community. The document probably carried this authority because it marked the occasion on which the indigenous lords pledged fealty to their new lord.

Elsewhere in the Codex Aubin the impact of a book as news-carrying document is even more striking because it is unrelated to questions of renewed loyalty to the Spanish Crown. In 11 House (1581) the Aubin historian paired a European book with a wrapped corpse, the indigenous convention for death (Fig. 11.5b).[5] The Nahuatl text elaborates that in this year, on 15 June, came the paper announcing the deaths of the Spanish Queen and the wife of the Viceroy (Dibble 1963: 88; Lehmann and Kutscher 1981: 50–1, 172 n. 6, 7). This notice, or 'paper', could not have had the same political impact on the community as did the accession decree of Philip II, yet, again, it is the book that becomes such a major part of the event. The pictured books in these two instances are not so much books *per se* as they are the crucial containers of knowledge about events external to the community.

Books, or folded and scripted papers containing alphabetic writing, figure in the annals history in other ways as well. When they appear, they represent the creation of official records that will affect the community, as with the taking of censuses (Aubin 52r) and the assessment of taxes (Aubin 54v, 55r) (Dibble 1963: 72–3, 77, 78; Lehmann and Kutscher 1981: 40, 43, 44, 167–8 n. 9, 169 n. 10, 170 n. 7). In a record of an Inquisition trial, the book stands as written testimony (Aubin 59r; Dibble 1963: 83–4; Lehmann and Kutscher 1981: 48). In these instances, the books represent the documentary interface between Spanish officialdom and the Indian community, and they stand as vehicles by which truth is conveyed.

In religious contexts the pictographic appearance of script referenced doctrinal texts and also conveyed the concept of truth. For example, books represent the Gospels when they appear with the evangelists in the dominical calendar in the Codex Mexicanus (5, 6; Mengin 1952: 402). This iconography of the evangelists shown writing their books continues a strong European tradition, which in Mexico coincided with the native tradition of picturing writers with their books.

Books or writings also signify documentation and truth (*veritas*) as abstract concepts, as exemplified by their use in a pictorial catechism from the Mixtec region (Fig. 11.6).[6] The catechism is a sheet made from native bark paper on which the Articles of the Faith and the Ten Commandments are recorded pictographically. The content is presented over seven registers, which are segmented into units by vertical lines that define discrete cells. The cells read in a linear boustrophedon track, beginning in the upper left corner, reading left to right, then right to left on the next register down, then left to right on the third register, and so forth down the page. This cell structure is common to the almanacs in preconquest divinatory books, and the boustrophedon reading pattern is common to the preconquest Mixtec screenfolds (e.g. Smith 1973: Fig. 1). The Articles of Faith open in the upper left cell with the pictorial equivalent of the statement: 'Here begin the Articles of Faith, which are fourteen.' A pointing hand stands for 'beginning', a piece of paper with rows of painted lines stands for the written articles, the cross is the glyph for 'faith', and the linked disks, clustered in groups of five (as they are in preconquest pictography) signify '14' (Seler 1904: 222). Each time the canonical passage recorded in registers 1–4 calls for the word 'article', the word is so signified by the sheet of scripted paper, whose dimensions vary according to the space it occupies. This glyph for the articles is more like an indigenous document than a European one, for it varies in shape and lacks the spine of European books.

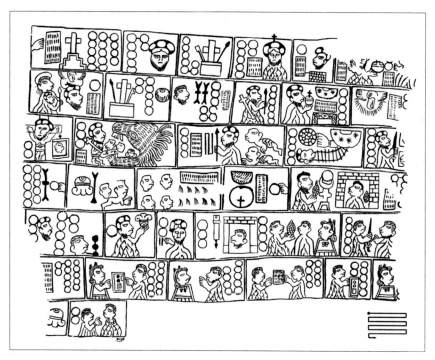

Figure 11.6 Pictorial catechism, recording the Fourteen Articles of the Faith and the Ten Commandments. Humboldt Fragment 16.

In the Ten Commandments on the lower registers, the scripted paper takes on a different meaning. Commandment Eight in register six—'Thou shall not bear false witness against thy neighbour'—is signified by two men facing each other; one hands the other a sheet of paper that is messily covered with marks. The marks are not the clear and orderly lines of the articles but here are crowded, jumbled, and cross-hatched. Lacking order and logic, they effectively convey the meaning of 'falsity' to a people who valued moderation and self control. The book, to the colonial manuscript painters, was more than an icon signifying record-making and record-keeping, although it served that purpose too. It had a potent agency as a container of information, and it represented truth value.

By means of new pictorial conventions, such as are used in the catechism, in the property dispute, and in the annals histories, Mexican pictography drew European events, ideas, and persons into its own script system. This new pictorial vocabulary gave it a resiliency that served it well for nearly 100 years.

Mimicry of European Script

In addition to developing new images and symbols to accommodate the new colonial reality, pictography changed in other ways as well. It began to take on some of the structural and semantic characteristics of European writing. One sees a slight increase in the linearity of its organization. Glottography increased in name signs, and there was more of an effort to record the contents of speech acts. Concurrently, pictography also began to split in two, moving from a single pictographic system to a dual code of script and image.

Linearity

Linearity had always been a feature of preconquest pictography: the Mixtec genealogical histories and the Aztec annals (e.g. Fig. 11.2b) both proceed from unit to unit in linear sequences, as do many divinatory almanacs. This seems to have increased, however, after the conquest. The Mixtec catechism just discussed follows the boustrophedon pattern of earlier indigenous manuscripts. Other catechisms, however, take on a strict left-to-right pattern similar to European script (e.g. Griffin 1968; León-Portilla 1979). The third part of the Codex Mendoza—a 1541 ethnographic account of the life cycle of Aztec people, which is usually considered a colonial construct without preconquest prototypes (Robertson 1959: 97; Calnek 1992: 82-4)—also organizes its material in registers that read left to right.

Greater linearity extends to genealogies and ruler lists as well. In preconquest histories from the Mixteca, the story progresses serially in registers: first an individual ruler's deeds are recounted, followed by his or her marriage statement and offspring; the deeds, marriage, and offspring of the next ruler then follow (e.g. Codices Bodley, Selden). In manuscripts painted after the conquest, the ruler's deeds and dependents often fall away, leaving only the sequent ruling couples, as in *lienzos* and *tiras* from the Mixteca and the Coaixtlahauca Valley (Parmenter 1982; Boone 2000: 127–61). These sequent couples were also stacked in straight columns that read bottom to top (e.g. Mapa de Teozacoalco and the Lienzo of Ihuitlan). M. E. Smith (1994: 121) has suggested that this stacking reflects the Spanish requirement that rulers and other indigenous landholders had to be descended from their forefathers 'por linea recta' in an unbroken continuum. The colonial painters seem purposefully to have omitted any confusing side lines or challenges to rule.

Glottography

Mimicry extended also to glottography, as pictography moved toward greater phoneticism in name signs and the representation of speech acts. Phoneticism had always been a part of the preconquest system of name signs, but the new Spanish names with their strange combinations of sounds encouraged this development. Some names could be easily represented ideographically or metonymically. Pedro de Alvarado, Hernan Cortés's second in command, came to be known as Tonatiuh (Sun) because of his light hair, and his name glyph was the sun (Fig. 11.7a). Saints' names were also indicated symbolically—e.g. St John was represented by the chalice, St Peter by a sword, St Sebastian by an arrow, and the Virgin by a crown (Codex Osuna 38r)—but since these objects were associated with these saints in Christian iconography, this glyphic signification should be recognized as a simple extension of the European tradition.

Most other names had to be phonetically referenced, however, requiring a rebus that joined Spanish and Nahuatl sounds through an intermediary image (Arreola 1922; Boornazian 1996; Dibble 1960; Galarza 1980). The name sign chosen for the judge Alonso de Zorita, for example, was a quail (*zollin*) (Fig. 11.7b). Viceroy Antonio de Mendoza's name had many variants, but the most common was a maguey leaf (*metl*) and a gopher (*tozan*), which, once these Nahuatl words lose their endings, combine to yield *me-toza* (Fig. 11.7c). For the title of 'Virrey' (Viceroy) the colonial manuscript painters consistently chose an eye (*ixtli*) and a bean (*etl*) which yield *ix-e* (pronounced as 'ee-shay') (Fig. 11.7d). Sometimes a painter would combine it with a speech-scroll (the ideogram that characterizes a speaker [*tlatoani*] or ruler) to clarify that it is the authority or person of the Viceroy that is being signified (Fig. 11.7e). A number of the rebuses were quite long and complex.

Concurrently with this development of rebus name signs, pictography also increased its capacity to record actual speech. This was not a totally new phenomenon; like rebus it developed from precolumbian precedents. What does seem to be new is a greater emphasis on speech acts in the colonial histories.

Before the conquest, speech scrolls were used both as signifiers of position and as indicators of actual speech. A speech scroll emerging from a mouth of a

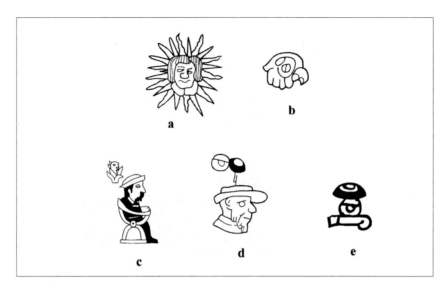

Figure 11.7 Glottography in colonial name signs: a, a sun for Pedro de Alvarado, known
as Tonatiuh (Sun); b, a quail (*zollin*) for Alonso de Zorita; c, a maguey leaf
(*metl*) and a gopher (*tozan*) for Antonio de Mendoza; d, an eye (*ixtli*) and a
bean (*etl*) for the title "Virrey"; e, "Virrey" with the added speech scroll to
signal rulership.

man seated on a woven mat signalled his identity as a ruler or *tlatoani* (speaker).
Speech scrolls from the mouths of others, however, usually represented their
act of speaking or singing. Occasionally the scrolls were embellished with qualifying symbols that indicate the general character of the speech: a flower to
denote the 'flowery speech' or especially rich quality of sacred orations, songs,
or prayers (Codex Borbonicus 5), or jade to denote preciousness (Codex Laud
2). More specific adjectival elements were also used on occasion: e.g. corn perhaps to refer to life and fertility (Fig. 11.8a), wavy lines that with the chevron
path signal war (Codex Zouche-Nuttall 44), and fuzzy white curls that probably
indicate fog, the latter issuing from the mouth of the water goddess (Codex
Fejérváry-Mayer 8).[7] In a Mixtec history (Fig. 11.8b), a speech scroll qualified
with the calendrical construction '7 Flower' specifies that the speech probably
referred to the Lord 7 Flower, who had earlier been sacrificed in the War of
Heaven (Byland and Pohl 1994: 112; Boone 2000: 58, 256). These examples demonstrate that preconquest painters did use images to signify the quality or content of speech, although they did so very rarely.

Two early colonial manuscripts that reveal minimal European influence
have more elaborate and specific reproductions of speech acts, which may also
reflect the preconquest practice or an expansion of speech rendering after
the conquest. In the Aztec Codex Boturini (21), the subject of a conversation

between the ruler of Culhuacan and the two Mexica (Aztec) vassals who stand before him concerns a war with Xochimilco during which Mexica warriors cut off the ears of their captives and brought them back to the ruler in a sack (Fig. 11.8c). This event was also recorded alphabetically by the native author of the Crónica X and preserved in Diego Durán's (1994: 114) history. In the painted account, the elements of the discussion are pictured between the men: the place sign of Xochimilco (Flower Field, its sign being a rectangular patch of ploughed field with two flowers on top), the shield-and-club war symbol, and the sack, to which the seated ruler points. An additional war symbol is connected by a dotted line to one of the Mexica's speech-scrolls, as if to emphasize that the topic is war. The specific instructions to sever the ears are pictured above another conversation, where the ruler's diadem and the ears are linked by a dotted line to a warrior holding up an obsidian blade (Fig. 11.8d).

The Codex Selden, a Mixtec genealogical history, contains several pictographic conversations. When the historian depicts the priestess Lady 9 Grass betrothing Lady 6 Monkey and Lord 11 Wind, he paints the long scrolls of her speech reaching out to touch the tops of the couple's heads, thereby joining them (Fig. 11.2, top register). Later the historian represents Lady 9 Grass and Lady 6 Monkey discussing the need to go to war; this subject is signified by a stack of symbols between then, including the shield and spear combination, the chevron path, and parallel crinkled lines, all references to war or conflict (Fig. 11.8e).

This potential to designate the content of speech acts expanded after the conquest, as exemplified in the Codex Xolotl, a cartographic history composed of a series of maps that cover the same geographic region but pertain to progressively later times. In the later maps, several strings of images compose the specific content of instructions, invocations, and conversations (Maps 6, 7, and 8; Dibble 1980: 86, 90–2, 105, 106). On Map 7, for example, the painter has recorded several orders issued by the tyrant Tezozomoc (Fig. 11.8f). A line of three pictorial elements contains the war symbol, the name sign for the Acolhua people (water, arm), and the place sign of Ecatepec (wind, bean, three dashes), which calls for war against the Acolhua of Ecatepec. The name sign Acolhua and the place sign of Ecatepec rely on multiple phonic referents: Acolhua is water (*atl*) and arm (*acolli*); Ecatepec is wind (*eecatl*), bean (*etl*), and three (*yei*) (Dibble 1980: 160–1). A second and longer speech line just below includes the diadem of rulership, the Acolhua name sign, a bale of cotton, and a cloak. The indigenous historian Fernando de Alva Ixtlilxochitl, who used this codex to write his own alphabetic history, explains this famous episode when Tezozomoc began to send cotton to the Acolhua ruler and insultingly ordered him to have his people make mantles from the cotton (Dibble 1980: 90; Alva Ixtlilxochitl 1985, 1: 327–8). The contents of some other speeches extend as sequences of eight or nine elements (Fig. 11.8g). The length and complexity of these speech lines suggest that

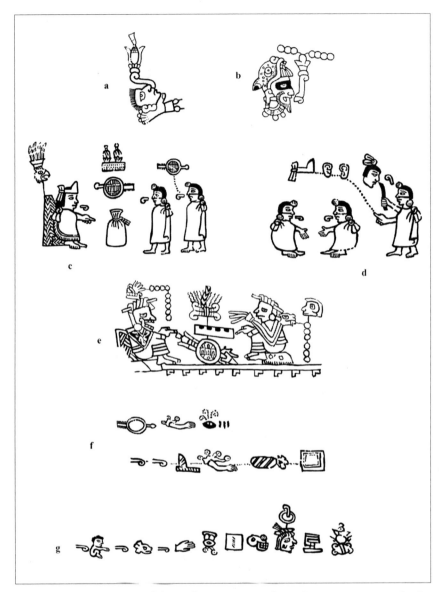

Figure 11.8 Representation of the quality or content of speech in preconquest and colonial manuscripts: a, oral expression involving corn; b, words probably about Lord 7 Flower; c, discussion of severed ears presented to the ruler of Culhuacan; d, the instructions to sever the ears; e, Lady 6 Monkey and Lady 9 Grass discuss war; f, Tezozomoc calls for war against Etla and requires the Acolhua to make cloaks for him; g, a long stream of sequent symbols representing the content of a speech act.

the painter has come under the influence of European script, although, except for the appellatives, the painter still works in ideograms rather than in phonic rebus elements.

Other colonial histories illustrate what seems to be a new interest in speech acts in general, although they do not necessarily record the content. Several histories of the Aztec migration represent the Aztec tribal patron Huitzilopochtli as extremely vocal when he commands the Aztec people to leave Aztlan. Copious amounts of speech scrolls fairly bubble forth from his mouth (e.g. C. Boturini 1, C. Mexicanus 18, Mapa Sigüenza). In the Codex Xolotl, the participants become more visually talkative as time progresses. In the earlier maps, a few protagonists are shown speaking rather simply, with a single speech scroll or occasionally two. In some of the later maps, it seems as if practically everyone is talking with great animation (Map 8). The quietness of the earlier maps seems to give way to a visually rendered cacophony toward the end.

Bifurcation into image and text

As pictography developed a new colonial vocabulary and became more linear and glottographic, it also began to bifurcate into figural image and text. In this way it came increasingly to imitate the dual but separate graphic codes of Europe. Scripted texts were progressively added to explicate, then to complement, and ultimately to replace some of the images. At the beginning short glosses and even some longer texts were added to name or explain the images to those not versed in pictography. In this way the oral voicing of the painted image was permanently fixed in European script. Such are the short glosses that name many of the actors and places in the Codex Boturini, which repeat but do not replace any of the painted information. The more copious glosses and texts in the Codex Mendoza also translate the pictographic message into Spanish script and add some extra commentary. Soon, however, scripted glosses and short texts came to replace parts of the pictography. The parts they replaced first were appellatives, the very parts where the most indigenous phoneticism was found and the very parts that are often considered 'true writing'.

We see this process clearly in a property plan from Tlaxcala, which records the sequential inheritance of contiguous plots of land (Fig. 11.9) (Boone 1998: 174–9). The original owner, Lord Jaguar by his name sign, is pictured seated in a palace, a sign of his royal situation. A genealogical cord links him to his son, Lord Eagle, in a second palace to the left. Both father and son are identified by their personal name signs, the jaguar and eagle heads located just above them. Glosses provide the Nahuatl voicing of their names but do not otherwise interfere with or add to the meaning. Below on the left are pictured Lord Eagle's two sons, also attached to him by lineage cords. These two sons lack name signs, however; scripted glosses alone record their names: Don Pedro Chichimecatecuhtli (who had clearly been baptized by this time and may have been the

Tlaxcalan lord of that name who allied himself with Cortés during the conquest) and his brother Teohuaonohualli. Their equal size and parallel presentation signal that they jointly held the land when the document was created. The painter either did not know their pictorial name signs or felt their alphabetically written names were more appropriate to his audience. Sometime later, another scribe brought the record of sequential inheritance up to date. Unskilled in pictography, he drew a circle and then a smaller circle to signify the subsequent heirs, and he linked them to Teohuaonohualli with a simple ribbon. Glosses, which seem to be in the same hand as the circles, identify the circles as specific individuals: Don Julián García and Diego García. In this amendment, pictography retains its control only in the form of these circles, the ribbons, and the spatial relationships they have with each other. Alphabetic glosses began to substitute for name signs early after the conquest (e.g. Inquisition record of 1539; Boone 1998: 165–7).

As the sixteenth century progressed, scripted glosses increased in length and frequency. In some contexts they developed into texts of considerable length

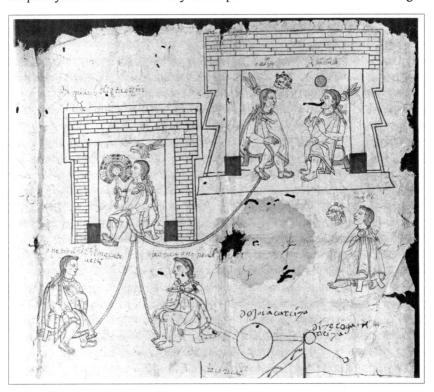

Figure 11.9 Record of the inheritance of lands in Tlaxcala. Detail of Properties of descendents of Quauhtliztactzin.

that conveyed information about indigenous culture equally with the images. One sees this especially in the cultural encyclopedia, one of the new genres of painted manuscripts that was developed after the conquest. Cultural encyclopedia were conceived, usually by the mendicant friars proselytizing in Mexico, to document a wide range of data about indigenous society. Native artists were assigned to paint images of the Aztec gods, feasts, calendar, and customs; they often also copied extracts of mythic and secular history, or included imagery from tribute lists. In the process, the artists extracted the images of indigenous reality from their original context and recontextualized them according to European categories of knowledge. These explanted images then served as the basis for explanatory texts written alphabetically.

Such is the Codex Tudela, which pictures the rain god Tlaloc as the patron deity of the feast of Etzalcualiztli (16r) (Fig. 11.10). The original source of such an image would most likely have been a divinatory almanac, where Tlaloc would have been put into graphic association with other gods and the day-signs in order to give prognosticatory meaning to units of time. The colonial artist has reconfigured this prognosticatory Tlaloc into a different kind of symbol. Painted as it is on European paper in a bound book, the image stands in a pristine space as a figural rendering of the divinity and a symbol of the feast. Its function is to illustrate the god and to be the source for the glosses and text that are written to describe the feast. The image remains prior to the text, but it has changed conceptually. It no longer exists as an element in Aztec pictography, but now stands as a figural replication of a deity which is intended to educate European eyes.

In the Codex Tudela, the image is the source from which the discursive text springs, but in later cultural encyclopedias, the two come to occupy parallel tracks as separate but associated equals. We see this in the Codex Ixtlilxochitl, where the Tlaloc being presented is a standing anthropomorphic object (Fig. 11.11). His body is controlled by European visual canons of *contrapposto, chiaroscuro*, linear perspective, and the contour line, which together describe to us a deity in human form standing in space on a sacrificial platform. Only the rain god's face mask and tunic—the features that characterize him as Tlaloc—remain within the flat conventions of Aztec pictography. He is half pictographic and half European figural, but his context is fully European. The text associated with this image exists on a separate page, as an autonomous statement. He and it are part of a report on Texcoco intended for the Spanish Crown (Juan de Pomar's *Relación de Texcoco*), and he is there to illustrate the likeness of the Aztec god.[8]

Ultimately texts like these came to dominate, and the images became mere accessories to the script. Diego Durán's (1971, 1994) treatise of 1579–1581 on the gods, rites, calendar, and history of the Aztecs is primarily a textual document, whose scripted descriptions are illustrated with paintings. Likewise, Bernardino de Sahagún's (1950–1982) *Historia general de las cosas de Nueva España* (Florentine Codex) of 1578–1579 has paintings that illustrate but follow the texts. In these cultural encyclopedias, pictography has completed its bifurcation; it has split and transformed itself into the dual graphic codes of alphabetic script and figural illustration.

Isolated Survivals

The use of pictography grew increasingly spotty toward the end of the sixteenth century, as alphabetic script came to dominate. Native tax and tribute records, censuses, and court depositions continued to be painted up to the 1570s but not much after that. The cultural encyclopedia, as a manuscript genre introduced by Spaniards, preserved pictography in artificial form until about 1600, when the last of these encyclopedias were produced, their images and texts copied from earlier versions. But vestiges of pictography did survive in two genres: the pictorial catechism and the painted history.

The pictorial catechism (also called Testerian manuscript, after Jacobo de Testera who preached using pictures) was developed by the mendicant friars to record canonical Catholic texts by means of conventional images (Fig. 11.5) (Normann 1985; Dean 1989). Testerian manuscripts employ sequences of symbols and figural images in various configurations to reference texts like the Pater Noster, Ave María, Articles of the Faith, and Ten Commandments. Brain-

Figure 11.10 Image of the rain god Tlaloc representing the feast of Etzalcualiztli. Codex Tudela 16r.

Figure 11.11. Image of Tlaloc. Codex Ixtlilxochitl, 110v.

child of the Franciscans, the genre was created specifically to teach these texts to the natives, who were so accustomed to reading and writing in images. The first pictorial catechisms may have appeared in Mexico as early as the 1520s; the catechism of the mendicant pioneer Pedro de Gante, who arrived in Mexico just two years after the conquest, has survived (Gante 1992). The last ones date from the nineteenth century; they are likely to be copies of earlier versions. It is not yet clear why pictography survived so long in these catechisms, except that they may have continued to be produced in the small backward communities where change was slow and alphabetic literacy nearly non-existent. As pictorial referents to a vocal discourse, they may have continued to help the native populations learn canonical recitations.

The other survival was the painted history. Aztec annals remained a valuable historical form through the sixteenth century and into the seventeenth. The traditional structure kept fundamentally steady, especially in the long *tiras* of native paper (e.g. Tira de Tepechpan), where the ribbon of the year count continued unbroken until the end of the strip. When annals were painted on sheets of European paper bound together as a book (e.g. Codex Aubin), the new page format forced the strip of year signs to break into segments. The imagery also changed to reflect the new colonial reality, and the figural style became less sure. More and more, glosses and short texts came to replace glyphic signifiers, but the content still concerned the events that affected the indigenous community.

At the end of the sixteenth century, four and five generations after the conquest, indigenous elites still valued the pictorial nature of their histories. The Codex Aubin, for example, was initially painted and written around 1576 by a native historian who chose to fashion a history that was primarily pictorial rather than alphabetic (Glass and Robertson 1975: 88; Lehmann and Kutscher 1981: xii–xvi). Although he spaced the images on the leaves of European paper to allow them to be embellished with alphabetic glosses and texts, the images still preceded the texts that explain and elaborate on them. This painted and glossed history was later continued up to 1596, after which another scribe added alphabetic texts to extend the account to 1603. Then a final historian reverted to a pictorial year count for the years 1604–1608. This final use of year signs tells us that pictography, even in this last reduced form, was still valued in the early seventeenth century.

Pictography signified ancient truth even for people who could no longer read the imagery. The Codex Colombino-Becker, a preconquest screenfold that records the dynastic history of the rulers of a coastal Oaxacan town, was reconfigured in the sixteenth century and later reused by two separate polities. Images were obliterated from it, the manuscript was divided into fragments, and the two fragments were glossed with the boundary names of separate polities. One set remained on the coast, where it was prized as an ancient record of land holdings until 1717, when it was entered as evidence into a boundary dispute with a neighbouring town. The other set of fragments, also annotated with boundary names, was presented as a land document in an 1852 case involving a entirely different polity in northern Oaxaca. In both cases, the scripted boundary names re-identified the screenfold fragments as maps, for their owners who needed ancient pictorials to prove their claims (Caso 1966: 113; Smith 1963, 1966: 165; Smith and Parmenter 1991: 70, 111 n. 21). It was the antiquity and pictographic nature of these documents that gave them their validity. A number of towns in Oaxaca and Puebla still today retain their sixteenth-century pictorials, which they guard as town charters, histories, and land records (e.g. Parmenter 1982: 46–8).

When no ancient pictorials remained, some towns in central Mexico had them created. Such are the Techialoyan codices, created in the late seventeenth and early eighteenth centuries as land titles for towns who had none of their own (Robertson 1975; Harvey 1986). They seem to have been mass-produced for several dozen towns who needed to submit ancient land documents to Spanish authorities, who, via *composiciones*, were trying to consolidate and regularize village landholdings. In pictures and alphabetic texts written on native *amate* paper, these Techialoyans usually picture and describe the moment when the towns' boundaries were first established, record aspects of preconquest and colonial history, and describe in detail the town and its lands. The texts attempt to reproduce sixteenth-century Nahuatl, but the paintings are European in style and conception; they lack pictographic conventions entirely. Still, the pictorial content of these manuscript was clearly crucial to their success. In the eighteenth century, ancient documents were understood to be pictorial documents, and although Aztec pictography had ceased to exist as a viable graphic form, the concept of a pictorial history as a container of knowledge and truth was still valid.

The Process of Extinction

Mexican pictography—so similar to other scripts as a graphic medium by which knowledge was permanently recorded, and so different from them in its figural properties and relative independence from spoken language—declined and went extinct in many of the same ways as did other scripts throughout the world. It died out when the culture that supported it was conquered by outsiders who introduced and privileged their own script; the new script suppressed and replaced the old. In its essence, there is little that is surprising here. What maintains our interest, however, and what makes the study of pictography's death relevant to the larger issue of script extinction, is that in tracking Mexican pictography into the colonial period, we are able to understand something of the general processes by which writing systems decline, survive for a time, and expire.

The essential cause of death for Mexican pictography was the Spanish conquest of Mexico. The Spanish invasion introduced European alphabetic writing, and the subsequent conquest assured that this form of writing would dominate. Within Mexico's European community, letters, words, and numerals were the only acceptable graphic forms for recording things European, and these forms were soon adopted by acculturated indigenous people as well. Mexican pictography, however, continued to remain strong within the indigenous community, employed for much of a century to record information about and for this community. Thereafter it retained its value as an antique, esoteric script for two more centuries. The manner in which it endured and expired was governed by changes in its graphic form, the nature of its users, and its cultural function.

Following the conquest, pictography's graphic properties adjusted to the new colonial reality, and this allowed it to survive. Its semantic corpus expanded to embrace data pertaining to the conquerors and colonial life: Spaniards and Spanish cultural features came to be characterized and recorded in figures and glyphs. Its syntactic structure also shifted to accommodate the expectations of users of alphabetic writing. In this way, glosses and texts entered the traditional domains of the indigenous script, first to amplify but eventually to replace figural elements. Pictography finally bifurcated and aligned itself more fully with the dual graphic codes of Europe (writing and figuration). At the same time that these semantic and syntactic adjustments diluted the purity of the indigenous system, they extended its usefulness to European readers, users of the dominant script.

Pictography primarily endured, especially in the first fifty years after the conquest, because Europeans and well as indigenous authorities needed the information it contained. Although the Spaniards quickly extinguished some genres (e.g. religious and divinatory books), they valued practical and historical documents. Thus, land records, tax and tribute lists, court depositions, and histories continued to be painted for an indigenous and Spanish readership, and a new genre, the cultural encyclopedia, was created for a purely European audience. By the late sixteenth century, however, indigenous script communities had shrunk, rendered largely irrelevant by alphabetic writing and their membership decimated by epidemics. As with other declining scripts, active practitioners were replaced by rememberers.

Also like other dying scripts, pictography lost its functional range and endured as a specialized prestige script. As alphabetic writing and Arabic numerals replaced it in legal and civic realms, its functional scope narrowed. Pictography retained its cultural importance as a container of information, but increasingly this information pertained solely to the Precolumbian past and to that part of the colonial present that was directly based on this ancient past. Indigenous elites and some colonial courts continued to value the painted books both for their antiquity and for their painted materiality, despite their inability to read the painted images, because they understood the painted books to be repositories of ancient knowledge.

Notes

1 For reviews of the pictorial conventions and symbols of Mexican pictography, see Smith (1973: 20–35), Marcus (1992), and Boone (2000: 33–61).

2. The glyphs can themselves have adjectival qualifiers that describe some characteristic of a place but do not otherwise contribute to the rebus system of the name sign. Such is the place sign for the Mixtec polity of Añute (Place of Sand), which, as M. E. Smith (1983: 252–5) has pointed out, is rendered by a mouth (*a*) with sand (*ñute*) coming out of it; the sign in the Codex Selden is additionally configured as a tall hill ringed by a platform lined in clouds, to signal Añute's location in the mountains.

3. Dibble 1981. Additions carry the history up to 1569, and a gloss mentions an event of 1603 (Glass and Robertson 1975: 115).

4. Mengin 1952. It contains an ecclesiastical calendar for 1570, and one hand carries the history up to 1571; additions extend the year count to 1590, although the last event is from 1583 (Glass and Robertson 1975: 166).

5. The Aztec corpse was flexed in a seated position before wrapping in preconquest times but came to be stretched prone after the conquest under the influence of Spanish burial practices (Boone 2000: 235).

6. Seler 1904: 221–9; Glass and Robertson 1975: 291–2. Although the document has no phonic referents to identify the language of its painter, the ninth Commandment— 'Thou shall not covet thy neighbour's wife'—pictures a woman whose *huipil* or blouse has chevrons, the Mixtec symbol for enemy, at the neck; this 'enemy woman' is the other man's wife who cannot be coveted. Additionally, the numerical disks are clustered and linked in groups of five in a particularly Mixtec manner (compare with Codices Bodley and Zouche-Nuttall).

7. See also, Codex Fejérváry-Mayer 14, 18; Codex Bodley 9b.

8. The Codex Ixtlilxochitl is composed of three separate manuscripts bound together before the eighteenth century; the second part contains text and paintings that were drafts or copies of Pomar's *Relación* (Glass and Robertson 1975: 147–8).

References

Alva Ixtlilxochitl, Fernando de
1985 *Obras históricas.* Edited by Edmundo O'Gorman. 2 vols. Mexico City: Universidad Nacional Autónoma de México.

Arreola, José
    1922   *Jeroglíficos de apellidos españoles*. Mexico City: Estudios Científicos de la Socie-
            dad Mexicana de Geografía y Estadística.

Berdan, Frances F., and Patricia Rieff Anawalt (trans. and eds)
    1992   *The Codex Mendoza*. 4 vols. Berkeley, CA: University of California Press.

Boone, Elizabeth Hill
    1998   'Pictorial Documents and Visual Thinking and Postconquest Mexico'. In
            Elizabeth Hill Boone and Tom Cummins (eds), *Native Traditions in the Postcon-
            quest World*. Washington, DC: Dumbarton Oaks, 149–99.
    2000   *Stories in Red and Black: Pictorial Histories of the Aztecs and Mixtecs*. Austin, TX:
            University of Texas Press.
    2003   'The Multilingual, Bi-visual World of Sahagún's Mexico'. In John Frederick
            Schwaller (ed.), *Sahagún at 500: Essays on the Quincentenary of the Birth of Fr.
            Bernardino de Sahagún*. Berkeley, CA: Academy of American Franciscan His-
            tory, 137–66.

Boornazian [Diel], Lori
    1996   'A Comparative Study of Personal and Place Names in the Aztec and Mayan
            Writing Systems.' MA Thesis, Tulane University, New Orleans, LA.

Byland, Bruce E., and John M. D. Pohl
    1994   *In the Realm of 8 Deer: The Archaeology of the Mixtec Codices*. Norman: University
            of Oklahoma Press.

Calnek, Edward
    1992   'The Ethnographic Content of the Third Part of the Codex Mendoza'. In
            Berdan and Anawalt 1992: 81–91.

Caso, Alfonso
    1966   *Interpretación del Códice Colombino / Interpretation of the Codex Colombino*.
            Accompanied by a facsimile of the codex. Mexico City: Sociedad Mexicana de
            Antropología.

Caso, Alfonso (ed.)
    1960   *Interpretación del Códice Bodley 2858 / Interpretation of the Codex Bodley 2858*.
            Accompanied by a facsimile of the codex. Mexico City: Sociedad Mexicana de
            Antropología.

Codex Aubin, See Dibble 1963.

Codex Bodley, See Caso (ed.) 1960.

Codex Borbonicus
    1974   *Codex Borbonicus, Bibliothèque de l'Assemblée Nationale—Paris (Y120)*. Graz: Akad-
            emische Druck- u. Verlagsanstalt.

Codex Boturini
 1964–67 In José Corona Núñez (ed.), *Antigüedades de México, basadas en la recopilación de
            Lord Kingsborough 2*. Mexico City: Secretaría de Hacienda y Crédito Público,
            6–29.

Codex Colombino. See Caso 1966.

Codex en Cruz. See Dibble 1981.

Codex Fejérváry-Mayer
1971   *Codex Fejérváry-Mayer 12014 M, City of Liverpool Museums.* Graz: Akademische Druck- u. Verlagsanstalt.

Codex Ixtlilxochitl
1976   *Codex Ixtlilxochitl, Bibliothèque Nationale, Paris (MS. Mex. 65–71).* Graz: Akademische Druck- u. Verlagsanstalt.

Codex Laud
1966   *Codex Laud. MS. Laud Misc. 678, Bodleian Library, Oxford.* Graz: Akademische Druck- u. Verlagsanstalt.

Codex Mendoza. See Berdan and Anawalt 1992.

Codex Mexicanus
1952   *Codex Mexicanus. Bibliothèque nationale de Paris, Nos. 23–4.* Facsimile published as a supplement to the *Journal de la Société des américanistes* 41, to accompany Mengin 1952.

Codex Osuna
1973   *Pintura del gobernador, alcaldes y regidores de México.* 2 vols. Madrid: Dirección General de Archivos y Bibliotecas, Ministerio de Educación y Ciencia.

Codex Selden
1964   Alfonso Caso (ed., *Interpretación del Códice Selden 3135 (A.2) / Interpretation of the Codex Selden 3135 (A.2).* Accompanied by a facsimile of the codex. Mexico City: Sociedad Mexicana de Antropología.

Codex Tudela
1980   José Tudela de la Ordén (ed.), *El Códice Tudela.* 2 vols., including a facsimile of the codex. Madrid: Ediciones Cultura Hispánica.

Codex Xolotl. See Dibble 1980.

Codex Zouche-Nuttall
1987   *Codex Zouche-Nuttall, British Museum, London (Add. MS. 39671).* Graz: Akademische Druck- u. Verlagsanstalt.

Dean, Carolyn S.
1989   'Praying with Pictures: A Reading of the *Libro de oraciones'. Journal of Latin American Lore* 15, 2: 211–73.

Díaz del Castillo, Bernal
1956   *The Discovery and Conquest of Mexico, 1517–1521.* New York: Farrar, Straus and Cudahy.

Dibble, Charles E.
1960   'Spanish Influences on the Aztec Writing System'. In *Homenaje a Rafael García Granados.* Mexico City: Instituto Nacional de Antropología e Historia, 171–7.

Dibble, Charles E. (ed.)
1963   *Historia de la nación mexicana. Reproducción a todo color del Códice de 1576 (Códice Aubin).* Madrid: José Porrúa Turanzas.

1980   *Códice Xolotl*. 2 vols. Mexico City: Universidad Nacional Autónoma de México.

1981   *The Codex en Cruz*. 2 vols. Salt Lake City: University of Utah Press.

Diel, Lori Boornazian.

2005   'Painting Colonial Mexico: The Appropriation of European Iconography in Mexican Manuscript Painting'. In Elizabeth Boone (ed.), *Painted Books and Indigenous Knowledge in Mesoamerica: Manuscript Studies in Honor of Mary Elizabeth Smith*. New Orleans, LA: Tulane University, Middle American Research Institute, 301-17.

Durán, Diego

1971   *Book of the Gods and Rites and The Ancient Calendar*. Fernando Horcasitas and Doris Heyden (trans. and eds). Norman: University of Oklahoma Press.

1994   *The History of the Indies of New Spain*. Doris Heyden (trans.). Norman: University of Oklahoma Press.

Galarza, Joaquín

1980   *Estudios de escritura indígena tradicional (Azteca-Nahuatl)*. Mexico, City: Archivo General de la Nación.

Gante, Pedro de

1992   *El catecismo de fray Pedro de Gante*. Madrid: Testimonio.

Glass, John B., and Donald Robertson

1975   'A Census of Native Middle American Pictorial Manuscripts'. In Robert Wauchope and Howard F. Cline (eds), *Handbook of Middle American Indians* 14. Austin: University of Texas Press, 81–252.

Griffin, Gillett

1968   *An Otomí Catechism at Princeton*. Princeton, NJ: Princeton University Library.

Harvey, H.R.

1986   'Techialoyan Codices: Seventeenth-century Indian Land Titles in Central Mexico'. In Victoria Bricker and Ronald Spores (eds), *Handbook of Middle American Indians, Supplement 4*. Austin: University of Texas Press, 153–64.

Houston, Stephen, John Baines, and Jerrold Cooper

2003   'Last Writing: Script Obsolescence in Egypt, Mesopotamia, and Mesoamerica'. *Comparative Study of Society and History* 45: 430–79.

Lehmann, Walter, and Gerdt Kutscher (trans. and eds)

1981   *Geschichte der Azteken: Codex Aubin und verwandte Dokumente*. Berlin: Gebr. Mann.

Leonard, Irving A.

1949   *Books of the Brave*. Berkeley: University of California Press.

León-Portilla, Miguel (ed.)

1979   *Un catecismo Náhuatl en imagines*. Mexico City: Cartón y Papel de México.

Lienzo of Ihuitlan. See Boone 2000: Fig. 180.

Mapa de Teozacoalco

1949   'Alfonso Caso, "El Mapa de Teozacoalco".' *Cuadernos Americanos* año 8, 47, 5: 145–181.

Mapa Sigüenza See Boone 2000: Figs. 105–110.

Marcus, Joyce
1992 *Mesoamerican Writing Systems*. Princeton, NJ: Princeton University Press.

Mengin, Ernst
1952 'Commentaire du Codex Mexicanus no. 23–4 de la Bibliothèque nationale de Paris'. *Journal de la Société des américanistes* 41: 387–498, with a separate, accompanying facsimile of the codex.

Noguez, Xavier (ed.)
1978 *Tira de Tepechpan: Códice colonial procedente del valle de México*. 2 vols. Mexico City: Biblioteca Enciclopédica del Estado de México.

Normann, Anne Whited
1985 'Testerian Codices: Hieroglyphic Catechisms for Native Conversion in New Spain'. PhD dissertation, Tulane University, New Orleans, LA.

Parmenter, Ross
1982 *Four Lienzos of the Coixtlahuaca Valley*. Studies in Pre-Columbian Art and Archaeology 26. Washington, DC: Dumbarton Oaks.

Pomar, Juan Bautista de
1986 'Relación de la ciudad y provincia de Tezcoco'. In René Acuña (ed.), *Relaciones geográficas del siglo XVI: México* 3. Mexico City: Universidad Nacional Autónoma de México, 21–113.

Robertson, Donald
1959 *Mexican Manuscript Painting of the Early Colonial Period: The Metropolitan Schools*. New Haven, CT: Yale University Press.
1975 'Techialoyan Manuscripts and Paintings, with a Catalog'. In Robert Wauchope and Howard F. Cline (eds), *Handbook of Middle American Indians* 14. Austin: University of Texas Press, 253–80.

Sahagún, Bernardino de
1950–82 *Florentine Codex: The General History of the Things of New Spain*. Charles E. Dibble and Arthur J. O. Anderson (trans. And eds). 12 books in 13 vols. Santa Fe, NM: School of American Research and the University of Utah.

Seler, Eduard
1904 'The Mexican Picture Manuscripts of Alexander von Humboldt in the Royal Library at Berlin'. In Charles P. Bowditch (ed.), *Mexican and Central American Antiquities, Calendar Systems, and History*. Smithsonian Institution, Bureau of American Ethnology Bulletin 28. Washington, DC: United States Government Printing Office, 123–229.

Smith, Mary Elizabeth
1963 'The Codex Colombino: A Document of the South Coast of Oaxaca'. *Tlalocan* 4, 3: 276–88.
1966 *Las glosas del Códice Colombino/The Glosses of the Codex Colombino*. Bound with Caso 1966 and accompanied by a facsimile of the codex. Mexico City: Sociedad Mexicana de Antropología.
1973 *Picture Writing from Ancient Southern Mexico: Mixtec Place Signs and Maps*. Norman: University of Oklahoma Press.

1983 'The Mixtec Writing System'. In Kent Flannery and Joyce Marcus (eds), *The Cloud People: Divergent Evolution of the Zapotec and Mixtec Civilizations*. New York: Academic Press, 238–45.

1994 'Why the Second Codex Selden Was Painted'. In Joyce Marcus and Judith Francis Zeitlin (eds), *The Caciques and Their People: A Volume in Honor of Ronald Spores*. Ann Arbor: Museum of Anthropology, University of Michigan, 111–41.

Smith, Mary Elizabeth, and Ross Parmenter

1994 *The Codex Tulane*. New Orleans, LA: Middle American Research Institute, Tulane University.

Tira de Tepechpan, See Noguez (ed.) 1978.

12

Late Khipu Use

Frank Salomon

Quechua khipu (pl. *khipukuna*) and Aymara *chinu* (pl. *chinunaka*), both mean 'knot', and both denote objects of cord used in the Andes to store and share information. Peruvian schoolbooks and popular media locate the khipu in a triangle together with Inka rule and Quechua speech. But all three sides of the triangle crumble under research pressure. Dialectology and diachronic linguistics (Cerrón-Palomino 1987: 79–217; Parker 1963; Torero 1974) have shown that the 'Quechua II' dialect which served as an administrative language of the Inka state is only one of a family of Quechuas spoken before, during, and after Inka rule. Likewise archaeology and ethnography show that the Inka khipu (Urton 2003), though by far the most common kind of khipu, belonged to a family of fibre-based media originating long before Inka rule (Conklin 2003; Splitstoser *et al.* 2003) and outlasting it, as we shall see, by over 400 years. Early cord media spread through space and time independently of Quechua diffusion, casting doubt on whether there is any more than a chronological and geographical overlap between khipu and the Inka-promoted Quechua language. Indeed, there is room for doubt about whether khipu included signs for components of any particular language at all, i.e. whether it was 'writing' in Boltz's (1994: 16–28) sense of the word. (For Boltz, 'writing' includes only codes whose signs stand for segments of the speech stream.) The khipu's decline from political medium par excellence under Inka rule (c. 1430–1532) to illegible cultural emblem in our time cannot therefore be explained either as a consequence of the Inka state's collapse under Spanish invasion (1532–1535), or as a consequence of Quechua's gradual demotion from political-administrative language to peasant vernacular.

The Khipu Problem

I will argue that late khipu use, especially political khipu use, had a trajectory of its own. This trajectory was linked to the Inka state and to the Quechua speech community but separable from them, and in the event determined by other factors. I will also argue against the idea that the functional power of Spanish (i.e. Castilian and Latin) literacy inflicted a death sentence on khipu. Rather, I hold that khipu and the alphabet coexisted in a colonial pattern of semiotic pluralism until fairly recent changes in the authoritative value of knotted versus alphabetic information undercut khipus' cogency.

We know more about the context of khipu than we do about the actual nature of the script. The problem is not lack of evidence, for khipus are far from rare (some 600 being held in museums, and more emerging continually from the sands of coastal Peru and Chile). Nor is the problem lack of effort. After a long lull following the initial recovery of khipu arithmetical code (a base-ten positional notation reconstructed by Locke 1923, 1928), khipu studies regained vitality in the 1980s (Mackey *et al.* 1990) and 1990s (Quilter and Urton 2002). The difficulty of khipu decipherment comes, rather, from lack of toeholds for understanding the anchoring of meanings in cord signs. For reasons that are far from obvious, no early-colonial Spaniard seems to have learned and explained khipu. This leaves a field of basic disagreement wide open.

The common but implausible assertion by grammatologists (e.g. Gaur 1984: 22–3, 77–9) that khipu were 'mnemonics' peculiar to their individual makers has been amply rebutted (Urton 2003: 15–26). Roughly speaking, three positions remain in play. An eighteenth-century thesis (Sansevero di Sangro 1750) holds that, besides the 'numerical' code clarified by Locke, a separate kind of 'royal' khipu contained a Quechua-based syllabography. The eighteenth century formulation embodies a neoplatonistic speculation about 'philosophical language', related to then-current erroneous 'symbolic' interpretation of Chinese and Egyptian scripts. (It deviates from these, however, by postulating a phonography built up from syllabic analysis of philosophical keywords in Quechua.) This thesis has been promoted anew by advocates of materials discovered in Naples in the 1980s and continuing to tumble forth in the 1990s from a private collection (Domenici and Domenici 2003; Laurencich Minelli 1996; Animato *et al.* 1989). A less naive version of the phonographic thesis (Hyland 2003) holds that a reworking of khipu code by the early colonial mestizo intellectual Blas Valera yielded real, but post-Inka, khipu phonography. A second thesis suggests that khipus are a semasiography (using Gelb's 1963 term as revived by Sampson [1985: 26–45]; Boone and Mignolo 1994)—that is, a code whose signs are, in Boltz's terms, semantically full but phonetically empty, like sheet music or mathematical formulae. Finally, Gary Urton (2003) launched a third thesis, namely that khipu signs are a neutral underlying code, each sign being assignable to surface meaning according to contexts. That is, their status is similar to eight-bit binary sequences, which 'stand for' different surface entities depending what any particular program makes of them. The future of these theses is in debate.

The Spanish Conquest (1532–1535) and Inka Inscription

For comparability's sake, I will sketch the beginnings of the colonial transition under the three rubrics which Houston, Baines, and Cooper suggest (2003: 435).

The first rubric is sociolinguistic status: the standing of khipu in relation to co-existing modes of inscription, in terms of prestige and authority. Imperial khipu were Peru's most authoritative data source. The god-king Inka himself is reported to have been involved in their production. From an array of such testimonies (Sempat Assadourian 2002), the words of Juan de Betanzos, married into an Inka royal household, will do as an example:

> [Inca Yupanque] ordered many woollen cords in a variety of colours. Bringing each cacique before him in the presence of those lords of Cuzco and making knots in those cords, he made a record for each one of them of what he was to bring in tribute to the Inca and to the city of Cuzco. [...] The Inca ordered two of each one of these quipos and records to be made, one for the cacique to take and another to remain in the possession of those lords.[1]

Khipus are well attested as sources of calendrics, censuses, tribute records, royal deeds reportedly recited in verse, genealogies, ritual records, and inventories. In no testimony did co-existing modes of Inka inscription (e.g. the *tuqapu* or woven heraldic code) trump khipu. As will be seen below, Spaniards quickly came to share the opinion of khipu as authoritative for Andean matters, though they never adopted its use; sociolinguistic demotion is a later development.

The second or 'sphere of exchange' variable asks in what kinds of transactions a script was considered to yield legitimate records. The functional sphere of khipu was conditioned by its non-congruence to language. The first Quechua–Spanish dictionary and grammar were in print as early as 1560 (Santo Tomás 1951 [1560]; 1995 [1560]; Itier 2001; Taylor 2001) and Quechua soon functioned as a colonial lingua franca. But not a single person who claimed the status of 'pure' Spaniard is known to have claimed khipu competence: 'We have been dealing with them [Peruvians] for more than seventy years without ever learning the theory and rules of their knots and accounts, whereas they have very soon picked up not only our writing but also our figures' (Blas Valera, quoted by Garcilaso Inca de la Vega 1966 [1609]: 824). An ethnically separate khipu sphere of exchange arose wherever an 'Indian' institution claimed ownership of a body of information.

The third or 'demographic' variable considers script networks by analogy with language demography. How did the number and social density of writers and readers affect cross-generational transmission? As with much else of Andean culture, Inka informants tried to project the idea that khipu use was a restricted elite privilege, but this is likely to be untrue. What little we know about the demography of Inka khipu use suggests competence far beyond the charmed circle of Inka descent. The half-Inka chronicler Garcilaso Inca de la Vega wrote that each village had four to thirty khipu masters (1966 [1609]: 331). If so, the number of authorised masters within the empire would have been at least in the tens of thousands. The attested Inka manner of aggregating and verifying tribute rolls (Julien 1988) implies a well-developed grass-roots recording base. By wrecking apical institutions like the high priesthoods, the conquest did not so much shrink the khipu-using community as decentralise it. Without a central authority, from about 1535 to about 1970, khipus afforded local margins of independence from the 'lettered city' of scribes and notaries (as Angel Rama called it, 1996 [1984]). But the resulting fragmentation was such that not a single one of the modern khipu-holding or khipu-remembering communities which this researcher has visited is aware of other communities also having retained them.

Arenas of Late Khipu Use

The politicised search for 'Inka history'

Convinced by Inka informants that khipus contained ancient *memoriales*, chroniclers often compared them to histories. As early as 1542 a Spanish governor took the khipu-based deposition of four cord masters in order to clarify dynastic claims, which unfortunately reach us only as quoted within a lawsuit in 1608, sixty years *ex post facto* (Collapiña, Supno et al. 1974 [1542, 1608]). In 1559 and 1569 royal descent groups (*panaka*) claimed to have consulted cords to explain the deeds of long-dead Inka kings (Rowe 1985; Julien 2000: 134) and thereby vindicate their Inka privileges as nobility. Many chroniclers claimed to probe prehispanic times by khipu. Among the best informed were the 'soldier-chronicler' Cieza de León (1985 [1553]: 57–60), Juan de Betanzos, (1987 [1551]: 96–7), Cristóbal de Molina 'cuzqueño' (1959 [1573]), and Juan Polo de Ondegardo (Julien 2000: 55; Fossa 2000), who by 1559 was convinced that khipu masters really could 'configure' laws, royal successions, and dynastic marriage records on cord (Sempat Assadourian 2002: 126). Polo put khipu lore to the test by using it to sniff out politically dangerous foci of Inka royal cult. These and a few others had already begun looking into khipus before Spanish officials began to influence production of cords for trials and tribute records. Their assertions may therefore be taken as referring to Inka khipu work.

As the conquest evolved from warlordism to colonial governance, Spanish demand grew for a politically innocuous version of American antiquity. This occurred while prehispanically trained khipu masters still lived. The viceroy who shaped the 'mature colony', Francisco Toledo, had a panel of them interviewed by his official historian, Pedro Sarmiento de Gamboa, in 1571–1572, so as to establish a 'true' history of the 'tyrannical' Inka state and thereby immunize the viceroyalty against future challenges to its basic legality (Sarmiento de Gamboa 1942 [1572]). In opposition, Garcilaso Inca, relying on another half-indigenous chronicler, Blas Valera, averred that Inka knot masters had recorded Spaniards' usurpations in Peru even as they occurred (1966 [1609]: 676, 682, 687, 689).

Khipus and colonial administration

Hardly had the Pizarro brothers invaded Peru when they found themselves startled by 'Indians'' ability to keep accounts on strings. In 1533, an eyewitness noticed an Inka storehouse-keeper knotting down goods the invaders were taking from a state storehouse (Pizarro 1920 [1533]: 175). Untying some knots and tying knots on other cords, the Inka official may have been using a double-entry method. Because double entry was at that time Europe's newly invented state-of-the-art accountancy (Pizarro 1920 [1533]: 175), and because Indo-Arabic base-ten arithmetic, though familiar to Spaniards as a shortcut used by merchants (*guarismo*, from Arabic *alhuwarizmi*), did not yet have bureaucratic respectability, Andean functionaries' adroitness with numbers impressed early Spaniards as almost uncanny. Although early Spanish warlords and missionaries usually were anything but credulous about native intellect, personal familiarity with cord-medium experts convinced many that Andean cord records were tenable accounts. By 1555 Agustín de Zárate's proto-Lockean understanding of cord accountancy was in print (1995 [1555]: 28). When, in 1549, the crown sent its intervener Pedro de la Gasca to inventory the ex-Inka wealth which conquistadores had been ransacking, he sent seventy-two inspection teams a few of whose khipu-based reports are now fundamental sources.[2]

The core of post-Inka media history is thenceforward a story of coexistence and interaction effects, not one of simple replacement. The resulting 'paper khipus', transcriptions of khipu testimony made by colonial scribes, recently compiled by Martti Pärssinen (2004), are a key resource for decipherment.

Garcilaso Inca de la Vega wrote that in his youth, the 1540s and 1550s, local ethnic lords requested that he read them the Spanish ledgers as a check against falsification of knotted tribute data (1966: 333). Platt (2002) details a Bolivian case where natives tracked tribute abuses in 1548–1551 so accurately that they could convincingly litigate them twenty-one years later. Similarly, in 1554, Wanka ethnic lords adduced their khipus as accounts of goods seized by Spanish armies during the early days of the Spanish invasion. At first the jurists could hardly believe that *indios* equipped only with strings could account for every bag of corn or pair of sandals seized in the hurly-burly of war decades before. But the conjoint cord–paper technique in which native political authorities oversaw the recitation, translation, and writing of cord contents proved persuasive, and the courts did recognize such presentations as valid 'accounts' (*cuentas*, Murra 1975) even though the Council of the Indies never authorised them. The early *visitas* or inspections by which the viceroyalty converted ex-Inka tribute systems into European levies also relied on khipus. One case (Ortiz de Zúñiga 1967, 1972 [1562]) even specifies how khipus were compiled. Details about presentation of khipu to colonial courts are now under close study for clues about how cord signs were realised as speech (Howard 2002: 29). Marcia and Robert Ascher's (1997 [1981]) hypothesis that cord structures signified stereotyped '-emes' of narrative structure or genre format remains in play.

Do any extant khipus actually attest colonial practice? Few if any museum khipus have been radiocarbon-dated, so we have no idea how many colonial khipus now exist. But Urton's persuasive (2001) analysis of one of the khipus from Laguna de los Cóndores argues that it represents a triennium of colonial tribute payments.

From 1570 onward changing khipu use reflected the microscopically interventionist policies of Viceroy Francisco de Toledo (who ruled 1569–1581). Philip II sent Toledo to hammer down nonstandard practices that had arisen during thirty-seven years of haphazard royal administration and indigenous–Spanish dealmaking. In the early Toledan years colonial policy passed beyond receiving khipus toward regulating their usage and even requiring indigenous lords to maintain specific kinds of cords which would supposedly complement notarial-scribal records. Juan de Matienzo, theorist of the Toledan regime, prescribed that 'every six months the tucuirico [supervisor] is to send a memorandum by writing or by khipu of the Indians who have died, or increased, or reached the age of eighteen, or fled' (1967 [1567]: 67). Toledo in 1572 ordered that khipu masters were to aid judges in receiving native cases (Toledo 1986–1989 [1572]: 237–8) and ranked them as equal in standing to assistant scribes (Loza 1998: 155). In this way the colonial khipu proper came into being. It was solidly inserted into Quechua- and Aymara-speaking political practice as early as the 1570s (Del Río 1990: 107–108; Abercrombie 1998: 259–61).

Indeed, some Spaniards thought the Toledan regime went too far in legitimating cord accountancy. Functionaries found political-economy reason to denounce the old art. A good example is a 1589 memo by a certain Dr Murillo de la Cerda, expressing opinions about 'cord-plus-paper' accountancy as the Toledan age practised it (BN/M Manuscript 5938 f.433–5). In part Murillo says:

> [T]oday [1589?] there continues the use of some quypos, which we call books of account [although] the Indians had no such [thing as account books] except those quipos, which are some woollen cords of various colours and on them many knots as is here shown [an illustration may be missing]. Some [are] different from others, such that by the difference they recognize and know the

amounts that entered and left the account, and the gold and silver pesos which have been given and paid and received. The Spanish did not grasp this kind of account when they won that kingdom, nor have they been able to learn it up to today. [This accounting] has good faith and credit only through some trustworthy Indians in those towns, whom they call quypo camayos, as majordomos of those accounts and as senior accountants. The accounting of all the livestock, and fruits and fields of the communities is in their charge [...] and these quipo camayos do the accounting before the judicial authorities, and verbally give account of everything. Up until today they have saved a great infinity of these knotted cords. Although the cunning and aptitude of some leading Indians has already extended in that kingdom as far as learning Romance [i.e. Spanish] and Latin and to singing and playing various instruments, and counting with Arabic numerals, in reality they do not use them [Arabic numerals], nor do the crown district governors allow them to take anything or give anything according to our counting and numerals, but rather through these quipos. And the quipocamayos themselves choose these same instruments, before the crown district governor, in their town council. This order is maintained today. The other order, our own, serves as a curiosity and refinement of the leading Indians who choose to learn it.

Murillo tells us that a half-century after the conquest, Andean notables had learned Spanish numeracy but considered it a mere affectation of biculturalism, by comparison to the real working technology of cords. Khipu technology had evidently worked its way deep into the viceregal order. The regime not only allowed pluralism in data systems, it positively gave Andean people a mandate to create records that Spaniards could not read. This helps one understand why, in later times, when Spaniards lost interest in cords, natives felt entitled to maintain them.

Khipus of the 1580s concerned secular matters such as service to the way-stations (*tampu*) of the Inka trunk road (Espinoza Soriano 1960: 264–5; Cobo 1964 [1653] vol. 2: 143), or as labour chits in the crown's gunpowder factory at Santa Inés de Chíchima (BN/M Manuscript 12965 No. 9). Up to about 1600 local lords were expected to 'bring their khipus' to *visitas* or tribute censuses and assessments (e.g. AGN/BA 1588 f.8r).

Most scholars say that as the scribal establishment flourished after 1600 the khipu art was marginalised or that khipu masters practised in a poorly documented space of informality (Pease 1990; Loza 1998: 156). A closer look shows more than marginalised contraband. After all, it hardly seems likely that the elaborate khipu–paper interface, which Spaniards had themselves helped to build, vanished without a trace while the institutions and relationships that mandated it stayed in place. It would be puzzling if *indios* willingly sacrificed their independent database *vis-à-vis* distorted Spanish data (or, for that matter, missed the chance to 'cook' data before presenting it to Spaniards). In 1653 a report on a textile plant (*obraje*) in the jurisdiction of Quito said (Costales de

Oviedo1983: 276-7; see also Meisch 1998):

> A khipu master is needed in the obrajes so that he too can keep account of the days that the factory hands have worked. He should make a large khipu with different strings according to the Indians who work at different tasks. By this means the workers will be able to check what is shown (señalado) by the khipu master and what his administrator has noted down, and in this way they may reach agreement.

As Spaniards stopped admitting khipu masters to official functions, the khipu art apparently lodged in folk-legal proceedings off the colonial ledger. These records, though not procedurally visible within the legalistic orbit, were vital in preparing indios' positions when they litigated. One fateful case was the 1607 ecclesiastical trial in which members of several villages turned against their curate, Francisco de Avila (AA/L Capítulos Leg. 1 Exp. 9), who soon afterwards sponsored the compilation of the only known Quechua-language book about the pre-Christian deities, and then promoted the persecutions known as 'extirpations of idolatry'. While the importance of Avila's trial has been amply recognised in researches of Antonio Acosta Rodríguez (1979, 1987), its khipu-based evidentiary structure has not been noted. It indicates that a multilevel khipu data collection system existed, even though more than seventy years had passed since the Inka state ceased to co-ordinate khipu registry. Overall, the trial confirms, as the chronicler Murúa had affirmed in 1590 (1946: 124), that local ethnic groups had developed khipu resources apart from Inka bureaucracy.

The 'indigenous chronicler' Felipe Guaman Poma de Ayala finished his stupendous illustrated history in 1615.[3] Guaman Poma drew khipu in specifically colonial use (see Figs. 12.1 and 12.2), and in his 'Buen Gobierno', a utopian prescription, he urged continued use as the lower tier of a dual-media empire. His drawings of khipu match with startling accuracy the modern patrimonial specimens discussed in 'Khipus in community politics and self-government' below (1980 [1615]: 335, 348, 358, 360, 800 in the original pagination). From the later seventeenth century to the end of the early Republican era information on local administrative khipus is very scarce. A 1725 idolatry trial reported on 'the Indian who always has his khipu of strings' by which he knew all of the people from his panaca, their duties and their wealth (Sempat Assadourian 2002: 136). As late as 1778 inhabitants of Chorrillos, a fishing village near Lima, litigated about who was to be their quipocamayo (Rojas 2004).

Administrative khipus emerge from this shadow only with the beginnings of modern travel literature and ethnography. In the era of independence, which recognized no specifically 'Indian' authorities as such, khipus shown to outsiders served primarily to administer private latifundist estates. Max Uhle in 1897 published the first full description of an 'ethnographic khipu', a herder's log of animals from Cutusuma, Bolivia (see 1990 reprint). Twentieth-century reports of other herding khipus (Nuñez del Prado 1990 [1950]; Prochaska 1983;

Figure 12.1 A colonial village councilman drawn by the bilingual chronicler Felipe Guaman Poma de Ayala. The headline says, 'THE COUNCILMAN SHALL KEEP BOOK AND KHIPU OF ACCOUNTS'. The khipu in his hand closely resembles patrimonial specimens from Tupicocha.

Figure 12.2 Guaman Poma's colonial 'ASTROLOGER POET WHO KNOWS the cycle of the sun and moon and of the stars and comets...' carries the same sort of khipu. Some modern Tupicochans also regard khipus as a source for auguries.

Soto Flores 1990 [1950–1951]) stimulated Carol Mackey's important but unpublished 1970 study of twenty-four modern specimens, some of whose owners
were competent in the art. She judges rural competence of the 1960s to represent a reduced or simplified residue of the Inka art with many nonstandard
features. Absence of basic common norms reflects the 'gerrymandering' of the
pan-Andean user community into local peasantries (Holm 1968). These herding
khipus' very small audience allowed herder-supervisor dyads—user communities as small as one person, plus one other to whom content was verbalised—to
influence the selection and arrangement of signs.

Khipus *and Catholicism*

Peru's Third [archiepiscopal] Council of Lima, 1581–1583, condemned khipus because its experts judged them likely to contain 'testimonies of ancient
superstitions [... and] secrets of their rituals, ceremonies, and iniquitous laws'
(Mannheim 1991: 66–71; Sempat Assadourian 2002: 134). Khipus were ordered
confiscated. Yet up to this date and long afterwards, some clerics felt 'Indians'
would learn the doctrine better if allowed to use the old medium. Some even
sought to promote it for Christian ends (Duviols 1977: 305.) In her biography
of the daring half-indigenous Jesuit Blas Valera, Hyland (2003) suggests that
Valera or his peers in a Church brotherhood with Inka sympathies developed a
syllabographic reworking of the cords before 1580.

   Indeed, conciliar doctrine to the contrary notwithstanding, quite a few
'Indian' Christians did go on using khipus for Catholic purposes. Towards 1590
the Jesuit Father José de Acosta observed that women used 'threads' to record
their sins for confession, and elders to itemize points of catechism. He explicitly contrasted alphabetic characters, which he understood as referring to
sub-meaningful sound segments, with khipu codes, which referred to a class
which he called 'significations of things' (*significaciones de cosas*) (Harrison 2002:
267; Acosta 1954 [1590]: 190, 275, 280, 287; see also Sempat Assadourian 2002:
126–37). In the early seventeenth century, according to the Mercedarian Martín
de Murúa, lay specialist confessors tallied Indian congregants' sins on confes-
sional khipus. One even worked up 'the entire Roman calendar' on cords, at his
own initiative (Sempat Assadourian 2002: 138–9). A 1602 Jesuit letter from near
Cuzco says that a blind man brought in 'an eighteen-foot khipu that had certain
objects (stones, bones, feathers) enmeshed in it that represented various sins
[...] so intricate [...] that he needed four days to render up his tally, crying all the
while' (Harrison 2002: 281). Juan Pérez Bocanegra's 1622 confessors' manual,
prepared for those serving around the old Inka capital, goes into detail about
how 'Indians, and specifically the female Indians, teach the others to confess
by means of these knots and signs, which they have in many colors' (Harrison
2002: 271). Pérez Bocanegra warned that khipu users could easily deceive cler-

ics. He, like other colonial Spaniards, seemed oddly resigned to not understanding them, and he too reached the conclusion that it would be better to burn them.

Perhaps just because the Andean medium gave lay people a margin of autonomy, Church coercion seems to have unintentionally encouraged unofficial khipu use. In 1609, on the eve of Peru's massive 'extirpation of idolatries' campaigns (Mills 1997), a Jesuit *carta annua* reported that amid the uproar of attack on the gods and ancestors, converts eager to get on the right side of enforced Christianity engaged in a furore of khipu activity. 'Everywhere people were making quipos to confess, to learn what they didn't know about the doctrine in order to confess, to fast, and discipline themselves, and [...] generally attend, each one, to the salvation of his soul' (Polia Meconi 1999: 273). Church observers wrote of khipu use as general lay activity and not as the work of cord specialists. Seemingly, a demotic cord art already existed.

The hybrid khipu-alphabetic objects known as 'khipu boards' seem to have been invented on the ecclesiastical side. Two drawings which may show khipus-tablas in the catechesis of women comes from the remote north coast around 1789 (Martínez Compañón 1985 [c. 1779–1789]: 53–4). In 1852 the scientific traveller Mariano Rivero observed that 'in some parishes of Indians, the khipu were attached to a panel with a register of the inhabitants on which were noted their absences on the days when Christian doctrine is taught' (Sempat Assadourian 2002: 136). As late as 1968 another specimen of nineteenth-century origin was discovered, in disuse, at the church of Mangas in central Peru (Robles Mendoza 1982: 9).

The most recent credible data on church khipus were captured in 1963 in the church of Tuanta, an Aymara-speaking village of Chipaya Bolivians (Gisbert and Mesa 1966). It is in church context that one most often hears of women as khipu users. We do not yet know whether this has to do with a prehispanic female role in the recording of sacred acts, or with missionary practices.

Khipus in community politics and self-government

This section concerns khipus that were never shown to Spanish authorities but used in the internal business of villages. I have suggested that the viceroyalty's waning interest in khipus promoted their refunctionalization, from public, inter-ethnic, and even lingua franca usage, toward usage as the in-group vernaculars of ethnically bounded regional or local populations. The specifically intra-ethnic address of khipus by 1750 comes to the fore in the field diary of Sebastián Franco de Melo, a bilingual Spanish mine operator who repressed the rebellion led by Francisco Ximénez Ynga of Huarochirí Province (MM/BA 1761; see Salomon and Spalding 2002). In such rebellions, letters and interception often provided the intelligence keys to tactical success. Franco de Melo invented a disinformation trick to disable rebel villages by setting them against each other: he disseminated twenty-two fake letters that would cause each rebel village to think its allied villages had switched sides. He had a herdswoman of his acquaintance, María Micaela Chinchano, make one khipu for each letter, and tie the letter up in it. Melo wrote that the khipu 'is the way they communicate' ('es el modo con que ellos se entienden'), using a distancing third-person pronoun that implies he himself, though bilingual and largely bicultural, did not so communicate. A khipu-like device was also said to have conveyed conspiratorial messages in a rebellion far beyond the old Inka heartland, in Araucanian Chile, in 1792 (Stevenson 1825, vol. 1: 50–1).

In the early nineteenth century, villages gained a margin of autonomy as creoles fought off the Spanish empire while creating only a spotty republican administration to replace it (Thomson 2002: 269–80). The new states depended on a *modus vivendi* with self-governing peasantries (Platt 1982). This gave communities in some provinces a chance to prolong the use of khipu in self-administration. In other provinces, as the nineteenth century advanced, latifundia engulfed communities whole. In the latter case, the new estate-bound context of the old art gave rise to the kind of herders' khipus already reviewed.

Towards 1923 the pioneer archaeologists Tello and Miranda (1923: 534) saw villagers of Casta, Huarochirí, use 'khipu boards' to record participation in communal canal-cleaning and the rites for non-Christian water-owning deities. Two other communities conserved the khipu art as a tool of internal administration into the twentieth century. One, Rapaz, in Oyón Province (Ruíz Estrada 1982; Salomon, Brezine, de las Casas, and Falcón 2006), possesses a large mass of khipu (see Fig. 12.3) in its own storage house. Arnold and Yapita (2000: 339–76) and Pimentel (2005) claim cord use in modern Aymara village organization but present no specimens.

The other documented patrimonial case is Tupicocha, in Huarochirí, Peru. Tupicocha owns ten khipus (Salomon 2002, 2004). In the period 1994–2003, nobody claimed competence to read or make khipus. These khipus are of medium size, and in overall design resemble canonical Inka type. They show little if any of the 'reduction' or 'defectiveness' characteristic of moribund scripts.

Like many Andean villages Tupicocha is a confederation of corporate kin groups (*ayllu*). In such a system the core social contract is equitable contribution. When the khipus were in full function each *ayllu* owned a pair of presentation khipus, which it used to plan its member-households' duties to each other, and the *ayllu*'s collective duties to the federation. Knots added or removed in ritual intervals that punctuate collective tasks recorded compliance. The khipus were displayed at the annual village plenary meeting (*Huayrona*) as proof of good standing. Today, the ceremony of draping a khipu upon the chest of each incoming *ayllu* president (*camachico*) is still the climactic moment (see Fig. 12.4).

The impact of Spanish writing could not be the reason Tupicocha abandoned khipus, because late use and abandonment happened when the village had been

Figure 12.3 The patrimonial khipus of Rapaz, accompanied by local officials (*balternos*) in charge of community fields and pastures.

Figure 12.4 In Tupicocha, new presidents of *ayllus* (corporate descent groups) are installed by draping patrimonial khipus upon them.

involved with writing for over 300 years. Tupicochan khipus yield ambiguous radiocarbon dates, with nineteenth-century dates being most prevalent as dates of manufacture. Internal *ayllu* books give clues about when cords ceased to be official media. One (APM/SAT 01 1889: f.13r) in 1898 mentions the *quipocamayos* as artefacts 'de anterior' ('of former [times]'). This may reflect discontinuities caused by the Chilean–Peruvian War of the Pacific (1879–1883), which brought combat to Tupicocha. War led to Peruvian defeat and a wide questioning of pre-war institutions. If khipu had still been made in the nineteenth century but became obsolescent by 1898, people rising to community office after the end of the War of the Pacific are likely to be the ones who relinquished khipu practice. In the 1920s, the time when people born around 1880 were reaching peak power, khipu sets were broken up by *ayllu* fission, suggesting their functionality was no longer important. In the 1920s, too, the *ayllus* responded to the national state's 'indigenist' campaign to include traditional governments within government structures by writing themselves modernist constitutions. These were understood as replacements for 'customs' such as khipu. Official recognition of the community in 1935 probably set the seal on an already advanced transition from cords to books. Yet from 1958 to 1974, one *ayllu's* secretaries still described, as opposed to merely inventorying, its khipu. This registry shows some change over time, suggesting some residue of 'rememberer' competence and perhaps a final round of knotting activity.

Pseudo-Khipus

The decline of khipu yielded and still yields a profusion of khipu-derived objects which, unlike patrimonial khipus, do show 'reduction', 'defectiveness', and arbitrary innovations. In these cases, unlike the Egyptian, Mayan, and Mesopotamian cases, the creators are hardly ever members of patrimonial khipu-inheriting groups.[4] The reason is that the esoteric prestige which khipus have acquired in cosmopolitan society since the eighteenth century scarcely registers in rural Andean society, whereas the stigma on 'Indian' things is a constant burden. In the nineteenth century a number of 'quipolas' incompetently mimicked the tradition (Loza 1999), and suspicion of similar activity falls upon the 'Naples objects'. The majority of pseudo-khipus, however, are products of public schools, where the khipu is fetishized as an emblem of pristine Inka wisdom.[5] Other examples, like the rainbow khipu displayed in Cuzco's festival of Inti Raymi, are expressions of recent indigenism. When demonstrators in Lima in 2000 publicly laundered Peruvian flags to protest the disrepute that the dictatorial President Alberto Fujimori had brought on their country, one man washed a neo-khipu bearing the flag's red-white-red colours.[6] Many pseudo-khipus reflect international appreciation of what are seen as sublime, exotic design objects.[7] Grete Heikes produces 'quipu Andean rope art'[8]; one dealer in Shangdong, China, is now supplying fanciful 'quipu folk art' wholesale. It is only a matter of time before someone produces a frankly neo-khipu legible code.

Discussion

In the case of the khipus it proved only equivocally true that 'a subordinate script is a despised script' (Houston *et al.* 2003: 434, quoting R. Grillo). The supremacy of Spanish alphabetic writing did grind away at the Andean notation in most places and times. But where the content of khipus was identified with the owners' communal or even factional interests, khipus garnered tenacious support. After central, long-distance, long-term institutions of Andean society were destroyed—that is, after the 1530s—the institutions whose data were vested in khipus became more and more local. As a result, khipus became less standardized. Yet very small usage communities sufficed to transmit the art as long as even a few remained convinced that cords were indispensable to data integrity. It is surely significant that in the Andes, unlike Mesoamerica, alphabetic paperwork in indigenous languages remained rare (Durston 2008), while the indigenous medium outlasted the institution of the bilingual 'scribe for natives'.

The areas where khipu use is well documented into republican times form sharply contrasting cases. In the Cuzco highlands and Lake Titicaca basin (and, to some degree, far-northern Cajamarca), khipus articulated relations between herding estates or churches and peasant households. Most commentators have perceived "reduction" or "defectiveness" here. These examples conveyed a range of meanings associated at best with humble household needs and at worst with the misery of enserfment. As a result the complex was ill equipped to survive the land reform era (1969–1973).

The other region of republican survival is the Sierra de Lima, a part of the central Peruvian highlands. Here khipu endured as the apparatus for collective labour and ritual at *ayllu* and community level. Some of these khipus closely resemble Inka khipus in design. The associations of these cord regalia remain lofty and positive. But after traditional polities were co-opted by the state under the 1929 Law of Communities, they were considered redundant.

How does the khipu case look in comparison to other scripts' obsolescence? First, the khipu's fate is non-congruent to that of any language. This fact may be accidental, but it seems more likely that the reason lies in khipu semiosis itself. Unlike Egyptian, Mesopotamian, and Maya writings, the khipu seems to have used an inventory of signs unconnected to speech except insofar as monolingual users will take a sign with a familiar meaning as a 'virtual logogram', or insofar as specific languages may have supplied patterns for deploying the signary (e.g. Quechua SOV word order as pattern for cords expressing transitive statements).

Second, the durability of the medium owed much to its opacity to the Spanish eye. In the Andean countryside, assembling signs on khipus may have been a 'parallel language' in the sense entertained by Benveniste (1985 [1969]). I think that like proto-Elamite tablets as explained by Nissen, Damerow, and Englund (1993), khipu specialised in displaying information as patterned by a social task other than speech. This principle seemingly escaped Spaniards, a population intensely focused on the authenticity of the word. Andean payers of tribute and workers in forced labour (*mita*) were excluded from the literacy that regulated these institutions. Maintaining an impermeable parallel record increased chances to check up on accounts that privileged ethnic lords tendered to colonial officials.

Third, late khipu use owed little to refunctionalization as 'true writing'. Of course, there is no inherent reason why cords could not signify speech sounds, nor is there any doubt that some people made them do so. The doubt is whether these people were conducting vernacular Andean community business, or experimenting with khipu phonography as a new prestige medium for colonial native elites, or faking antiquities for a European audience (Adorno 1999; Estenssoro and Bustamante 1997; Hyland 2003). There is no evidence of vernacular retooling towards phonetic use.

Fourth, limited khipu spheres of exchange sufficed for retention when the medium carried vital, proprietary information. Narrow use puts a script in danger, but a subordinated script may nonetheless be a valuable asset. We have already mentioned the uses of privacy: Seventeenth-century labour khipus, eighteenth-century political khipus, and nineteenth- and twentieth-century herding khipus provided authenticated information on one side of an ethnic divide even when actors on both sides shared a language. In the Sierra de Lima, the narrowly taught khipu medium underwrote the integrity of intra-group governance.

So it was not the demographic or prestige factors that decided the fate of Andean media. Their death sentence was, rather, the end of a situation in which what Cummins calls incommensurability between media served user interests (1994: 192-98). By incommensurability, Cummins means a situation in which codes differ in basic semiotic principles, and therefore cannot be bridged by translation alone. From 1783 to the 1910s it was sometimes illegal, and never a state responsibility, to teach Spanish writing to plebeian *indios*. But in the wake of the disastrous War of the Pacific the state reversed this policy. Under the Leguía administration (1919–1930) indigenist pressures to retool the *ayllu* as a part of state apparatus tipped the khipus' obsolescence past the point of no return—the point at which no potential learner believed code transmission to be indispensable. Community recognition and access to schools convinced villagers that the alphabet would be the only way to defend their titles and data. Despite the presence of elders who knew elements of khipu into the second half of the twentieth century, villagers by that time counted khipu-use among stigmatizing 'Indian' habits harmful to 'modernization' interests. Yet the few villages where people conserve khipu specimens because they embody links to divinity may still offer one last chance at an exchange of knowledge between the Andes' two pristinely different graphic traditions.

Notes

1. Betanzos 1987 [1551]: 96–7. All translations are my own unless otherwise stated.

2. Their bibliography is summed up in Urton 2002: 7.

3. The entire book is available on the web pages of Denmark's Kongelige Bibliotek: http://www.kb.dk/elib/mss/poma/index-en.htm, last accessed 14 March 2007.

4. One exception, a young Tupicochan interested in making khipu simulacra, is mentioned in Salomon 2004.

5. The word khipu, or more usually quipu, is commonly folklorized as title for writings that claim association with Amerindian heritage. *Quipu* is the title of the newsletter published by the New Mexico State Records Center and Archives, and also of a Mexican social science journal. *Kipu* is the annual repertory of indigenous affairs news published by Quito's Abya Yala press and *Kipus* the bulletin of the US Embassy in Bolivia. *Khipu* is a publication of a German association for Latin American cultural exchange. The Chilean poet Cecilia Vicuña has written a book *Quipoem*. *Quipu* is also the title of a serious archaeological website at http://infodome.sdsu.edu/research/guides/quipu/, a cyber-gallery in Peru http://quipu.uni.edu.pe/gAleRiA/pinacoteca/pin6.htm, and various jejune personal pages. Links last accessed 14 March 2007.

6. http://www.americas.org/News/Features/200108_Public_Art/200109Lauer.htm, last accessed 14 March 2007.

7. http://janhaag.com/ospt.htm, last accessed 14 March 2007.

8. http://www.usd.edu/library/art/contemporary.htm, last accessed 14 March 2007.

References

AA/L (Archivo Arzobispal / Lima)
    1607   Capítulos. 1607–1609. Leg. 1 Exp. 9. Proceso remitido por el señor dean y provisor al doctor padilla vicario general de capitulos contra el doctor francisco de avila cura y beneficiado de el [sic] doctrina de san damian y sus anejos.

Abercrombie, Thomas A.
    1998   *Pathways of Memory and Power: Ethnography and History Among an Andean People.* Madison: University of Wisconsin Press.

Acosta, José de
    1954 [1590] *Historia natural y moral de las indias.* In Francisco Mateos (ed.), *Obras del P. José de Acosta*. Madrid: Ediciones Atlas. Biblioteca de Autores Españoles, vol. 73.

Acosta Rodríguez, Antonio
    1979   'El pleito de los indios de San Damián, Huarochiri, contra Francisco de Avila, 1607.' *Historiografía y Bibliografía Americanistas* 23: 3–33.
    1987   'Francisco de Avila Cusco 1573(?)—Lima 1647.' In Gerald Taylor (ed. and trans.), *Ritos y tradiciones de Huarochirí del siglo XVII*. Historia Andina, No. 12. Lima: Instituto de Estudios Peruanos [and] Instituto Francés de Estudios Andinos, 551–616.

Adorno, Rolena
    1999   'Criterios de comprobación: un misterioso manuscrito de Nápoles y las crónicas de la conquista del Perú.' In I. Arellano and J. A. Rodríguez Garrido (eds.), *Edición y anotación de textos coloniales hispanoamericanos*. Pamplona and Madrid: Universidad de Navarra-Iberoamericana and Vervuert, 15–44. Biblioteca Áurea Hispánica 6.

AGN/BA (Archivo General de la Nación / Buenos Aires).
   1588   Padrones de La Paz. 13-17-5-1. Revisita de Sisicaya.

Animato, Carlo, Paolo A. Rossi, and Clara Miccinelli
   1989   *Quipu: il nodo parlante dei misteriosi Incas.* Genoa: Edizioni Culturali Internazionali Genova.

APM/SAT 01
   1889   Archivo de la Parcialidad Mújica / San Andrés de Tupicocha. [Libro primero de la Parcialidad de Mújica,1875(?)–1918.]

Arnold, Denise Y., and Juan de Dios Yapita
   2000   *El rincón de las cabezas: Luchas textuales, educación y tierras en los Andes.* La Paz: Facultad de Humanidades y Ciencias de la Educación, Universidad Mayor de San Andrés, and Instituto de Lengua y Cultura Aymara.

Ascher, Marcia, and Robert Ascher
1997 [1981] *Code of the Quipu: A Study of Media, Mathematics, and Culture.* New York: Dover.

Benveniste, Emile
1985 [1969] 'The Semiology of Language.' In R. E. Innis (ed.), *Semiotics. An Introductory Anthology.* Bloomington: Indiana University Press, 225–46.

Betanzos, Juan de
1987 [1551] *Suma y narración de los Incas,* ed. María del Carmen Rubio. Madrid: Ediciones Atlas.

BN/M (Biblioteca Nacional / Madrid)
1589   Manuscrito 5938 fos. 433–435. Sobre la escritura de los indios del Peru por el Doctor Murillo de la Cerda.

Boltz, William G.
   1994   *The Origin and Early Development of the Chinese Writing System.* New Haven, CT: American Oriental Society.

Boone, Elizabeth H., and Walter D. Mignolo (eds.)
   1994   *Writing Without Words: Alternative Literacies in Mesoamerica and the Andes.* Durham, NC: Duke University Press.

Cerrón-Palomino, Rodolfo
   1987   *Lingüística quechua.* Cuzco: Centro de Estudios Rurales Andinos 'Bartolomé de Las Casas'.

Cieza de León, Pedro de
1985 [1553] *Crónica del Perú. El señorío de los Incas.* Edited by Manuel Ballesteros. Madrid: Historia 16.

Cobo, Bernabé
1964 [1653] *Historia del Nuevo Mundo.* In *Obras de P. Bernabé Cobo.* F. Mateos (ed.). 2 vols. Madrid: Ediciones Atlas. Biblioteca de Autores Españoles 92, vol. 1: 3–427, vol. 2: 7–476.

Collapiña, Supno *et al.*
1974 [1542/1608] *Relación de la descendencia, gobierno, y conquista de los Incas.* Lima: Universidad Nacional Mayor de San Marcos.

Conklin, William J.
    2003   'Strings of Meaning: The Two Millennial Evolution of the Inka Khipu.' Paper presented at 22nd Northeast Conference on Andean Archaeology, Cambridge, MA, 2 November 2003.

Costales de Oviedo, Ximena
    1983   *Etnohistoria del corregimiento de Chimbo 1557-1820.* Quito: Mundo Andino.

Cummins, Thomas B. F.
    1994   'Representation in the Sixteenth Century and the Colonial Representation of the Inca.' In E.H. Boone and W.T. Mignolo (eds.), *Writing Without Words: Alternative Literacies in Mesoamerica and the Andes.* Durham, NC: Duke University Press, 188-219.

Del Río, Mercedes
    1990   'Simbolismo y poder en Tapacarí.' *Revista Andina* 8(1): 77-113.

Domenici, Davide, and V. Domenici
    2003   *I Nodi segreti degli incas.* Milan: Sperling and Kupfer.

Durston, Alan
    2008   'Native-Language Literacy in Colonial Peru: The Question of Mundane Quechua Writing Revisited'. *Hispanic American Historical Review* 88(1): 41-70.

Duviols, Pierre
    1977   *La destrucción de las religiones andinas (Durante la conquista y la colonia),* trans. Albor Maruenda. Mexico City: Universidad Nacional Autónoma de México.

Espinoza Soriano, Waldemar
    1960   *El alcalde mayor indígena en el virreinato del Perú.* Anuario de Estudios Americanos 17: 183-300.

Estenssoro F., Juan Carlos, and J. Bustamante
    1997   'Falsificación y revisión histórica: informe sobre un supuesto nuevo texto colonial andino.' *Revista de Indias* 57(210): 563-78.

Fossa, Lydia
    2000   'Two Khipu, One Narrative: Answering Urton's Questions.' *Ethnohistory* 47(2): 453-68.

Garcilaso Inca de la Vega
1966 [1609] *The Royal Commentaries of the Incas,* trans. H. Livermore. 2 vols. Austin: University of Texas Press.

Gaur, Albertine
    1984   *A History of Writing.* London: The British Library.

Gelb, Ignace J.
    1963   *A Study of Writing,* revised edition. Chicago, IL: University of Chicago Press.

Gisbert, Teresa, and José de Mesa
    1966   'Los chipayas.' *Anuario de Estudios Americanos* 23: 479-506.

Guaman Poma de Ayala, Felipe
1980 [1615] *Nueva corónica y buen gobierno del Perú.* J. V. Murra and R. Adorno (eds.), J. L. Urioste (trans.). 3 vols. Mexico City: Siglo XXI.

Harrison, Regina
   2002   'Pérez Bocanegra's *Ritual formulario*: Khipu Knots and Confession.' In J. Quilter and G. Urton (eds.), *Narrative Threads: Accounting and Recounting in Andean Khipu*. Austin: University of Texas Press, 266–90.

Holm, Olaf
   1968   'Quipu o sapan: un recurso mnemónico en el campo ecuatoriano.' *Cuadernos de historia y arqueología*. 18(34/35): 85–90.

Houston, Stephen, John Baines, and Jerrold Cooper.
   2003   'Last Writing: Script Obsolescence in Egypt, Mesopotamia, and Mesoamerica.' *Comparative Studies in Society and History* 45(3): 430–79.

Howard, Rosalind.
   2002   'Spinning a Yarn: Landscape, Memory, and Discourse Structure in Quechua Narratives.' In J. Quilter and G. Urton (eds.), *Narrative Threads: Accounting and Recounting in Andean Khipu*. Austin: University of Texas Press, 26–49.

Hyland, Sabine
   2003   *The Jesuit and the Incas: the Extraordinary Life of Padre Blas Valera, S. J.* Ann Arbor: University of Michigan Press.

Itier, César
   2001   'La propagation de la langue générale dans le sud du Pérou.' In *Le Savoir, pouvoir des élites dans l'empire espagnol d'Amérique*. Paris: Université Sorbonne Nouvelle—Paris III, Centre de recherche sur l'Amérique espagnole coloniale, 1, 63–74.

Julien, Catherine J.
   1988   'How Inka Decimal Administration Worked.' *Ethnohistory* 35(3): 257–79.
   2000   *Reading Inca History*. Iowa City: University of Iowa Press.

Laurencich Minelli, Laura
   1996   *La Scrittura dell'antico Perú*. Bologna: Cooperativa Libraria Editrice Universitaria Bologna.

Locke, Leland L.
   1923   *The Ancient Quipu, or Peruvian Knot Record*. New York: American Museum of Natural History.
   1928   'Supplementary Notes on the Quipus in the American Museum of Natural History.' *Anthropological Papers of the American Museum of Natural History* 30: 30–73.

Loza, Carmen Beatriz
   1998   'Du bon usage des *quipus* face à l'administration coloniale espagnole (1500–1600).' *Population* 1–2: 139–60.
   1999   'Quipus and quipolas at the Museum für Völkerkunde, Berlin. Genesis of a Reference Collection (1872–1999).' *Baesler Archiv* 47(1): 39–75.

Mackey, Carole, Hugo Pereyra, Carlos Radicati, Humberto Rodríguez, and Oscar Valverde (eds.)
   1990   *Quipu y yupana: Colleción de escritos*. Lima: Consejo Nacional de Ciencia y Tecnología.

Mannheim, Bruce
   1991   *The Language of the Inka since the European Invasion.* Austin: University of Texas Press.

Martínez Compañón y Bujalda, Baltasar Jaime
1985 [c. 1779–89] *Trujillo del Perú.* Vol. 2. Madrid: Instituto de Cooperación Iberoamericana.

Matienzo, Juan de
1967 [1567] *Gobierno del Perú,* ed. G. Lohmann Villena. Paris and Lima: Travaux de L'Institut Français d'Etudes Andines.

Meisch, Lynn A.
   1998   'Qumpi and Khipucamayuks: New Perspectives on Textiles in Colonial Ecuador.' Paper presented at the 38th Meeting of the Institute of Andean Studies, Berkeley, CA, 10 January 1998.

Mills, Kenneth
   1997   *Idolatry and its Enemies: Colonial Andean Religion and Extirpation, 1640-1750.* Princeton, NJ: Princeton University Press.

MM/BA (Museo Mitre / Buenos Aires)
   1761   Diario histórico del lebantamiento de la provincia de Huarochirí, y su pacificación. Escrito por Don Sebastián Fran.co [i.e., Francisco] de Melo...

Molina, Cristóbal de, 'el cuzqueño'
1959 [1573] *Ritos y fábulas de los Incas.* Buenos Aires: Editorial Futuro.

Murra, John V.
   1975   'Las etno-categorías de un *khipu* estatal.' In *Formaciones económicas y políticas en el mundo andino.* Lima: Instituto de Estudios Peruanos, 243–54.

Murúa, Martín de
1946 [1590] *Historia del origen y genealogía real de los reyes Incas del Perú.* Madrid: Biblioteca Missionalia Hispánica, Instituto Santo Toribio de Mogrovejo; Consejo Superior de Investigaciones Científicas.

Nissen, Hans J., Peter Damerow, and Robert K. Englund
   1993   *Archaic Bookkeeping: Writing and Techniques of Economic Administration in the Ancient Near East,* trans. Paul Larsen. Chicago, IL: University of Chicago Press.

Núñez del Prado, Oscar
1990 [1950] 'El kipu moderno.' In C. Mackey *et al.* (eds.), *Quipu y yupana: Colleción de escritos.* Lima: Consejo Nacional de Ciencia y Tecnología, 165–82.

Ortiz de Zúñiga, Iñigo
   1967, 1972 [1562] *Visita de la provincia de León de Huánuco (1562).* Vol. 1: *Visita de las cuatro waranqa de los chupachu.* Vol. 2: *Visita de los yacha y los mitmaqkuna.* Huánuco, Peru: Universidad Nacional Hermilio Valdizan.

Parker, Gary J.
   1963   'La clasificación genética de los dialectos quechuas.' *Revista del Museo Nacional* (Lima) 32: 241–52.

Pärssinen, Martti, with Jukka Kiviharju
   2004   *Textos andinos. Corpus de textos khipu incaicos y coloniales.* Vol. 1. Madrid: Insti-

tituto Iberoamericano de Finlandia y Departamento de Filología Española I, Facultad de Filología, Universidad Complutense de Madrid.

Pease, Franklin
  1990   'Utilización de quipus en los primeros tiempos coloniales.' In C. Mackey *et al.* (eds.), *Quipu y yupana: Colección de escritos.* Lima: Consejo Nacional de Ciencia y Tecnología, 67–72.

Pimentel, H., D. Nelson
  2005   *Amarrando colores: La producción del sentido en khipus aymaras.* Oruro, Bolivia: Latinas Editores.

Pizarro, Hernando
  1920 [1533] 'A los señores oydores de la audiencia real de su Magestad.' In H. H. Urteaga (ed.), *Informaciones sobre el antiguo Perú.* Colección de Libros y Documentos Referentes a la Historia del Perú, vol. 3 (2nd series). Lima: Imprenta Sanmartí, 16–180.

Platt, Tristan
  1982   *Estado boliviano y ayllu andino: Tierra y tributo en el norte de Potosí.* Lima: Instituto de Estudios Peruanos.
  2002   '"Without Deceit or Lies": Variable *Chinu* Readings During a Sixteenth-Century Tribute-Restitution Trial.' In J. Quilter and G. Urton (eds.), *Narrative Threads: Accounting and Recounting in Andean Khipu.* Austin: University of Texas Press, 225–65.

Polia Meconi, Mario (ed.)
  1999   *La cosmovisión religiosa andina en los documentos inéditos del Archivo Romano de la Compañía de Jesús, 1581-1752.* Lima: Pontificia Universidad Católica del Perú.

Prochaska, Rita G.
  1983   'Ethnography and Enculturation of Weaving on Taquile Island, Peru.' MA thesis, University of California at Los Angeles.

Quilter, Jeffrey, and Gary Urton (eds.)
  2002   *Narrative Threads: Accounting and Recounting in Andean Khipu.* Austin: University of Texas Press.

Rama, Angel
  1996 [1984] *The Lettered City,* trans. J. C. Chasteen. Durham, NC: Duke University Press.

Robles Mendoza, Román
  1982   *Quipu y mashas en la comunidad de Mangas.* Lima: Seminario de Historia Rural Andina, Universidad Nacional Mayor de San Marcos.

Rojas, Alejo
  2004   Personal communication, 9 January 2004.

Rowe, John H.
  1985   'Probanza de los Incas nietos de conquistadores.' *Historica* (Lima) 9(2): 193–245.

Ruíz Estrada, Arturo
  1982   *Los quipus de Rapaz Huacho.* Huacho, Peru: Centro de Investigación de Ciencia y Tecnología de Huacho.

Salomon, Frank

2002 'Patrimonial Khipu in a Modern Peruvian Village: An Introduction to the "Quipocamayos" of Tupicocha, Huarochirí.' In J. Quilter and G. Urton (eds.), *Narrative Threads: Accounting and Recounting in Andean Khipu*. Austin: University of Texas Press, 293–319.

2004 *The Cord Keepers: Khipus and Cultural Life in a Peruvian Village*. Durham, NC: Duke University Press.

Salomon, Frank, Carrie Brezine, Gino de las Casas, Víctor Falcón

2006 'Los khipus de Rapaz en casa: Un complejo administrativo-ceremonial centroperuano.' *Revista Andina* 43: 59–92.

Salomon, Frank, and Karen Spalding.

2002 'Cartas atadas con khipus: Sebastián Franco de Melo, María Micaela Chinchano, y la represión de la rebelión huarochirana de 1750.' In J. Flores Espinoza and R. Varón Gabai (eds.), *El hombre y los Andes: Homenaje a Franklin Pease G. Y.* Lima: Fondo Editorial de la Pontificia Universidad Católica del Perú, 857–70.

Sampson, Geoffrey

1985 *Writing Systems: A Linguistic Introduction*. Stanford, CA: Stanford University Press.

Sansevero di Sangro, Raimondo

1750 *Lettera apologetica dell'Esercitato Accademico della Crusca contenente la difesa del libro intitolato Lettere d'una Peruana per rispetto alla supposizione de 'Quipu' scritta alla duchessa d'S** e dalla medessima fata pubblicare*. Naples: n.p.

Santo Tomás, Domingo de

1951 [1560] *Lexicon o vocabulario de la lengua general del Peru*, ed. R. Porras Barrenechea. Lima: Instituto de Historia [de la] Universidad Nacional Mayor de San Marcos.

1995 [1560] *Grammatica o arte de la lengua general de los indios de los reynos del Perú*, ed. R. Cerrón-Palomino. Cuzco: Centro de Estudios Regionales Andinos 'Bartolomé de Las Casas.'

Sarmiento de Gamboa, Pedro

1942 [1572] *Historia de los Incas*. Buenos Aires: Emecé.

Sempat Assadourian, Carlos

2002 'String Registries: Native Accounting and Memory According to the Colonial Sources.' In J. Quilter and G. Urton (eds.), *Narrative Threads: Accounting and Recounting in Andean Khipu*. Austin: University of Texas Press, 119–50.

Soto Flores, Froilán

1990 [1950–1] 'Los kipus modernos de la localidad de Laramarca.' In C. Mackey *et al.* (eds.), *Quipu y yupana: Colección de escritos*. Lima: Consejo Nacional de Ciencia y Tecnología, 183–90.

Splitstoser, Jeffrey C., Dwight T. Wallace, and Mercedes Delgado Agurto

2003 'Bound to be Important: Wrapped Sticks and Cords in a Late Paracas Burial at Cerrillos, Ica Valley, Peru.' Paper presented at 22nd Northeast Conference on Andean Archaeology, Cambridge, MA, 2 November 2 2003.

Stevenson, William Bennett

1825 *A Historical and Descriptive Narrative of Twenty Years' Residence in South America*. 3 vols. London: Hurst, Robinson and Co.

Taylor, Gerald
    2001   *Introducción a la lengua general (quechua)*. Lima: Instituto Francés de Estudios Andinos.

Tello, Julio C., and Próspero Miranda
    1923   'Wallallo. Ceremonias gentílicas realizadas en la región cisandina del Perú central.' *Inca. Revista Trimestral de Estudios Antropológicos* 1(2): 475–549.

Thomson, Sinclair
    2002   *We Alone Will Rule: Native Andean Politics in the Age of Insurgency*. Madison: University of Wisconsin Press.

Toledo, Francisco de
1986–9 [1572] *Disposiciones gubernativas para el virreinato del Perú*, ed. Guillermo Lohmann Villena. Seville: Escuela de Estudios Hispanoamericanos, Monte de Piedad y Caja de Ahorros de Sevilla.

Torero, Alfredo
    1974   *El quechua y la historia social andina*. Lima: Universidad Ricardo Palma.

Uhle, Max
1990 [1897] 'Un kipu moderno procedente de Cutusuma, Bolivia.' In C. Mackey *et al.* (eds.), *Quipu y yupana: Colección de escritos*. Lima: Consejo Nacional de Ciencia y Tecnología, 127–34.

Urton, Gary
    2001   'Calendrical and Demographic Tomb Text from Northern Peru.' *Latin American Antiquity* 12(2): 127–47.
    2002   'An Overview of Spanish Colonial Commentary on Andea Knotted-String Records'. In J. Quilter and G. Urton (eds), *Narrative Threads: Accounting and Recounting in Andean Khipu*. Austin: University of Texas Press, 3–25.
    2003   *Signs of the Inka Khipu: Binary Coding in the Andean Knotted-String Records*. Austin: University of Texas Press.

Vicuña, Cecilia.
    1997   *Quipoem / the Precarious: the Art and Poetry of Cecilia Vicuña*. M. C. de Zegher (ed.), Esther Allen (trans.). Hanover, NH: University Press of New England.

Zárate, Agustín de
    1995 [1555]   *Historia del descubrimiento y conquista del Perú*, ed. F. Pease and T. Hampe. Lima: Pontifica Universidad Católica del Perú.

13

Disappearance of Writing Systems: The Manchu Case

Giovanni Stary

Introduction

The Manchu language has been called the 'guoyu' in Chinese and 'gurun-i bithe' in Manchu, that is, the 'state' or 'dynasty language'—a definition which seems unequivocally to connect the destiny of the dynasty to that of its language and script. This definition, however, is true only in part and shows three substantial exceptions: they are the result of the unique development which the Manchu people and its culture—and the script is part of it—have undergone in the course of their extraordinary history. The Manchus arose more as a political than an ethnic unit within a couple of decades at the beginning of the seventeenth century, under the tribal leader Nurhaci (1559–1626), who was able to unify the dozens of Jurchen tribes living over a large territory east of present day's Shenyang up to the banks of the Amur river (Roth Li 2002). Already in 1644, the Manchus occupied the Chinese throne in Peking, completing within less than half a century their evolution from a 'hunting and fishing society' into the ruling class of the Chinese empire (Elliott 2001). Manchu, in both its spoken and written form, became the tool for the administration of that vast empire, side by side with Chinese, and in military and court affairs it became the prevalent and sometimes exclusively used language (Crossley and Rawski 1993). A lot of ink has been spilled on the decay of the Manchu language starting from the nineteenth century, which is generally explained with the sinicization of the Manchu people and the consequent loss of its autochthonous Tungusic culture (Stary 1994; Kane 1997). Debate on this issue is still open and far from being resolved: in fact, newly accessible archive documents show a longer 'survival' of the language (or a mixed Manchu–Chinese pidgin language) than had previously been supposed. The script, however, seems to have permanently disappeared with the fall of the dynasty—at least, as we will see, in China proper.

A Few Words on the History of the Manchu Script

According to the official historiography of the Qing dynasty, which in China as elsewhere had the duty to glorify the achievements of its rulers, the Manchu script was 'created' by an order of Nurhaci in 1599, who ordered two of his learned men (*baksi* Erdeni and Gagai) to adapt the Mongolian script to the Manchu language. In fact, the first 'Manchu' script is none other than Mongolian which, however, was quite insufficient to express clearly the pecularities of the Manchu language. Again, according to official historiography, this script was reformed in 1632 by Dahai who introduced diacritical marks (the point and circle—*tongki* and *fuka*), improved some letters and created new graphemes for Chinese sounds in order to reproduce, in the most precise way possible, the growing number of Chinese loan words (for a more detailed history of this script reform see Pang 2003; Weiers 1999). This new script became the 'National Manchu Script' and remained untouched until the present day—with a very few exceptions introduced in recent times for the so-called Sibe minority (Stary 1997). Like Mongolian, the Manchu script is written in vertical lines from left to right.

The fall of the Qing dynasty determined the official end of the Manchu language as a 'state and dynastic' language. It survives in some remote villages in Manchuria, in some cases through to present times—but in its spoken form only: the script itself was no longer taught and used among the Manchu people (for details see Jin Qicong 1981; 1984).

But if the fall of the dynasty saw the end (with some exceptions) of the language, the script itself survived, and we can establish three 'survival complexes' (see map Fig. 13.1):

1. Survival as a *scriptura* (and sometimes as a *lingua*) *franca* among some minority peoples of the border areas of Manchuria.

2. Survival (or better: revival) for political reasons in order to underline and highlight the autonomy of the 'Manchu autonomous counties' recently created in Manchuria.

3. Survival among the Sibe people living in the 'Chabchal Sibe autonomous county', located in the Ili valley in Xinjiang, at the border with Kazakhstan.

The first 'complex': the survival among local 'minority' peoples living in China's north-eastern border areas, such as the Solons, Dagurs, and Oroqen

Already during the Qing dynasty these peoples—who never had their own

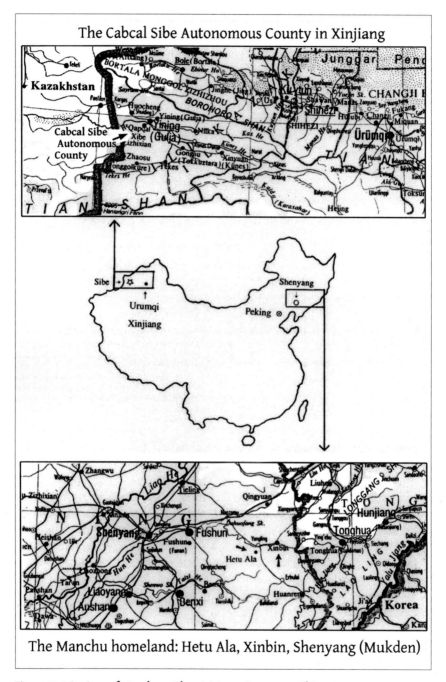

Figure 13.1 Regions of Manchu settlement in contemporary China.

script—used the Manchu language for their written relations, even after the fall of the dynasty. The best known evidence of the survival of Manchu until the 1930s is given by four newspapers published in the area around Hailar, northern Manchuria (for examples see Stary 1989). Another famous example is given by a 'passport' issued in Manchu by a local *solon* chief (at Aigun on the Amur river) to the German explorer Walther Stötzner in 1928. This document is considered the last witness of the once-ubiquitous Manchu language and script (facsimile reproduction and analysis in Hauer 1929).

But if the language itself gradually disappeared, the script continued to be used among these 'national minorities' (as they are called in China) for a longer period, at least until the 1950s. It was then substituted for a brief period, more on an experimental level than in real life, with the Cyrillic alphabet, which was soon substituted with the Latin alphabet—evidently under the influence of the Chinese *pinyin* transcription system.

In this area the Manchu alphabet had already been adopted and adapted in the nineteenth century for the Dagur and other languages (examples in Ivanovskij 1894; see also Humphrey 1996). The most recent witness is a Chinese–Dagur dictionary (by Nashundalai) published in Hohhot, Inner Mongolia, in 2001, bearing the trilingual title *Nikan Dahûr buleku bithe* (curiously enough in both Manchu language and script), *Niakan Daor bulku biteg* (in Dagur but with Latin letters), and *Han-Da cidian* (in simplified Chinese). Opening a page of this dictionary, we find the Dagur term written with Manchu letters, followed by its form in Latin letters according to its actual pronunciation (e.g. Nashundalai 2001: 204; Fig. 13.2):

1. 13th line from left: Chinese *mao jinxing* 'Venus'—[Manchu writing] *nidu es gali garabai* > [Latin] *nidees gali garbei*.

2. 11th line from left: Chinese *maoshi* 'to be audacious'—[Manchu writing] *peekeseleebei* > [Latin] *peekeesleebei*, where 'e' is doubled in Manchu *script*, that is, an impossible vowel repetition in Manchu *language*.

Another interesting example is found on p. 222, in the word for 'clay'—Chinese *niantu*, which in Manchu script is given as *taogalji*, but in Latin with *taogalj*: specialists of the Dagur language have to tell us if the 'Manchu' form with '-i' is an old form, or if it was attached to it because in Manchu no word could have a final '-j'.

As already mentioned, the Manchu letters are no longer in use today but can be found sometimes in special works on linguistics. So the chapter on the use of Manchu alphabet among the minority peoples of Manchuria should be considered closed.

Second 'complex': revival for political reasons

~olicy established in China in the 1980s consisted also in a new orien-
ınic minorities, for whom the concept of 'self-administration'

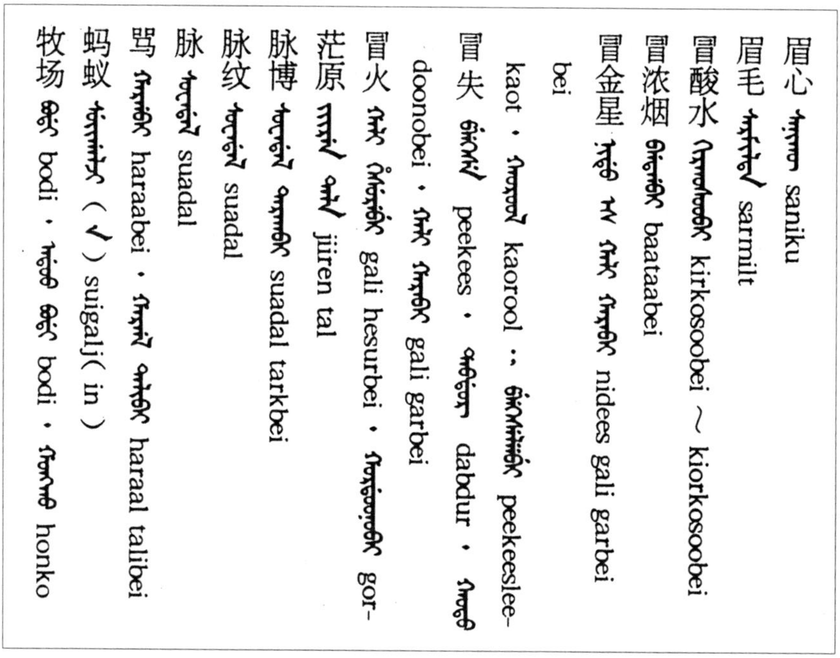

眉心 ᠰᠠᠨᡳᡴᡠ saniku
眉毛 ᠰᠠᡵᠮᡳᠯᡨ sarmilt
冒酸水 ᡴᡳᡵᡴᠣᠰᠣᠣᠪᡝᡳ kirkosoobei ~ kiorkosoobei
冒浓烟 ᠪᠠᠠᡨᠠᠠᠪᡝᡳ baataabei
冒金星 ᠨᡳᡩᡝᡝᠰ ᡤᠠᠯᡳ ᡤᠠᡵᠪᡝᡳ nidees gali garbei

bei

kaot · ᡴᠠᠣᡵᠣᠣᠯ kaorool ·· ᡦᡝᡝᡴᡝᡝᠰᠯᡝᡝ peekeeslee-
冒失 ᡦᡝᡝᡴᡝᡝᠰ peekees · ᡩᠠᠪᡩᡠᡵ dabdur ·

doonobei · ᡤᠠᠯᡳ ᡤᠠᡵᠪᡝᡳ gali garbei
冒火 ᡤᠠᠯᡳ ᡥᡝᠰᡠᡵᠪᡝᡳ gali hesurbei · ᡤᠣᡵ gor-
茫原 ᠵᡠᡳᡵᡝᠨ ᡨᠠᠯ juiren tal
脉博 ᠰᡠᠠᡩᠠᠯ ᡨᠠᡵᡴᠪᡝᡳ suadal tarkbei
脉纹 ᠰᡠᠠᡩᠠᠯ suadal
脉 ᠰᡠᠠᡩᠠᠯ suadal
骂 ᡥᠠᡵᠠᠠᠪᡝᡳ haraabei · ᡥᠠᡵᠠᠠᠯ ᡨᠠᠯᡳᠪᡝᡳ haraal talibei
蚂蚁 (ᠰᡠᡳ) suigalji(in)
牧场 ᠪᠣᡩᡳ bodi · ᠪᠣᡩᡳ bodi · ᡥᠣᠨᡴᠣ honko

Figure 13.2 Sample page from Nashundalai 2001, a Daur–Chinese dictionary that uses the Manchu script.

started to be introduced. In the case of the Manchus it brought a new ethnic consciousness which was also encouraged by the fact that the decennial anti-Manchu sentiments had disappeared seventy years after the fall of the 'barbarian' Qing dynasty. The Manchu rule over China started being judged in a more objective and well-balanced way, and also its positive sides (for instance in the field of cultural achievements under the Kangxi and Qianlong emperors) were no longer denied (for a discussion of this issue see Rhoads 2000). As a consequence, a certain number of 'self-administrated' or 'autonomous' counties (*zizhixian*) were created in territories with a Manchu majority, whose ethnic particularities were (and are) given by their historical memory and their customs still being preserved or brought to revival. The Manchu language, however, disappeared in all these counties a long time ago. The first Manchu autonomous county[1] was founded in 1985 in Xinbin, the territory from where the Manchu dynasty arose at the beginning of the seventeenth century. To express and emphasize this self-administration, tablets with bilingual Manchu-Chinese inscriptions were fixed to all public offices; the inscriptions, however, *not* understood by the population, are sometimes indecipherable, being made by handicraftsmen with no knowledge of the script, often with mistakes, and mainly consist in transliterations of the Chinese terms (examples in Stary 1991).

The same phenomenon is seen in the inscriptions found in newly restored (or even reconstructed) historical places—for example in the first capital of the Manchu khanate, Hetu Ala: the script looks artificial and badly proportioned, an imitation which recalls but does not correspond to the 'real' Manchu script (Fig. 13.3). The Manchu script as sign of self-administration is also found on local products and even on postmarks and cars, and as titles on scientific publications, to underline the 'Manchuness' of its content (examples in Stary *et al.* 1995: 75, 83–4).

All these facts, however, are nothing more than curiosities since they do not express a revival of the script, which remains incomprehensible for the local population.

Third 'complex': survival of the script among the Sibe settlements in the Chabchal autonomous county of the Sibe

A unique phenomenon of the Manchu script's survival is found in the Sibe Chabchal autonomous county situated in the Ili valley at the border with Kazakhstan, in Xinjiang. Its history goes back to the conquest of Turkestan by the Qing dynasty in the second half of the eighteenth century. In order to protect and fortify the newly conquered territory, the Manchu government ordered a mass transfer of Sibe soldiers, together with Mongols, Solons, and Dagurs, from

Figure 13.3 Palace inscription in classical style (right, Shenyang Palace Museum, eighteenth century) and modern imitation with grammatical mistake 'amgambi' (left, Hetu Ala, Xinbin county, Liaoning Povince).

Figure 13.4 Trilingual inscription 'Sin hûwa bithei puseli / Xinhua shudian / Xinhua Bookstore' from Cabcal City, Cabcal Sibe autonomous county, Xinjiang Province.

native Manchuria, and assigned them to the southern bank of the Ili river (Stary 1985). In such an isolated place, where in 1954 the Chabchal autonomous county of the Sibe was created, that tribe was able to preserve its language and script to the present day. A newspaper (*Cabcal serkin*, 'Chabchal Messenger') is published three times a week using a computer-created Manchu script, together with an annual or biannual journal entitled *Sibe šuwen* ('Sibe Culture'). Even if seriously endangered by the growing influence of Chinese (Stary 2003a), the Sibe language and its Manchu script are still in everyday use, as can be seen from inscriptions on public offices, shops (Fig. 13.4), street names, and public notices in the market (examples in Stary *et al.* 1995: 98, 102). The language—in contrast to that used in inscriptions in Manchuria—is still alive, and is not limited to simple transcriptions of Chinese terms. It is, however, difficult to say how long this situation will continue, since progress requires and necessarily favours the spread of Chinese; bearing in mind the experience in Manchuria, one cannot exclude that in the future the Manchu script will continue to be used for political reasons only, to underline the administrative autonomy and cultural particularities of the county. On the other hand, cultural and intellectual circles are making notable efforts to counteract this trend: in opposition to the rapidly diminishing number of books for the general reader (see Jin Ning 1989; Stary 1992; Stary 2003b: 874–82, 949; Harris 2004), new editions of schoolbooks are continuously republished on a local level, and the Manchu script itself is becoming (as happened in Qianlong times) an object of calligraphy and art (Fig. 13.5).

Retrospect and Prospect: In Lieu of a Conclusion

The creation of the Manchu script was an essential step in the building of the Manchu Empire at the beginning of the seventeenth century: no state administration, no military enterprise, no highly developed state form was possible without a clear

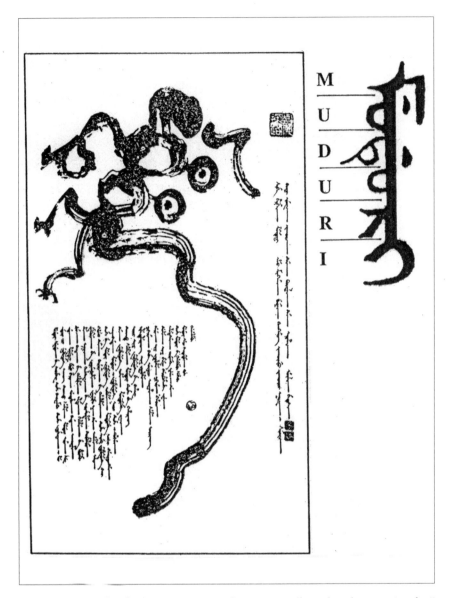

Figure 13.5 Example of contemporary Manchu artistic calligraphy: the term 'muduri' (dragon) is written in such a way to depict graphically the mythological animal. The letter 'm' is transformed in the animal's right foreleg, the letter 'd' in the animal's left foreleg. The two 'u' letters form the body, whereas the two diacritical marks of the 'u' letters represent the dragon's eyes. The 'r' letter represents the two hind legs, whereas the 'i' letter is utilized to represent the dragon's tail. A work of the Sibe artist Getuken (1989:4).

writing system, as it is shown from the ancient empires of the Middle-East (Mesopotamia, Egypt), of Central-East Asia (Runic Turkic, Phags-pa in Mongolia), and East Asia (China, Japan, Korea), and so on. What distinguished the history of the Manchu from other writing systems is the fact that Manchu, after the conquest of China, had to develop in less than half a century from a local, ethnic-based system to a 'universal' writing-system, co-existing on an administrative level with Chinese script, established for over 3000 years. Furthermore, it also served as a *scriptura (et lingua) franca* for reciprocal understanding between the many ethnic minorities of the Chinese Empire. It was therefore rightly called the 'Latin' of the Qing dynasty. It also gave the possibility to several previously illiterate peoples of North-East China to learn how to express themselves in a written form (for instance, Dagurs and Solons).

With these characteristics, the Manchu script survived the fall of the Manchu Qing dynasty in 1911 and continued to be used in Manchuria until the 1930s—that is, until Chinese language and script became dominant due to political and ethnic reasons (immigration policy, spontaneous or forced expansion of the Han-Chinese element, economic interactions).

The second stage in the history of Manchu writing is its artificial revival for political-cultural reasons, in connection with the new Chinese policy toward the so-called 'national minorities', which started around the 1980s. A series of autonomous Manchu counties were created in order to develop the economy and cultural inheritance of certain areas of Manchuria: this autonomy found its visible expression in bilingual inscriptions (Chinese–Manchu) in all public institutions. These inscriptions, however, never lost their pure symbolic character, since the local Manchu population was already entirely sinicized and unable to speak its own native language, or read and write its own original script. Thus the revival of Manchu writing became a political tool with the purpose of underlining political self-administration. As a positive consequence of this artificial revival one may note a growing interest among the local population for their own history and culture, a restoration and rediscovery of indigenous folklore such as dancing or shamanic performances and, in some rare cases, a tentative, experimental introduction of Manchu language classes.

The third stage in the history of Manchu writing is its constant and uninterrupted use by the Sibe people until today. The Sibe are a small Manchu group which in the second half of the eighteenth century transferred from native Manchuria to the western borders of the newly conquered territories known as Xinjiang (Sinkiang). They settled down on the southern branch of the Ili river and here their duty was to protect the new frontier: they kept their language and (Manchu) script as a result of their isolated position. In 1956, their territory was transformed into the Sibe Cabcal autonomous county, facing the border with Kazakhstan. Language and script are still taught in local schools and through the media: a local newspaper, a radio, and a television channel. Moreover, a rich publishing activity in Sibe contributes to keep the language alive. In recent times, however, the constantly growing Chinese economic influence and other contingent reasons have determined a contraction in the use of the Manchu script and Sibe language in favour of Chinese: without its knowledge—according to local people—'there is no future outside the boundaries of the autonomous county'. At present, it has been calculated that around 20,000 people, or perhaps even fewer, still use Sibe-Manchu, which is spoken mainly within the family.

Note

1. After Xinbin, eleven Manchu autonomous counties have been founded: Beizhen, Benxi, Fengcheng, Fengning, Huanren, Kuancheng, Kuandian, Qinglong, Qingyuan, Xiu-yan, and Yitong; a Manchu–Mongol autonomous county has been founded in Weichang. In addition, there exist more than 100 Manchu autonomous 'townships' (*xiang*).

References

Crossley, Kyle P., and Evelyn S. Rawski
    1993   'A Profile of the Manchu Language in Ch'ing History'. *Harvard Journal of Asiatic Studies* 53: 63–102.

Elliott, Mark C.
    2001   *The Manchu Way*. Stanford, CA: Stanford University Press.

Getuken
    1989   *Getuken faksingga hergen isamjan / Getuken shufa ji*. Urumqi: Xinjiang renmin chubanshe.

Harris, Rachel
    2004   *Singing the Village: Music, Memory and Ritual among the Sibe in Xinjiang*. Oxford: Oxford University Press.

Hauer, Erich
    1929   'Ein Reisepaß in Mandschusprache aus dem Jahre 1929'. *Mitteilungen des Seminars für Orientalische Sprachen / Ostasiatische Studien* 32: 153–6.

Humphrey, Caroline, with Urgunge Onon
    1996   *Shamans and Elders*. Oxford: Clarendon Press.

Ivanovskij, A. O.
    1894   *Mandjurica* vol. 1: *Obrazcy solonskogo i dachurskogo jazykov*. St Petersburg: Akademiya Nauk. Reprint: *Mandjurica* vol. 1: *Specimens of the Solon and the Dagur Languages*. Budapest: Akadémiai Kiadó 1982.

Jin Ning
    1989   *A Catalogue of Sibe-Manchu Publications 1954-1989*. Wiesbaden: Harrassowitz.

Jin Qicong
    1981   *Manzu de lishi yu shenghuo*. Harbin: Heilongjiang renmin chubanshe. German translation, Jin Qicong 1984. *Geschichte und Leben der Mandschu*. Preface by Giovanni Stary. Hamburg: C. Bell.

Kane, Daniel
    1997   'Language Death and Language Revivalism: The Case of Manchu'. *Central Asiatic Journal* 41: 231–49.

Nashundalai
    2001   *Nikan Dahûr buleku bithe / Niakan Daor bulku biteg / Han-Da cidian.* Hohhot: Nei Menggu renmin chubanshe.

Pang, Tatiana A.
    2003   'The Manchu Script Reform of 1632: New Data and New Questions'. In J. Janhunen and V. Rybatski (eds), *Writing in the Altaic World.* Helsinki: Finnish Oriental Society, 201–6.

Rhoads, Edward J. M.
    2000   *Manchus & Hans: Ethnic Relations and Political Power in Late Qing and Early Republican China 1861-1928.* Seattle: University of Washington Press.

Roth Li, Gertraude
    2002   'State Building before 1644'. In Willard J. Peterson (ed.), *The Cambridge History of China* IX, 1: *The Ch'ing Empire to 1800.* Cambridge: Cambridge University Press, 9–72.

Stary, Giovanni
    1985   *Geschichte der Sibe-Mandschuren.* Wiesbaden: Harrassowitz.
    1989   'Manchu Journals and Newspapers'. In G. Stary (ed.), *Proceedings of the XXVIII Permanent International Altaistic Conference, Venice 8-14 July 1985.* Wiesbaden: Harrassowitz, 217–32.
    1991   'Le iscrizioni mancesi di Hsin-pin'. *Aetas Manjurica* 2: 204–19.
    1992   'Alcune aggiunte sull'attività editoriale in lingua Sibe'. *Aetas Manjurica* 3: 213–21.
    1994   'Disappearance and Survival of a Dominant Nation: The Manchu Case'. In *The East and the Meaning of History.* Università di Roma 'La Sapienza', Studi Orientali 13. Rome: Bardi, 469–79.
    1997   'Die Orthographie-Reform der modernen Schriftsprache der Sibe'. *Central Asiatic Journal* 41: 76–121.
    2003a 'Sibe: An Endangered Language'. In M. Janse and S. Tol (eds), *Language Death and Language Maintenance.* Amsterdam and Philadelphia, PA: John Benjamins, 81–8.
    2003b *Manchu Studies: An International Bibliography* IV. Wiesbaden: Harrassowitz.

Stary, Giovanni, Nicola Di Cosmo, Tatiana A. Pang, and Alessandra Pozzi
    1995   *On The Tracks of Manchu Culture.* Wiesbaden: Harrassowitz.

Weiers, Michael
    1999   'Ein Blockdrucktext betreffend die orthographische Präzisierung der Buchstaben ohne Punkte und Kreise durch Dahai'. *Zentralasiatische Studien* 29: 87–96.

14

Revelatory Scripts, 'the Unlettered Genius', and the Appearance and Disappearance of Writing

John Monaghan

There is a basic assumption in many areas of the world that the gods control events and are the ultimate sources of human institutions and technologies. Their intentions are sometimes revealed to select individuals who are able to deliver their messages. Writing may be one such revelation (Dalby 1968; Gelb 1963: 231; Goody 1968) in that the creator of the system states that he or she has been inspired through dreams, visions, or visitation by divine beings. There are a number of examples of this, from almost every region in the world. In North America such writing systems appeared among the Yupik of Alaska and the Apache of Arizona. In the latter case the revelation was experienced in 1904 by Silas John Edwards. In his vision, God taught him sixty-two prayers, and also the graphic symbols with which to write them (Basso and Anderson 1975: 8–9). In Asia a Hmong man, Song Lue, had a writing system revealed to him in the late 1950s (Smalley et al. 1990). In Africa there are the celebrated examples of the Baumon of Cameroon (inspired by a dream that occurred to King Njoya of the Baumon around 1910), and the Vai syllabary of Liberia, which may date to 1823. In Surinam the Djuka script and the Paramaribo are further examples of revealed writing (Dalby 1968). Other cases will be cited. A curious fact about these writing systems is that, frequently, the human instruments of the revelation were illiterates or, in the words of William Smalley, 'the unlettered genius' (Smalley et al. 1990: 151). This chapter builds on the work of those who have linked writing and revelation and consider these scripts as a class of writing systems that develops with some frequency among peoples who are being colonized by expanding nations and empires. It suggests that scripts this sort are not uncommon, and that although they sometimes enter into conventional usage, it is more likely they disappear without leaving much of a trace.

Revelatory Scripts

Typologies of scripts tend to be of two sorts. They are historical, in the sense that they are based on script traditions, such as the East Asian line of writing systems, or they classify scripts based on their connection to language and the properties of its signs, such as being logosyllabic, syllabic, and so on. Classification, of course, is essential for making sense of things, but the result is an analytical creation that in the process of illuminating some aspects of a phenomenon—historical connections, sign relationships—can obscure other aspects. For example, historical classifications tell us little about how a script tradition is transmitted from one generation to the next, and the stress on language leaves certain script-like codes off to one side. Basso and Anderson observed that in Silas John's script, there are two kinds of signs—those that 'tell what to say' and those that 'tell what to do', in other words, the code conveys non-linguistic as well as linguistic information (Basso and Anderson 1975: 27). Some purists might say that Silas John's script is not *really* writing, and I agree there is good reason to distinguish between writing and other sorts of symbolic codes. But the point is there are other ways to consider a phenomenon such as Silas John's script without getting stuck over what is and what is not writing.

How does calling such scripts 'revelatory', as opposed to characterizing them in terms of their genetic connections to other scripts or the ways in which they reflect language (both valid exercises), improve our understanding of them? It draws our attention to the broader religious phenomena of which they are a part, and the context in which these movements develop. Specifically, revelatory scripts seem to be part of what students of comparative religion call millennial movements. The term was inspired by the Book of Revelation of John, which predicted the coming of a 1000-year reign of Jesus Christ's Kingdom on Earth, followed by a final struggle for divine salvation. Millennial movements in a broader sense may not have much to do with early Christianity, but they do espouse an end to the existing order of things and the possibility of creative change. Typically, in a millennial movement, a prophet proclaims a divinely inspired message, which may contain a new creed, the outlines of new rites, and new social practices. These, the prophet assures audiences, if followed, will allow people to transform their lives. If they do not heed the prophet's teaching, they risk disaster or a life of continuing misery. Close associates of the prophet, who often are the most active in spreading the movement, may elaborate upon the prophet's message. These followers are the ones who take over the leadership of the movement after the prophet's death. Often couched in a vocabulary of salvation, and proclaimed with the zeal of the true believers, millennial movements have been both ubiquitous (a review counted no less than 6000 cases reported in the literature [Daniels 1992]) and the root of some of the most far-reaching and durable mass movements in human history. After all, many of the great world religions began as millennial movements. Anthropological attention has been drawn to such movements because they can be found among peoples whose lives have been profoundly altered by colonial conquest and domination. Although this is not the only context in which millennial movements might develop—with 6000 cases there are bound to be exceptions to nearly every generalization—they frequently are found among groups whose lives have been profoundly altered by recent events, and most students of the phenomenon view them as one kind of response to an unsatisfactory or unjust state of affairs.

Returning to the authors of revelatory scripts, we can see that many of them were already religious leaders or connected to religious organizations before receiving their visions. Thus, Albert Edward Tritt was a former Kutchin shaman before leading a millennial movement around 1910, preaching the Christian gospel and making a central part of the cult an orthography developed by Robert McDonald, an Anglican Archdeacon (Walker 1996: 176). Uyaquq was the son of an Alaskan Yupik shaman and became a preacher and missionary before receiving his revealed script (Walker 1996: 182; Henkelman and Vitt 1985). Silas John had an association with Lutheran missionaries on the Fort Apache reservation, and after his visions declared himself a messiah and began to preach (Basso and Anderson 1975: 7, 9). The author of Yoruba holy writing, Josiah Olunowo Oshitelu, had visions as a child, and was known as someone who could identify witches. After he received the script from god he believed he had been called as a prophet, and established the Church of our Lord in 1930 (Dalby 1969: 175).

In 1968 David Dalby wrote a paper that specifically addressed the question of revealed scripts in West Africa. Despite this relatively early consideration, the literature surprisingly does not view revelation as important for understanding script origins or their nature. Dalby, for example, suggests the revelatory idiom in which the invention of these new scripts is announced serves to legitimize the new script and promote its acceptance (Dalby 1968). Another sympathetic observer of a revealed script, the missionary linguist William Smalley, seems to want to view revelation as an expression of the psychological processes of human creativity (Smalley *et al.* 1990: 176–9; see Wallace 1956). In both cases revelation is a proxy for something else: the legitimization of a new practice, or the local idiom for cognitive processes. While not incorrect, it is important to realize when considering something as complex as a religious movement interpretations such as these are only partial explanations. Taken to an extreme, the argument that prophets claim writing was revealed to them in order to get people to accept the script confuses cause and consequence and makes no attempt to understand religious phenomena in terms of themselves—that is, as creed, doctrines, and theologies. And perhaps the most distorting element of all this is that it assumes that underneath all the fluff of rituals, prayers and stated beliefs there is nothing more than a material and instrumental rationality at work.

However if we begin by viewing these scripts as serious expressions of faith, perhaps even as a kind of devotional exercise with intended spiritual effects, then certain patterns begin to emerge. This is perhaps best illustrated in the theology of Shong Lue's religious movement, where the practice of writing is key to practitioners' religious development and well-being. According to the revelation of Shong Lue he was told that the group that accepts the Hmong writing system will be blessed, while those who do not accept it will remain poor, 'the servant to other nations for the next nine generations' (Smalley *et al.* 1990: 24). In other words, learning the script and using it are key to salvation. We should not be surprised then if the uses and distribution of these scripts fail to conform to the kind of logic one expects in linguistically derived communication. Indeed, it is hard to see anything other than concern with one's spiritual well-being and sincere religious devotion behind the tremendous efforts Shong Lue's followers made to preserve the script while fleeing persecution, first into the wilds of Laos, then to refugee camps in Thailand, and then to the United States, where several of them used their earnings to develop a mechanical type for Hmong characters.

The millennial origins of such scripts can be seen in the kinds of restrictions placed on their use. The distribution of some of these scripts may be confined to a circle of adepts, who have attained the highest levels of spiritual training. It appears that Silas John's script was limited to the twelve 'assistants' he initiated in 1920 and their replacements. This was intentional since Silas John felt that, if the writing was known widely, people might not respect it or they might try to change it. It should be noted that in Native American religions there is a unity of things in time, so that what is sacred is unchanging and to speak of the eternal is also to speak of the holy. Thus for Silas John it was important that the writing be exactly, in the words of one Apache man, 'the way it was when it came to this earth from God' (Basso and Anderson 1975: 10). The script itself was used only to record the sixty-two prayers that were revealed to Silas John by God. In this sense it is similar to Na-khi script of Southern China. Of the 10,000 or so Na-khi books extant, ninety percent are duplicates. They are exclusively ritual guides, produced by and for religious specialists known as dto-mbas. Because dto-mbas never numbered more than about 100, literacy in this script was highly restricted (Jackson 1979: 62). The kind of information encoded in the script may also be highly restricted. In the Apache case, Silas John's writing was never used to record anything but the prayers sent by God. As long as this theology controlled the writing it would also not be subject to the kind of tinkering one sees in some other writing systems, where users reduce the number of signs and alter it in other ways so it may more accurately reflect phonology and syntax.

As noted, the leaders of millennial movements often articulate a doctrine of salvation, particularly those that arise where colonial policy promotes missionization by ethical religions such as Christianity. As such the prophet diagnoses a 'fallen' condition to his or her people's situation and much of the movement's activities are directed toward redemption. This extends to writing. James Mooney reproduced an account from an elderly Cherokee from the mid-eighteenth century: 'God gave the red man a book and a paper and told him to write, but he merely made marks on the paper, and as he could not read or write, the Lord gave him a bow and arrows, and gave the book to the white man' (cited in Bender 2002: 27). Although the accounts of Sequoyah's invention of writing are second hand, this widespread account suggests that the Cherokee would have seen writing as divinely inspired. Sequoyah, in the course of working on the script, was suspected of being involved with the occult, and it is even today closely associated with religious texts and curing (Bender 2002). Indeed, certain types of knowledge or enlightenment, especially concerned with curing and conjuring, are only accessible through the syllabary, and one must feel called to read and write it (Bender 2002: 97, 100–101). The Kachin of Burma hold that each tribe was given a book by the civilizing deity. However, the Kachin, who did not understand what they were given, ate the book and have been without a script as a consequence. The Hmong, where writing in the visions of Shong Lue was directly linked to salvation, also had a tradition of having lost writing, and its recovery was a consistent theme in millennial moments in general among them, not just with Shong Lue (Smalley *et al.* 1990: 87–8; Lemoine 1986). In West Africa, the human author of the Loma script, Wide, was frustrated that they had been left in ignorance by God, and when God appeared to him in a dream in 1930, demanded that God give them the benefits of writing. God feared the Loma would leave their traditions and become arrogant. After Wide promised to remain faithful, and never to teach it to a woman, God revealed the script to him (Dalby 1967: 26).

Writing as fetish

As far back as the 1930s anthropologists began to classify millennial movements based on their proclaimed goals: nativistic, a return to an idealized past state; utopian, movement into a future ideal state; and revitalistic, which aims to adjust individuals and groups to a changed state of affairs. Although couched in the language of salvation, these goals are not solely religious ideals, since they are also about building a community that has a shared past, but more importantly, a future that is their choice to make. These are some of the very same ideals that underwrite nationalist movements, and, indeed, there are examples of millennial movements that have transformed over the years into political parties. It is clear that nationalist ideals also inspire some of the human authors of revealed scripts. After Momolu Duwalu Bukele, the author of the Vai syllabary, brought the revealed writing to the attention of his king, Fa Toro, the king was delighted since it 'would raise his people upon a level with the Portuguese and Mandingos' (S. E. Keolle, cited in Dalby 1967: 8). Likewise, Dalby provides a long footnote (1968: 164 n. 24) where he discusses the general feeling among the human inventors of revealed West African scripts where the lack of writing, in comparison to Europeans and some competing groups, were the source of frustration and feelings of inferiority.

It is not hard to understand why a lack of writing would be the focus of a group's feelings of inferiority. Many have pointed out how groups might feel diminished or behind the times by their lack of a script when confronted with the use of writing by officials or when the face of colonization is that of a missionary bearing the Bible or the Koran. Accounts such as these are also replete with vaguely apocryphal stories where people have been awed by the ability to transmit a person's words over distances without being uttered. But what is missing in these observations is a sense of the degree to which people experience writing as an immediate manifestation of colonial power. For example, the Cree word 'to write' comes from a root that means 'to go into debt' because they first encountered writing through the accounts of traders such as those associated with the Hudson Bay Company (Laughlin 1988: 133). But the connection is even more vivid in cases of revealed writing. Let me begin with the dream that gave rise to the Vai syllabary which occurred in 1833 to Bukele. According to an interview conducted by the German linguist Koelle, Bukele recounted the dream in this way (cited in Dalby 1967: 7):

> About fifteen years ago, I had a dream, in which a tall, venerable looking white man, in a long coat, appeared to me, saying 'I am sent to you by other white men [...] I bring you a book'. [...] I am sent to bring this book to you, in order that you should take it to the rest of the people.

The messenger then showed Bukele his book, and taught him to write signs in the Vai language. They then began to read the book together. When he awoke and told his relatives about it, they were all quite sure it was a divine revelation. Another man claimed to have dreamed that the book had come from God (Dalby 1967: 7–10).

It is obvious from the account of Bukele that the spirit messengers who revealed the book look like nineteenth-century Europeans. This can also be seen in the account of Afaka Atumisi, the human author of the Djuka script, who had the writing system revealed to him by a spirit, in the form of a white man, who was sent by God (Dalby 1968: 163). A variation can be seen in the visions of Shong Lue: although his visions do not identify the holy messengers by ethnicity, they are identified as bureaucrats. In one of Shong Lue's visions, which occurred after he was instructed by the spirits to smoke opium and they were teaching him the Pahawh Hmong, a group of people in the uniforms of officials arrived, and called the spirits the saviours of the people. They then told Shong Lue that they had money for them and showed him where to dig. After doing so he found a jar of silver bars. He then realized that those people dressed in the clothes of officials had come from heaven (Smalley *et al.* 1990: 21–2).

As we all know, colonized people find themselves enmeshed in relationships where they are subordinated politically, economically, socially, and culturally to a dominant group. The source of the power of the colonizers is thus a matter of acute interest to the colonized. Millennial movements, as pointed out earlier, are often found among groups that have only recently experienced colonial subjugation. One of the things that we see generally as a consequence of this situation in millennial movements is that the prophet, in providing an explanation for the present state of affairs, goes on in creeds, rituals, symbols, and practices to fetishize elements of the colonizer's culture and society. In other words, things take the place of relationships, so that objects alone are viewed as the reason the colonizers are able to dominate others. It then becomes the work of the prophet to provide a formula through which these things can either be overcome, or come under the dominated group's control. In the Ghost Dance millennial movement of the 1890s, native peoples in the American West were inspired by a prophet to believe that the life they knew before would be restored to them, and in some versions European colonizers would disappear. Among the Sioux in particular there appeared Ghost shirts, which were believed to be a kind of body armour that would protect warriors against bullets, the single thing that they viewed as most responsible for US Army victories over the Sioux, which coincided with the introduction of rapid-fire Hotchkiss guns on the Great Plains. Another example is provided by the cargo cults that appeared in the Pacific during the first half of the twentieth century. Followers of these cults cut landing strips into the forest and made wooden replicas of airplanes, thinking that these things would attract the wealth they observed delivered to colonists or soldiers stationed on their islands during World War II. Other rituals had participants sitting at desks and speaking into telephones made out of bamboo connected by vines stretched among the trees.

The evidence suggests that, in the case of revealed scripts, writing is identified—like landing strips, the telephone, or the bullet—as one of the key sources, if not the key source of colonial power. It is given to the prophet by divine beings who themselves have some of the characteristics of the powerful—white skin, European dress, the badges of officials. This helps us to understand, without detracting from the intellectual achievement of the author of a new script, that writing, in these instances, is an idea whose time has come. Indeed, it is remarkable how often it is the case that there are several scripts that come into existence about the same time. Among the Central Alaskan Yupik, three different individuals developed scripts around 1900, and at least two of the authors believed them to be sudden gifts from God (Walker 1996: 181). There were at least two cases of revealed Hmong writing about the same time (Smalley *et al.* 1990). Dalby also remarked that the appearance of so many revealed West African scripts around 1900 cannot be a coincidence, although he does not explore the historical context of these revelations in any great detail, preferring to focus on the possible genetic connections these scripts have with other traditions (Dalby 1968). It also helps us to understand why many of the authors of these revealed scripts are illiterates: 'the unlettered genius', Smalley's phrase to describe Shong Lue. Although Shong Lue had been exposed to writing, he himself was an illiterate until he developed the Pahawh Hmong. The author of the revealed Yupik script, Uyaquq, was also illiterate, although it should also be pointed out there are many examples of revelatory writers who were literate in other scripts. But given the way writing can be fetishized in millennial movements, it is perhaps not surprising that those prophets who observe colonial regimes from the most marginalized positions, and who are the least familiar with the techniques of writing, can have writing as such a central part of their revelatory visions.

The Appearance and Disappearance of Revelatory Scripts

Given the vast number of human groups that have found themselves enmeshed in colonial relations, and the smaller, but still very large subset that have responded to conquest and colonization with millennial movements, why have just a handful of groups made revealed writing a central aspect of a religious cult? There are several answers to this. First, colonized people over time revise their understandings of the technologies and practices of colonialism. Thus, as people in the Pacific were drawn into more sustained contact with Europeans, the ritualistic mimicking of European practices ceased, and the cargo cults began to disappear, or were transformed into established churches and political parties. One could argue then that ignorance of writing—not the general principle of representing ideas or language by means of graphs, but a technical understanding of how scripts work—would promote its fetishization. Conversely, in areas where local writing systems were widely used before colonization, we would not tend to see writing as part of the revealed knowledge central to a millennial cult.

Second, the historical record is biased toward the success stories. I would even suggest that on the margins of colonialism the work of the 'unlettered genius' might not have been as rare as it seems. In the Yupik and Hmong case we know that multiple scripts were revealed about the same time, but some did not catch on. Likewise Dalby records examples of fully developed scripts that do not seem to extend beyond a small group or even the individual prophet himself. These scripts are recorded on wood and paper, and Dalby could find few extant traces of some of them just a few decades after they fell into disuse (Dalby 1968; 1969). Given the limited extent of these scripts and the perishable materials on which they are written, it is probably the case that a large number of revealed scripts are simply not recorded. It has already been noted that the Apache writing of Silas John was largely unknown despite the fact that the Apache had been put on reservations and been the subject of countless ethnographic studies. Moreover, since colonial powers are suspicious of millennial movements for their nationalistic aspirations, the prophet and his or her followers often come under attack. Shong Lue is good example. He was persecuted by the Royal Lao government, who saw him as a communist sympathizer, and by the communists, who suspected him of being a supporter of the Royal Lao government. Both sides tried to eliminate him, and he spent three years in prison after being arrested by the Lao government. After his release in 1970, he was murdered by solders of an anti-communist opium warlord. His followers scattered, and anyone using the writing system came under suspicion. In suppressing a millennial movement, the revelatory script associated with a prophet might also be suppressed.

The implication here it that the creation of writing alone is not an exceedingly rare or singular event, nor the disappearance of a script in these contexts surprising. Following Houston, Baines, and Cooper, who urge us to view origins and collapse in terms of one another (Houston *et al.* 2003: 431), the critical issue for a revelatory script is its entry into conventional usage as a means of communication. The literature on writing identifies a number of factors that bear upon this: how scripts can become nationalist symbols, how people recognize writing as a technological advance in communication, and so on. One variable in the success and persistence of a millennial movement that might be extended to writing in this context is the ability of the prophet to build a cadre of utterly committed followers, who become responsible for spreading the prophet's message. These followers are the ones who take over the leadership of the movement after the prophet's death and may substantially extend or revise the prophet's teachings. In the revealed scripts that tend to persist, such a cadre was formed by the prophet, and initiation into the writing system was vital for initiation into the prophet's inner circle. In other words the success or demise of a revelatory writing system hinged on the success of the movement within which it developed, so that the presence or absence of things that tend to give a millennial movement a lasting historical presence (such its connections to ethnic or nationalist political agendas, the development of a committed circle of followers around the prophet, who take over the movement) are the same factors that can lead to a revelatory writing system entering into sustained usage or dying off with its creator.

Finally, and to go back to a point made earlier, I think the number of revealed scripts can be expanded if we consider as examples of 'revealed writing' phenomena that might not pass muster as writing in other contexts. For example, adherents of Pacific cargo cults not only built airstrips and strung vines in trees like telephone wires, but some of them also began writing. The marks they produced were not readable, but the motivation for their writing was substantially similar to the motivations of those who developed recognizable scripts in other millennial movements. Some transitional cases are perhaps provided by 'the holy writing' of the Yoruba man Josiah Olunowo Oshitelu, which was inspired by a dream he had in 1926, in which he saw in the dream 'an open book, written in strange Arabic language' (Dalby 1969: 175), and the Oberi Okaime script, written down by two men of Nigeria, who began a religious movement after the script was revealed to them (Dalby 1968: 162). These are certainly much more complex than the writing produced in the cargo cults, but in both cases the revealed scripts were used for a revealed language (Dalby 1968: 158; 1969: 175) so it is difficult to see just how they could enter into conventional usage. To go even further, I think the experience of revealed knowledge through the medium of writing or the book can be quite widespread among people at the margins of modern nations. Maria Sabina, one of the best-known Mesoamerican curers, or 'people of knowledge' in her native Mazatec, often referred to herself as 'a book woman' (Munn 1983: 476). This is related to a vision she had under the influence of hallucinogenic mushrooms she ate to cure a patient. I quote from two separate interviews with her concerning the revealed source of her knowledge:

> Some people appeared who inspired me with respect. I knew they were the Principal Ones of whom my ancestors spoke. They were seated behind a table on which there were many written papers [...]. I knew this was a revelation that the saint children were giving me [...]. On the Principal Ones' table a book appeared, an open book that went on growing until it was the size of a person. In its pages there were letters. It was a white book, so white it was resplendent. One of the Principal Ones spoke to me and said 'Maria Sabina, this is the book of Wisdom. It is the Book of Language. Everything that is written in it is for you.'
>
> (Estrada 1981: 47)
>
> I thumbed through the leaves of the Book, many and many written pages, and alas I thought, I did not know how to read [...]. And suddenly I realized I was reading, and understanding all that was written on the Book, and it was as though I had become richer, wiser and in a moment I learned millions of things, I learned and learned.
>
> (Wasson *et al.* 1974: xxviii)

This is not an isolated phenomenon, since curers throughout Mesoamerica say they learn how to cure and divine from a book that divine beings showed them in a dream (Boege 1988: 178; Dow 1986: 51; Lipp 1991: 151; Tedlock 1985). Parenthetically, the person claiming to read is sometimes identified as illiterate (e.g. Dow 1986: 51), as was Maria Sabina. Leaving aside questions of just how reading is constructed in these traditions (Monaghan and Hamann 1999), this shows that the symbol of the book, and the idiom of reading and writing, are used throughout the world by people on the margins of colonial and neo-colonial states to conceive of and understand revelation, even if they are illiterate. Moreover, people have books and scripts revealed to them, without necessary going so far as to develop a writing system that we would recognize as such, or even jotting the script down.

What these phenomena suggest is that revealed scripts form a kind of continuum. On the one end are those like Shong Lue's script, which are complete writing systems. At the other end are scripts that may never have been set down, and are not used in conventional communication, but nonetheless have an important place in the religious movement that gave birth to them. It has only been the ones that can be considered complete writing systems that catch our attention. But there is good reason for connecting visions where knowledge is revealed through the medium of writing to the so-called pseudo-writing as found in cargo cults and to the full-blown writing systems like those revealed in West Africa, since they are all parts of similar religious phenomena, and begin in areas where writing is widely fetishized. It may even be that they co-occur. Smalley and his colleagues speculate that the Hmong tradition of diviners who go into trance, make marks on paper, and then read the writing, giving a prediction, may have influenced Shong Lue to develop the Pahawh Hmong (Smalley *et al.* 1990: 97–9). So it seems that the revealed writing system might be the tip of the iceberg, so to speak, of widespread revelations and divinely inspired writing practices, that not only co-occur, but form the vital context out of which such systems can emerge and disappear.

References

Basso, Keith H., and Ned Anderson
    1975   *A Western Apache Writing System.* Lisse: The Peter de Ridder Press.
Bender, Margaret C.
    2002   *Signs of Cherokee Culture: Sequoyah's Syllabary in Eastern Cherokee Life.* Chapel Hill: University of North Carolina Press.
Boege, Eckart
    1988   *Los Mazatecos ante la nacion.* Mexico City: Siglo XXI.
Dalby, David
    1967   'A Survey of the Indigenous Scripts of Liberia and Sierra Leone: Vai, Mende, Loma, Kpelle and Bassa'. *African Language Studies* 8: 1–51.
    1968   'The Indigenous Scripts of West Africa and Surinam: Their Inspiration and Design'. *African Language Studies* 9: 156–97.
    1969   'Further Indigenous Scripts of West Africa: Manding, Wolof and Fula Alphabets and Yoruba Holy Writing'. *African Language Studies* 10: 161–81.
Daniels, Ted
    1992   *Millennialism: An International Bibliography.* Hamden, CT: Garland Publishing.
Dow, James
    1986   *The Shaman's Touch.* Salt Lake City: University of Utah Press.
Estrada, Alvaro
    1981   *Maria Sabina: Her Life and Chants.* Santa Barbara. CA: Ross Erikson.
Gelb, Ignace J.
    1963   *A Study of Writing,* revised edition. Chicago, IL: University of Chicago Press.

Goody, Jack
    1968   *Literacy in Traditional Societies.* Cambridge: Cambridge University Press.

Henkelman, James W., and Kurt Vitt
    1985   *Harmonious to Dwell: The History of the Alaska Moravian Church 1885-1985.* Bethel, AK: The Moravian Seminary and Archives.

Houston, Stephen, John Baines, and Jerrold Cooper
    2003   'Last Writing: Script Obsolescence in Egypt, Mesopotamia, and Mesoamerica'. *Comparative Studies in Society and History* 45: 430–79.

Jackson, Anthony
    1979   *Na-khi Religion: An Analytical Appraisal of the Na-khi Ritual Texts.* The Hague: Mouton.

Laughlin, Robert
    1988   'What is a Tzotzil?' *RES: Anthrology and Aesthetics* 15: 133–55.

Lemoine, Jacques
    1986   'Shamanism in the Context of Hmong Resettlement'. In Glen L. Hendricks, Bruce T. Doming, and Amos S. Deinard (eds.), *The Hmong in Transition.* New York: Center for Migration Studies.

Lipp, Frank
    1991   *The Mixe of Oaxaca.* Austin: University of Texas Press.

Monaghan, John, and Byron Hamann
    1999   'Reading as Social Practice and Cultural Construction'. *Indiana Journal of Hispanic Literatures* 13: 131–40.

Munn, Henry
    1983   'Writing in the Imagination of an Oral Poet'. In Jerome Rothenberg and Diane Rothenberg (eds.), *Symposium of the Whole: A Range of Discourse Toward an Ethnopoetics.* Berkeley: University of California Press, 474–9.

Smalley, William A., Chia Koua Vang, and Gnia Yee Yang
    1990   *Mother of Writing: The Origin and Development of a Hmong Messianic Script.* Chicago, IL: University of Chicago Press.

Tedlock, Dennis
    1985   *Popol Vuh: The Definitive Edition of the Mayan Book of the Dawn of Life and the Glories of Gods and Kings.* New York: Simon and Schuster.

Walker, Willard B.
    1996   'Native Writing Systems'. In William C. Sturtevant (gen. ed.) and Ives Goddard (vol. ed.), *Languages.* Handbook of North American Indians 17: 158–84. Washington, DC: Smithsonian Institution.

Wallace, Anthony F. C.
    1956   'Revitalization Movements'. *American Anthropologist* 58: 264–81.

Wasson, R. Gordon, George Cowan, Florence Cowan, and Willard Rhodes
    1974   *Maria Sabina and her Mazatec Mushroom Velada.* New York: Harcourt Brace Jovanovich.

15

History without Text

Chris Gosden

In the Western academic mind, history without text might seem a contradiction in terms. This view manifested itself in a long debate about whether oral history was really history at all, or was far too unreliable as a means of accurately recalling the past (see Thompson 2000; Vansina 2006; Wolf 1982 for discussions and positive advocacy of oral history). Of course, this is a culturally (and historically) specific view and history is a term with a variety of meanings, ranging from the written records that are kept of past experiences or events, on the one hand, to the more general transmission of culturally significant knowledge, on the other. All cultural forms have history in this latter sense, but only some people write histories. History in the former sense derives from textual sources, involving the rewriting of primary archival sources into more synthetic, narrative forms of history. It follows from this view that people without texts are people without history. The loss of a script or the destruction of documentary sources means a loss of contact with the past which might well threaten the nature of identity in the present.

In some sense the past is being lost all the time, as events are forgotten or modes of thought and feeling die out to be supplanted by newer sensibilities. The means by which the past is conserved, which we call history, is linked intimately to the manner of its loss. In societies with texts loss is changed through the fact of writing: the possibility of recording the past in words leads to greater possibilities for curation, but might lead to loss of memory. In societies without texts the curation of the past is primarily through memory and the various mnemonics that exist in performances, artefacts, and landscapes. The existence of texts does not mean that the past is better preserved in a straightforward way, but it is differently curated. Consequently, the loss of a script does not mean that a society's ability to curate the past atrophies, but rather that it is reconfigured, and we can guess that the material mnemonics of memory might become more important.

The close and necessary link between text and history is one I want to nuance, making the point that the construction of the past can draw on many materials and modes of action, which include both oral histories and actions involving objects and landscapes. These sources of connection to the past have at least two effects: landscapes or artefacts can preserve memories, acting as prompts or mnemonics for stories, genealogies, and mythologies, helping to extend people's abilities to narrate and think about the past; landscapes also guide patterns of work, congregation, or movement, so that, although no conscious memories of the past may be preserved, that past has an impact on the present, for instance through trackways, buildings, field systems, or the layout of towns. In practice, the remembered landscape and the landscape as lived interact in complex ways, the conscious and the habitual reinforcing each other. Much has been made of the links between place and memory, which have a recursive relationship—places help store and channel memories, while it is the memories of people and events attached to a particular locale that make places what they are (Basso 1996). Pierre Nora's huge compendium of *lieux de mémoire* explores the importance of realms of memory (the English translation generally used for the French term) in the context of French national identity (Nora 1996–1998).

This leads us to a deeper point: all human life is made up of elements of which we are consciously aware and which can be put into words, to talk or write about and consciously examine, but it is deeply influenced by habit which is culturally based and specific, but which represents a set of dispositions so taken for granted that they are hard to put into words. The loss of a script or change of language causes a shift of major importance in people's appreciation of the world, but may not always change the world of habit, which is so important to everyday life and long-term patterns. The loss of scripts changes key elements of life without erasing all of them—the balance of change in any situation between the conscious and the habitual needs to be established empirically, rather than being assumed.

In what follows I shall look first at oral histories and how such histories might be rooted in the landscape, before looking at unconscious forms of history (flirting with oxymoron here for those who think history is always conscious) deriving from working in an old human landscape, the past shaping of which affects present actions.

Oral and Genealogical Histories

There has been a long debate over the accuracy and time-depth of oral histories. The overall tendency for many parts of the world has been towards accepting that oral history and genealogy can preserve accurate information over remarkably long periods of time (Finnegan 1992; Thompson 2000; Vansina 2006). It has been recognised that oral history does not exist purely as words, but is linked in many ways to features of the material world and perhaps especially landscape. An excellent example of the anchoring of history in landscape is provided by the work of Ballard (1995) amongst the Huli, who live in the Tari Basin of the Southern Highlands of Papua New Guinea (see Fig. 15.1).

The Huli have a very specific attachment to land. This attachment is anchored in genealogies which are remarkable in their time-depth, going back some twenty-four generations, telling a consistent story which can be traced over large areas of the Tari Basin. Ballard has collected a huge amount of genealogical information, and this has provided the basis for a history of the Huli. Over a maximum period of 500 years the genealogies outline rights to the ditches which are used to drain the swamps of the Tari Basin, as well as qualifying individuals to participate in ritual and trade. Specific ditches are named after known people, often those who dug them, so that a map of the ditches also forms a map of the historical social landscape. These ditches were used for growing an indigenous root crop, taro, supplemented more recently by the sweet potato introduced ultimately from South America. These crops form the basis for pig herds, which are central to exchange systems in Tari. Sweet potato has brought about massive changes in Huli society since its introduction around 250 years ago. At that time, people were already engaged in intensive agriculture, and the pig was the principal valuable (Ballard 1995: 246). The sweet potato laid the basis for rapid population increase and a greater concentration on intensive wetland agriculture than previously, with the main use of the swamp in the Tari basin beginning in the 1840s and 1850s (Ballard 1995: 175). The changes in the wealth economy encouraged new forms of leadership and ritual, especially the *tege pulu*, a ceremony involving the exchange of much larger numbers of pigs than in any previous form of ritual. This was controlled by secular leaders, unlike the older ritual forms, which could only be conducted by hereditary specialists (Ballard 1995: 241–6). The agricultural economy of the swamps forms the basis for pig herds, which are central to exchange systems in Tari. Ritual and trade are linked by a concern with directions and lines of power which are ritually charged. These lines of power, known as *dindi pongone*, are seen as being the tracks of ancestral spirits who created the present-day features of the landscape, and these obviously have parallels with Dreaming tracks, known from Australia. For Australian Aboriginal groups the Dreaming is a time in the distant past when ancestral figures moved across the landscape creating hills, rivers, lakes, or ocean bays. Huli beliefs are akin to these. Certain rituals have to be carried out at cosmologically important spots on the landscape, using material culture obtained from particular ritually charged directions, or substances

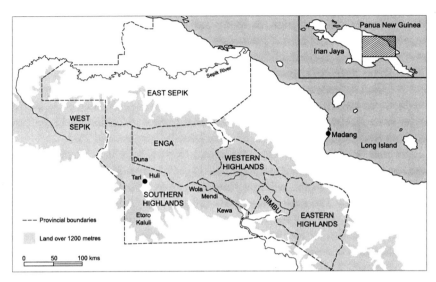

Figure 15.1 Papua New Guinea, with indication of the home regions of groups mentioned in the text.

such as pig fat, which have the correct properties to hold back the forces that lead the world to decline physically or cosmologically.

A number of layers of attachment to land anchor forms of history. First is the imprinting of the human group onto the ditches of the swamps, so that constructed features of the landscape provide the basis for understanding the past connections that contribute towards creating human groups in the present. The circle is completed by the fact that histories maintained through the land also help in maintaining the genealogies which form the basis for claims to land. The importance of swamp cultivation to personal power and to the ritual system helps explain why people put so much effort into maintaining long-lasting and accurate genealogies, without which their descent-based claims to land would lack force. The age of the cosmological landscape is unknown, but it may be of some antiquity, forming a basic orientation to Huli life, which found its expression in the last half millennium during which foodstuffs, new and introduced, have become the basis for personal wealth, but also as a means of intervening with the spirit world.

Findings from Tari are complemented elsewhere in New Guinea, where genealogical systems also have considerable time-depth, even in situations of marked change, as is shown in the material presented in Polly Wiessner and Akii Tumu's (1998) massive treatment of Engan oral history. The Engan language belongs to the same family as Huli, but they live at some distance from them. Some eight to ten generations ago, the Enga started consciously compiling a body of historical traditions in order to understand the history of each tribe and their interconnections (Wiessner and Tumu 1998: 2). Wiessner and Tumu's work, which draws on interviews from people in all 100 tribes of Enga speakers, lays out a structure to Engan history spanning at least the last 400 years. Within that time the sweet potato was introduced, and this brought complex changes in different parts of Enga, as well as promoting a population explosion from between 10,000 and 20,000 people 400 years ago, to over 100,000 some 220 years later (Wiessner and Tumu 1998: 355), with continued growth to around 200,000 people today. This saw a shift from agriculture, complemented by hunting and gathering, which took place in a sparsely populated landscape, to the intensive forms of agriculture, in a densely packed landscape, found today (Wiessner and Tumu 1998: 1).

Inter-group dynamics became much more complex, but there is little evidence of greatly increased warfare over the last 400 years. Instead, the stresses of inter-group competition were mediated through exchange networks, especially the *Tee* exchanges, which started in eastern Enga and spread throughout the region. The changes precipitated by the introduction of the sweet potato were so great that the networks along which wealth and knowledge flowed needed to be restructured each generation (Wiessner and Tumu 1998: 3). In all areas, however, the greatest changes occurred in the raising of pigs, whose social and symbolic value rose throughout the last 400 years (Wiessner and Tumu 1998: 360). This increased intensification was connected to the rise of leaders who could organize agricultural production, finance exchange events and the theatre involved in their staging, and keep up with the flows of knowledge throughout the region. Constant change has made Engan society open to change, experiment, and the import of cults and ideas. Rituals were regularly purchased from neighbouring groups, and these were very important historically in providing new values attached to relations between people and things and novel emotional or intellectual environments relevant to changed circumstances (Wiessner and Tumu 1998: 361–3). By the time of contact with the first patrol, that of the Sepik–Hagen patrol in the 1930s (Gammage 1998), the fabric of Engan society was strained by pressure on land, the levels of work needed to support pig herds and put on ceremonial events, and competition between groups.

One has the impression that amongst the Enga great effort has gone into maintaining oral histories because of the destabilizing level and pace of change; history can be used and debated as a means of putting present problems in perspective, enabling people to see their genesis and causes. Similar motives may underlie much of the interest in history in Western societies. Other Pacific societies also have considerable genealogical depth, and in places like Tonga this is used partly to anchor the claims of ruling families, which are also attached to features such as mounds and temples (Kirch 1984). Thus, for a variety of motives people are able to construct and to keep their own histories over many centuries and with some degree of accuracy. In principle, a fictitious history might be as useful as an accurate one. However, an agreed narrative for the past shared amongst different groups is necessary if conflicting claims to land or power are to be resolved.

What implications do such histories have for our understanding of people with written histories? We now have access to such histories which go back to the beginnings of writing. But histories which may be in some sense continuous with our own might not be of any greater longevity than those of the Huli or the Enga. Coincidentally we can date the start of Western modernity to around 500 years ago, at the same time as the Huli might see the start of their modernity, should they ever use such a difficult and loaded term. In Europe at that date a class system antecedent to that of today started to emerge from feudal society, colonial expansion was just beginning and starting to set up so many of the conditions of contemporary life, and the intellectual and cultural changes of the Renaissance created philosophical forms, modes of pictorial representation and, indeed, of history writing which still have some effect today. I do not want to posit some 500-year rule which would hold that continuity cannot be maintained over longer periods, but to make the point that such oral histories do not suffer from a shallow time-depth in comparison with those which possess written records. The Huli case might be at the maximum end of the genealogical effort, but it is not the case that oral societies suffer constant amnesia that would deny them the long past which provides historical perspective to those with writing. Such a view opens up the possibility of a broad comparative study of when, where, and how different lengths and qualities of history become important, and under what sorts of circumstances people will put social effort into curating and maintaining historical materials, irrespective of whether these are written or held in memory, or transmitted through material referents and cultural practices. Such broad comparisons might also throw extra light on why, on occasions, scripts are lost.

Landscape, Action and Memory

There is also the more subtle question of how far landscapes and indeed objects (although I will not consider the latter here) maintain continuity through the fact that past features of the land shape and channel people's actions in the present. I shall take as a brief example the potentially huge topic of the transitions from late Iron Age into the Roman period and the further shift to Anglo-Saxon society in Britain (see Fig. 15.2). This major set of transformations involved changes in language from Celtic to Latin and Germanic, alongside the coming of dense written records with the Romans and their loss in the early Anglo-Saxon period. These are very big themes on which I am only partially qualified to write, but which have considerable interest here, as they involve issues of continuity through the use of the landscape and basic cultural practices, but also changes of language and the introduction and local loss of scripts.

Let us start with the landscape and the forms of continuity it might have created. At first sight these are unpromising periods in which to look at landscape continuities, as changes seem so overwhelming and obvious.

In the late Iron Age of southern Britain, starting around 100 BC, there was a considerable re-organization of some elements of the landscape, the emergence of the so-called territorial oppida. These occupied a range of positions, from plateau areas, such as Wheathampstead in Hertfordshire, or lowland positions, like Camulodunum (Colchester) or Verlamion (St Albans). In many cases these new proto-urban settlements were surrounded by dyke systems which enclosed large areas of land, perhaps brought into something like private ownership for the first time, that might have provided controlled grazing land for horses, an increasingly important element of wealth at this time (Cunliffe 2005). Such changes went along with an intensification of agriculture and greater trade with the continent, as well as locally increased mass-production of pottery, metals, and other objects. All these changes, considerable through they were, pale into insignificance in comparison with the massive alteration of the landscape and all areas of life brought about by the invasion of the Romans in AD 43. This brought first a military infrastructure of roads, camps, and forts, with the road system being extended progressively over the next few centuries, which also saw new towns, some of them based on Iron Age oppida and other new foundations, the layout of new field systems which extended, changed, or erased earlier ones, as well as rural villas of various sizes and styles of magnificence (again often sited on earlier Iron Age structures). These formal changes to the urban and agrarian landscapes were accompanied by the introduction of a new range of crops including grapes, together with a greater intensity of agricultural production as well as various forms of consumption. Such a bald list cannot convey the scope and depth of the change to the landscape and other aspects of life (see Mattingly 2006 for a rather fuller account). These changes were compounded in the early fifth century AD by the withdrawal of the Roman legions and the coming of the Anglo-Saxons. Over the next few centuries the road network, urban forms, and some of the rural landscape were re-ordered and reused, so that some old towns initially fell into decay, but later new centres emerged.

The movements from the Iron Age to the Roman period, and from there to the Anglo-Saxons, represent two of the great transitions in British prehistory/history, both seeming to constitute a considerable break with what came before and in turn laying the basis for long-lasting developments to follow. Surprisingly, considerable evidence for continuity exists in the rural aspects of the landscape. From the late Bronze Age (around 1200 BC) onwards so-called linear ditches were constructed in many areas of Britain to divide territories, for reasons that we do not clearly understand. The tradition of constructing and maintaining linear ditches lasted around 1000 years until the Romano-British

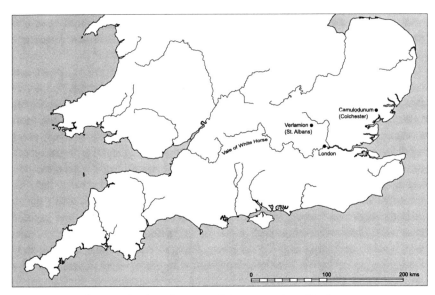

Figure 15.2 Southern England, with names of places mentioned in the text.

period. Ditches such as these, the longest of which stretch some 13 km, had not only to be dug, but also cleared regularly, as water and frost eroded their sides. These features of the landscape may have had names attached to them, perhaps of ancestral significance, and would have been part of the temporal round of maintaining the landscape.

Also beginning in the late Bronze Age around 1000 BC, hilltops came to be enclosed, initially by relatively small ditches and banks, some of which were later enlarged in the Iron Age a couple of centuries later to become what we know as hillforts, with relatively massive ramparts and ditches which were subsequently remodeled in new forms (Cunliffe 1990; Bradley *et al.* 1994: 143–7). Originally interpreted as primarily defensive places, as the name hillfort implies, these are now more generally viewed as sites which make a statement in the landscape to help assert social claims and to support power. I would add that the effort of constructing these sites, together with the regular practices of maintenance and work on them were as important as their final forms. In some sites, such as the famous Maiden Castle in England's West Country, the ramparts seem to have been subject to regular alterations by dumping soil in small amounts. The activity of construction may have been as important as the end result (Sharples 1991). The sites of late prehistoric southern Britain are often impressive features which now look relatively static and enduring. This should not blind us to the fact that it was actions of construction and reconstruction that may have been as important as their final form, since the sites required regular and repeated work that was part of the temporality of the landscape.

As mentioned above, the transition from the prehistoric to the Romano-British landscape is often seen as having been due to the imposition of new forms and changes in spatial sensibility. However, there is a possibility in some areas that the linear ditches and other prehistoric features had some impact into the Romano-British period. In the Vale of White Horse and the neighbouring Berkshire Downs some of the linear ditches may have been used to delimit Romano-British villa estates, as is indicated by the correlation between pottery scatters and those features (Gaffney and Tingle 1989; Tingle 1991). It is also possible that Romano-British villa estates then provided the plan for parish boundaries as these were laid out during the earlier Anglo-Saxon period, as suggested by estate boundaries in some parts of the Vale of White Horse (for the complexity of the evidence, see Hooke 1998). Here some of the parish bounds run along the Bronze Age linear ditches, pointing not just towards a use of convenient features but also to some ongoing structure to patterns of work and community over long periods of time.

Beneath all the obvious changes entailed in incorporation into the Roman Empire and emerging out the other side, there may have been important aspects of group life that were attached to landscape features and ordered the nature of work and modes of kinship that laid the basis for forms of group aggrandizement. These landscapes were named and formed the basis for stories, linking human beings to the features of the land, in ways that are analogous to the links the Huli make with their ditches.

These complex attachments to landscape need much more exploration and substantiation, but continuity of attachment took place despite changes in language and varying degrees of literacy. We assume that the majority of people in Iron Age Britain spoke Celtic languages—although it is now speculated that there may have been considerable numbers of Germanic speakers in Britain prior to the Roman invasion (Oppenheimer 2006)—and that these were groups whose histories were transmitted orally. The linguistic and textual situation changed drastically with the arrival of the Romans. It is now hard to grasp the breadth and depth of textual evidence that once existed for Britain in the Romano-British period, where together with a mass of official documentation there would have been letters, journals, and accounts by individuals, as the exceptional evidence from Vindolanda indicates (see Vindolanda Tablets Online). Mattingly (2006) pulls the textual evidence together with the archaeology, using inscriptions on buildings, curse tablets, and the like to provide insights into the manner in which writing was used as an element of power as well as a medium of record, or as a medium to write about daily life. The linguistic situation of Roman Britain is hard to know in any detail, but there probably existed a plethora of languages, spoken by small immigrant groups, as well as Latin and various Celtic languages.

All this changed very rapidly in the fifth century AD with a decline in people able to read and write as well as the destruction of textual evidence. Languages changed with the widespread replacement of Celtic by Germanic speakers. The landscape appears to have been renamed from what we can presume to have been a complex mode of Celtic naming. Once historical evidence for the landscape emerges in the form of Anglo-Saxon charter bounds, over 1000 of which exist, most in medieval copies (Hooke 1998), we find that even very small elements of the landscape were named and recognized. Place names which survive into the present also indicate the erasure of Celtic names, with some survivals, such as river names, representing the exception to an overall rule of replacement of Celtic by Germanic in this domain (Gelling 1988).

Given this radical set of changes in the linguistic basis of society and in its use of writing, the possibilities for continuity in landscape use assume great importance. Human cultural forms represent a balance between continuity and change, and it is a rare situation where everything changes at once. The loss of a script, with or without a shift in language use, represents a profound set of alterations influencing the manner in which people create and represent their world. It is possible that the more profound the change, the greater the need there is to create and maintain some forms of continuity. The landscape may be the key locus in which such forms of continuity are maintained.

Final Thoughts

I have written this text and you are now reading it, which means that both of us are particularly attuned to the importance of texted language and likely to be saddened by its loss. I have tried to make clear that text is not the only basis for histories stretching beyond a few human generations. Indeed, our reliance on text may well have resulted in an atrophy of memory and of the mechanisms by which aspects of history are maintained and transmitted in physical and spoken form. Most of us have short memories of family or community histories, unless we write them down. This is not true of many communities, who, if it is important enough, can preserve accurate and useful memories of the past stretching back a long way. Frequent spurs to memory occur when claims to things in the present, such as land, exchange relations, or sources of ritual power, are made through genealogy. Land may play a double role here, both as something to be claimed and as the medium through which memory, which supplies the basis of claims, is perpetuated.

Even when conscious memories of human acts on the landscape do not survive, as when they are erased or altered by incoming peoples, the landscape of work and territory may form the basis for continuity and may be important even when unacknowledged. New modes of work in the landscape may be influenced by older ways of dividing territory or creating fields, and this continuity can be reinforced when older inhabitants still remain active on the landscape, even if they have adopted the new forms of language and tropes for discussing the world. For us bibliophiles there seems to be a division of a large and important kind between societies with writing and those without, and I am certainly not trying to deny the difference that writing makes. But we need to recognize that knowledge and an appreciation of the past take many forms, some spoken, some not put into words at all but evident, and some written. Ultimately it is the interaction between varying modes of curating the past and attaching oneself to it that is vital and deserves more study. In order to understand exactly what is lost when a script vanishes, we need to look at other modes of human engagement and what role they play. A larger comparative study of human modes of relationship with the world of the past and the present should not stop at the divide between the literate and the oral, but should pursue comparisons and contrast across what has come to be seen as a key divide.

References

Ballard, Christopher
    1995   'The Death of a Great Land: Ritual, History and Subsistence Revolution in the Southern Highlands of Papua New Guinea', unpublished PhD dissertation, Division of Archaeology and Natural History, Australian National University, Canberra.
Basso, Keith
    1996   *Wisdom Sits in Places: Landscape and Language amongst the Western Apache.* Albuquerque: University of New Mexico Press.
Bradley, Richard, Roy Entwhistle, and Frances Raymond
    1994   *Prehistoric Land Divisions on Salisbury Plain.* London: English Heritage Archaeological Report 2.
Cunliffe, Barry
    1990   'Before Hillforts'. *Oxford Journal of Archaeology* 9: 323–36.
    1994   'After Hillforts'. *Oxford Journal of Archaeology* 13: 71–84.
    2005   *Iron Age Communities in Britain: An Account of England, Scotland and Wales from the Seventh Century BC until the Roman Conquest,* fourth edition. London: Routledge.
Finnegan, Ruth
    1992   *Oral Traditions and the Verbal Arts: A Guide to Research Practices.* London: Routledge.
Gaffney, Vincent, and Martin Tingle
    1989   *The Maddle Farm Project: An Integrated Survey of Prehistoric and Roman Landscapes on the Berkshire Downs.* Oxford: British Archaeological Reports 200.
Gammage, Bill
    1998   *The Sky Travellers: Journeys in New Guinea 1938-1939,* Melbourne: Melbourne University Press.

Gelling, Margaret
    1998   *Signposts to the Past: Place-Names and the History of England.* Chichester: Phillimore.

Hooke, Donna
    1998   *The Landscape of Anglo-Saxon England.* London: Leicester University Press.

Kirch, Patrick Vinton
    1984   *The Evolution of Polynesian Chiefdoms.* Cambridge: Cambridge University Press.

Mattingly, David
    2006   *An Imperial Possession: Britain in the Roman Empire 54 BC - AD 409.* London: Allen Lane.

Nora, Pierre
    1996–8 *The Realms of Memory.* Trans. A. Goldhammer. New York: Columbia University Press.

Oppenheimer, Stephen
    2006   *The Origins of the British: A Genetic Detective Story.* London: Constable and Robinson.

Sharples, Niall
    1991   *Maiden Castle: Excavations and Field Survey 1985-6.* London: English Heritage Archaeological Report 19.

Thompson, Paul
    2000   *The Voice of the Past: Oral History.* third edition. Oxford: Oxford University Press.

Tingle, Martin
    1991   *The Vale of the White Horse Survey.* Oxford: British Archaeological Reports, British Series 218. Oxford: Tempus Reparatum.

Vindolanda Tablets Online, http://vindolanda.csad.ox.ac.uk, last accessed 3 December 2007.

Vansina, Jan
    2006   *Oral Tradition: A Study in Historical Methodology.* New Brunswick, NJ, and London: Aldine Transaction.

Wiessner, Polly, and Akii Tumu
    1998   *Historical Vines: Enga Networks of Exchange, Ritual and Warfare in Papua New Guinea.* Bathurst, NSW: Crawford House Publishing.

Wolf, Eric
    1982   *Europe and the People without History.* Berkeley: University of California Press.

16

Writing and its Multiple Disappearances

John Baines

Introduction

In the Preface to this book we present briefly the gap in scholarship that we have sought to address, describing the conference at which we brought scholars together with the intention of addressing that gap and going as far as we could beyond the article in which Stephen Houston, John Baines, and Jerrold Cooper (2003) had made an initial exploration of relevant issues and given short case studies. Probably the vast majority of the writing systems that have existed in the world have fallen out of use and, if now known at all, either are no longer intelligible or have been deciphered in the last couple of centuries. Yet the process of loss of writing systems has hardly been studied, even though such systems constitute the most developed mode of visual–verbal communication in material form that many societies have created, as well as generally, but not always, having profound meaning for those societies.

In planning the conference, we set our parameters broadly, thinking in terms of systems of communication that have a material form as marks or artefacts and are made up from defined repertories of signs (compare, for example, the 'communication systems' evoked by Michalowski, 1990). We did not focus on writing narrowly defined. We therefore included both Mexican pictography, a system whose classification as writing is disputed because it does not have a straightforward relation with the words and sounds of language, and the Andean khipu, a complex system of recording through knotted cords that is still not well understood but also appears not to be closely linked to language. We also extended the range of practices under consideration by including a paper on the preservation and loss of traditions in societies that do not have either practices comparable with those institutions or with writing systems, or that sustain significant traditions past civilizational breaks, exhibiting marked continuities in material practice and the memorialization that it offers.

The aim of this short concluding chapter is to present some thoughts arising from reading the individual chapters, and in the process to offer a few pointers toward a synthesis. With a few exceptions, principally for Mesopotamian cuneiform, the volume of research published in this area is so modest that significant developments can be expected in the future. The lists of references for the chapters represent more the primary materials under examination than secondary discussions (the references are so diverse that they have not been gathered into a single bibliography). Moreover, numerous other cases of marginal, disappearing, or vanished scripts exist around the world today, while hitherto unknown and otherwise lost writing systems from the past continue to be discovered, most recently a system of the early first millennium BC in the ancient Olmec region of Mexico (Rodríguez Martínez *et al.* 2006). Coverage in this volume is very incomplete, and is affected not only by the availability of expertise but also by what could be fitted into the framework of a conference and a reasonably sized volume of proceedings. (In what follows, citations of authors' names without further details are references to their chapters in this book.)

Point of Departure

In order to review what is at stake when a writing system disappears, I sketch some features that are common to many systems and thus are likely to lie at the core of what is lost with a whole system.

Writing systems and comparable institutions are specialized modes of communication in physical form. They materialize memory in explicit fashion, in a style that is markedly different from many other ways in which material culture conveys meaning (some important aspects of this materialization are reviewed by Chris Gosden). Essentially they bring together the two institutions that distinguish human beings from other animals: an elaborate material culture; and language. They are far more specific in reference and more extensive in potential or actual coverage than almost all other material codes. Some of them may not have been invented or developed in order to notate a particular language, or language in general, but rather to store information through a system of signs (see the range of examples discussed in Houston 2004). Nonetheless, they become closely identified with language, and in analysing them scholars often find it difficult not to adopt a linguistic perspective without first asking whether it is the right one. If writing systems are viewed through the lens of language and linguistic theory, they appear to share its salient characteristic of being able in principle to communicate content of an indefinite range of types.

In practice, however, few writing systems are as broad in character and application as such a formulation might imply. Moreover, for all of them it should be borne in mind that they do not include domains such as the purely visual, the musical, or the numerical/mathematical, which require other notational or more broadly representational systems (see e.g. Chrisomalis 2004), even if some of these are integrated with writing. Most writing systems are not very extensively developed or do not encompass more than a small subset of the domains of social action that pass through speech, while many create modes of communication that are substantially different from spoken ones. Among those that focus on small subsets, cultural factors often predominate: writing is used to set down matters that are in varied ways important. Writing absorbs great cultural energy. Once it is set up as a working system, it must be learned and transmitted. Institutions that can sustain it need to have redundancy built into them. Most societies train more literate people than will use writing in adult life, either professionally or, for a smaller group, as part of a high-cultural lifeway. Until modern times, the physical materials used for writing in many or most traditions have been costly in terms of resources or craftsmanship.

One widespread but not universal function of writing is in forms of elite display. These may be more or less public. So far as they can, elites control what writing is used for and how it is disseminated. Display accentuates the broader tendency of the visual media and forms of writing to be strongly aesthetic, while vast resources can be expended on creating display pieces, often without any strong expectation that the result will be read. Much that is written belongs only in the domain of writing and has no close counterpart, or no counterpart at all, in the spoken realm.

Writing systems are generally institutions of complex societies and civilizations. The inventors of some systems in small societies have been aware of writing's existence in a dominant neighbour society, as with the revelatory scripts discussed by John Monaghan. The numerically small-scale society of Rapanui (Easter Island), which produced the largely undeciphered Rongorongo tablets (see e.g. Fischer 1997: 552–60), was among the world's most unusual, earlier creating colossal statuary with a prodigality in relation to its size that has few if any parallels. Rongorongo seems to have been invented after contact with the Spanish, so that the script is an example of 'stimulus diffusion' rather than fully independent invention.

Most complex societies either are multilingual, or encompass speakers of dialects that range into mutual incomprehensibility, or both. The main script of a society that uses anything other than an alphabetic script typically writes one among the many languages or dialects that are present. Moreover, the often unexamined modern assumption, that a writing system can notate languages other than the one for which it was devised, has seldom been widespread. In Italy, as Kathryn Lomas shows, the Greek and Etruscan scripts, which were ultimately variants of each other, were adapted to form distinct scripts for local languages, although some of those languages were written in more than one script. The Arabian peninsula and India are examples of regions where each written language generally has a script of its own, even if it differs only in minor ways from neighbouring scripts. Major exceptions to that pattern are cuneiform, in Mesopotamia and adjacent regions, and some alphabetic scripts, notably Latin, Greek, and Arabic. If a script is closely identified with a language, the latter's disappearance may condemn the former to the same fate.

Because most scripts that were not devised on the periphery of other script cultures developed for centuries before they represented a language at all fully, the form of language they record tends to be conservative, archaic, or obsolete. Another reason for this preference is that writing is used for symbolically important purposes for which the everyday language would be inappropriate in an analogous spoken context. Often the written language is not the one that is normally spoken in the society; it may even belong to a different language family.

All these features, which are found in varying patterns and probably in most societies that use writing, contribute to making writing systems into specialized, value-laden institutions, many of them closely identified with the core values of a society or civilization. The range of uses of writing, the extent to which it is employed—that is, its penetration through different sectors of society—and rates of literacy vary enormously. Often writing is specialized for sacred, high-cultural, or economic purposes. In the quite numerous societies that use more than one script, each of them may occupy a different social register, as among the Vai in Liberia (Scribner and Cole 1981). Perhaps only in relation to the last couple of centuries can one think of usages of writing in a single script as in any way not carrying a heavy cultural load (I mention the partial exception of India below). Writing now tends to be seen as a self-evident good, with universal literacy a goal to which the world as a whole should aspire; in the West, such aspirations are unreflectingly linked to alphabetical writing and phonetic representation of language. The small extent to which today's discourse takes into account the culturally and politically hegemonic character of such an assumption is striking.

In considering the loss of writing systems, one needs to get behind such modern, often Eurocentric assumptions, and in particular to detach oneself from the mindset which assumes that writing is a routine matter for most people in a society—something that scholars often find hard to do. In order to make progress, one must address the roles that scripts had in individual past societies, as well as present societies in which specific scripts or comparable communication systems are under threat. This is what the chapters of this book do. Now that a range of case studies is available, documented and persuasively analysed by the contributors, it becomes meaningful to ask what patterns emerge among the results they present, to point out gaps in our understanding, and to suggest hypotheses for examination in future studies of these examples, or of ones that are not covered here.

Disappearance of Language, Culture, and Script

At the core of the questions raised by our authors is the fact that disappearances of more than one entity among scripts, languages, polities, and cultures or civilizations mostly overlap. It is not common for a writing system to disappear without one or more other major institutions being lost from the culture in question. The cases presented in this volume cover various combinations among these possibilities, as well as offering significant examples of survival of scripts and comparable entities long past the eclipse of the states and civilizations that created them. Similarly, the principal language of a culture or civilization can continue in existence after the original cultural configuration to which it belonged has vanished, or it can be superseded by another language at the spoken level while the older language continues to be used in writing.

One reason for this separability of civilization and language is the simple fact that language is a human necessity. The successor society, or the continuation of the same society, must use language, which may be the same one as was spoken by the previous civilization in the same place. Another, more or less converse reason is that, even if a civilization's language is no longer spoken and fundamental ideological change has taken place, the language may retain cultural and/or religious prestige in the new context. An obvious case is the survival of Latin in Europe into modern times despite its progressive disappearance as a mother tongue, which was complete more than a thousand years ago. Scripts can be replaced largely for reasons of politics and identity, with a greater or lesser involvement of other cultural factors. Salient instances in the modern world are the shift from Arabic to Latin script for writing Turkish, or the oscillation among Cyrillic, Latin, and other scripts for many languages of eastern Europe and the former Soviet Union.

Developments of this type are part of wider-ranging ideological changes. After the early twentieth century reforms of Kemal Atatürk, the transformation of the Turkish language through vocabulary replacement, together with the shift from Arabic to Latin script, has been so thorough-going that only a small minority in Turkey can read Ottoman Turkish in Arabic script. Before very long, that combination of script and language will effectively have disappeared. There is no immediate prospect that Ottoman Turkish will need to be deciphered, because a vast amount of material and information relating to it remains and it continues to be studied. It is, however, easy to imagine how a comparable change could lead to the same situation as existed for more than 1200 years up to the eighteenth century in relation to Egyptian hieroglyphic, where civilizational transformation had brought with it loss of knowledge of the script's workings. The change in Turkish is particularly striking since the society's religion has remained the same throughout the process, but it has been bound up with important social transformations and issues of national and cultural identity.

This volume offers the comparable case of Manchu (Giovanni Stary), where the language and newly devised script of a hitherto peripheral people were of central political importance to the largest state in the world for 250 years but were marginalized by historical developments in which their ethnic group first became assimilated culturally and then fell from power. The Manchu script and language have nonetheless survived into the present, but are threatened with disappearance by forces comparable with those which have affected many other past scripts. The character of the threats involved differs in two regions of China that are remote from each other. In a sense, Manchu offers a laboratory where it is possible to observe at work similar forces to those that we can only posit for most of the historical examples treated in this book.

Common features of different cases?

A simple point, which stands behind the chapters of this book, is of central importance to studies of the role of writing in societies. This is that writing is highly diverse as a phenomenon and as an institution. We have sought to address this diversity and to set it in a still broader context by including studies of cognate phenomena that may or may not be included within a particular definition of what constitutes writing. Moreover, one should not ascribe necessary effects or consequences to the appearance of writing in any society. The emergence of more nuanced approaches is visible within the œuvre of Jack Goody (e.g. Goody and Watt 1968 [1963]; Goody 1977; 1986; 2000), who was a prime mover in research in this area but happens not to have addressed the disappearance of writing systems; his later studies ascribe less instrumentality to writing than his earlier ones did. A specific rejection of causal models is visible in a number of other writers, among whom one might pick out Brian Street (e.g. 1984; 1993; 1995; 2001; see also Halverson 1992). Neither author tests his interpretations against the disappearance of writing. Their approach is not as unilinear as that of Eric Havelock (1982), for example, but it should be borne in mind that the disappearance of writing in itself shows that its impact sits within a societal context and cannot be absolute.

But if writing has no single role in society, studies may be in danger of separating into a mass of incommensurable detail. How can some generality and comparability in analysis be achieved? One answer is that comparison should be based on informed understanding of examples rather than superficial similarities, and such understanding is what the preceding chapters offer. They also present as wide a range of societies as possible. While the juxtaposition of examples shows that no one mode of analysis can be applied to them, it also throws into relief commonalities among societal factors that influence the loss of writing. The most important of these are probably two: the relative weight ascribed to the oral and performed on the one hand, or to materially encoded on the other hand, with writing having a special status among forms of material encoding; and the degree of integration of writing systems with central values of a society or civilization and with how these change. An overarching issue, related to those, is the extent to which a society or social group identifies itself with its writing system. These are more promising lines of analysis than any assumption that the presence of writing brings about a particular effect while its disappearance marks the end of that effect. In what follows I explore briefly approaches that relate to these broad issues.

Loss of language in relation to loss of script

Language 'death' is a much-studied phenomenon and has become a matter of great concern because so many of the world's languages are endangered or becoming extinct (see e.g. Dorian 1989; Grenoble and Whaley 1998; Crystal 2000). Still more than with scripts, the overwhelming majority of the languages that have been spoken in the world must be lost. It is, however, a little easier to define what constitutes the end of a script than when a language disappears. One script can be the ancestor of another (or of more than one), but the two can mostly be distinguished, whereas one language can evolve almost seamlessly into another. Nonetheless, scripts can survive for centuries in restricted usages that bear little resemblance to their societal penetration when they were flourishing. Much of this book deals with such attenuated modes of existence, of which Mesopotamian cuneiform, Egyptian hieroglyphic and demotic, and Maya provide good examples. These cases offer good generalized parallels for language death, notably in that they mark allegiance to an identity, and sometimes a culture or civilization, that is in the long run overwhelmed by a later form or by one introduced from outside. In some cases scripts can be more strongly diagnostic than languages, because they are major and deliberate creations of their originators, whereas languages are not intentionally devised in the same way.

Some of the short-lived scripts discussed by John Monaghan had a significant role of a different kind in their communities, enhancing the standing of their inventors and distinguishing the small group who used them. In other cases scripts of longer standing and more intensive use were lost very quickly, one example being Aegean Linear B, writing a form of Greek, which seems to have disappeared in just a few years as the palaces in which it was used were destroyed around 1200 BC. Since the language of the successor communities was probably Greek, one must assume that they had no use for writing or for the institutions which supported it. While a couple of generations of scholarly work on Linear B have established that it was a matter for elites and had a significant role in social organization, no public, display, or literary writing survives (see e.g. Bennet 2001; 2007; Palaima 2003). Perhaps the lack of diversity in the script's role made it particularly easily dispensable. I return to this example below.

Some cases covered in this book, alongside others that are not the subject of chapters, exemplify the complexity of the distribution of languages and scripts in the expanding empires of the first millennium BC (J. David Hawkins; David Brown); comparable complexity probably existed in other regional polities and periods. Language and script did not coincide in any neat way, and the survival of languages that were no longer spoken, such as Akkadian and still more Sumerian, appears to have been because they provided the content of the inherited and highly prestigious writing system, while the spoken language had become Aramaic, which was hardly written in cuneiform. In the Achaemenid Empire, Elamite writing may have survived after the Elamite language had ceased to be spoken (Jeremy Black). By contrast, the Old Persian cuneiform script, which was identified with modes of display developed from earlier Mesopotamia and Elam, disappeared from use with the demise of the political entity which had created it. The Persian language, however, has continued both to evolve and to retain highly traditional forms until today, using first scripts derived from Aramaic and later the Arabic script. The Achaemenid Empire may also have been the first political entity controlling a multitude of former states, often themselves multilingual and with their own languages and writing systems, in which there was no single dominant written language, while the principal language of administration, Aramaic, was not that of the ruling group (in itself a common situation). Despite this heterogeneity, the only scripts that can be said to have disappeared with the demise of the empire were Elamite and Old Persian cuneiform, which belonged in its heartland, and they seem to have been in decline long before the empire's destruction in the campaigns of Alexander the Great.

No single pattern can be derived from this range of different cases, but it seems clear that script and language can be mutually reinforcing in surviving and resisting assimilation by dominant identities and cultures. In such contexts, language relates closely to the identity of ethnic groups, while script is particularly associated with complex cultural systems, whether of administration, belief, literary expression, or a combination of two or more of these.

A case of a rather different type, where scarcity of evidence limits what can be said, is that of the non-Roman Italic scripts treated by Kathryn Lomas. These alphabets, which notated local languages, some cognate with Latin and others not, disappeared essentially with the demise of their polities, mostly under the pressure of Roman expansion but in a complex range of patterns. It seems impossible to say whether the languages in question ceased to be spoken when the scripts fell out of use, in part because their limited attestation does not permit deductions about uses they may have had beyond display; a variety of evidence suggest that uses could have been quite various (see Cornell 1991, for a rather maximalist view). It seems clear that the scripts were important elite vehicles of regional polities, but they do not appear to have been retained long after the Italian peninsula was united by Rome.

Cultural status of scripts and script types

None of the scripts of pristine civilizations was exclusively phonetic/phonemic in its encoding of language, and all seem to have had a high cultural status. In specialized ways, that characterization applies to separate inventions such as the Aegean scripts, although to a lesser extent than to Mesopotamia, Egypt, China, and Mesoamerica. More or less the same can be said about the less unambiguously defined Mexican pictography (Elizabeth Hill Boone) and Andean khipu (Frank Salomon). (The undeciphered script of the third and early second millennium Indus Valley civilization may not have been very salient, but hardly anything about its status or function is understood, so that it cannot well be drawn into a discussion; see e.g. Parpola 1994.) By contrast, the status of alphabetic scripts is quite diverse in different cultures. Some, such as various ancient alphabets of the Arabian desert and peninsula, seem almost to have been hobbies or pastimes and to have been lost with changes in cultural practice, whether or not these were accompanied by the eclipse of the societies in question.

An especially revealing instance of an alphabetical script is that of Kharoṣṭhī in north-west India, which was used for the full typical range of civilizational purposes of writing but disappeared quickly in its heartland, being replaced by Brāhmī. Richard Salomon suggests that a major reason why this change was so rapid and seemingly untraumatic was that the core values of Indian traditions were altogether more oral than written in focus and that Sanskrit and Pali, as the chief carriers of traditional Indian culture or of the Theravada Buddhist tradition, could be written in a variety of scripts. The writing system was therefore secondary to other focuses of civilizational values. The same probably applies to Aegean Linear A and B, both of which had limited use in societies that seem to have attributed great value to oral and performed high culture (see Bennet 2007, and this volume).

Those who see ease of learning and the associated goal of universal literacy—rather than such purposes as extension of memory, communication, and cultural enrichment—as an ultimate purpose of writing systems tend to focus on the alphabet as the vehicle of this aspiration. Accordingly, many writers view the history of scripts as one of progressive improvement toward an alphabet that will achieve a complete and simple phonemic representation of a language; that was indeed the basic premise of the classic work of I. J. Gelb (1963). A little of a similar vision may have underlain the original creation of alphabetic scripts, whether this occurred in smaller-scale societies in western Asia or north-east

Africa, between the civilizations of Egypt and Mesopotamia (recently e.g. Gold-wasser 2006), or among people of immigrant stock in Egypt (Hamilton 2006: esp. 320–1). These communities will not have had the same amount of resources to invest in writing systems as did their larger neighbours, but by the same token, their commitment to its potential and the media and forms in which it was used was not always so extensive. The early history of alphabetic scripts, from the appearance of the 'Protosinaitic' script first attested from around 1800 BC to their wider dissemination in Syria-Palestine and the Arabian peninsula from 1300 BC or later, is likely to include types that were invented in small societies and then disappeared and are now unknown. The only well attested example is the consonantal cuneiform script of Ugarit, which disappeared around 1200 BC at the end of the Bronze Age; there is no reason to suppose that it was unique, although it is possible that the same consonantal cuneiform was disseminated over much of Syria-Palestine (see e.g. Naveh 1987: 28–31). Ugaritic has been recovered principally because it was written in the prestigious cuneiform manner on clay and belonged to the international 'palace culture' of its time (Van De Mieroop 2007); it is significant that material in Mesopotamian cuneiform was also recovered from the city.

The integration of visual and written culture, which is most marked in Egypt and in the Maya region cases among obsolete writing systems, and in East Asia among systems with continuing traditions, is a generally less prominent feature of alphabetic systems, although the artistic importance of the alphabetical Arabic script shows that this difference is not a consequence of script type. More probably, alphabetical writing systems have tended to belong with inherited or common artistic forms rather than initiating new ones from scratch. An instance would be Aramaic inscriptions of the south Anatolian and Syrian polities of the first half of the first millennium BC, many of which are on monuments in regional styles originally elaborated for combination with cuneiform or Hieroglyphic Luwian (J. David Hawkins). It is striking here that the monument of Darius I at Bisitun, the pre-eminent public inscription of the Achaemenid Empire, which was a cultural descendant of the same regional forms, includes Akkadian cuneiform, Elamite, and Old Persian cuneiform—an alphabetic script but modelled on culturally hallowed Mesopotamian forms—but not Aramaic, the most widely current language and alphabetical script of the period. The civilizational complex of cuneiform writing and the languages that it wrote was threatened, more immediately in Iran, where an Aramaic-based written culture emerged in the centuries after the Achaemenid Empire, and less strongly in Mesopotamia, where it survived in progressively weakening form for another three centuries. In both cases, scripts and civilizations were identified, and the disappearance of the scripts marked the end of the traditional high culture of the regions; in the case of Achaemenid Persia, that high culture had lasted only a couple of centuries.

Persistence, Transformation, and Disappearance

As noted, heavy and continuing investment is required to maintain a writing system that is used for a range of functions. Even very limited systems absorb much of their practitioners' attention. Late phases of a script's existence are often contemporaneous with the presence of other scripts in the same societies— as seems to be the case for Linear A both when it was the principal Cretan script and during the period when Linear B was becoming the norm (John Bennet)—so that competition for resources compounds the problems facing those who work to preserve it.

The survival of writing systems in adverse conditions is a testimony to their great significance for the actors. Eloquent examples included in this book include Mesopotamian cuneiform (David Brown and Jerrold Cooper), Egyptian hieroglyphs and demotic (Martin Stadler), Meroitic (Claude Rilly), and Maya (Stephen Houston). These focus around religious and high-cultural institutions, but in a variety of ways. What all have in common is a gradual diminution in the range of writing practised and a reduction in the costliness of the media used for inscription. In Mesopotamia cuneiform became largely confined to very specialized usages, whereas in Egypt traditional high culture, as seen in papyrus texts and in temple inscriptions, was remarkably resilient until the third century AD, not becoming severely restricted until the fourth century. In the Maya case, after the collapse of the Classic, use of the script fragmented among the many polities of the region and persisted only on smaller, movable objects.

The resilience of writing traditions and difficulties in evaluating evidence are strongly evidenced by Meroitic. The Meroitic script was in existence for about 650 years, but attestation of its range of use is poor because find conditions do not favour cursive or documentary materials, although it is known that they existed. Monumental inscriptions, which are most of what is now extant, cease to be known a couple of centuries before the principal successor language, Old Nubian, was written down in Greek letters with some additions as part of the Christianization of the region; this process was presumably influenced by the rather earlier parallel development of Coptic writing in Egypt. Despite this apparent gap, the Old Nubian alphabet includes sign forms that seem to derive from Meroitic. While oral tradition might transmit even an alphabetical order, it is unlikely that shapes could be handed down the same way, so that the signs in Old Nubian provide indirect evidence for the survival of the Meroitic script for some time after the latest documented finds. Such a survival, in successor polities to the Meroitic state that were much smaller than it and different in social organization, is striking testimony to the script's importance, even if it is impossible to say what it may have been used for.

Stephen Houston introduces the valuable notion of 'script communities' to the discussion of these late survivors of previously widespread writing systems.

Whereas writing that pervades a complex society, or a social stratum within that society, does not distinguish a community except in the most general sense, the smaller groups who sustain a script, either in peripheral societies or among survivors of larger entities, form distinct communities. Even here, the distribution of the evidence may mislead us. Thus, the cities of Roman Egypt have left hardly any evidence for indigenous writing (as against the dominant Greek), whereas it is well known from the more rural Fayyum, much of which was abandoned in the following period. But the use of writing in Upper Egypt at Thebes (e.g. Riggs 2003) and Armant (Grenier 1983), and especially at Philae (Martin Stadler), from which the very latest inscriptions come, seems clearly to be a local rather than a general phenomenon.

The resilience of these communities was closely related to traditional religious practice in major temples, which continued even after Christianity became the official religion of the Roman empire. This resilience can be compared with the pattern in Mesopotamia, where the indigenous civilization did not generally survive so long (for an exception, see Green 1992). Experiments with writing Egyptian in Greek letters began in Ptolemaic times, receiving stimulus in the Roman period from the desire to notate the pronunciation of magical spells in obsolete Classical Egyptian. Ultimately this development flourished with the cultural and ethnic identification of Egyptian language and the new religions of late antiquity, among which Christianity triumphed, resulting in the stabilization of Coptic as the successor to ancient Egyptian. Meanwhile, the ancient hieroglyphic and demotic were closely identified with traditional religious culture, especially in their time of final decline. The period of about 600 years required for this process to be completed—and subsequently to be followed by the transition to Islam—is indicative of the robustness of the complex of beliefs and of their material expression through material culture and writing. That duration can be approximately compared with two other, very different examples discussed in this volume, which are the slow disappearance of Maya writing (Stephen Houston) and the double transition from Iron Age to Anglo-Saxon England through transformations in material and written culture in a more slowly changing landscape that acted as a repository of memory and value (Chris Gosden). The persistence of the Andean khipu almost 500 years after the Spanish conquest of Peru, even without their original administrative functions, is another case of the centrality for ideology and identity of record systems that can also be forms of display and of specialized communication (Frank Salomon).

In other cases, writing systems came and went or were transformed into other systems. The salient instance of such transformation is that of the Nabataean version of the Aramaic alphabet into Arabic, where numerous scripts that were well suited to writing their South Semitic languages in Arabia were ultimately succeeded by one dominant script writing another South Semitic language that also came to dominate (M. C. A. Macdonald). Nabataean was chosen as the vehicle for Arabic not because it was suited to its phonology but because it was the prestige script of the region that was the cultural centre for the developing group out of which the founders of Islam emerged. This pattern of emergence sealed the fate of the other scripts and inhibited the invention of further alphabets in the Arabian peninsula. The extraordinary spread of the Arabic script relates most closely to the rise of Islam, but the rapid evolution of Islamic society into a civilization with urban centres and complex institutions that inherited much from precursor civilizations in the region meant that its use of writing had little in common with that of the pre-Islamic peoples of Arabia.

Among scripts studied in this book, those which disappeared quickly either were limited in their range of use or belonged to cultures that valued oral forms over written ones—notably Kharoṣṭhī (Richard Salomon)—or both—as is probably the case with Aegean Linear A and B. Partly similar points apply to the revelatory scripts studied by John Monaghan, but most of these were in any case sited in communities undergoing rapid change and great stress from encroaching societies. A rather different case is that of Manchu (Giovanni Stary), which rapidly became a significant script in the vast empire of China, but was altogether less well rooted there than the traditional Chinese script and culture. The marginalization of Manchu since the fall of the Qing dynasty appears to share features with the end of very different scripts such as Egyptian in late antiquity. These examples exemplify the value of comparative study of the role of writing systems: despite their diversity, they exhibit mutually illuminating characteristics that might be overlooked if they were not brought together.

Conclusion

As central achievements and institutions of cultures and civilizations, writing systems are both highly significant in themselves and indexes of wider societal change. Analysis of their role needs to be detached to some extent from study of the still more fundamental institution of language, because the two do not change at the same rate and often not for the same reasons. Since language as such is not accessible through archaeology, much of what can be said about radical change and how it may relate to linguistic phenomena in past complex societies must focus on the material record. The multiple inventions of writing systems and complex recording techniques in the Near East, East Asia, and the Americas, provide material traces of their existence, decline, and disappearance. These, as well as gaps in the record of use of such systems, offer a way of entry into thinking about how societies change radically and at what point they can be said to have lost their cultural ancestry. Disappearances of writing are the polar opposite of inventions, but are neglected in today's context of all-pervasive writing. Writing systems that have been lost are often better understood than those for which we try to establish their process of formation. Their loss may be just as revealing as their first appearance.

References

Bennet, John

2001 'Agency and Bureaucracy: Thoughts on the Nature and Extent of Administration in Bronze Age Pylos'. In Sofia Voutsaki and John Killen (eds), *Economy and Politics in the Mycenaean Palace States: Proceedings of a Conference Held on 1-3 July 1999 in the Faculty of Classics, Cambridge.* Cambridge Philological Society, Supplementary Volume 27. Cambridge: Cambridge Philological Society, 25–37.

2007 'Representations of Power in Mycenaean Pylos: Script, Orality, Iconography'.In Felix Lang, Claus Reinholdt, and Jörg Weilhartner (eds), ΣΤΕΦΑΝΟΣ ΑΡΙΣΤΕΙΟΣ *[Stephanos Aristeios]: Archäologische Forschungen zwischen Nil und Istros, Festschrift für Stefan Hiller zum 65. Geburtstag.* Vienna: Phoibos, 11–22.

Chrisomalis, Stephen

2004 'A Cognitive Typology for Numerical Notation'. *Cambridge Archaeological Journal* 14: 37–52.

Cornell, Tim

1991 'The Tyranny of the Evidence: A Discussion of the Possible Uses of Literacy in Etruria and Latium in the Archaic Age'. In *Literacy in the Roman World.* Journal of Roman Archaeology, Supplementary Series 3. Ann Arbor, MI: Journal of Roman Archaeology, 7–33.

Crystal, David

2000 *Language Death.* Cambridge: Cambridge University Press.

Dorian, Nancy C. (ed.)

1989 *Investigating Obsolescence: Studies in Language Contraction and Death.* Studies in the Social and Cultural Foundations of Language 7. Cambridge: Cambridge University Press.

Fischer, Steven R.

1997 *Rongorongo, the Easter Island Script: History, Traditions, Texts.* Oxford Studies in Anthropological Linguistics 14. Oxford: Clarendon Press.

Gelb, Ignace J.

1963 *A Study of Writing,* revised edition. Chicago, IL: University of Chicago Press.

Goldwasser, Orly

2006 'Canaanites Reading Hieroglyphs: Horus Is Hathor?—The Invention of the Alphabet in Sinai'. *Ägypten und Levante* 16: 121–60.

Goody, Jack

1977 *The Domestication of the Savage Mind.* Cambridge: Cambridge University Press.

1986 *The Logic of Writing and the Organization of Society.* Cambridge: Cambridge University Press.

2000 *The Power of the Written Tradition.* Smithsonian Series in Ethnographic Enquiry. Washington, DC, and London: Smithsonian Institution Press.

Goody, Jack, and Ian Watt
1968 [1963] 'The Consequences of Literacy'. In Jack Goody, (ed.), *Literacy in Traditional Societies*. Cambridge: Cambridge University Press, 27–68.

Green, Tamara M.
1992   *The City of the Moon God: Religious Traditions of Harran*. Religions in the Graeco-Roman World 114. Leiden: Brill.

Grenier, Jean-Claude
1983   'La stèle funéraire du dernier taureau Bouchis (Caire JE 31901 = Stèle Bucheum 20) Ermant 4 novembre 340'. *Bulletin de l'Institut Français d'Archéologie Orientale* 83: 197–208.

Grenoble, Lenore A., and Lindsay J. Whaley (eds)
1998   *Endangered Languages: Language Loss and Community Response*. Cambridge: Cambridge University Press.

Halverson, John
1992   'Goody and the Implosion of the Literacy Hypothesis'. *Man* 27: 301–17.

Hamilton, Gordon J.
2006   *The Origins of the West Semitic Alphabet in Egyptian Scripts*. Catholic Biblical Quarterly, Monograph Series 40. Washington, DC: Catholic Biblical Association of America.

Havelock, Eric A.
1982   *The Literate Revolution in Greece and Its Cultural Consequences*. Princeton, NJ: Princeton University Press.

Houston, Stephen D. (ed.)
2004   *The First Writing: Script Invention as History and Process*, Cambridge: Cambridge University Press.

Houston, Stephen D., John Baines, and Jerrold Cooper
2003   'Last Writing: Script Obsolescence in Egypt, Mesopotamia, and Mesoamerica'. *Comparative Studies in Society and History* 45: 430–79.

Michalowski, Piotr
1990   'Early Mesopotamian Communicative Systems: Art, Literature, and Writing'. In Ann Gunter (ed.), *Investigating Artistic Environments in the Ancient Near East*. Washington: Smithsonian Institution Press, 56–69.

Naveh, Joseph
1987   *Early History of the Alphabet: An Introduction to West Semitic Epigraphy and Palaeography*, second revised edition. Jerusalem: Magnes Press, Hebrew University.

Palaima, Thomas G.
2003   '"Archives" and "Scribes" and Information Hierarchy in Mycenaean Greek Linear B Records'. In Maria Brosius (ed.), *Ancient Archives and Archival Traditions: Concepts of Record-Keeping in the Ancient World*. Oxford Studies in Ancient Documents. Oxford: Oxford University Press, 153–94.

Parpola, Asko
1994   *Deciphering the Indus Script*. Cambridge: Cambridge University Press.

Riggs, Christina
    2003   'The Egyptian Funerary Tradition at Thebes in the Roman Period'. In Nigel Strudwick and John H. Taylor (eds), *The Theban Necropolis: Past, Present and Future (International Colloquium, 27–28 July 2000)*. London: British Museum Press, 189–201.

Rodríguez Martínez, Maria del Carmen, Ponciano Ortíz Ceballos, Michael D. Coe, Richard A. Diehl, Stephen D. Houston, Karl A. Taube, and Alfredo Delgado Calderón
    2006   'Oldest Writing in the New World'. *Science* 313: 1610–14.

Scribner, Sylvia, and Michael Cole
    1981   *The Psychology of Literacy*. Cambridge, MA: Harvard University Press.

Street, Brian V.
    1984   *Literacy in Theory and Practice*. Cambridge Studies in Oral and Literate Culture 9. Cambridge: Cambridge University Press.
    1995   *Social Literacies: Critical Approaches to Literacy in Development, Ethnography and Education*. Real Language Series. London and New York: Longman.
    2001   *Literacy and Development: Ethnographic Perspectives*. Literacies. London: Routledge.

Street, Brian V. (ed.)
    1993   *Cross-Cultural Approaches to Literacy*. Cambridge Studies in Oral and Literate Culture 23. Cambridge: Cambridge University Press.

Van De Mieroop, Marc
    2007   *The Eastern Mediterranean in the Age of Ramesses II*. Oxford and Malden, MA: Blackwell.

Index

References to notes are entered as, for example, 22n. References to tables and figures are entered as 116t or 37f respectively. References in parentheses following site- or place-names are to modern countries.